CRITICAL THEORY FOR LIBRARY AND INFORMATION SCIENCE

CRITICAL THEORY FOR LIBRARY AND INFORMATION SCIENCE

Exploring the Social from across the Disciplines

Gloria J. Leckie, Lisa M. Given,
and John E. Buschman, Editors

 LIBRARIES UNLIMITED

AN IMPRINT OF ABC-CLIO, LLC
Santa Barbara, California • Denver, Colorado • Oxford, England

Library of Congress Cataloging-in-Publication Data

Critical theory for library and information science : exploring the social from across the disciplines / Gloria J. Leckie, Lisa M. Given, and John E. Buschman, editors.
    p. cm.
  Includes bibliographical references and index.
  ISBN 978-1-59158-938-9 (acid-free paper) — ISBN 978-1-59158-940-2 (ebook)
 1. Library science—Sociological aspects. 2. Library science—Philosophy.
3. Information science—Sociological aspects. 4. Information science—Philosophy.
5. Critical theory. I. Leckie, Gloria J. II. Given, Lisa M. III. Buschman, John.
  Z665.C778 2010
  020.1—dc22   2010012813

ISBN: 978-1-59158-938-9
EISBN: 978-1-59158-940-2

14 13 12 11 10   1 2 3 4 5

This book is also available on the World Wide Web as an eBook.
Visit www.abc-clio.com for details.

Libraries Unlimited
An Imprint of ABC-CLIO, LLC

ABC-CLIO, LLC
130 Cremona Drive, P.O. Box 1911
Santa Barbara, California 93116-1911

This book is printed on acid-free paper ∞

Manufactured in the United States of America

Contents

Introduction: The Necessity for Theoretically Informed Critique in Library and Information Science (LIS)

Gloria Leckie
University of Western Ontario

John Buschman
Georgetown University

THE EVOLUTION OF CRITICAL THEORY

The rise of critical theory is usually identified with the Institute for Social Research (Institut für Sozialforschung), formed in 1923 and associated over the years with the University of Frankfurt am Main in Germany.[1] The institute was the home of what became known as the Frankfurt School of social thought/critique. Particularly under the leadership of Max Horkheimer during the 1930s, the institute became a focus for the radical critique both of the fabric of society (including the economy and its attendant sociopolitical formations) and the social theories that were purported to be explanatory of social phenomena. Dahms (2007) remarks that

Critical theory began as the project of illuminating how "traditional" theories of modern society, conceptions of social science, approaches to studying social life, and practices of doing research start out from largely implicit yet highly problematic assumptions about the relationship between social science and society, in the sense of social science and concrete socio-historical context. Since the early 1930s, critical theory has stood as a reminder that the specific economic, political, cultural and ideological configurations of socio-historical contexts have a direct bearing on the form, content, practice and normative orientation of both social life and social sciences (18).

Early critical theorists of the Frankfurt School included Theodor Adorno, Walter Benjamin, Erich Fromm, Max Horkheimer, Herbert Marcuse, Wilhelm Reich, and later, Jürgen Habermas. While this group of scholars had a wide-ranging intellectual agenda, they were united in their neo-Marxist thinking and analyses, which they brought to bear on issues such as the sociohistorical origins of capitalism and the nature of work/ labor in a capitalist system, historical materialism, the characteristics and functioning of the modern state, processes of cultural hegemony/domination, exclusion and ideology, alternate views of existence, the nature of reality, and the psychosocial processes of everyday life. In addition, members of the Frankfurt School took aim at contemporary social theory, including logical positivism and pragmatism, and the nature of dialectics. Although the Frankfurt School now refers to a particular historical period and group of theorists, the Institute for Social Research continues, with the current director being Axel Honneth, and associated prominent scholars including Nancy Fraser, Seyla Benhabib, and Agnes Heller, among others.

While in some academic circles the term *critical theory* is still used as shorthand specifically for the Frankfurt School, this was not the only group of theorists who offered a penetrating critique of the social. Dant (2003) points out that there was an "overlapping but slightly later Gallic tradition" (3) of critical theory, including the writings of Roland Barthes, Jean Baudrillard, Andre Gorz, Henry Lefebvre, and Alain Touraine. Dant notes that both the Germanic and Gallic critical theorists took "Marx's analysis of the mode of production as a starting point that needs to be developed to cope with the changes in capitalism that had become apparent by the middle of the twentieth century," and from there attempted "to extend the 'critique of political economy' towards a broader critique of society and culture as a whole" (4). However, the critique does not end there; rather the

emphasis shifts towards what we might call the "culturisation" of the economy: the way that modern culture follows the underlying rationale of the economy.... What emerges in both the Germanic and Gallic critical theory traditions is a concern to modify Marx's analysis, sometimes drawing on Freud, to mount a critique of culture and society beyond the critique of political economy. At times this critique is of society as *culture*, in distinction to Marx's critique of society as *political economy*, but consistent is a critique that addresses society as a totality and treats culture not as epiphenomenal, as Marx was prone to do, but as the form in which the modern mode of production resides (4).

In addition to those noted by Dant, there were other French scholars whose work has come to be considered in the realm of a loosely defined critical theory, but who did not see themselves as aligned with the project of the Frankfurt School and who rejected, or at least resisted, the Marxian and Hegelian foundations of the Frankfurt scholars. Among these are included both structuralist and poststructuralist theorists, most notably Pierre Bourdieu, Jacques Derrida, Michel Foucault, Jacques Lacan, and Jean-François Lyotard.[2] These thinkers, and the areas of scholarship they have influenced, have attacked a wide-ranging set of issues and contradictions, from the hegemony of various socioeconomic systems, to unexamined forms of domination and social regulation, forces of marginalization, and the constraints of a curriculum and pedagogy based upon a privileged canon of literature. Their critique is rooted in a shift in emphasis to aesthetic, textual, and quasi-political strategies, demonstrating a commitment to celebrating those who have been defined as the Other by those with power. Pluralism has thus become a primary value, justifying movements to dismantle processes and hierarchies of power that have enabled the divisive selecting and sorting of people, thus creating the Other (Rose 1989).

These notions dovetail with the refusal to accept Western privileging of mathematical and scientific definitions of reality at the expense of other ways of knowing. The overall project supports inclusion and democratic justice for persons of color, women, and gay men and lesbians in society, bringing a refreshing poignancy to conceptions of fairness. These critical theorists "drew attention to the inadequacy of class reductionist accounts of human society [and] the marginalization of women and minorities" in ways that other forms of critical analysis were not able to do (McCarthy and Apple 1988, 18).

The recognition of the complex heterogeneity of people is now a core idea, and the relationship between genuine multiculturalism and democracy was established. Furthermore, critical theorists have shown that the actions of professionals are implicated in power—asymmetrical relations based on class, race, ethnicity, and sexual preference. Edward Said (in Leonard 1993, 388) has pointed out that " 'all cultures are involved in one another; none is single and pure, all are hybrid, heterogeneous, extraordinarily differentiated';...that we are in our 'history-making' less the 'symphonic whole'...than 'an atonal ensemble' of complementary and interdependent...rhetorics.' "

In earlier phases, critical theory has had to overcome two resulting problematics: radical pessimism (Held 1980) and the later conflation of culture and philosophy. Hall (1986) made this second point some time ago on the danger of collapsing analysis and prescription and going beyond "identifying new trends or tendencies, new cultural configurations, but in learning to love them" (45). While some still find in critical theory a tendency towards these two problematics, nonetheless, as the definition of critical theory has shifted in the last few decades, new critical approaches, such as poststructuralism, postcolonialism, feminist and queer theory, have developed and solidified. In this wider sense, critical theory is evident across more diverse disciplines than ever before, including education, literary studies, philosophy, management, communication/media studies, international relations, political science, geography, language studies, sociology, and psychology, to name a few. Yet while the idea—or definition—of what critical theory is may have broadened in recent decades (see, for instance, Sinnerbrink, Deranty, and Smith 2006; Badminton and Thomas 2008, 1–5), within its theoretical heritage are two concepts that have been carried forward and form underlying assumptions within this volume. The first is that critical theory opposes all theory that "renders its own validity claim dependent on the concealment of its grounds" (Bauman 1991, 277). In this sense, critical theory as it is manifested in this volume is not "theory in the ordinary sense, but a theory of the foundation and validation of theory" (Bauman 1991, 277). The second is that critical theory now culturalizes the interpretation of the world instead of naturalizing it (Bauman 1991, 284). In other words, it is a short leap in post-Frankfurt critical theory to move from the earlier basis of the analysis of categories of social relationships to now say that:

- History is made by human beings, but in turn history shapes human experience and "produces outcomes which [people] neither intend nor foresee" (Giddens 1987, 156);
- The mode of production, as it exists in various societies, is embedded within all sociocultural practices and institutions and cannot be separated from the analysis of culture;
- Knowledge is socially constructed and must be understood in its sociocultural context. The "genesis of what has heretofore seemed to be natural and necessary involves contingent relations....Categories, principles, rules, standards, criteria, procedures, techniques, beliefs, and practices formerly accepted as purely and simply rational may come to be seen as in the service of particular interests" (McCarthy 1991, 45, 47; see also Sim 2005, vii–xiv);
- Finally, the critic herself must both conduct a "theoretically informed analysis of social phenomena" while at the same time acknowledging that she is unable to assume a superior or neutral position. The critic is always and only a "partner in dialogue, a participant, even when observing or criticizing" (McCarthy 1991, 128).

Critical theory now speaks to this ensemble of approaches. While "it is clear that critical theory is situated in the Marxist tradition...it is equally clear, however, that critical theory is an attempt to adapt Marx's insights in the face of profound social and economic change" (Granter 2009, 3). Accordingly, critical theory questions the grounds of claims; it situates human action and structures within culture and history as contingent; it questions categories; and it insists that the critic/theorist is neither neutral nor above the social circumstances being theorized. At the same time, there is still a desire to uncover and distinguish between the just and the unjust, the reasonable and the irrational, the consensual/dialogic and the coercive and unspoken (McCarthy 1991, 54–55). Critical theory seeks, above all, to reveal the irrational societal contradictions (cloaked in the ideologies of supposed rationality) that enable

individuals and indeed nations to annihilate one another, as they continue to do. It is irrational to condemn, structurally, whole sectors of populations to poverty, toil, unhappiness and servitude, as continues to be the case...Critical theory seeks to identify and penetrate the ideologies that cloak this domination (Granter 2009, 2–3).

In this sense, then, critical theory is viewed as liberationist and transformative (Matustik 2001, vii–xi; Granter 2009, 1–5). Along these lines, Matustik calls for a new or re-invented critical theory in the New World Order (ix), a critical theory that will "speak about liberation in plural and multidimensional voices and yet do so while being historically and materially linked to ongoing struggles" (xi). Thus, as it is understood here, critical theory has both a scholarly and a normative purpose.

Can critical theory realize this dual purpose? Despite its seeming uptake across many different areas of scholarship, Dahms (2007) is skeptical that critical theory is truly making a difference, particularly in the established disciplines of the social sciences (where one might think that critical theory should be very strong). He comments that in mainstream (i.e., traditional, noncritical and established) social science

resistance to considering the specifics of socio-historical context takes many forms, the following being among the more prominent:

- the strict separation between the logic of scientific method and the analysis of the characteristic features of socio-historical context;
- the determined refusal to acknowledge that the centrality of contradictions to modern society influences concrete research agendas and modes of research, to scrutinize concrete contradictions and implications resulting from their centrality, and to determine the nature of the link between contradictions and social forms; and
- the ingrained unwillingness to ensure that claims made about the purpose and consequences of research coincide with its actual orientation and effects within socio-historical contexts (Dahms 25).

Dahms further remarks that "the goal and purpose of critical approaches is to direct research efforts at providing representations of modern society that reveal to its members and to social scientists their problematic features as integral components of its concrete socio-historical form, and thus, its very possibility" (48). Given the resistances noted above, can critical theory move us forward toward this goal? Dahms concludes that it can, at the very least by holding mainstream research agendas and practices to account, and by reading much of mainstream research "against the grain," as it were (49).

THE NEED FOR CRITICAL THEORY IN LIS

We argue that an understanding of critical theory is important to scholarship in LIS for a number of important reasons, not the least of which is reading much of our own scholarship against the grain. First, while there certainly are scholars in LIS who are known for their critical-theoretical work (including John Budd, John Buschman, Ron Day, Bernd Frohmann, Michael Harris, Hope Olson, and Sanna Talja, to note a few) overall, there is not a strong tradition in LIS of producing metatheoretical discourse in the vein of Foucault, Bourdieu, Habermas, or Negri, for example. Accordingly, there is a tendency in LIS to adapt theoretical perspectives from other disciplines, often doing so without a critical or complete understanding. The chapters in this volume by Ron Day and Andrew Lau on psychoanalysis and Sanna Talja on Lave's situated cognition are cases in point: psychoanalytic and cognitive research concepts have crept into LIS in the form of the cognitive paradigm, but that paradigm is not based on a thorough understanding of the original theoretical frameworks or their deficiencies. While all disciplines borrow theory from other disciplines to a certain extent, in LIS, we need to be more aware and/or critical of what and how we borrow or adapt. In LIS, analyses that describe forms of power so pervasive and complex, with so many root causes, make it almost impossible to direct critique against any one source of power, or to communicate effectively to oppose further incursions of the current neoliberal *grand récit* (like the market or managerialism) into library content and services. A more critical-theoretical approach, therefore, is warranted and necessary.

Second, the incorporation of critical theory into LIS research is beneficial in that it forces us to be more in tune with the current understandings and scholarly trends in other disciplines. As a practice-oriented field tied to large institutions, a certain lag in theory use might be understandable (although in a comparable field, education, critical theory is much more in evidence). However, LIS cannot forever remain innocent of the debates and the progressions of thought that have characterized broad realms of theoretical influence in the humanities and social sciences and still maintain its place within those constellations of research and practice. Sophisticated use of critical theory makes our scholarship and practice more relevant to a larger academic society and wards off the dangers of LIS isolationism.

Third, critical theory in the LIS fields of research and practice *should* both encourage sophisticated adaptation *and* enable articulate responses to current issues facing the field: tax revolts, cultural conservative demands to cleanse the contents of libraries (and their screens), the incursion of ever more advertising into content, and the overwhelming demands to make libraries responsive to (and reflective of) the neoliberal idea of the market (Brosio 1994; Buschman 2003). Our "discourse...tends to favor technical and managerial language use," which in turn prevents librarians from critically examining and evaluating information resources and systems (Andersen 2005, 21).

Library technologies continue to be seriously undertheorized, with a consequent research focus on their technical facility, look, feel, appeal, popularity, and connection to other media products of postmodern culture. These issues should be explored in depth. In an obvious case, Google's plan, in conjunction with some major research library collections, to digitize millions of books in a single collection is another enormously important project largely untouched by an LIS critical theory. The project has been greeted with immense fanfare and outright triumphalism, but Google is becoming a powerful portal for targeted advertising marketing to library audiences in the process. Another glaring example is that there are notable intellectual freedom concerns, aside from the obvious invasion of private inquiry, over the technologies to track book searching and reading in an age of secret information gathering (such as under the umbrella of the USA PATRIOT Act), all to be blessed by libraries. Nor is there sufficient skepticism within library research to question the use or abuse of this information in private, corporate hands (generally), or the participation of the university administrators at public institutions in this privatizing digitization project (Buschman and Brosio 2006).

Critical theory expands the boundaries of what we know and how we think, and thus opens up new possibilities and avenues for LIS research. However, critical-theoretical perspectives are not and should not be confined just to our academic endeavours, but need to be incorporated into the very essence of our professional practices. As it stands now, major areas of practice conduct a great deal of research that is pragmatic, but highly uncritical. A better understanding of critical-theoretical approaches would serve to sharpen the research lens when we examine problems relating to professional practice and real-world applications. To this end, Gerry Benoit (2002, 462–63) suggests that critical theory in LIS would help to counter the influences of positivism, particularly in the areas of the discipline that examine information systems. He comments that

If the field is considered from a critical theoretic stance, questions are raised also about the performance of LIS research and practice, such as whether LIS research ought to rely solely on evidence of causality, as user studies often do, or to reflect what is believed is happening (subconsciously) in the mind of the user…LIS research that drives professional training and system design often reduces the individual's need to a representation of group behaviors. To some philosophies, holding the user at arm's length may be merely a concession to today's understanding of professionalism, or the limits of computer architecture. To more radical philosophies, it suggests that reliance on this type of scientific methodology, that is, one that prefers a quantifiable aggregate, permits researchers to abrogate the right of individuals (the end users) to critique the researcher, which, in an extreme reading, renders the method and practice self-legitimating (464).

Critical theory can help us to break, or at least expose, the self-legitimation cycle by allowing us to examine the unexamined and question the unquestioned, both in terms of our accepted bodies of knowledge and their associated research agendas and methodologies. Frohmann (2004) explores why it is that a particular view of information as an abstract object (11) has permeated our field and to a certain extent, our culture. This is especially true with respect to science and our taken-for-granted understanding of the production of scientific knowledge, which we (in LIS, but also elsewhere) have tended to view in a particular way. Frohmann notes that

All the attention paid to improving information systems seems somewhat odd when knowledge production is seen less as a matter of producing, processing and exchanging information than as making things work in the laboratory and manipulating material things, processes and techniques. Scientists would appear to have been quite successful at such work since the sixteenth century… [until] today, when their labours enjoy huge military and corporate support.…What then, is the source of the conviction that a perfected science information system would necessarily increase scientific productivity? (93)

As Frohmann's work suggests, science is, in the end, essentially a product of complex social forces, specific institutionalized and documentary practices and a rather entrenched story "of the objectivity and universality of scientific knowledge" (22; see also

Kuhn 1996). This understanding runs counter to traditional views of the way in which science operates and how it produces a body of scientific knowledge. Critical theory gives us the tools to undertake such an investigation, to hold our assumptions up to the light, and to examine the refracted beams in a new way.

Finally, as a quintessentially social field, LIS is interested (in one way or another) in how society, people, institutions (including but not limited to libraries), governments, and information technologies work, and the interactions among them. Furthermore, LIS is also very interested in the betterment of society, from the development of national information policies, to the provision of user-friendly and equitable access to information, the inclusion of diverse and/or marginalized clienteles, the support of citizen lifelong learning, the nurturing of the library in the community, and many other proactive areas of research and practice. Critical theorists give us an array of perspectives or approaches to the very concerns that we have in LIS and help us to think about/examine those issues in new ways. For instance, an act of information seeking might be viewed as an individual and isolated event, but a critical framework allows us to see how information seeking is part of a larger milieu that has many social dimensions in play, such as ideologies, hegemony, socioeconomic forces ("cognitive capitalism"), spatial practices, and so forth. Similarly, critical-theoretical perspectives help us to understand how large-scale changes in society, such as globalization and the permutations of capitalist production, affect what might seem to be routine and local practices, such as collections development or the purchase of catalog records, thus bringing fresh insights on who we are and what we do, collectively and individually.

The educational philosopher Maxine Greene (1986) writes in language that is startlingly close to the critical-theoretical sense of LIS we are attempting to describe:

Who knows better how important it is to look at things, whenever possible, as if they could be otherwise? To speak that way is to summon up the idea of imagination. Imagination is, in part, the capacity to apply concepts to things, to recognize the range of applications, and to invent new concepts. It is the possibility to move between…"spontaneous concepts" and more formal or schematic ones. It is the capacity to make metaphors, to create new orders in experience and to realize that there is always more in experience than anyone can predict. It is, also, the power to perceive unexpected relationships, to envisage alternative realities, and to reach beyond the taken-for-granted towards possibility (26–27).

INTRODUCTION TO THIS VOLUME

This edited text, therefore, seeks to introduce into the field a number of sources of theory of potential interest or relevance to current and future researchers. There is no claim here that this subset of theorists is either exhaustive or represents the "best" theorists who should concern LIS. Rather, the text was the product of negotiation between the editors, potential chapter authors, the extant LIS literature, and the necessary practical choices to realize what might be possible in such a volume. In other words, this volume illustrates one of the primary tenets contained in the title of the volume: it is the product of *the social*. Further, this volume—with its proliferation of sources of theory from the vantage point of the social—illustrates another of the primary tenets contained in the title of the volume: it is a *critique* of these unexamined assumptions and the scientivistic/positivistic undertones of much LIS research and practice.

The number of theorists presented, the welter of theoretical assertions, and the incommensurability of many of these thinkers here may well be cause for complaint. This is not taken lightly, but there are two broad answers to this objection. The first is that these thinkers help us make important distinctions between the *theoretical* and the "technical in nature [that which is pointed toward] the most expeditious means of achieving goals...agreed on beforehand." The *theoretical* should be concerned with the " 'systematically mistaken': mistaken arrangements and wrong action[s]" that are not "random consequences of a system...." Theoretical work "seeks to displace" the systematically mistaken, often ending in critique (Wolin 1969, 1080). The clear implication here, and in this volume, is that, as an undertheorized field (in the critical theory sense), LIS can benefit significantly from more (and deeper use of) critical-theoretical perspectives.

The second response is that the welter of theory is perhaps less of a welter than it may seem. Bernstein (1983), McCarthy (1991), and Sim (2005) all variously argue that critical-theoretical disagreements (in the broader debates) have been emphasized, and this has masked substantial areas of common concern such as those outlined earlier: for example, questioning the grounds of claims and categories, insisting that the theorist is neither neutral nor above what is being theorized; asserting the contingency of action and structures within culture and history; desiring to uncover and distinguish between the consensual and the coercive, and so on. The contributions to this volume exhibit some parallel characteristics. While it is true that there are a wide variety of approaches, there does seem to be agreement on the broad issues of the socially constructed nature of knowledge and information (variously defined) in LIS; critique and uncovering of assumptions and interests to guide research and practice; and perhaps even a hope for *praxis* in LIS. The chapters here perhaps represent a response to our theoretical heritage—a heritage that has not led to the discipline of LIS being recognized as fountainhead of theory development nor a strong player among her sister disciplines. This volume then, is an explicit attempt to break open the theoretical floodgates for a variety of sources of observation, analysis, and theory-informed practice.

Because of the conceptual difficulties that would immediately arise, we have chosen not to attempt to group the theorists in this volume into artificially constructed categories but rather simply to order the chapters alphabetically by theorist. Accordingly, we begin with an overview of the work of Michel Aglietta, the French Marxist economist whose pioneering doctoral thesis provided the foundation for what has become known as French school regulation theory. In this chapter, Siobhan Stevenson demonstrates the explanatory potential of this relatively underutilized approach for some of the more vexing questions facing LIS scholars and practitioners today. Following a brief description of those aspects of Michel Aglietta's biography and specifically his experiences as a student during the social and political ferment associated with Paris during the late 1960s, which directly influenced his scholarship, Stevenson highlights the main analytic tools associated with the approach and their application to date across a range of LIS subfields including library history, the organization and representation of knowledge, and the political economy of the contemporary public library. Through the use of concepts such as Fordism and post-Fordism, modes of social regulation, and regimes of accumulation, French school regulation theory supports the reading of all manner of information phenomena, institutions, and occupations from a political economy perspective. As such, the importance of history as a means of distinguishing between historical continuities and discontinuities, particularly the identification of the truly novel; the social dynamism created by the tension between capital and the broader social factor; and the implications of neoliberal political philosophy on the role of the state, its institutions, and its citizens, are problematized. One aspect of the approach that bears emphasizing is its inherent optimism regarding the power of people and the emancipatory potential embedded in productive technologies (today's ICTs) to create positive and lasting social change. This is most powerfully captured in the following quote from the regulationist Alain Lipietz, who has done much to extend Aglietta's work: "democracy is not a sphere to be managed or enlarged. It is a continent to be discovered, from one century to the next" (1995, 341). Notably, particularly for practitioners, is Aglietta's framing of solutions to social and economic instability and inequality within capitalism and not, for instance, an alternative system of social organization dependent upon a socialist revolution. This fact will appeal to the practical and pragmatic concerns associated with the field. Finally, there is a consonance between the values underpinning the approach and the service ethos that defines much of the work undertaken in the field of LIS.

Hans Dam Christensen's chapter on Roland Barthes takes, as its primary focus, the theorist's stance as a semiologist. Christensen presents a brief biography and overview of Barthes' key works, including "Death of the Author," and discusses how Barthes' work extends the writings of other key theorists, such as Ferdinand de Saussure, and contests those of other writers, such as György Lukács. The chapter also presents an overview of Barthes' influence on LIS, with a focus on classification, taxonomies, and subject indexing of images. The chapter closes with a brief discussion of the implications of Barthes' theories for examinations of social media, folksonomies, and other new points of focus for research in the field.

John Budd writes on Roy Bhaskar—a very new figure for LIS. He notes that, in clarifying differences between the natural and the social sciences, Bhaskar states that inquiry in the social sciences might not be able to achieve the positivist goal of prediction. The human aspect of dialectic critical realism obviates predictability, requiring deep and thoroughgoing research to reach understanding. Critical realism thus differs from empiricism and from idealism, conditioning our analysis of how real social reality is, and how can we best study complex social events with information seeking and use. Bhaskar's work, Budd argues, provides a sound theoretical grounding for a critical appraisal of existing underlying (historical) assumptions that have contributed to the present state of LIS. Dialectic provides a framework through which inquiry and praxis in librarianship can be examined in his idea of the social sciences as encompassing the two forms of reality. Bhaskar's stance is that there are varying ontological existences that must be accounted for, that human relations cannot be reified, and the very concept of "information" can be revisited in light of the dialectic he details. Bhaskar provides a corrective for an abundance of information seeking and information retrieval work that has been heavily influenced by information-processing cognitive inquiry. The potential is not limited to those topics of inquiry; the breadth of LIS could benefit from the critical-realist eye.

Lisa Hussey's chapter on French sociologist Pierre Bourdieu explores his focus on the construction and presentation of the social world. Hussey examines Bourdieu's central concepts of habitus, power, and capital, as well as social structures and fields of production, which shape his explorations of a general theory of practice—or how individuals (within society) function day to day. Hussey examines Bourdieu's influence across disciplines, including LIS, and summarizes key works that make use of Bourdieu's body of theory. The chapter also provides an overview of the potential implications of

Bourdieu's work on future research; Hussey highlights the possible extensions of Bourdieu's theory to studies of user services in libraries and museums, as well as studies of information centers as sites of cultural production. She also calls for an examination of LIS education, using Bourdieu's work as a lens for critical analysis.

Paulette Rothbauer examines the promise that French cultural theorist Michel de Certeau's work holds for scholarship related to individuals' everyday information practices. Rothbauer presents an overview of de Certeau's key works, such as *The Practice of Everyday Life* (1984), which focuses on the ways that people "make do" within institutions like education, the military, and large corporations. The chapter explores the implications of de Certeau's work for practices of reading and writing, in particular, as well as his explorations of space and place. Rothbauer summarizes the current use of de Certeau's work in LIS, noting that most scholars employ this theorist's writing to explore research participants' active or resistant agency in various contexts. She also provides guidance on potential future uses of de Certeau's work, including the extension of his theories to studies of everyday life information seeking and the information practices of library users.

The work of French theorist Jacques Derrida, whose name is most closely aligned with the concept of deconstruction, is reviewed by Joseph Deodato. Deodato notes Derrida's influence on poststructuralism, particularly the value to numerous academic disciplines of providing alternate readings of social texts related to gender, race, class, and sexuality. The chapter summarizes Derrida's key concepts, including the metaphysics of presence, logocentrism and phonocentrism, and *différance*. Deodato also explores the influence of Derrida's work on LIS, with a focus on scholars' work in the areas of bibliographic description and classification. The author notes that this body of theory poses a challenge to librarians' traditional ways of knowing and conducting their work, given that Derrida's work problematizes notions of truth, meaning, and objectivity.

Michael Olsson's chapter on Michel Foucault explores his highly influential work across a broad range of disciplines, from history and sociology to gender studies and literary criticism, as the central figure in the development of postmodernism. Despite this prominence, Foucault remains a largely underutilized theorist in contemporary LIS research, as witnessed by the continuing focus on searching behavior and mental processes of the individual information seeker to the exclusion of social factors. A Foucauldian research paradigm would focus on language use and people's engagement with existing, intersubjective networks of power/knowledge. The growing body of LIS research drawing on social-constructivist and discourse-analytic approaches indicates the time may be ripe for a wider appreciation of the significance of Foucault's work in the LIS community, and a greater application of his ideas in LIS research.

Martina Riedler and Mustafa Yunus Eryaman introduce Brazilian educator Paulo Freire, whose critical pedagogy—in particular, his notions of dialogue, praxis, and conscientization—presents a useful framework for examining transformative library pedagogy in community-based contexts. Riedler and Eryaman examine Freire's most famous text, *Pedagogy of the Oppressed*, alongside his other key works. The chapter presents a critical framework based on Freire's critical pedagogy and identifies the characteristics of a transformative and community-based library. The end result is an alternative conception of library pedagogy that positions it as a dialogic accomplishment.

Ron Day and Andrew Lau provide a wide-ranging overview of psychoanalysis and its potential role as a critical framework in LIS. In particular, the chapter begins with a discussion of Freud, but then broadens to include Lacan, and Deleuze and Guattari in terms of their critiques and conceptualizations of the subject. As such, the works of these thinkers are reviewed in terms of their critical contributions, as well as some of their conceptual overlaps and differences. The chapter engages psychoanalysis as a critical discourse on subjectivity, knowledge, and action, and it suggests that such a discourse can be useful in a critique of the concept of the subject as it is traditionally theorized in LIS, particularly in the information-user tradition. Further, the chapter suggests that a critical-cultural discourse on psychoanalysis may offer a means for understanding the subject in contemporary developments and expressions of new and social media.

Howard Rosenbaum's chapter on Anthony Giddens examines the broad influence of the theorist's work on LIS to date, and explores the possibilities for future work in this area. The chapter focuses primarily on Giddens' "structuration theory," along with his other central ideas. Rosenbaum presents a citation analysis of top journals in LIS to demonstrate how Giddens' theories have been used in the field. The chapter also explores the various ways of citing Giddens' work; these include ceremonial citations, as well as more substantive modes of incorporating the theorist's ideas into research in the field.

Mustafa Yunus Eryaman examines the work of Henry Giroux, with a particular focus on the implications of Giroux's "border pedagogy" for library education and community empowerment within public libraries. The chapter connects Giroux's work to research on the limitations of information and communication technologies and explores the implications for libraries as transformative organizations. The chapter closes with an overview of research pointing to the potential for libraries (and librarians) to be agents of democratic change; in all of these areas, Giroux's theories can guide LIS science scholars in their investigations of transformative change.

Writing on Antonio Gramsci, Doug Raber remarks that of the critical social theorists included in this volume, only a handful have actually participated in direct political action or work to change a social order. Raber notes that Gramsci was actively engaged in the prewar European socialist movement, earning a reputation as an effective political journalist, and that he can be regarded as an incidental theorist who intended his writing to be a direct and practical guide. Gramsci's philosophy of praxis, scattered across many different texts, offers a surprisingly coherent understanding of how modern capitalism works and provides a profound reinterpretation of the relationship between Marxist concepts of base and superstructure and new insights into the relations between the material conditions of human existence and human consciousness as aspects of human history. Raber concludes with a summary review of the few LIS uses of Gramsci and the liberatory potential of Gramsci's ideas for LIS scholarship.

John Buschman provides a thematic overview of the work of Jürgen Habermas. Buschman devotes much of his chapter on Habermas' attempts to working through and beyond the aporia of foolproof transcendental arguments and the dead end of relativism. Since Habermas' work is vast, Buschman concludes that the use of Habermas in LIS is partial, at best. The chapter is selective, focusing on some of Habermas' earlier ideas that still percolate through the increasingly subtle and abstract refinements of his later work: the emancipatory interest in knowledge, the theory of knowledge as social theory, communicative action, and the public sphere. Habermas' work is highly interrelated, but these categories give some notion to the framing power of his thinking and its applicability to LIS.

Ron Day's second chapter discusses the works of Martin Heidegger and his critique of information as a late stage in the Western metaphysical tradition. In particular,

Heidegger's critique of technological modernity is reviewed, from his critique of ontology as metaphysics to his critique of language and art as metaphysics. Additionally, this chapter attempts to articulate the centrality of representation, particularly within the arena of LIS discourse, and ultimately advocate for a richer and more nuanced view of the relationship between information, language, and thought. The chapter argues that an understanding of Heidegger's work is essential not only for understanding many other critical theorists, but also that Heidegger's work constitutes an extraordinarily deep and broad critique of the ideology and the rhetoric of information in modernity and today.

Bruno Latour is the subject of the chapter by Will Wheeler. In this chapter, Wheeler argues that Latour demonstrates that evidence from scientific practice controverts entirely both our understanding of objective external reality "out there" and our received understanding of the internal, socially constructed world of our minds "in here." Latour stands on *neither* side of the objective/subjective divide. Rather, he is repositioning his work outside of critical theory per se, and starting over with new premises based on how we actually work in practice via detailed evidence and meticulous studies across a wide range of scientific disciplines. Thus Latour is indispensable to an understanding of humans, technology, and information society. Wheeler reviews nine essential things to know about Latour's recent (versus earlier) work to give researchers exploring the social in LIS a sense of what is particularly relevant.

Sanna Talja presents the situated cognition or practice theory approach of Jean Lave. Through her explication of Lave's key ideas, Talja seeks to clarify the theoretical assumptions that underpin the ongoing conceptual shift from information behaviour to information practices. Talja points out that Lave's key argument that problem solving and decision-making have been given an exaggerated role in cognitive research is particularly relevant to LIS. Talja argues that the legacy of cognitive science influenced basically all major theories of human information behavior developed between the late 1970s and 1990s, which are, in essence, theories of problem solving and decision-making. In practice theory, problem solving does not have a broad or central role to play in everyday activity in its customary settings. Rather, it is the activity setting with its structures and material conditions that entails particular selves, skills, values and sensibilities, and ways of acting and doing. Talja also points out that the widespread popularity of Lave's later work on communities of practice (Lave and Wenger 1991) has, to a large degree, left Lave's earlier criticism of research on human information-processing as decision-making and problem solving in its shadow. While most studies applying Lave and Wenger have focused on communities and not theorized the concept of practice, Talja's chapter concentrates on the key ideas underpinning Lave's concept of practice, also explaining how practice theory differs from other social theoretical approaches, such as textualism.

Gloria Leckie and Lisa Given discuss the work of Henri Lefebvre, who was early on known for his writings on Marx and on historical materialism. The chapter focuses on a work completed relatively late in his career, *The Production of Space*, which appeared in English in the 1980s. The translation of this particular work propelled Lefebvre into prominence in Anglo-American scholarly circles, spawning "sociospatial Marxism" (Merrifield 2006, 102). Lefebvre's premise that social space is a social product has implications or consequences, such as natural spaces becoming background décor. Lefebvre asserts that, historically, every society's space looks and feels different from those spaces that preceded or followed because of the particular interrelationships between the social relations of production and the relations of production. The specific ways that these interrelationships are played out produces a specific and historically contingent configuration of space. Lefebvre introduced his now famous conceptual triad of space (spatial practice, representations of space, and representational spaces), which the authors review. Lefebvre, the authors argue, is a relatively underutilized scholar in LIS but one whose theoretical approach could help to shed light on issues ranging from the place of the library in a globalizing world order, to the conceptualization of libraries as places within the public sphere and the everyday uses of library spaces by patrons.

Herbert Marcuse (1898–1979), who was an important and influential philosopher, public intellectual, and social activist of the 20th century, is covered by Ajit Pyati. Among Marcuse's many works, *One-Dimensional Man* (1964) and *Eros and Civilization* (1955) remain his most famous. The themes of domination and liberation animated much of Marcuse's writings, as he was concerned with the technological rationality and repressive tendencies of advanced industrial societies. Marcuse was a utopian thinker who envisioned the potential of radical revolutionary moments to create an aesthetically rich and nonrepressive society. Marcuse's critiques of technological rationality and the technological society have particular relevance for LIS. Specifically, a Marcusean approach to LIS can highlight some of the gross inequities of the information society, critically assess modern constructions of information, influence discourses of technology, and provide inspiration for a new generation of socially conscious scholars and professionals.

Hansson's chapter on Chantal Mouffe explores her social analysis of (post-Marxist and post-Gramscian) hegemony. Hansson argues that Mouffe's work on politics and the political in society approaches those topics in a different way. He argues for this by reviewing, in turn, her related groundbreaking work on discourse theory, on the political, and "agonistic pluralism." LIS has been exceptionally empirical and not theoretically oriented, with critical and emancipatory perspectives rarely seen. Mouffe, Hansson argues, contributes to new efforts to summarize and use existing empirical knowledge in defining emancipatory elements in both LIS as an academic field of research and librarianship as a social practice. Her theories can be fruitful as a framework for critical analyses of library and information institutions and practices.

Nick Dyer-Witheford argues that the work of Antonio Negri is an overlooked source of inspiration for critical theorists in LIS. After tracing Negri's early and dramatic involvement in Italian "workerism" in the 1970s, the chapter focuses on his later work, and, in particular on his concepts of the socialized worker, Empire, and multitude. Here, Dyer-Witheford suggests, we find an audacious rewriting of the traditional Marxian account of conflict between labour and capital adapted for an era of information capitalism and what Negri terms "immaterial labour." Negri's work is, however, not only important for his description of an era where the dynamics of exploitation centers on issues of communication and knowledge. Even more significant is his effort, undertaken with coauthor Michael Hardt, to think through the possibilities of a new order alternative to capitalism—a commonwealth—of which an information commons would be a vital component.

Paul Solomon's chapter on Saussure explores both the crucial processes by which his work has been assembled and understood and the *langue* and *parole* distinction that has provided a means to assess the value and utility of linguistic formalizations and for understanding the pragmatic and discourse aspects of conversations in information seeking contexts. Much of the intellectual use of Saussure has been about interpretation and application. The contrast of understanding, comprehension, interpretation, and application provides an approach to the role of language in LIS and Saussure's contributions, and Solomon reviews a number of those uses.

Rosamund Stooke's examination of the work of Dorothy Smith explores this American theorist's influence on sociology, women's studies, and other disciplines, including LIS. Stooke first examines Smith's early work, which explored issues related to the social organization of knowledge (e.g., standpoint theory). Stooke then examines Smith's best-known work—institutional ethnography—that provides a technique for investigating ruling relations through an empirical lens. Stooke describes her own use of this approach in exploring the work done by children's librarians, summarizes others' use of Smith's work in the field, and then explores the implications of Smith's work for future research. The chapter closes with a discussion of the ways that Smith's work can inform both research and practice in library and information settings, with a particular focus on issues of equity and social justice.

In the final chapter of the volume, Hope A. Olson and Melodie J. Fox interpret the rich writings of Gayatri Chakravorty Spivak, illustrating her unique blend of feminist, Marxist, deconstructionist, and postcolonial theory with an eye to application in LIS. Her work is sometimes regarded as impenetrable, so Olson and Fox translate Spivak's interpretations of each of these four epistemic stances into clear, scholarly prose, including explanations of background concepts from Derridean deconstruction to the progression from colonialism to postcoloniality. The authors suggest how Spivak's theoretical lenses, which are shaped by her lived experience, may also serve to ground research questions in LIS. Spivak derives in her work several semantic constructs, which she has defined in her own terms. Olson and Fox introduce five of these concepts: the subaltern, ideology, strategic essentialism, translation and representation, and the telematic society of information command. They describe the potential for direct application of Spivak's concepts to issues in LIS. In the end, Olson and Fox reveal Spivak's cerebral position to be a highly pragmatic vehicle for a text-based humanities approach to research that bridges theory and practice, particularly in LIS.

REFERENCES

Andersen, Jack. 2005. "Information Criticism: Where Is It?" *Progressive Librarian* 25 (Summer): 12–22.

Badmington, Neil, and Julia Thomas, eds. 2008. *The Routledge Critical and Cultural Theory Reader*. London: Routledge.

Bauman, Zygmunt. 1991. Critical Theory. In *The Renascence of Sociological Theory: Classical and Contemporary*, ed. Henry Etzkowitz and Ronald M. Glassman, 277–303. Itasca, IL: Peacock.

Bernstein, Richard J. 1983. *Beyond Objectivism and Relativism: Science, Hermeneutics, and Praxis*. Philadelphia: University of Pennsylvania Press.

Benoit, Gerry. 2002. "Toward a Critical Theoretic Perspective in Information Systems." *Library Quarterly* 72 (4): 441–71.

Brosio, Richard A. 1994. *A Radical Democratic Critique of Capitalist Education*. New York: Peter Lang.

Buschman, John E. 2003. *Dismantling the Public Sphere: Situating and Sustaining Librarianship in the Age of the New Public Philosophy*. Westport, CT: Libraries Unlimited/ Greenwood.

Buschman, John, and Richard A. Brosio. 2006. "A Critical Primer on Postmodernism: Lessons from Educational Scholarship for Librarianship." *Journal of Academic Librarianship* 32 (4): 408–18.

Dahms, Harry F., ed. 2007. *No Social Science Without Critical Theory*. Bingley, UK: JAI Press.

Dant, Tim. 2003. *Critical Social Theory*. London: Sage.

Dews, Peter. 1995. *The Limits of Disenchantment: Essays on Contemporary European Philosophy*. London: Verso.

Frohmann, Bernd. 2004. *Deflating Information: From Science Studies to Documentation*. Toronto: University of Toronto Press.

Giddens, Anthony. 1987. *Sociology, A Brief but Critical Introduction*, 2nd ed. New York: Harcourt Brace Jovanovich.

Granter, Edward. 2009. *Critical Social Theory and the End of Work*. Farnham, UK: Ashgate.

Greene, Maxine. 1986. "Liberal Learning and Teacher Education." In *Excellence in Teacher Education Through the Liberal Arts: Proceedings of the Conference*, ed. Michael Carbone and Ann Wonsiewicz, 23–27. Allentown, PA: Education Department, Muhlenberg College.

Hall, Stuart. 1986. "On Postmodernism and Articulation." *Journal of Communication Inquiry* 10: 45–60.

Held, David. 1980. *Introduction to Critical Theory: Horkheimer to Habermas*. Berkeley: University of California Press.

Kuhn, Thomas S. 1996. *The Structure of Scientific Revolutions,* 3rd ed. Chicago: University of Chicago Press.

Lave, Jean, and Etienne Wenger. 1991. *Situated Learning: Legitimate Peripheral Participation*. Cambridge: Cambridge University Press.

Leonard, John. 1993. "Novel Colonies: Review of Edward W. Said, *Culture and Imperialism* and Ahmandou Kourama, *Monnew*." *The Nation* 256 (March 22): 383–90.

Lipietz, Alain. 1995. "Post-Fordism and Democracy." In *Post-Fordism: A Reader*, ed. Ash Amin, 338–57. Cambridge: Oxford University Press.

Matustik, Martin Beck. 2001. Foreword. In *New Critical Theory: Essays on Liberation,* ed. William S. Wilkerson and Jeffrey Paris, vii-xiii. Lanham, UK: Roman and Littlefield.

McCarthy, Cameron, and Michael W. Apple. 1988. "Race, Class and Gender in American Educational Research: Toward a Nonsynchronous Parallelist Position." In *Class, Race, and Gender in American Education*, ed. Lois Weiss, 9–42. Albany: State University of New York Press.

McCarthy, Thomas A. 1991. *Ideals and Illusions: On Reconstruction and Deconstruction in Contemporary Critical Theory*. Cambridge, MA: MIT Press.

Merrifield, Andy. 2006. *Henri Lefebvre: A Critical Introduction*. New York: Routledge.

Rose, Mike. 1989. *Lives on the Boundaries*. New York: Penguin.

Sim, Stuart, ed. 2005. "From the Modern to the Postmodern." In *The Routledge Companion to Postmodernism*, 2nd ed., vii–xiv. New York: Routledge.

Sinnerbrink, Robert, Jean-Philippe Deranty, and Nicholas H. Smith. 2006. "Critique, Hope, Power: Challenges of Contemporary Critical Theory." In *Critique Today*, ed. Robert Sinnerbrink, Jean-Philippe Deranty, Nicholas H. Smith, and Peter Schmiedgen, 1–22. Leiden: Brill.

Wolin, Sheldon S. 1969. "Political Theory as a Vocation." *American Political Science Review* 63 (4, Dec): 1062–82.

NOTES

1. Many thanks to colleagues Nick Dyer-Witheford and Tom Carmichael for reading drafts of this chapter and providing very helpful commentary.

2. For a more detailed discussion of the relationship between the Frankfurt School and poststructuralist theorists, see Peter Dews, *The Limits of Disenchantment: Essays on Contemporary European Philosophy*. London: Verso, 1995.

1

Michel Aglietta and Regulation Theory

Siobhan Stevenson
University of Toronto, Canada

BIOGRAPHICAL BACKGROUND

Michel Aglietta (b. 1938) is a French Marxist economist. Currently, he is a professor of economic sciences at the University of Paris X Nanterre and a policy advisor with the Centre d'Etudes Prospectives et d'Informations Internationales (CEPII). In 1979, he published an expanded version of his pioneering doctoral thesis entitled *A Theory of Capitalist Regulation: The U.S. Experience,* thus laying the foundation for what has become known as French school regulation theory. Drawing on the dominant intellectual traditions of the time including Marxism and structuralism (Boyer 2002, 13), Aglietta's general theory of capitalism was both an intellectual project and a political one. Intellectually, it represented a critique of and alternative to dominant neoclassical economic theories, particularly given their inability to explain the widespread social and economic crises of the late 1960s and early 1970s (Aglietta 2000, 15). As a political project, Aglietta was concerned with developing a set of analytic tools within a reading of capitalism as a social creation (19) and the political sphere as the central site in which collective interests and the democratic principle could be brought to bear on the establishment of a new capitalist regime.

As a student, Aglietta was struggling with these questions against a backdrop that included the May 1968 general strike in Paris, the largest wildcat strike of its kind, in which 11,000 workers and students took to the streets in a revolt against the status quo. Within this context, appreciation for Aglietta's concerns with the need to forge real-world connections between theory and empirical reality for the purpose of creating a more just, prosperous, and peaceful world is enhanced.

Since the publication and translation of his thesis in 1979, theorists working across a range of disciplines including policy studies, economics, urban development, geography and, more recently, information science have elaborated on Aglietta's work. In 2000, a new edition was released containing a postface in which Aglietta considers the approach's continued relevance.

REVIEW OF AGLIETTA'S MAJOR CONTRIBUTIONS

Introduction

Aglietta is credited with having developed an approach to the study of social change within the context of capitalism's evolution over the course of the 20th century. Based on Marx's general theory of capitalism, Aglietta's analysis of capitalist regulation in the United States is informed by the precepts of historical materialism mapped onto the inherent contradictions underpinning wage societies and which provide them with their technological dynamism. Having said that, Aglietta's approach diverges from Marxism in one significant respect. Where Marx theorized that the inherent contradictions within capitalism, namely the class tensions embedded in the wage relationship, would inevitably lead to the system's demise and replacement by socialism, Aglietta foresees no such eventuality (Aglietta 2000, 396). Indeed, Aglietta is clear that the purpose of his work is to provide the analytic tools necessary to engage society (in France but also beyond) in a political debate over how best to strengthen democracy, rekindle solidarity, maintain social harmony, and improve living conditions for all *within* the context of capitalism's globalization. In the words of Aglietta, "The purpose of the political debate is to devise a means of giving expression to people's social rights so that the new growth regime can put wage societies back on the road to social progress" (445).

Since the goal of this chapter is to demonstrate the value of Aglietta's theory of capitalist regulation for questions in library and information science (LIS), three points of additional clarification will facilitate the process of making connections between Aglietta's work and the interests and concerns of LIS researchers and students.

First, reference to social change and transformation refers specifically to the emergence since the early 1970s of what has been variously labeled as the post-industrial society, the information society, the information economy, the digital economy, the global information economy, and so forth. Indeed, theorizing the shift in the West from predominantly industrial-based economies to information and service-based economies and its ripple effects around the globe is a central source of contestation and debate among social theorists, government bureaucrats, and corporate leaders. Given the interests involved, the outcomes of these debates bear directly on the world's population as citizens, workers, and consumers. In order to appreciate Aglietta's contribution, it is useful to situate him within this wider political context. In brief, theorizations of contemporary social change can be roughly divided into two camps. On the one side are those who take their inspiration from social theorists such as Daniel Bell and his work during the 1970s and 1980s on postindustrial society (1973). A distinguishing feature of his work was the transformative potential ascribed to the new information and communication technologies (ICTs). Within this new and historically discontinuous world, the old antagonisms between industrial labour and capital disappear in what has been called the "end of ideology" thesis, the tenets of which have been enthusiastically appropriated by the global neoliberalist project. On the other side are those, primarily on the left, like Aglietta, who conceive of contemporary conditions as more or less historically continuous. Thus, despite the seeming novelty of the new ICTs and their transformative effects on all aspects of life, their production and distribution unfolds squarely within the social (class) relations that constitute capitalism as an inherently contradictory and unstable system of social and economic integration.

Second, as a work of political economy, it is helpful to review the main tenets of the political economy perspective. In *The Political Economy of Communication: Rethinking and Renewal* (1996), Vincent Mosco has produced a particularly succinct summary of the theoretical requirements of the political economy approach, of which Aglietta's *Theory of Capitalist Regulation: The U.S. Experience* is an exemplar. (1) As evidenced by the above discussion, and because capitalism is conceived of as historically continuous, history and social change or transformation are intrinsically linked. Analytically, this is particularly valuable for distinguishing between those qualitative social and economic changes that are truly novel, and those that represent a continuation of past practices and social relations, albeit in a different form. (2) Political economy analyses take into account the totality of social life; this, in sharp contrast to classical economic theory that conceives of the economy as abstracted from the complexities and contradictions of the human condition and the dialectic within capitalism between the economic and noneconomic realms. (3) The concept of moral philosophy is used "to refer to social values (wants about wants) and to conceptions of appropriate social practices. The goal of this particular form of analysis is to clarify and make explicit the moral perspectives of economic and political economic perspectives, particularly because moral viewpoints are often masked in these perspectives" (Mosco 1996, 34). As such, it is impossible to analyze public policies without attending to their ideological import. (4) Praxis. The research needs to be action oriented and its findings geared towards the real world of policy development. Within this context, the political economy perspective frames the public policy process as a central site of social struggle over the power to decide how society's resources, including information resources, are to be produced and distributed. Given the service-oriented nature of the discipline and its contemporary philosophical concerns regarding the tension between information as a public good and information as an economic resource, an increasing number of LIS scholars are integrating this perspective into their research practices.

The third point of clarification concerns the pattern of scholarly communication within which Michel Aglietta is embedded as the founder of French school regulation theory. Except for the publication in 2000 of a new edition of *A Theory of Capitalist Regulation: The U.S. Experience* with its updated postface, there exist few other translated texts of Aglietta's work in English. For this reason, the elaboration of his ideas and the application of his analytic concepts to new areas of inquiry beyond the field of economics have been undertaken by a heterodox mix of scholars from around the world (Jessop 2006, 2). This has given rise to the theory's characterization as an approach and a research programme rather than a unified theory of fully refined concepts (Aglietta 2000, 388). That said, there are a number of theorists whose contributions cannot be ignored in any general introduction to the approach. These include Alain Lipietz (1987, 1992), David Harvey (1989), Robert Boyer (1990), Jamie Peck and Adam Tickell (1992), and Bob Jessop (2006).[1]

French School Regulation Theory: Aglietta's Contribution to Marxist Scholarship

Aglietta's contribution to Marxist scholarship has been the conceptualization of capitalism's history into distinct periods as a means of interpreting how an inherently contradictory and crisis-prone system of social and economic organization manages to reproduce and transform itself over time. Aglietta's theory of capitalist regulation is based on his analysis of the history of capitalism's evolution in the United States from the Civil War through to the 1970s. Within this historical frame, Aglietta focuses our attention on key moments in that society's development, paying particular attention to the complex interplay between the emergence of new productive technologies and their impact on social relations of production and reproduction. Having traced the history of American capitalism's cyclical boom and bust periods and attendant social (class) struggles dating from the 1880s and culminating in the Great Depression of the 1930s, Aglietta sets the stage for his detailed analysis of America's postwar years of unprecedented prosperity and relative social harmony up until the late 1960s.

Significantly, Aglietta was less concerned with analyzing the reasons behind the social and economic crises of that period than with explaining why they hadn't occurred sooner. He was specifically interested in exploring the kinds of social compromises, alliances, and negotiations that unfolded between capitalism's two central and competing social identities (labour and capital) and which resulted in the world hegemony of American capitalism. To this end, Aglietta theorized that a deeper and more concrete understanding of the dynamics underpinning American Fordism and which distinguished it from past experiments would provide clues to the way out of the contemporary crisis.

Aglietta posited that in order for capitalism to function and reproduce itself for any period of time, it required the development of a historically specific regime of accumulation and a complementary mode of social regulation (MSR). The concept regime of accumulation refers to the ways in which surplus value (profit) is realized during the twin processes of production (work) and circulation (consumption), or, in other words, how capital is accumulated within a wage society. However, the pivot upon which accumulation rests and from which the system takes its energy and growth dynamic is the wage relationship. Indeed, for Aglietta, appreciating the social energy generated within capitalism through the ongoing process of constituting the wage relation formed the basis for his work on modes of social regulation.

The theory we will seek to elaborate here is in reality a theory of development of the wage relation. Our aim is to grasp the source of this dynamic in order to be able to interpret the modes of societal cohesion from which economic relationships can be derived (Aglietta 2000, 72).

Aglietta posited that a mode of social regulation did the important work of legitimating and reproducing the wage relationship through the establishment of a wide range of social institutions in both the economic and non-economic realms. Regulationist Alain Lipietz provides a particularly useful description of the dialectic between a regime of accumulation and mode of social regulation: "if a regime of accumulation is to be realized and to reproduce itself for any length of time, there must also be institutional forms, procedures and habits which either coerce or persuade private agents to conform to its schemas" (Lipietz 1987, 33). It is important to note that the concept of modes of social regulation actually originates with Antonio Gramsci's work on the dynamics of American Fordism (Aglietta 2000, 29). As such, modes of social regulation extend to all aspects of social and cultural life, which, in their organization and functioning, serve to socialize individuals to the requirements of the regime of accumulation and legitimate the social relations that underpin that regime. The structural integration of a regime of accumulation and mode of social regulation results in the temporary stabilization of capitalism as a system of social and economic integration.

Finally, as theorized by Aglietta, these periods of relative stability exist on either side of periods of social chaos as one regime becomes destabilized and the process of establishing a new or transformed regime is negotiated among the system's central social identities. Within this context, Aglietta highlighted the centrality of the nation-state for any project aimed at mediating relations between capital and labour and creating conditions conducive to capital accumulation, on the one hand, and social harmony and cohesion on the other. He credits the work of James O'Connor in the United States, Manuel Castells in France, Tony Negri in Italy, and Joachim Hirsch in Germany with influencing his conception of the state within capitalism (Aglietta 2000, 28). From a political perspective then, in order for capitalism to work, it requires the active participation of three social identities without which prosperity *and* harmony are impossible: the state, capital, and labour. As well, periods of social and economic stability are completely dependent upon the successful negotiation of these competing interests with respect to defining both a regime of accumulation and mode of social regulation. Further, this process of stabilization is not based on consensus building but rather on compromise, negotiation, trade-offs, and complex class and interclass alliances. At the heart of the process is the class struggle over the power to control the production and allocation of society's resources.

In summary, capitalism, as a system of social and economic integration, bears the imprint of these underlying social relations. The implications of this dynamic include, but are not limited to, the following: (1) Social change is inevitable. Given that periods of stability are built upon a foundation of negotiation and uneasy compromises, such settlements can only ever be temporary. An important source of constant change (and as highlighted within the approach) is the meaning of technological innovation for social relations of production, particularly when read through the differing hegemonic projects of labour and capital. (2) Power is never assured. While the trio of social identities remains constant, the relative power among these three is historically variable. (3) Each regime of accumulation requires for its successful reproduction a complementary mode of social regulation and vice versa. (4) The period of transition between one regime and another is not linear; rather it occurs over an extended period of time, with cracks appearing here and there in either the regime of accumulation or the mode of social regulation. Part of the transition to a new regime involves attempts to save the old via the renegotiation of terms between capital, the state, and labour. Inevitably, however, and in large part as a result of the opportunities for emancipation through technological innovation, the system fails and the process of establishing an entirely new regime begins again.

Fordism and Post-Fordism

Aglietta used the terms *Fordism* and *neo-Fordism* as a means of distinguishing between what he perceived as two historically specific regimes of capital accumulation and modes of social regulation. Although he was conducting his research "in the midst of the crisis of Fordism, and the new interactions [were] only little visible" (2000, 127), his detailed and nuanced analysis of American Fordism and an emerging neo-Fordism or post-Fordism (as it is more commonly termed) continues to inform the work of scholars more than 30 years later. To follow is an overview of Aglietta's (2000) treatment of American Fordism, its collapse, and the features of a newly emerging regime. This chapter will then conclude with a summary of its analytic value and its applications (actual and potential) within LIS.

The term Fordism is a direct reference to Henry Ford's introduction in 1914 of the semi-automated assembly line (for the mass production of cars) combined with a five-dollar, eight-hour day (which would ensure that the mass of workers could afford to buy the cars produced). Ford's innovative program with respect to the management of social relations of production both inside and outside his factory's walls was the result of a culmination of historical forces. His system represented a specific response to the chaos and social instability that characterized the transition to industrial capitalism from approximately 1870.

Ultimately, Ford's program is significant because it represented one of the first attempts to manage the inherent contradictions of the system by establishing a connection between the central role of the worker within the two moments of capital's circuit: production and circulation. Hence, while workers needed to be habituated to the discipline of life on an assembly line, they also needed to be educated in a new set of values that equated quality of life with the ability to purchase the commodities they produced. In this way, a virtuous cycle was produced which resolved a number of earlier problems, not the least of which was the effective management of surplus value. It is important to note that an insatiable desire for commodities was an unnatural condition, as were hours of monotonous and routine labour. Both had to be learned and then the learning curve had to be forgotten, as the requirements of the regime of accumulation for life inside and outside of work became internalized as commonsensical and inevitable.

It was not, however, until the establishment of the Keynesian welfare state following the Second World War that Fordism, as a regime of accumulation and mode of social regulation, would become stabilized. Regulationists refer to this period as the "real golden age of capitalism" (Lipietz 1992, 1). Within this new configuration, state powers were expanded to enable it to function as an effective countervailing force to the vagaries of the market. State intervention vis-à-vis a comprehensive set of social and economic regulations, including the guarantee of full employment (via employment insurance and pensions), coupled with the power to adjust interest rates and otherwise intervene in the business cycle, ensured that despite its inevitable cycles of boom and bust, individuals would be able to maintain their purchasing power, and capital could enjoy uninterrupted accumulation. In addition to its economic powers, the welfare state also took on a significant role in the reproduction of labour, thus freeing capital from this burden. Public spending on social infrastructure including schools, health care, social services, housing, and libraries (to name a few) expanded exponentially.

A full explication of Aglietta's in-depth and nuanced treatment, in his 2000 study, of this period of history in the United States is beyond the scope of this chapter, but a brief example should suffice to illustrate the size of the canvas on which he was working and the spaces he left for others to contribute and complete the picture. Aglietta effectively weaves together a number of social threads that comprised the social fabric within which economic relations unfolded during the 1950s and 1960s in the United States. The purpose of this historical analysis was to demonstrate the ways in which seemingly disparate phenomena including the family (157), the educational system, racism and sexism (173), the institutionalization of class struggle through collective bargaining (190), and the growth of the automobile and standardized housing markets (159) served to reproduce dominant ideologies of individualism, social mobility, and equality of opportunity despite the reality of labour's stratification into a rigid and relatively permanent social and economic hierarchy.

Some of the salient features of this regime, and which ultimately became the sources of its crises, included: the growth of large bargaining units ("big labour"), the mass production of homogenous goods coupled with mass consumption, vertical organization structures and authoritarian command, an emphasis on scientific management and the fragmentation of unskilled labour into discrete activities, the emergence of large national monopolies ("big capital"), and the mediating influence of the welfare state ("big government").

This period of prosperity lasted until the early 1970s, when, as interpreted through the regulationist lens "the whole miraculous balance of the Fordist compromise was jeopardized" (Lipietz 1992, 16). For a myriad of complex economic and social reasons, including global competition from the recovered, technologically innovative, and nimble German and Japanese economies, and the global oil crisis, the United States experienced a period of protracted economic and social crises in both its regime of accumulation (chronic inflation, unemployment) and mode of social regulation (strikes, student protests, and the emergence of a numerous social movements rebelling against the rigidities of Fordism, such as the civil rights, antiwar, environmental, and women's movements, to name a few). Indeed, even within the apparently pacific domain of American Library Association, the spirit of resistance was present in emergence of the social responsibilities movement and the concept of library activism in the 1960s (Samek 1998).

Post-Fordism is an umbrella term used by regulationists to describe the process of Fordism's transformation since the early 1970s into a new, yet to be stabilized, regime of accumulation and mode of social regulation. Not surprisingly, perhaps, the emerging features of post-Fordism "as a system designed to meet the crisis in such as way as to safeguard the wage relation—in other words, perpetuate capitalism" (Aglietta 2000, 122), stand in stark contrast to Fordism's social relations of production and reproduction. Table 1.1 outlines some of the key differences between Fordism and an emerging post-Fordism in the Western world.

Table 1.1
Characteristics of Fordism and Post-Fordism

Fordism (1945–1965)	Post-Fordism (1973–present)
Manufacturing economies based on a cycle of mass production and mass consumption for a mass national market.	**Information economies** based on the production of just-in-time and customizable products for niche global markets.
Rigid and mechanistic structures vis-à vis semiautomated assembly line production requiring the establishment of capital intensive and relatively immobile factories reliant on the local population for workers. The concomitant labour force was semiskilled or unskilled within a technocratic order that diminished worker responsibility.	**Flexible and networked structure** vis-à-vis highly automated systems employing distance- and time-shrinking information and communications technologies to create a flexible, 24/7 production cycle enabled by access to an international workforce. This global workforce is polarized by a small core of highly skilled, well-compensated elite workers at one end, and a mass of lower-skilled workers subjected to an intensification in surveillance as a result of new technologies (i.e., counting keystrokes, ongoing monitoring of transaction logs, etc.).

Table 1.1 (continued)

Fordism (1945–1965)	Post-Fordism (1973–present)
Corporate culture based on **scientific management** practices and the increased rationalization of labour into minute, routinized, and repetitive tasks. Authoritative and top-down command within a highly formalized and rigid hierarchy of job classes and the stratification of the labour force into permanent and recognizable socio-economic categories, that is, assembly line workers, supervisors, professionals, paraprofessionals, managers, owners, and so on. A worker's position within the hierarchy, including salary, benefits and opportunities for advancement, were dependent upon clearly articulated requirements with respect to qualifications, including such factors as educational credentials, experience, and seniority. In this way, the economic class struggle became institutionalized in the form of collective bargaining and structural inequalities were legitimated.	Emphasis on the concept of **contingent management** premised on the assumption that no single management style will suffice, rather a more eclectic and flexible approach is required in an operating environment that is conceived of as highly competitive, fluid, evolving, and ever changing. The clearly demarcated job classes of Fordism are replaced with more fluid organizational structures and post-Fordist workers often find themselves in project-based work teams comprised of a heterogeneous mix of workers. Unlike the clear demarcation between workers within Fordism, the steady erosion of unions and collective bargaining has led, among other things, to the negotiation of employment conditions on an individual basis, hence, the possibility for more ambiguous and flexible job descriptions and the move to merit based pay schemes as opposed to negotiated rates for classes of workers. One result of this shift has been the increase in the number of part-time and limited-contract positions and a decrease in permanent positions.
"Job for life."	"Job for now."
Cultural aesthetics: **uniformity** and **standardization**	Cultural aesthetics: **difference, diversity,** customization, intense individualism
The Keynesian welfare state provided a countervailing balance to capitalism as a regime of accumulation through the regulation of market relations both nationally and internationally; the guarantee of "full employment" or a living wage to ensure full consumption and a virtuous cycle between production and consumption; the establishment of a social safety net ensuring the reproduction of labour through generalized standards of living for all citizens (health, education, pensions, consumer protections, living standards); the establishment of protective labour legislation (health and safety, minimum wages, benefits, the right to collective bargaining). Within this context, there was a clear division between the public and private spheres, and the citizen identity and social solidarity were privileged in public discourses, thus creating conditions for a viable political sphere.	**The neoliberalist state** emphasizing market deregulation (free trade), increased privatization of formerly public functions and a privileging of the market as the best mechanism for social cohesion and coordination; the repeal and/or weakening of protective labour legislation and protections, austerity in public spending; increasing emphasis on public-private partnerships, entrepreneurship and innovation; the constitution of government as revenue generating, the dismantling of the welfare state and the devolution of roles and responsibilities to the community and individual level. The relative withdrawal of the state from the public sphere and the extension of the market into previously uncommodified areas of life, the blurring of lines between public and private sphere, the emergence of the citizen as consumer identity.
Regime stabilized vis-à-vis class compromise characterized by "big business, big labour, and big state."	Regime remains unstable due to class imbalance based on the emergence of a global information capital and neoliberal state power bloc.
Small nuclear families with members occupying strongly defined, gender-based roles.	Diverse family groupings.

Analytic Value

The value of regulation theory's twin analytic concepts of Fordism and post-Fordism is that they provide a framework and set of comparators with which to make connections between a regime of capital accumulation and the ideological work performed by the mode of social regulation for the purpose of achieving social and economic stability and cohesion. Further, as a conceptual framework, the mode of social regulation is particularly fruitful for questions about, and critical research into the evolution of those social institutions, professional practices, and behaviors that blossomed under the auspices of the Keynesian welfare state, including libraries and librarianship, and which, at first glance, appear a far remove from contemporary class struggles in the transition to a globalized capitalism.

Currently, within the field of LIS, researchers and practitioners are struggling to make sense of the meaning of fundamental social change as a result of the forces of capitalism's globalization including the production and diffusion of perpetually innovating ICTs, the near hegemony of the neoliberalist project,[2] and the very real impact of these on the full range of research and professional concerns that comprise the field. Evidence of this change dynamic's influence on the field abounds from the emergence of the i-school movement and the introduction of new specializations (i.e., information policy, knowledge management, and health informatics, to name three), through on going anxiety regarding the future of the library. The concept of mode of social regulation provides a powerful analytic tool with which to engage with this change dynamic, bridge institutional specific research with larger global trends, and forge theoretical connections not obvious otherwise. The following expanded description of a mode of regulation speaks to the concept's explanatory potential for a wide range of information phenomena within capitalism's globalization.

A mode of regulation is a set of mediations which ensure that the distortions created by the accumulation of capital are kept within limits which are compatible with social cohesion within each nation. This compatibility is always observable in specific contexts at specific historical moments. The salient test for any analysis of the changes that capitalism has undergone is to describe this cohesion in its local manifestation. It involves understanding why such cohesion is a short-lived phenomenon in the life of nations, why the effectiveness of a mode of regulation always wanes. And it requires grasping the processes that occur at times of crisis, confusion and changing behaviour patterns. Lastly it involves trying to perceive the seeds of a new mode of regulation in the very midst of the crisis afflicting the old one (Aglietta 2000, 391).

Regulation Theory and LIS

Although underutilized in the field of LIS, when regulation theory is employed, it has proven particularly useful for critical analyses of the role of the public library as a mode of social regulation. In an article entitled, "Regulating Readers: The Social Origins of the Readers' Advisor in the United States" (2001), Brendan Luyt employs regulation theory in a historical study of the rise and decline of readers' advisory services in American public libraries during the 1920s and 1930s. Within this context, Luyt provides discursive evidence of the concrete links between the organization and delivery of this public library service and the disciplining of the population to the requirements of an early Fordism, particularly with respect to new consumptive norms. In a period that predates the golden age of Fordism, Luyt situates the rise and decline of the readers' advisor within this experimental period in U.S. capitalism's evolution. The connections that Luyt makes between the library profession and the publishing industry, on the one side, and the readers' advisor and individual readers, on the other, go a long way in demonstrating the role the public library played in advancing the interests of capital, notably the legitimization of mass culture by encouraging an appetite for mass-produced books and magazines. Beyond consumption, Luyt describes the number of ways in which the readers' advisor contributed to the normalization of the social relations underpinning assembly-line production. From the constitution of the readers' advisor as expert and the reader in need of guidance, through the development of an individualized reading program designed to ensure "purposeful reading" (460) and the concomitant emergence of the concept of rationalization "that came to stand for the efficient control and use of resources" (462), Luyt skillfully demonstrates how a seemingly autonomous activity like reading became embedded in capital's requirements for accumulation and which "fit nicely with the world of the assembly line" (461).

However, as emphasized by Luyt in his final paragraph, his concern is not with evaluating the relative success or failure of the readers' advisory experiment in the early decades of the 20th century, but rather with what a historical analysis of this service has to tell us about the role of the public library within an emerging mode of social regulation.

The readers' advisory service was just one attempt or experiment among many (psychological testing, social work reform, consumer credit, state welfare, and union organization are a few examples), not all of which succeeded in establishing a place for themselves in the new mode of social regulation that eventually developed. The key point, however, does not revolve around the degree of success that the library or these other institutions achieved, but the recognition that they were connected in a society-wide project, as opposed to being in isolation from those wider trends. The rise of the readers' advisor in the 1920s reflects the fact that the library was and still is embedded within a particular kind of capitalist society (464).

The use of regulation theory for research into the public library as a mode of regulation in the early years of the 20th century builds upon a strong foundation of critical scholarship in the field concerned with demonstrating the links between the practices of librarianship and an emerging industrial economy's requirements for workers, consumers, and citizens (Garrison 1979; Harris 1982; Van Slyck 1995; Frohmann 1997). It also complements critical research on contemporary librarianship's role within today's global information economy (Schiller and Schiller 1988; Blanke 1996; Buschman 2003).

Regulation theory was also used by this researcher for the purpose of developing a political economy of the contemporary public library during the current transition from industrial-based to information-based economies (Stevenson 2005). To this end, the influence of large-scale philanthropies on the development of the American public library was analyzed. The parallel concepts of Fordism and post-Fordism provided the ideal framework for considering the influence of Andrew Carnegie and Bill Gates' philanthropies on all aspects of the library's functioning. Given the significant parallels between both men as captains of industry and philanthropists, and the historical timing of their entry into philanthropy, these twin concepts enabled a nuanced reading of not only the similarities between conditions at either side of the 20th century, but, as significantly, those differences that open onto the novel features of capital's updated project. As a result of this analysis, connections between Gates' project to bridge the digital divide vis-à-vis his library automation project and larger social struggles over free versus proprietary software, the expansion of intellectual property rights, and the social and economic significance of software as the new means of production were possible. Once again, the role of the public library in legitimating conditions conducive to capital accumulation was uncovered.

Beyond the sphere of the public library, a recently published study considered library OPACs and web portals as technologies of social regulation. Leckie, Givens, and Campbell (2008) use regulation theory to

argue that library catalogs and Web portals should be viewed as information technologies that are, first and foremost, commercial entities within the production system of advanced capitalism. The fact that library catalogs and Web-management systems are designed, sold and purchased for purposes deemed to be a social good sometimes obscures the fact that such technologies are not necessarily socially neutral or benign but operate very much in the capitalist marketplace and framework (221).

The authors use the concept of mode of social regulation to "disentangle and reveal the elements of the MSR that have been at work over the past 30–40 years that may account for the relative lack of change to, and persistent problems with, library OPACs" (249). Consistent with the requirements of this approach, the researchers' primary concern is with developing a more critical appreciation among practitioners (librarians) regarding the reality of capitalist relations on professional practices (past and present) and particularly where these intersect with the potentially competing needs of library users within spaces (library catalogues) often assumed to exist separate from the sphere of market relations. The application of regulation theory to the area of cataloging and classification represents a significant development in the use of the approach by LIS scholars. It also demonstrates the analytic potential of the concept mode of social regulation for a wide range of information phenomena.

Concluding Remarks

Having acknowledged the value of the theoretical tools developed by the regulation school and specifically the parallel concepts of Fordism and post-Fordism, it is important to note that the legitimacy of this approach is the subject of some serious debate among the left, particularly because of the assumption that the solution to the Fordist crisis resides within the context of labour's reconciliation with rather than liberation from capital (Sivanandan 1989; Peláez and Holloway 1991; Dyer-Witheford 1999). Indeed, within Aglietta's work, it is assumed that the road out of the crisis of Fordism will be another capitalist regime, the result of a second "grand compromise" between capital and labour. This model of class cooperation, coupled with the ways regulation school's Marxism intersect with the anti-Marxist perspectives of conservative industrial analysts such as Piore and Sabel (1984) leads to some serious misgivings regarding its meaning for the larger Marxist project. Indeed, because of these issues, theorists such as Nick Dyer-Witheford have come very close to rejecting it, for as he reminds us, "[t]he Marxist project has never been to help capitalism find its way out of a crisis. It has been to find a way out of capitalism. This is precisely the possibility that much post-Fordist writing abdicates" (Dyer-Witheford 1999, 60). However, while the danger of such abdication is real, it is not an inevitable consequence of adopting regulation school theory (as it has been subsequently developed).

In the final analysis, the analytic concepts underpinning Aglietta's theory of capital regulation have great explanatory potential for many of the more vexing questions and problems confronting LIS as a field of research and a professional practice within this period of rapid and fundamental social change.

REFERENCES

Aglietta, Michel. 2000. *A Theory of Capitalist Regulation: The U.S. Experience;* with a new postface by the author. New York: Verso Press.

Amin, Ash, ed. 1994. *Post-Fordism: A Reader.* Cambridge: Blackwell.

Bell, Daniel. 1973. *The Coming of Post-Industrial Society: A Venture in Social Forecasting.* New York: Basic Books.

Blanke, Henry. 1996. "Librarianship and Public Culture in the Age of Information Capitalism." *Journal of Information Ethics* 5:54–69.

Boyer, Robert. 1990. *The Regulation School: A Critical Introduction.* New York: Columbia University Press.

Boyer, Robert. 2002. The Origins of Régulation Theory. In *Regulation Theory: The State of the Art*, eds. Robert Boyer and Yves Saillard, 13–21. New York, NY: Routledge.

Buschman, John. 2003. *Dismantling the Public Sphere: Situating and Sustaining Librarianship in the Age of the New Public Philosophy.* Westport, CT: Libraries Unlimited.

Dyer-Witheford, Nick. 1999. *Cyber-Marx: Cycles and Circuits of Struggle in High Technology Capitalism.* Urbana: University of Illinois Press.

Frohmann, Bernd. 1997. " 'Best Books' and Excited Readers: Discursive Tensions in the Writings of Melvil Dewey." *Libraries and Culture* 32:349–71.

Garrison, Dee. 1979. *Apostles of Culture: The Public Librarian in American Society, 1876–1920.* New York: Free Press.

Harris, Michael. 1982. "The Purpose of the American Public Library: A Revisionist Interpretation of History." In *Public Librarianship: A Reader,* ed. J. Robbins-Car, 63–72. Littleton, CO: Libraries Unlimited.

Harvey, David. 1989. *The Condition of Postmodernity: An Enquiry into the Origins of Cultural Change.* Oxford: Blackwell.

Harvey, David. 2005. *A Brief History of Neoliberalism.* Oxford: Oxford University Press.

Jessop, Bob, and Ngai-Ling Sum. 2006. *Beyond the Regulation Approach: Putting Capitalist Economies in Their Place.* North Hampton, MA: Edward Elgar.

Leckie, Gloria, Lisa Givens, and Grant Campbell. 2008. "Technologies of Social Regulation: An Examination of Library OPACS and Web Portals." In *Information Technology in Librarianship: New Critical Approaches,* ed. Gloria Leckie and John Buschman, 221–60. Westport, CT: Libraries Unlimited.

Lipietz, Alain. 1987. *Mirages and Miracles: The Crisis of Global Fordism.* London: Verso.

Lipietz, Alain. 1992. *Towards a New Economic Order: Postfordism, Ecology and Democracy.* New York: Oxford University Press.

Luyt, Brendan. 2001. "Regulating Readers: The Social Origins of the Readers' Advisor in the United States." *Library Quarterly* 71 (4): 443–66.

Mosco, Vincent. 1996. *The Political Economy of Communication: Rethinking and Renewal.* London: Sage, 1996.

Peck, Jamie, and Adam Tickell. 1992. "Accumulation, Regulation and the Geographies of Post-Fordism: Missing Links in Regulationist Research." *Progress in Human Geography* 16 (2): 190–218.

Pelàez, Elonia, and John Holloway. 1991. "Learning to Bow: Post-Fordism and Technological Determinism." *Science as Culture* 8:15–27.

Piore, Michael, and Charles Sable. 1984. *The Second Industrial Divide: Possibilities for Prosperity.* New York: Basic Books

Samek, Antonio. 1998. "Intellectual Freedom and Social Responsibility: An Ethos of American Librarianship, 1967–1973." PhD diss., Univ. of Wisconsin-Madison.

Schiller, Herbert, and Anita Schiller. 1988. "Libraries, Public Access to Information, and Commerce." In *The Political Economy of Information,* ed. Vincent Mosco and Janet Wasko, 146–66. Madison: University of Wisconsin Press.

Sivanandan, Ambalavaner. 1989. " 'All That Melts into Air Is Solid': The Hokum of New Times." *Race & Class* 31 (3): 1–23.

Stevenson, Siobhan. 2005. *The Post-Fordist Public Library: From Carnegie to Gates.* PhD diss., Univ. of Western Ontario.

Van Slyck, Abigail. 1995. *Free to All: Carnegie Libraries & American Culture, 1890–1920.* Chicago: University of Chicago Press.

NOTES

1. Ash Amin's 1994 edited collection, *Post-Fordism: A Reader,* is an excellent introduction to the theory and its applications across a range of social phenomena and includes essays by many of post-Fordism's major theorists.

2. *Neoliberalism* is the term used to describe the dominant political ideology associated with globalization. The prefix *neo-* indicates its most recent incarnation in the 1980s in the fiscal and social policies of the Thatcher government in the United Kingdom and the Reagan government in the United States. At issue are questions regarding the power of the state to intervene in the workings of the market in light of the societal consequences of its inevitable boom and bust tendencies. Liberal political philosophy promotes a model of the state that does best when it does least. Here, a self-correcting market mechanism is constructed as the most effective and efficient means of achieving economic growth and social cohesion. As the successor of the Keynesian welfare state, some of the features associated with neoliberalism include austerity in social spending, market deregulation, and the privatization of once public goods. The policies of Thatcherism/Reaganism were not uncontested, and more than 30 years later, alternative social movements continue to resist, citing the increasing wealth gap, the criminalization of the poor, and the erosion of labour's power as direct fallout from the neoliberalist agenda. The concept of project is useful in discussions of ideology and social struggle because the ultimate goal of hegemonic achievement can only ever be partial. David Harvey provides an excellent account of the neoliberal project in *A Brief History of Neoliberalism* (2005).

2

Roland Barthes: On Semiology and Taxonomy

Hans Dam Christensen
Royal School of Library and Information Science, Denmark

BIOGRAPHY AND INTRODUCTION

Roland Barthes was born in Normandy, France, in 1915, and died from the injuries incurred in a street accident in Paris, 1980. From 1935 on, he studied classical literature, grammar, and philology at Sorbonne University, Paris. These studies were delayed by his suffering from tuberculosis. As a consequence of this illness, he gained his final degree only in 1948.

Barthes started his professional teaching career by taking short-term positions at French lycées (1939–46) as well as, after graduating, the French Institute in Bucharest, Rumania, and University of Alexandria, Egypt (1948–50). In 1952 he became affiliated with the distinguished Centre National de la Recherche Scientifique; from 1960 to 1976 he was a director of studies at École Pratique des Hautes Études; and from 1976 to 1980 he was the chair of literary semiology at the prestigious Collège de France, the highest position in the French academic system. Along the way, Barthes gradually gained more and more recognition for his research on semiology and literature as well as his writings on wide-ranging cultural and personal topics. By the late 1960s he had achieved an international reputation.

In the company of prominent intellectuals such as Jacques Lacan, Claude Lévi-Strauss, Jacques Derrida, and Michel Foucault, Roland Barthes became a leading figure in structuralist and poststructuralist circles of postwar France. He gained his reputation as a literary critic, a cultural philosopher and, not the least, a semiologist. Barthes' ideas were set forth in a series of essays originally published in Albert Camus' journal, *Combat*, and compiled in the volume *Le degré zéro de l'écriture* (Barthes 1953). These texts established Barthes as a prominent critic of French Modernist literature.

In the early 1950s Roland Barthes' writings also came in contact with semiology. This very quickly engaged him in a rethinking of the notion of signs with profound associations of a Marxist critique of the *mythe petite-bourgeoise* (Barthes 1957a). Moreover,

Barthes had an impact on the development of semiology as a research field as he expanded on the work of Ferdinand de Saussure. Saussure, one of the founding fathers of modern semiology, focused on theoretical relationships between signs in a closed system, more or less ignoring the role played by the interpreter. Barthes, however, integrated and elaborated on this idea; his expanded notion of signs included analyses of (for example) theatre, fashion, popular culture, tourism, images, and social conventions as semiotic systems. He embraced a theoretical approach to semiology as well as a cultural criticism in which meaning production, the *signification*, was central.

In the following sections, it is primarily as a semiologist that the influence of Roland Barthes is discussed. It is a semiology that in different, partly overlapping phases touched upon and had an impact on existentialist, Marxist, and phenomenological, as well as structuralist and (later) poststructuralist thinking. My brief departure is to pay attention to Barthes' most important contribution to current semiology. Next, I map out phases in his writings, in particular facilitated by his own taxonomy from *Roland Barthes par Roland Barthes* (Barthes 1975). This mapping of his ideas and writings incorporates taxonomy as an important tool in his semiological thinking, for example, in *Système de la mode* (Barthes 1967a). Last, I discuss subject analysis in picture indexing, classification, and so on, in terms of Barthes' writings on images as sign systems.

In sum, Roland Barthes is important from the perspective of library and information science (LIS) because he is interested in meaning production in a variety of contexts and, hence, important for domains that touch upon representation of information as well as models of communication and taxonomy.

BARTHES AS SEMIOLOGIST

It is not an unreasonable claim that Roland Barthes' writings do have a certain chameleon character, when he so easily adapts to the state-of-the-art versions of existentialist, Marxist, structuralist, and poststructuralist theories. As early as the 1940s, but especially from the 1950s on, Barthes' ideas shift according to the development and changes of leading critical theory. It is, however, crucial to bear in mind that his ideas at the same time add force to those larger theoretical transformations.

In retrospect, Barthes' work (including key terms and theoretical displacements) points in manifold directions. With reference to his semiological project, it is pertinent to assert that Barthes' oeuvre (considered as a *sign*) manifests itself as a *signifier* (for example, the huge collection of essays, books, comments, reviews, and interviews collected by Éric Marty in *Roland Barthes: Oeuvres complètes* [Barthes 2002]) referring to a *signified* (the meaning of this oeuvre). This distinction between *signifier* and *signified* is, of course, modeled on Saussure's *signifiant,* the form that the sign takes, and *signifié,* the concept the sign represents; the intrinsic relation between *signifiant* and *signifié* is arbitrary (Saussure 1916).

According to Barthes, among others, the signified can further be divided into two types: the *dénotation* (the first order of signification) and the *connotation* (the second order of signification). The denotative signified is what the signified actually appears to be, in this case a group of writings that bears the mark of "Roland Barthes" and which can be read and intuitively understood. In Barthes' view, however, the reception of the denotative signified is marked or already imprinted by the connotative signified; here, the reader (e.g., of Barthes' work) brings a deeper meaning (consciously or unconsciously) to the signified. The connotation produces the denotation as a natural sign, that is, a meaning that intuitively or, rather, apparently goes without saying (e.g., "*This is what Roland Barthes meant*"). However, the denotation is just another connotation. It is part of a second-order semiological system, the connotative system, which incorporates the sign of an initial system (the denotative system) that becomes the signifier of the second system. For example, we expect the author-subject Roland Barthes to be present in the writings that bear this name, even though it is as difficult for Barthes as for his interpreters to state who he really is or what he truly intended at the time of the writings. Furthermore, this approach presupposes a Roland Barthes who was a more or less unambiguous subject from his early writings in 1940s to the posthumous publications.

In other words, the connotations are the possible interpretations of the singular pieces of Barthes' work, the different taxonomies of his oeuvre, the theoretical and historical contextualizations, the implied biographical readings, and so on, which all are colored by conventions, presuppositions, and ideologies (e.g., in Ungar 1983; Jouve 1986; Bensmaïa 1987; Barthes 1993–95; Calvet 1995; Culler 2002; Allen 2003; Stafford 2004; Badmington 2009). In Barthes' view, for example, discourses on and practices of text interpretation mistakenly assume the aforementioned relation between author and text, that is, signified and signifier, although the intrinsic relation is arbitrary. Despite his famous challenge of this perception between author and text in "The Death of the Author" (Barthes 1968), it is difficult not to infer something about his lifelong, very close relationship with his mother while reading some of his texts, given the presuppositions in a modern Western society with plenty of gay stereotypes.

The explanation of this intricate play of connotations and denotations represents Barthes' most remarkable supplement to semiology. It is an adjustment of Saussure's model of the sign, which focused primarily on the formal settings of the sign system (that is, the relations of first order of signification as an enclosed entity); instead, Barthes underlines the importance of the connotation (and the reader) in the signifying processes. In *S/Z*, for example, Barthes states that "la dénotation n'est pas le premier des sens, mais elle feint de l'être. Sous cette illusion, elle n'est finalement que la dernièredes connotations (celle qui semble à la fois fonder et clore la lecture, le mythe supérieur grâce auquel le texte feint de retourner à la nature de langage, au langage comme nature" (Barthes 1970a, 561). This complexity between levels of signification will resurface in the following sections.

BARTHES AS TAXONOMIST

The prevalent optics of literary criticism, which first and foremost has embraced Barthes' thinking, segregate his writings into three phases that approximately correspond to the decades of the 1950s, 1960s, and 1970s. They can, accordingly, be viewed as the ideological-critical phase, the structuralist phase, and the hedonic phase (Norris 1974, 250–57; Culler 2002); this last one is also sometimes referred to as "the late, nostalgic or sentimental Barthes" period (Culler 2001). A partly alternative account is the author's own classifications. In line with his predilection for taxonomies and personal, more or less autobiographical notes, the elder Barthes completes no less than two: the lecture "L'aventure sémiologique," published as an article in the French newspaper *Le Monde* (Barthes 1974), and, shortly after, the book *Roland Barthes par Roland Barthes* (Barthes 1975). In the following, I will use these partly overlapping taxonomies as a guiding principle.

In "L'aventure sémiologique" Barthes describes three stages of the development of semiology as a science correlating to his own advancements, and in the succeeding year he literally charts five periods or phases of his academic maturity in *Roland Barthes par Roland Barthes*. While the stages from the lecture have numbers followed by explanatory paragraphs, the five phases in the book are mapped by three columns with the interrelated headings *Intertexte, Genre,* and *Oeuvres*. Put simply, *Oeuvres* refers primarily to Barthes' own books, *Genre* refers to his methodological or rather theoretical approaches doing these writings, and *Intertexte* refers to Barthes' inspiration, or in the elder Barthes' own words, the infinite signifying processes of poststructuralism: "L'intertexte n'est pas forcément un champ d'influences; c'est plutôt une musique de figures, de métaphores, de pensées-mots; c'est le signifiant comme sirène" (Barthes 1975, 148).

(L'ENVIE D'ÉCRIRE)

By using *Genre* as a structuring principle the first phase is "(L'envie d'écrire)" supplemented by "(Gide)" as an *intertexte* (both in Barthes' parentheses). As such, the *intertexte* relating to the genre of "the desire for writing" refers to the young Barthes' inspiration from the French avant-garde writer André Gide (1869–1951). The *Oeuvres* were yet to come.

Three partly correlated periods between book and lecture then follow. They are introduced by the following sentences in the lecture: "1. Le premier moment a été d'émerveillement; 2. Le second moment fut celui de la science, ou du moins de la scientificité; and, 3. Le troisième moment est en effet celui du Texte"; in the last section of this lecture, they are referred to as "l'Espoir", "la Science" and "le Texte" (Barthes 1974, 39). In the concise mapping of the book, the corresponding phases are entitled "mythologie sociale," "sémiologie," and "textualité," supplemented by the fifth and final "moralité". It should be noted that Barthes does not consider these phases in a strict chronological order without some overlap in the concepts. On the contrary, they dissolve into each other, "entre les périodes, évidemment, il y a des chevauchements, des retours, des affinités, des survies; ce sont en général les articles (de revue) qui assurent ce rôle conjonctif" (Barthes 1975, 148). Thus, it should be added that Barthes' writings go beyond the books assigned to the *Oeuvres* column. The abundance of minor essays, reviews, comments, interviews, and so forth forms an important addition to his oeuvre as pretexts, sketches, revisions, and further reflections.

MYTHOLOGIE SOCIALE

Comprising the genre "mythologie sociale," Barthes refers to works such as *Le degré zéro de l'écriture* (Barthes 1953) and different essays on the theatre, as well as *Mythologies* (Barthes 1957a) with Sartre, Marx, and Berthold Brecht as *intertextes* (Barthes was a leading French authority on Brecht in these years). In "L'aventure sémiologique" he elaborates on this section. He makes known that after reading Saussure's *Cours de linguistique générale* (1916) in the early 1950s, he merged his ideological critique of the "mythes petits-bourgeois" (Barthes 1974, 37) with the scientific approach of semiology. According to Barthes, semiology hitherto had not had the outline to become a fundamental approach in ideological critique. After reading Saussure, Barthes aims at investigating how bourgeois culture naturalizes its ideology as appearances of universal values in semiological terms.

As a starting place Barthes regards "les représentations collectives" as sign systems in order to describe "la mystification qui transforme la culture petite-bourgeoise en nature universelle" (Barthes 1970b, 563). His methodological tool is the play between the denotative and connotative systems. The denotative system represents the system, as the meaning of the sign is more or less intuitive. At the level of the connotative system the denotative system is, however, unmasked, because its ideological codes are exposed. This second level of signification deals, according to Barthes, with "fragments of an ideology.... These signifieds have a very close communication with culture, knowledge and history and it is through them, so to speak, that the environmental world [of the culture] invades the system [of representation]" (Barthes 1967b). In other words, it is the system of connotations that forms the meaning of the denotative system, although it seems as if the latter anchors the signifying processes.

Barthes exemplifies this relation between first-order signification and second-order signification in *Mythologies* (Barthes 1957a). A rather well-known case in point is his analysis of a front cover of *Paris-Match* that demonstrates how bourgeois culture consequently treats cultural conventions as natural rather than contrived signs. The magazine shows a young black soldier ("un jeune nègre vêtu d'un uniforme français"), with his eyes uplifted, apparently saluting the French flag, the *Tricolore*. Instantly, Barthes reads this denotative meaning of the signifier. Next, he interprets the connotative meaning of this saluting: "that France is a great Empire, that all her sons, without any colour discrimination, faithfully serve under her flag, and that there is no better answer to the detractors of an alleged colonialism that the zeal shown in this black ("ce noir") in serving his so-called oppressors" (688). However, there is a presence of the signified through the signifier as the saluting black soldier is not a natural symbol of the French Empire, but "a fabricated, quality of colonialism." The signified is, in fact, already formed by the signs of language helping France to sustain her imperial status.

SÉMIOLOGIE

The subsequent period of Barthes' thinking in *Roland Barthes par Roland Barthes*, "sémiologie" with Saussure as *intertexte*, is obviously interrelated with the previous. Yet, the allocated *oeuvres*, *Éléments de sémiologie* (Barthes 1965) and *Système de la mode* (Barthes 1967a), indicate a structuralist strengthening of his semiological methodology and, partly, a move beyond the ideological-critical approach. As mentioned, the opening paragraph in "L'aventure sémiologique" reads: "Le second moment fut celui de la science, ou du moins de la scientificité." While Saussure, although he defined the sign in linguistic terms, envisaged semiology as "a science which studies the life of signs as part of social life" ("On peut concevoir une science qui étudie la vie des signes au sein de la vie sociale...nous la nommerons sémiologie," (Saussure 1916)), Barthes sees semiology as just one part of linguistics; for example in his introductory remarks for the French journal *Communications*' 1964 issue devoted to the state of semiological research, he states: "la linguistique n'est pas une partie, meme privilège, de la science générale des signes, c'est la sémiologie qui est une partie de la linguistique" (Barthes 1964a, 1413).

This stance comes into view in the period from 1957 to 1963, where Barthes' studies in fashion seek to reconstruct the grammar in the language (*langage*) of fashion, that is, it is a structural analysis of descriptions of women's clothing by writers about fashion, more precisely the fashion pages of a few women's magazines. In brief, his object of study is the verbal structures of the "written-garment" (*vêtement-écrit*) in contrast with the "image-clothing" (*vêtement-image*). "The image freezes an endless number of possibilities, words determine a single certainty," (Barthes 1967, 13) while the clothes themselves are the signs. The fashion code correlates particular kinds or combinations of clothing with certain concepts (elegance, formality, casualness, romance). These are the signifieds. This coding converts the clothes into signs, which can then be read as a language (e.g., Barthes 1957b, 746).

The poststructuralist Barthes emphasizes in his 1974 retrospective lecture, "L'aventure sémiologique", that this structuralist phase was not a matter of establishing semiology as a science, but the pleasure (*plaisir*) of practicing a "Systématique": "Il y a, dans l'activité de classement, une sorte d'ivresse créative qui fut celle grands classificateurs come Sade et Fourier...le plaisir du Système remplacait en moi le surmoi de la Science" (Barthes 1974, 38). In *Système de la mode,* this pleasure unfolds over several pages in listing "inventaire des genres" (Barthes 1967a, 219ff) and, literally speaking, making models of the signifying processes of the grammar of fashion as well as introductory definitions of graphic symbols which are used in the texts. Barthes' "pleasure" of classification and modeling in the years of *Éléments de sémiologie* (Barthes 1965) and *Système de la mode* (Barthes 1967a) is, however, akin to the structuralist venture of the time. Practices of taxonomy and classification are crucial for the semiological project, which Barthes also recognizes in, for example, "Littérature et discontinu," where he states, "On commence à savoir, un peu depuis Durkheim, beaucoup depuis Cl. Lévi-Strauss, que la taxinomie peut être une part importante de l'étude des sociétés," and, further, in his own italics, *"dis-moi comment tu classes, je te dirai qui tu es"* (Barthes 1962, 1302). On the one hand, taxonomy is very important in analyzing the formal signifying processes, because the single sign (separated in a signifier and signified combined with an intrinsic arbitrariness) means nothing, since it could stand for anything. It is its difference from other signs in the system, as well as signs that could replace it in the process of signification, that inform the meaning of the sign. On the other hand, Barthes is very alert to the social conventions of this taxonomy, as his analyses in *Mythologies* (1957) demonstrate. Principles of taxonomy always express values of some kind, be it societal, cultural, ideological, etc.

TEXTUALITÉ

The aforementioned "pleasure" gives access to Barthes' third period, "textualité" with Sollers, Kristeva, Derrida, and Lacan as *intertextes* and *oeuvres* such as *S/Z* (Barthes 1970), *Sade, Fourier, Loyola* (Barthes 1971a) and *L'Empire des signes* (Barthes 1970c). In particular, his notions of the partly interrelated text (*texte*), writing (*écriture*), and author (*auteur*) summarized in seminal essays such as "The Death of the Author" (1968) and "From Work to Text" (1971b), become imperative sources for the development of modern literary criticism in this phase. On the one hand, the meaning of a text in the Barthesian sense is not the intention of the writer, but the reader's active production of meaning in reading the text. Barthes' focal points are the performances of reading and meaning production. This view of the text tentatively sets up a practice of reading, which can be seen in contrast with the work as an enclosed system of meaning created by the author. In this way, he contests the notion of the author as a genius or the origin of meaning, "author-god," creating a work of art by the powers of his original imagination, which becomes the authority for interpretation. This is a delusion of Western bourgeois culture.

Despite his Marxist inclinations, Barthes also contests György Lukács' literary realism, which, from a Marxist perspective, opposed nearly all prominent avant-garde writers in Western modernist literature who deviated from 19th-century realism. According to Lukács they were making style an end in itself, whereas Barthes praises avant-garde writing for manipulating conventions of style, that is, its codes. Writing, in the Barthesian sense becomes marked by "intransitivity." The activity of writing invokes a condition in which the writing subject disperses into an almost irretrievable contemporaneity with its writing performance: "The modern *scriptor* is born *at the same time* as his text," Barthes writes in "The Death of the Author." "[H]e is not furnished with a being which precedes or exceeds his writing, he is not the subject of which his book would be the predicate; there is no time other than that of the speech-act, and every text is written eternally *here* and *now*" (Barthes 1968, 52). In contrast with the spoken language or the normative coded language, which is submitted to power, conventions, and institutions, Writing in Barthes' sense is deported or deviated from language as such. It seeks to avoid power, meaning, ideology, representation, and so on in order to (via pleasure, body, deviation) relate to the inexpressible of the conventional language.

The up-to-date dialogue with existentialist, phenomenological, and semiological thinking in Barthes' notions of writing and text" is evident. These issues merge with his poststructuralist approach in for example "The Death of the Author," where he also states that the "text is a tissue of quotations drawn from the innumerable centers of culture" (147) that is, a text always refers to other texts. This semiological approach is also obvious in his meticulous reading of Honoré de Balzac's *Sarrasine* in *S/Z*, when he in a similar way declares that, in fact, "le sens d'un texte ne peut être rien d'autre que le pluriel de ses systèmes, sa "transcriptibilité" infinite (circulaire)" (Barthes 1970a, 635). Furthermore, Barthes moves beyond structuralist semiology as he conducts the reader through the entirety of Balzac's short story, systematically noting and explaining the usage of five different codes ("Voix de l'Empire (les proaïrétismes), Voix de la Personne (les sèmes), Voix de la Science (les codes culturels), Voix de la Verité (les herméneutismes), Voix du Symbole" [Barthes 1970a, 568]) as they occur. They invite a plurality of readings that should not be reduced to any privileged interpretation. By way of this plurality, he highlights the manner in which the reader is an active producer of the meaning of the text, rather than a passive consumer. The term *hedonic,* in the introductory remarks on the prevalent classification of his writings, refers to this open-ended interpretation for the benefit of the reader and the text.

MORALITÉ

The last part of his writings, Barthes entitles "moralité" with "(Nietzsche)" [Barthes' parentheses] as *intertexte*, and *Le Plaisir du Texte* (Barthes 1973) and *R.B. par lui-même* (that is, Barthes 1975) as *oeuvres*. Obviously, this part only covers the period until the time of writing *Roland Barthes par Roland Barthes,* and not the period after 1975 until his death in 1980, but there is no need for a further phase. Jonathan Culler's perhaps unusual naming, "the late, nostalgic or sentimental Barthes," refers to the abundance of personal references in the 1970s as well as the pleasure of that period's writings, which Culler fears overshadow Barthes' semiological endeavors. For example, he considers *Roland Barthes par Roland Barthes* (Barthes 1975) and *La chambre claire* (Barthes 1980) to be "peculiar, yet compelling." The former is "a strangely detached account of the life and works of one 'Roland Barthes'" that "evades the conventions of autobiography" and the second consists of "meditations on favourite photographs rather than an analysis of the art of photography" (Culler 2002, 3). In particular, one photograph reveals the personal investment of Roland Barthes, that is, the one of his mother, Henriette Barthes, as a child, in the Winter Garden Photograph, which is described but not, as many others are, reproduced in the book. Barthes mourns the loss of his mother while he explores different concepts in order to name the *noem* of photography.

From two different points of view, *Roland Barthes par Roland Barthes* and *La chambre claire* both are Barthes' attempts to formulate the inexpressible of the conventional language. Among other things, family photographs and other photographs supplemented with the author's brief comments illustrate the first of these works. In many of these pictures, "Barthes" is present by his direct appearance as a child, student, young man, professor, and so on; in others his presence is less directly evident (for example, in photographs of his handwritten notes, his tuberculosis case sheet, or places where he once lived). On the one hand, it is not a matter of personal expressions, but, as mentioned earlier, the act of writing that merges subject and text; on the other hand, the photographs and the brief texts are not telling *the* story of his life, but should be considered as documentary traces that leave the reader to sense the meaning.

In *La chambre claire,* Roland Barthes takes up an earlier distinction from his essay, "The Third Meaning" (Barthes 1970d), an essay on some still pictures from S. M. Eisenstein's film *Ivan the Terrible,* between the *obvious* and the *obtuse* meaning, now naming them *studium* and *punctum.* In the 1970 essay he defines three levels of meaning: (1) the informational level, or the level of "intuitively" communication; (2) a symbolic level, or the level of signification, which loads the first level with referential meaning; and (3) the level of the third meaning, which he is unable to give a name because he does not know what its signified is. Later, he also makes a related distinction between the level of signification or the "obvious meaning" (the second level) and the level of *signifiance* or the "obtuse" meaning (the third level): "The obtuse meaning is not in the language-system (even that of symbols). Take away the obtuse meaning and communication and signification still remain, still circulate, still come through: without it, I can still state and read" (60). The term *signifiance* is introduced by Julia Kristeva (present as *intertexte* in the previous phase) to signify the mechanisms within language that permit it to deliver more than the simple communication of verifiable facts.

In *La chambre claire,* the concept of *studium* likewise concerns the symbolic characteristics of a photographic image that more or less intuitively can be understood by every viewer, while *punctum* "*punctuates* the meaning of the photograph (the *studium*) and as a result punctures or pierces its viewer" (27). The *punctum* is not part of a collective code of meaning and, therefore, the difficulty in naming it: it has no signifier. On the other hand, Barthes forces the *punctum* into *studium* when moving beyond photographs, to be expressed in language; here, as Derrida has argued, Barthes takes on an impossible task: his readers cannot avoid transferring what he writes about his mother into "the figure of the Mother," that is, into ideas of the love of a mother for a son and vice versa, the Oedipus complex. According to Derrida, Barthes turns "toward his mother, and not toward the Mother. But the poignant singularity does not contradict the generality, it does not forbid it from having the force of law, but only arrows it, marks, and signs it" (Derrida 2001, 46).

BARTHES AS IMAGE MAKER

La chambre claire and the essay "The Third Meaning" are but two of Barthes' writings on images. Among others are his earlier, seminal essays, "The Photographic

Message" (Barthes 1961a) and "Rhétorique de l'image" (Barthes 1964b), but references to images surface in countless places in his writings, for example, in "L'information visuelle" (1961b), where he also states his interest in images as widespread, albeit rather concealed, semiological systems in modern society: "Nous vivons entourés imprégnés d'images, et pourtant nous ne savons encore presque rien de l'image" (Barthes 1961b, 955). In "The Photographic Message," an essay on the signification of press photographs, he also states that "the text constitutes a parasitic message designed to connote the image, to 'quicken' it with one or more second-order signifieds," and goes on to say, "In other words, and this is an important historical reversal, the image no longer *illustrates* the words; it is now the words which, structurally, are parasitic on the image" (Barthes 1961a, 25). Barthes takes his position on the superiority of language because it, at the connotative level, loads the images with meaning.

In Barthes' writings from the 1950s and 1960s, one finds many reassurances of this hierarchy, for example, "nous sommes, bien plus qu'autrefois et en dépit l'envahissement des images, une civilisation de l'écriture" because "tout système sémiologique se mêle du langage" (Barthes 1964a, 1412–13; see also Barthes 1966, 116). The statement of "une civilisation de l'écriture" also appears in his most theoretically elaborated essay on images, "Rhétorique de l'image" (Barthes 1964b), notwithstanding a landmark text in visual semiology.

In "Rhétorique de l'image" as well as the earlier "The Photographic Message (1961a), the image is interesting from a semiological point of view because it apparently is a message without a code, that is, a pure denotation. The photograph is a perfect *analogon,* even though the image *is not* reality, but *represents* reality. However, at the same time it opens up a paradox at the levels of reception as well as production, mirroring Barthes' ideas of the complex play between connotations and denotations. In the early essay, he states that the reading of the photograph, thanks to its code of connotation, "is thus always historical; it depends on the reader's 'knowledge' just as though it were a matter of a real language [*langue*], intelligible only if one has learned the signs....To find this code of connotation would thus be to isolate, inventoriate and structure all the 'historical' elements of the photograph, all the parts of the photographic surface which derive their very discontinuity from a certain knowledge on the reader's part, or, if one prefers, from the reader's cultural situation" (28).

In the later essay, "Rhétorique de l'image," the structuralist Barthes attempts to outline the signifying levels of a photographic image by way of advertisements, which are chosen because they are supposed to be frank about their intended meanings. He breaks the system of signification into three sections, that of the linguistic message, the coded iconic message and the noncoded image. The first message, the linguistic, operates at two levels: the denotative level that points directly to what can be read in or around the picture, and the connotative level that loads the denotative signified with meaning. As a case in point, Barthes analyses an advertisement for pasta and pasta sauce. The name of the producer is Panzani, which "gives not simply the name of the firm but also, by its assonance, an additional signified, that of "Italianicity" (Barthes 1964, 33) that is, the linguistic connotation.

The next message, the coded iconic level, is the totality of all the messages that are connoted by the image itself, that is, the third message (which is different from the above-mentioned "third meaning"). It is the noncoded level that equals the denotative system, the "natural" signs that apparently go without saying. In other words, the reality effect of the photograph naturalizes the symbolic message. The straightforward image shows a half-open string shopping bag with Panzani products as well as a tomato, a mushroom, a pepper, and onions, which, of course, load the prefabricated products with "freshness," but they also "stand[s] in a relation of redundancy with the connoted sign of the linguistic message," that is, "the knowledge it draws upon is already more peculiar; it is a specifically "French" knowledge (an Italian would barely perceive the connotation of the name, no more than he would the Italianicity of tomato and pepper), based on a familiarity with certain tourist stereotypes" (Barthes 1964a, 34).

This is a crucial observation because the connotative level has several operative functions, which Barthes names the rhetoric of the image. The rhetoric of the image is the classification of its connotators, which in terms of lexical units vary according to observers, that is, they depend on the different kinds of knowledge of the observer that are invested in the image: "The variation in readings is not, however, anarchic; it depends on the different kinds of knowledge (i.e., practical, national, cultural, aesthetic) invested in the image and these can be classified, brought into a typology" (Barthes 1964a, 46). The connotators operate at a conscious level as well as an unconscious level, as Barthes' indirect reference to Lacanian psychoanalysis reveals, as he states that the image is "constituted by an architecture of signs drawn from a variable depth of lexicons...each lexicon, no matter how deep, still being coded, if, as is thought today, the *psyche* itself is articulated as an language" (122).

BARTHES AS PICTURE INDEXER

"Rhétorique de l'image" as well as Barthes' other writings on images have been appealing to several writers in LIS in order to elaborate on picture indexing as well as to rethink the theoretical basis of, for example, Sara Shatford-Layne's well-known efforts to establish a broad formula for subject analysis in picture indexing (Shatford 1986; Shatford-Layne 1994; Ørnager 1995; Shatford-Layne 2002; Rafferty and Hidderly 2007; Yoon 2008).

Shatford-Layne takes the art historian Erwin Panofsky's concepts of iconography and iconology as a starting point in her model. In a very influential article Panofsky defines three levels of interpretation: pre-iconographical description, iconographical analysis, and iconological interpretation (Panofsky 1955). The Panofskyian pre-iconographic level is a matter of intuitively recognizing the factual motif, the "primary or natural subject matter" and its expressional features (14). At the second order of meaning, Panofsky connects motifs or groups of motifs identified generically at the first order of meaning with iconographical schemes, literary sources, or concepts; he constitutes "the world of images, stories and allegories" (14). At the third level of meaning the interpreter in a hermeneutic manner recreates the essential tendencies of the human mind, "conditioned by personal psychology and *Weltanschauung*"; he constitutes the intrinsic meaning of the image (14).

In her essay, "The Language of Images: Enhancing Access to Images by Applying Metadata Schemas and Structured Vocabularies," Patricia Harpring (2002) summarizes this approach as it is used in the Getty Research Institute's *Categories for the Description of Works of Art* (CDWA).

Three sets of subcategories under the category Subject Matter in CDWA reflect this traditional art-historical approach to subject analysis, but in a somewhat simplified and more practical application of the principles, one better suited to indexing subject matter for purposes of re-trieval.... The following three levels of subject analysis are defined in CDWA:

- *Subject Matter—Description.* A description of the work in terms of the generic ele-ments of the image or images depicted in, on, or by it;
- *Subject Matter—Identification.* The name of the subject depicted in or on a work of art: its iconography. Iconography is the named mythological, fictional, religious, or histori-cal narrative subject matter of a work of art, or its non-narrative content in the form of persons, places, or things;
- *Subject Matter—Interpretation.* The meaning or theme represented by the subject mat-ter or iconography of a work of art" (3).

In her essay in the same volume, Shatford-Layne further elaborates on her distinction between *of-ness* and *about-ness* that clearly resembles Panofsky's pre-iconographic and iconographic levels as well (Shatford-Laynes 2002). In brief, her *of-* part relates to a ge-neric as well as a specific level, that is, at the pre-iconographic level an image is generi-cally, for example, *of* a woman, but also *about* a certain expressivity: if the woman is smiling, is sad, and so forth. At the iconographic level, *of* refers to the generic of Mary and the specific of, for example, *Maria Lactens,* and the *about-ness* refers to, for exam-ple, motherhood or Christianity. One has to keep in mind, as Shatford-Layne observes, "the range from generic to specific, from description to identification, can be more of a continuum than a dichotomy" (1).

Although Shatford-Layne applies the model to art images in general, Panofsky pres-ents a methodology that primarily allows interpretations of Renaissance art in light of philosophy, classical mythology, and general humanistic knowledge. Therefore, his levels tend to ignore or misrepresent works of art from other periods and cultures as well images that are not art, which can have an impact on the classificatory practices: "they did not translate well from the area of renaissance art to a more general domain," as Chen and Rasmussen summarize Enser and McGregor's 1993 article, "Analysis of Visual Information Retrieval Queries" (Chen and Rasmussen 1999, 173).

Faced with Barthes' discussion of the complexity between the denotative and con-notative levels, it is easy to see resemblances connecting denotative signifieds, pre-iconographic description and *of-ness* on the one side, and, on the other, connotative signifieds, iconographic analysis, iconological interpretation, and *about-ness.* In fact, Panofsky's (and Shatford-Layne's) model presents a straightforward methodology (in which the first step is description, the next analysis, and the last interpretation) that mirrors long-established humanistic interpretative practices. However, Panofsky and Shatford-Layne both do not take into account the signifying processes of the descriptive (classifying) and interpretive acts. In Barthes' terminology they are partly aware of the implications of the connotators or lexicons, but they do not fully realize their own limi-tations, and they utterly ignore the social implications. To different degrees, both con-sider the image the primary object with an intrinsic meaning that has to find its place in a preexisting web of meaning. Panofsky even parallels the interpretative act with the riddle of the Sphinx, that is, only one answer is correct, whereas Shatford-Layne is more concerned with the abundance of possible subject matters. In contrast, Barthes, on the one hand, points to the way the connotation re/produces the denotation; on the other hand, he indirectly challenges the limitations of picture indexing, when he examines the difficulties in naming the *punctum,* "the third meaning," or "the obtuse meaning."

Barthes' reverse model of the signifying processes does not destabilize either Panofsky's interpretative practice or Shatford-Layne's procedure for subject analysis as it is used in, for example, *Categories for the Description of Works of Art*, but it does refine the theoretical understandings of indexing practices as well as controlled and structured vocabularies. The apparently natural meaning in classificatory scheme is always the signifier of the second-order system that incorporates the signs of the initial system. For example, several writers have discussed the Eurocentric, nationalistic, or ideological implications in taxonomical practices of art history in survey books, study programs, classification systems, bibliographies, thesauruses, and such (e.g., Nelson 1997; Elkins 2002; Ørom 2003, Dam Christensen 2006). By classifying objects according to preexisting schemes, the indexer, the art historian, and other LIS professionals risk reproducing ideologies inherent in the structures of the practices. Art history is not a particular coincidence. The same problematic can be found in other domains as well; namely, everywhere that classical hierarchical, "universal" classification systems or, so to speak, meaning that goes without saying, are not properly questioned.

CONCLUSION

Roland Barthes' writings cover several decades, many genres, and a broad range of topics. In this chapter it has been the semiologist who has been presented in order to demonstrate Barthes' interest in meaning production and signification in a range of domains, but in particular the visual domain. In general, his accomplishments as a literary critic and cultural philosopher are very noteworthy, too, but it is as a semiologist that his relevance for domains that touch upon representation of information as well as models of communication and taxonomy is most evident. By way of his writings on images, the complex play between connotations and denotations, as well as the ideological implications in classificatory practices has been outlined as a more elaborated corrective to prevalent theories of indexing. In addition, it is worth mentioning that Barthes' poststructuralist notions on reading, text, author, and writing also confront, for example, network text, hypertext, user-driven innovation, folksonomies, social tagging, and so on. In short, the text is a tissue of other texts, writing is an act of performativity, the reader is decoding without dependence on the writer, and tagging is a matter of understanding the usage of connotators in the Barthesian sense.

REFERENCES

("Barthes" references in the text refer to first publication year of either French original or English translation)

Allen, Graham. 2003. *Roland Barthes.* London: Routledge.
Badmington, Neil. 2009. *Roland Barthes. Critical Evaluations in Cultural History.* 4 vols. London: Routledge.
Barthes, Roland. 1953. *Le degré zéro de l'écriture.* In *Roland Barthes: Oeuvres complètes,* ed. Èric Marty, Vol. 1. Paris: Éditions du Seuil, 1993.
Barthes, Roland. 1957a. *Mythologies suivi de Le Mythe, aujourd'hui.* In *Roland Barthes: Oeuvres complètes,* ed. Èric Marty. Vol. 1. Paris: Editions du Seuil, 1993.
Barthes, Roland. 1957b. "Histoire et sociologie du vêtement." In *Roland Barthes: Oeuvres complètes,* ed. Èric Marty. Vol. 1. Paris: Editions du Seuil, 1993. Originally published in *Annales* 3 (1957).

Barthes, Roland. 1961a. "The Photographic Message." In *Roland Barthes: Image – Music – Text,* ed. Stephen Heath. London: Fontana Press, 1977. Originally published as "Le message photographique" in *Communications* 1 (1961).

Barthes, Roland. 1961b. "L'information visuelle." In *Roland Barthes: Oeuvres complètes,* ed. Èric Marty. Vol. 1. Paris: Editions du Seuil, 1993. Originally published in *Communications* 1 (1961).

Barthes, Roland. 1962. "Littérature et discontinu." In *Roland Barthes: Oeuvres complètes,* ed. Èric Marty. Vol. 1. Paris: Editions du Seuil, 1993. Originally written in 1962.

Barthes, Roland. 1964a. "Présentation." In *Roland Barthes: Oeuvres complètes,* ed. Èric Marty. Vol. 1. Paris: Éditions du Seuil, 1993. Originally published in *Communications* 4 (1964).

Barthes, Roland. 1964b. "Rhetoric of the Image." In *Roland Barthes: Image – Music – Text,* ed. Stephen Heath. London: Fontana Press, 1977. Originally published as "Rhétorique de l'image" in *Communications* 4 (1964).

Barthes, Roland. 1965. *Eléments de sémiologie.* In *Roland Barthes: Oeuvres complètes,* ed. Èric Marty. Vol. 1. Paris: Éditions du Seuil, 1993.

Barthes, Roland. 1967a. *Système de la mode.* In *Roland Barthes: Oeuvres complètes,* ed. Èric Marty. Vol. 2. Paris: Editions du Seuil, 1994. English edition: *The Fashion System.* Trans. Matthew Ward and Richard Howard. New York: Hill, 1983.

Barthes, Roland. 1967b. *Elements of Semiology.* New York: Hill and Wang.

Barthes, Roland. 1968. "The Death of the Author." In *Roland Barthes: Image – Music – Text,* ed. Stephen Heath. London: Fontana Press, 1977. Originally published as "La mort de l'auteur" in *Mantéla* V (1968).

Barthes, Roland. 1970a. *S/Z.* London: Cape, 1973. In *Roland Barthes: Oeuvres complètes,* ed. Èric Marty. Vol. 2. Paris: Éditions du Seuil, 1994.

Barthes, Roland. 1970b. New preface. In *Mythologies suivi de Le Mythe, aujourd'hui. Roland Barthes: Oeuvres complètes,* ed. Èric Marty. Vol. 1. Paris: Éditions du Seuil, 1993.

Barthes, Roland. 1970c. *L'Empire des signes.* In *Roland Barthes: Oeuvres complètes,* ed. Èric Marty. Vol. 2. Paris: Éditions du Seuil, 1994.

Barthes, Roland. 1970d. "The Third Meaning." In *Roland Barthes: Image – Music – Text,* ed. Stephen Heath,. London: Fontana Press, 1977. Originally published as "Le troisième sens: Notes de recherche sur quelques photogrammes de S. M. Eisenstein," *Cahiers du cinéma* 222 (1970).

Barthes, Roland. 1971a. *Sade, Fourier, Loyola.* In *Roland Barthes: Oeuvres complètes,* ed. Èric Marty. Vol. 2. Paris: Éditions du Seuil, 1994.

Barthes, Roland. 1971b. "From Work to Text." In *Roland Barthes: Image – Music – Text,* ed. Stephen Heath. London: Fontana Press, 1977. Originally published as "De l'oeuvre au texte," *Revue d'esthetique* 3 (1971).

Barthes, Roland. 1973. *Le Plaisir du Texte.* In *Roland Barthes: Oeuvres complètes,* ed. Èric Marty. Vol. 2. Paris: Éditions du Seuil, 1994.

Barthes, Roland. 1974. "L'aventure sémiologique." In *Roland Barthes: Oeuvres complètes,* ed. Èric Marty. Vol. 3. Paris: Éditions du Seuil, 1995. Originally published in *Le Monde,* 7 juin 1974.

Barthes, Roland. 1975. *Roland Barthes par Roland Barthes.* Paris: Ecrivains de toujours / Seuil.

Barthes, Roland. 1980. *La chambre claire: Note sur la photographie.* In *Roland Barthes: Oeuvres completes,* ed. Èric Marty. Vol. 3. Paris: Éditions du Seuil, 1995.

Barthes, Roland. 1993–95. *Oeuvres complètes,* ed. Èric Marty, 3 vols. Paris: Seuil.

Barthes, Roland. 2002. *Oeuvres complètes,* ed. Èric Marty, 5 vols. Paris: Seuil.

Barthes, Roland, with Philippe Pilard. 1966. "Visualisation et langage." In *Roland Barthes: Oeuvres complètes,* ed. Èric Marty. Vol. 2. Paris: Éditions du Seuil, 1994. Originally published in *Bulletin de la radio-télévision scolaire* January 28–March 12 (1966).

Bensmaïa, Réda. 1987. *The Barthes Effect: The Essay as Reflective Text*. Trans. Pat Fedkiew. Minneapolis: University of Minnesota Press.

Calvet, Louis-Jean. 1990. *Roland Barthes*. Paris: Flammarion.

Calvet, Louis-Jean. 1995. *Roland Barthes: A Biography*. Trans. Sarah Wykes. Bloomington: Indiana University Press.

Chen, Hsin-Liang, and Edie M. Rasmussen. 1999. "Intellectual Access to Images." *Library Trends* 48 (2): 291–302.

Culler, Jonathan. 2001. "Barthes, Theorist." *Yale Journal of Criticism* 14(2): 439–46.

Culler, Jonathan. 2002. *Barthes: A Very Short Introduction*. Oxford: Oxford University Press.

Dam Christensen, Hans. 2006. "Which Art History?" In *Is Art History Global?* ed. James Elkins, 298–309. London: Routledge.

Derrida, Jacques. 2001. "The Deaths of Roland Barthes." In *The Work of Mourning*, ed. Pascale-Anne Brault and Michael Naas, 31–68. Chicago: University of Chicago Press.

Elkins, James. 2002. *The Stories of Art*. London: Routledge.

Harpring, Patricia. 2002. "The Language of Images: Enhancing Access to Images by Applying Metadata Schemas and Structured Vocabularies." In *Introduction to Art Image Access: Issues, Tools, Standards, Strategies*, ed. Murtha Baca. Los Angeles: Getty Research Institute.

Hollink, L., et al. 2004. "Classification of User Image Descriptions." *International Journal of Human-Computer Studies* 61 (5): 601–26.

Jouve, Vincent. 1986. *La littérature selon Roland Barthes*. Paris: Éditions de Minuit

Nelson, Robert S. 1997. "The Map of Art History." *Art Bulletin* 79 (1): 28–40.

Norris, Christopher. 1974. "Les Plaisirs des Clercs: Barthes's Latest Writing." *British Journal of Aesthetics* 14 (3): 250–57.

Ørnager, Susanne. 1997. "Image Retrieval: Theoretical Analysis and Empirical User Studies on Accessing Information in Images." *Proceedings of the American Society for Information Science Annual Meeting* 34: 202–11.

Ørom, Anders. 2003. "Knowledge Organization in the Domain of Art Studies—History, Transition and Conceptual Changes." *Knowledge Organization* 30 (3–4): 128–43.

Panofsky, Erwin. 1955. "Iconography and Iconology: An Introduction to the Study of Renaissance Art." In *Meaning in the Visual Arts*, 26–54. Garden City, NY: Doubleday.

Saussure, Ferdinand de. 1916. *Cours de linguistique générale*. Ed. Tuillio de Mauro. Paris: Editions Payot et Rivages, 1995. Orginally published by Charles Bailly and Albert Séchehaye in 1916.

Shatford, Sara. 1986. "Analyzing the Subject of a Picture: A Theoretical Approach." *Cataloging & Classification Quarterly* 6 (3): 39–62.

Shatford-Layne, Sara. 1994. "Some Issues in the Indexing of Images." *Journal of the American Society of Information Science* 45 (8): 583–88.

Shatford-Layne, Sara. 2002. "Subject Access to Art Images." In *Introduction to Art Image Access: Issues, Tools, Standards, Strategies*, ed. Murtha Baca, 1–12. Los Angeles: Getty Research Institute.

Stafford, Andy. *Roland Barthes, Phenomenon and Myth: an Intellectual Biography*. Edinburgh: University of Edinburgh Press.

Ungar, Steven. 1983. *Roland Barthes, the Professor of Desire*. Lincoln: University of Nebraska Press.

Yoon, Jung Won. 2008. "Searching for an Image Conveying Connotative Meanings: An Exploratory Cross-Cultural Study." *Library & Information Science Research* 30 (4): 312–18.

3

Roy Bhaskar's Critical Realism

John M. Budd
University of Missouri, USA

Roy Bhaskar was born in London in 1944 to an Indian father and an English mother. In 1963 he attended Balliol College, Oxford, on scholarship and graduated with first class honors. During his graduate studies he worked under the guidance of the philosopher Rom Harré, although his writings after he left Oxford diverged considerably from those of his mentor. In particular, Bhaskar developed his own conception of realism, which he initially placed in the tradition of critical realism and then reconceived as transcendental realism. Since 1995 he has worked with the Centre for Critical Realism and the International Association of Critical Realism.

What constitutes science and what constitutes the social? Some theorists examine science from the point of view of the social (Thomas Kuhn, Paul Feyerabend, Nelson Goodman), while others are careful to state that there are distinctions between science and social phenomena to be made (Imre Lakatos, Karl Popper). In short, there has tended to an either/or debate among those who study the practice of scientists. Roy Bhaskar does not fall neatly into either category; in fact, he finds both sides wanting. Imagine a scientific realist, a searcher after a naturalist alternative to positivism, who also embraces mysticism as a pathway to self-actualization. Over the course of a long career Bhaskar has developed and revised a set of ideas that bypasses method as such and attempts to address the most fundamental ontological and epistemological underpinnings of what can be called *wissenschaften* (the generic concept of science as ordered and reasoned inquiry).

The foundation he seeks to provide is undeniably postpositivist; his critiques are as informative as are his original stances. His alternative framework of critical realism is very rarely discussed in library and information science (LIS); this essay may help direct readers to Bhaskar's creative and imaginative thought. His work is not simple; his writing forces readers to work extremely hard. Further, as was just mentioned, his ideas are different; they cannot be placed into neat (and existing) categories. Since the body of Bhaskar's work has addressed a number of matters related to the philosophy of science and social science (as well as the work of the sciences and social sciences themselves), this essay will necessarily be limited to a selected body of ideas. Also, since I am doing the selecting, what is presented here is one person's judgment of the importance of the ideas to library and information science (LIS). The aim here is to demonstrate as clearly as possible that the ideas *are* important, that Bhaskar presents an alternative to several traditions of thinking that have, at some times and in some ways, retarded progress in LIS.

INTRODUCTION

While a linear treatment cannot do justice to the work of many theorists, it is the most legitimate way to relate Bhaskar's contributions. The reason for the linear approach, as is hinted at above, is that he revisited, revised, and sometimes reconceived his ideas over time. Each of his published works builds upon the others, so anyone interested in learning about his thought as it has developed should read his books in order of publication. For example, his earliest writings concentrated heavily on the natural sciences and how progressive inquiry can proceed. At the outset of one of his earliest books he (1997) writes, "The aim of this book is the development of a systematic realist alternative to positivism which since the time of Hume has fashioned our image of science" (12). His alternative is designed to be a corrective to an epistemology (logical empiricism or positivism) that has limited research in all fields. By dating positivism back to Hume he is tackling a long tradition of empiricism; Hume was not tolerant of ideas not grounded firmly in sensory experience. His opening salvo is a very important starting point for an energized critical approach in LIS.

It has to be admitted, and the foregoing quotation from Bhaskar demonstrates this, that a considerable amount of intellectual labor is necessary to comprehend and appreciate his thought as fully as possible. A construct that he developed early in his writings, and applies throughout his career, is a set of distinctions that can also be applied to LIS inquiry. His entire conceptual program is based on the existence of the "real." The real assuredly exists; it is ontological reality, but its clear discernment is elusive in the inquiry into open systems (any system where external influences cannot be eliminated or reduced, including the entirety of social structure). The real, then, is a domain that is somewhat separate from the actual (or what we could call the "actualized"). Experimentation, for example, structures study in such a way that the real cannot be clearly identified; mechanisms (conceptual and physical) intervene between the real and what is apprehended through experimentation. The events that do occur in life (including such things as people seeking and evaluating information, making decisions, establishing policy, and so on) are in the domains of the real and the actual. While the real is frequently elusive in terms of conforming to theory, the actual can be seen as manifest in many ways. The domains of possibility are further complicated in that, according to Bhaskar, perception (or observation) can be out of sync with events, so the empirical domain can be distinct from the actual and the real. The distance of the empirical from the actual and the real is one of the primary hallmarks of his program. Bhaskar (1997) illustrates his distinction graphically (13), as shown in Figure 3.1.

Since these points are so central to Bhaskar's program, they deserve some explication. Let us assume an interaction between a librarian and a student. The student asks for assistance with an assignment given by a political science instructor: discuss potential causes of Barack Obama's rise, in spite of seeming advantages of opponents such as Hillary Clinton. The assignment is a brief statement of the real; Obama did overcome obstacles and gain support from many quarters for many reasons. The actual is part of the student's challenge, to identify *some* explicable connections among events that are

Figure 3.1
Bhaskar's Three Domains

	Domain of Real	Domain of Actual	Domain of Empirical
Mechanisms	✓		
Events	✓	✓	
Experiences	✓	✓	✓

related to the instructor's assignment. If there should happen to be some natural laws explaining political action (and here we *must* remember that Bhaskar's model is limited to the natural sciences at this early stage in his career), then those laws are not fully confirmed by the events that the student can identify. In short, the student cannot provide a "perfect" answer. The librarian, removed yet another step from the assignment, is limited to the student's explanation of what she or he needs. The librarian is in the observer's role and concentrates, quite possibly, on information resources that the student can use to fulfill the assignment. The domains are related, but substantively distinct as reflections of what *is*.

The distinctions are extremely important to an understanding of critical realism. What Bhaskar asserts throughout his writings is that critical realism is not a simplistic statement of a narrow ontology that is unshifting and perpetually knowable. The figure is an effort to demonstrate different means by which humans perceive (and impose perception) upon what is. The differences are every bit as vital as is the admission of the existence of the domains. Bhaskar (1993) writes,

(α) they are categorically distinct and ontologically irreducible;
(β) they are normally disjoint or out of phase with one another;
(γ) the activity necessary to align them for epistemic purposes normally involves practical and conceptual distanciation, typically dependent on the past and the exterior; and
(δ) they may possess radically different properties (e.g., in fetishism, mediatization or visualization they may invert, or otherwise occlude, the properties they purport to describe) (234).

If we take "information" as an example here, it is possible to envision the differences among the real, the actual, and the empirical. What is it about information that can be observed; in other words, what are the limitations to an empirical investigation of information? There may be properties relating to media, symbology, signs, and so on that can be studied. Those properties are distinct from the actual; information in the domain of the actual is experienced differently (including semantically, grammatically, communicatively . . . in general, the interpretable). The lesson to take away from Bhaskar is that conflation of such things as the domains of possibility reveal the ways that the positivist epistemologies have obscured understanding of ontology.

One of Bhaskar's most valuable contributions to fields like LIS is his articulation of differences when it comes to *what* is studied. His early work suggests a simple way to assess the differences; some things are not the products of human manufacture, imagination, or activity. These objects have a reality that is independent of us. Some other things are created by humans, and their reality is apprehended as part of human Being. Bhaskar (1997) says,

If men ceased to exist sound would still continue to travel and heavy bodies to fall to the earth in exactly the same way, though ex hypothesi there would be no-one to know it. Let us call these, in an unavoidable technical neologism, the *intransitive objects of knowledge*. The *transitive* objects of knowledge are Aristotelian material causes. They are the raw material of science—the artificial objects fashioned into items of knowledge by the science of the day (21).

The two types, or species, of objects of knowledge require a new vision of ontology, what Bhaskar calls "transcendental realism." His explication of differences is especially important as our field contemplates just what information is (transitive or intransitive).

BHASKAR AND SCIENCE

Before delving into Bhaskar's transcendental realism an excursus into his position on philosophy more generally, as it can be connected to knowledge, is necessary. The position is related to the dynamics illustrated in Figure 3.1. If a scientific examination of society and social phenomena can be at all possible, then there must be a definable way that science works. In essence, Bhaskar provides a palliative for "science envy" by presenting unique definitions of what science is and what it does. He accomplishes this feat through critique and originality. His first step is to invoke Kant, but without any necessary commitment to scientific theories and with acceptance of a conditional quality of theorizing. Kant's categorical imperative—that one should act according to principles that could apply universally to all—is a starting point; the imperative does not over-individualize experience. The social, according to the categorical imperative, is not merely the product of individuals; it is a complex of physical, affective, and temporal interrelations. This is not a simple principle to grasp; Bhaskar intends that we, as scientific investigators of social action, avoid reifying laws of human action (making the error of confusing human action as intransitive objects of knowledge). As he (1998) says, "activity and its conceptualization may be historically transient; that the activity may depend upon the powers that people possess as material things rather than just as thinkers or perceivers; and that its analysis may establish transcendental realist, rather than idealist, and so epistemically relativist, rather than absolutist (or irrationalist) conclusions" (5).

The combination of ontological realism and epistemological relativism may appear to be discordant, but it is not. Transcendental realism, according to Bhaskar, is the basis of science. He uses the example of experimentation with intransitive objects of knowledge to make his point. The scientist has no alternative other than constructing a project aimed at producing a pattern of events. The construction is itself determinate, at least to a considerable extent, of the pattern of events produced. The determinism, says Bhaskar, is demonstrative of the failure of the Humean causal model; a different construction might produce a different pattern of events. He concludes that, as we apply the experimental results in open systems (in which the determinate construction usually will not obtain), the results can seem to be at odds with life in the open system. The results of the experiment do not conform to actual experience.

There is an illustration, possibly clearer, that suggests Bhaskar's transcendental realism is an effective philosophy of science. At a time, not long ago, cosmologists used then-existing theories and instrumentation to estimate the age of the known universe. When data from the Hubble telescope and other sources became available, cosmologists has to adjust their estimates. The knowledge according to which they had operated was no longer valid, so their epistemic responsibility was to reject many formerly held commitments to the erroneous estimates. This example deals with an intransitive object of knowledge, something that did not alter itself (the universe did not decide to play a prank on cosmologists). Bhaskar (1998) concludes, "There is an ontological gap between causal laws and their empirical grounds. . . . This not only renders standard positivist methodological injunctions patently inapplicable, but vitiates the most familiar hermeneutic contrasts" (11).

INCLUDING THE SOCIAL

The turn to constructivist theories of knowledge, including scientific knowledge, is not addressed directly by Bhaskar, but constructivism is opposed to transcendental realism. Bhaskar does mention Richard Rorty, as well as Kuhn and others in his critique of what (he argues) amounts to a dualist ontology. For example, Jan Golinski (1998) claims that "The constructivist outlook suggests . . . that science is shape by social relations at its very core—in the details of what is accepted as knowledge and how it is pursued" (17–18). Bhaskar claims that talk is real; it can be referred to again and again. Discourse cannot be misconstrued as the way people construct statements about things; the things about which they speak have some genuine referents, some ontological signifieds (the meaning to which a signifier refers) that are more than the ideological wishes of the speaker. Golinski's confusion illustrates a fundamental error in understanding ontology (this error will be elucidated shortly). Bhaskar's critique challenges the stance that knowledge is an emergent phenomenon that is generated solely by minds. His epistemological relativism does include admission that knowledge is fallible; in this way he could be read as sympathetic to some of those he critiques. However, the means by which knowledge is generated is not individualistic; that is, it is not the product of one person, one mind. Because of the complex social element, knowledge is corrigible; progress is possible.

Bhaskar, understanding the historicity of philosophy as well as anyone, recognizes the potential atomism of radical constructivism as a product both of bourgeois individualism (and he shares with Marx this target) and the 20th-century positivist quest for incorrigibility (the holy grail of irreducible knowledge). Radical constructivism, according to his critique, necessitates what would generously be called a blank slate, but what, in terms of transcendental realism, is actually an empty mind. In contrast to the empty mind Bhaskar's transcendental realism not only allows for, but explains, how epistemological progress is possible. He manages to explain, in part by refuting the opposing positions of Thomas Kuhn and Karl Popper, that knowledge is neither the mere agreement of a community nor the simple refutation of an existing hypothesis. Both Kuhn and Popper, by very different means (they disagreed with each other in print and in person), argue against a certainty and stasis in scientific practice, but ignore the potential for progress in the face of change: "For those philosophers, such as Popper and Kuhn, who, in opposition to the classical inductivist view, have drawn attention to the phenomenon of scientific discontinuity and change, have found it difficult to reconcile this with the idea that science involves a cumulative growth in our knowledge of nature" (Bhaskar 1998, 11). Bhaskar's epistemological relativism is, as is clear, not nihilistic; to reiterate, it admits to relativism by accepting correction, advance, and progress.

The other means Bhaskar employs in his critique is a refutation of what he calls the epistemic fallacy. In brief, the epistemic fallacy is a "taboo on ontology" (Bhaskar 2002, 9);

the central fallacy is to reduce ontology to epistemology; to reduce what *is* to what we can claim to *know*. The fallacy is closely related to radical constructivism. This fallacy follows from the Humean empiricist tradition in that it insists on a categorizing of experience and a presumption that the categories of experience are indeed atomistic and constant (Bhaskar 1998c 29–30). The presumption can only hold if knowledge is incorrigible (experience is universally shared and categorized once and for all). According to the fallacy only what we can claim to know—that is, only what we can make statements about—or agree that we know exists. More specifically, what we can propose about the meaning of something, including an idea, is the important philosophical point (which is the hallmark of the linguistic turn in philosophy). The epistemic fallacy, as Bhaskar notes, eliminates all intransitive objects of knowledge; nothing can be examined *as* real in itself. A variation on the epistemic fallacy is the linguistic fallacy (Bhaskar 1998a, 133). Peter Winch (1958) is a major proponent of what can be referred to as the conflation of philosophy and social science (that is, the practice of the social sciences as Winch would prescribe it *is* philosophy). Winch argues that philosophy and social science are concerned with meaning, that meaning is relative to cultures, places, and times, and that the method of the social sciences is conceptual and in no way empirical. Winch is featured here because his book, published more than 50 years ago, is still read and referred to as a model for some practices in the social sciences. If one accepts Bhaskar's transcendental realism, though, one must reject Winch. For example, at one point Winch (1958) writes that the "logical relations between propositions…depend on social relations between men" (126).

Bhaskar's refutation of Winch is thorough. He (1998b) points out that

Winch's two main arguments…are parasitic on a positivist ontology. Constant conjunctions of events are neither necessary nor sufficient either for natural or for social scientific understanding: both alike are concerned with the discovery of intelligible connections in their subject matter. Nor do the conceptual and the empirical jointly exhaust the real [refer, once again, to Figure 3.1]. Critical realism can allow that conceptuality is distinctive, without supposing that it is exhaustive, of social life.…The social world is characterized by the complete absence of laws and explanations conforming to the positivist canon" (xv).

It is here that another crucial aspect of Bhaskar's transcendental realism is introduced—dialectic (to which we will return shortly). In the instance of his critique of Winch (and of a persistent tradition in the social sciences), Bhaskar emphasizes the lack of laws, particularly covering laws, that could explain and predict human action in the social sphere. He traces the tendency to seek (and claim to find) such laws to the ancient world, and to Parmenides (who defined reality as immutable and timeless, and appearances as deception) who strongly influenced Plato. In attempting to correct the Platonic/Socratic conception of knowledge, Bhaskar (1994) suggests that "Knowledge-acquisition, to use my (not Plato's) terms, is a *pre-existing ongoing social* affair [italics in original]" (7). He means that human inquiry begins with some prior knowledge and assumptions that contribute to the search for answers, and which also leads to further questions requiring inquiry. He places this construction in terms of ontology; the prior knowledge exists not merely for one person, but for society, and the questions that emerge are also real for everyone.

Again, context is helpful. There is a tradition in LIS of inquiry into the ways people search for the information they want and need. The tradition had to begin at some point when, for example, the study of people's psychological states was at its beginning. What was known informed what would be examined, so there were limits to the conceptualization of searching activities. The contributions to knowledge (which have been *real*) in a variety of fields have led to LIS researchers being able to frame their questions and inquiry in evolving ways. Mechanistic kinds of studies were typical some years ago, but more sophisticated types of examination have been made possible by increased knowledge of the ways people think about texts (defined as broadly as possible). Stemming from the cross-fertilization and ongoing activity, work such as that by Birger Hjörland, Sanna Talja, Catherine Ross, and others could be published. This work illustrates the state of inquiry, the potential for future activity, and the ontological character of knowledge. The ontology of social action (and inquiry), for Bhaskar, is defined somewhat differently from the customary, rather rigid, manner. His is what he calls stratified; there are some realities that define our lives that are in conflict with simultaneously existing realities. While Margaret Archer's (1995) critical realism is substantively different from Bhaskar's, she helps to explain this idea: "To the social realist there is no 'isolated' micro world—no *lebenswelt* 'insulated' from the socio-cultural system in the sense of being unconditioned by it, nor a hermetically sealed domain whose day-to-day doings are guaranteed to be of no significant 'import'" (10).

INTRODUCING DIALECTIC

Bhaskar repeatedly uses the example of Marx's suggestion that, while humans are in fact free to envision their lives, they are also constrained by the exploitation of labor by capital. Suppose we take as an example for our purposes here the institution of the library. There is a presumption of freedom of information—even a presumption, stated by the profession as collective, of a responsibility to ensure that information is free. Librarians operate upon the reality of the presumption both as idea and as practice. Materials and access are intended to reflect the range of perspectives, influences, and possibilities, and are managed in ways to optimize the intention. At the same time there are financial constraints on purchases and licensing, as well as community preferences and/or objections, technological challenges, and other mitigating factors. Both of the elements are real and are faced by librarians continuously; librarians struggle to reconcile the freedom with the constraints, attempting to enhance the freedom and diminish the constraints. The elements create tension that demonstrates clearly the impossibility of isolation of one (preferable) state of affairs. In the effort to accentuate the freedom there can be an impetus to relegate the constraints, as negatives, to an effective absence. What this means is that librarians, understanding the financial and other tensions that exist, attempt to realize the freedom insofar as it is possible. In other words, it is inevitable that the positive and the negative coexist.

Bhaskar's more recent work focuses on the challenges of dialectic, but as a necessary component of the examination of social life. In the later works his attention has turned away (somewhat) from science and toward emancipation. The turn constitutes a reduced focus on the method of science and even of social science and enhanced attention to human lives as people are best able to live them. "I should make it explicit that I do not see science as a supreme or overriding value, but only as one among others to be balanced (in a balance that cannot be wholly judged by science) in ergonic, emancipatory and eudaimonistic activity" (Bhaskar 1993, 15). I would suggest that, while his attention did shift, the entirety of his philosophical program should be investigated;

there are consistencies that lead to the unified direction of the freedom of human action. He (1993) says that the dialectic that is central to critical realism is a *value*: "Dialectic is the yearning for freedom and the transformative negation of constraints on it" (378). The transformation, which must be an essential commonplace of every profession, carries a moral obligation based on personal agency. Agency, first-person action, is the means by which *ought* can be realized as *is,* and an ideal of a eudaimonistic society (a society that values both human autonomy and social good) can become a reality. Agency is limited, though, in that "we never create the social structure, we never create the social circumstances into which we are born. We never create it from scratch, it always pre-exists us. Therefore, we must acknowledge the presence of the past" (Bhaskar 2002, 20). Bhaskar's ideal is strongly stated, but it is in concert with the values—the axiological foundation—of librarianship.

The agency that Bhaskar champions is active, and requires intentionality on the part of actors. A person acting intentionally has considerable freedom, but some variation inheres in intentionality. Bhaskar (1993) explains the variation:

Four dialectically interdependent planes constitute social life, which together I will refer to as four-planar social being, or sometimes human nature. These four planes are (a) of *material transactions with nature;* (b) of *inter-personal intra- or inter-action;* (c) of *social relations;* and (d) of *intra-subjectivity.* Important discriminations must be made at each level, thus at (c) we can differentiate *power* (including hegemonic/counter-hegemonic), *discursive* and *normative* relations (to which there correspond at [b] power, communicative and moral relations) [emphasis in original] (153).

The rules of grammar and syntax constrain speech (discursive relations), but they by no means determine it; there are choices that people are able to make intentionally. In other words, even with constraints, there are an almost infinite number of meaningful things that *could* be said. Likewise, rules of logic constrain formal inquiry, but the application of the rules can only occur in certain circumstances. For example, an argument is a formal structure, but that structure does not determine the premise that a particular individual will posit at a given time. Social reality is not *determined* by discourse, even as that reality's existence is shaped by human action. Our profession could investigate in greater detail the extent to which reality's existence is shaped by what we call information.

Contexts, including contexts of science and social science practice, tend to be social. Society, in critical realism, is not an object separate from people, but neither do people at a point in time *make* society. It both preexists the individuals who live right now (to some extent society is *given* to a person at a point in time) and is shaped by those individuals. Society is comprised of many, each acting to some extent intentionally and (although at many times in some substantive purposive agreement) not entirely in concert. Further, society is human *and* historical; it is a product of what happens now, what has happened, and what future is intended. For these reasons no method that allows, much less embodies, atomism can have efficacy. Moreover, society is comprised of a complex set of interactions, as Bhaskar (2002) points out:

I would like to look at the social world in this way: there are four places of social being which ordinate it (the social world). There are material transactions with nature, so the social world is constituted by nature; there are inter-personal relations between agents...; underlying those there are social structures which pre-exist and form the conditions of possibility of our actions. Such things as languages, modes of production, modes of political practice, those are the social structures which provide the conditions, the means and materials for our transactions with nature and with each other. And then there is the depth stratification of the personality, of the psyche, of the individual, and in principle the collective human spirit (73–74).

Method in the social sciences relies on the historical, transitive element. For anyone to be able to ask a new question, one must be cognizant of previous questions and their answers. It also relies on the ontic structure that defines the world. The structural contribution of Bhaskar is very complex, but vital to method. He (1993) represents what he calls four-planar social being graphically (160), as shown in Figure 3.2.

The cube represents flow, not static being, so the study of human action and the social world can be studied as flows. The flows, though, have structure, a structure that accommodates the ontic (the real), the communicative, and the interpretive. The graphic also serves to illustrate that there are *both* enabling *and* constraining forces and that individuals/society are capable of *both* the simple reproduction of structures and actions *and* transforming those structures and actions. The complexity of the social cube holds a great deal of meaning for method.

An additional feature of Bhaskar's dialectical critical realism is an understanding that negativity is essential. It is in the negative that the positive is possible. Bhaskar clarifies his meaning in some mundane example—pauses and stops in speech make communication comprehensible; there must be some absences so that the presence of what is said can be heard. For fields such as LIS, though, the importance of negativity is even greater than the mundane. As nonpositivist practice, LIS has to reject the particular kinds of monisms (conceptual and methodological) that positivist empiricism imposed. That is,

Figure 3.2
Four-planar being encompassing the "social cube"

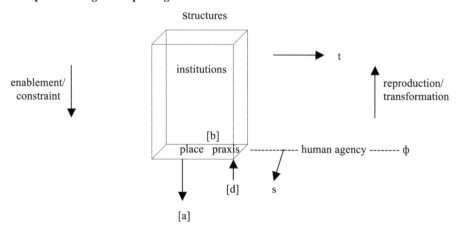

[a] = plane of material transactions with nature
[b] = plane of inter-/intra-subjective [personal] relations
[c] = place of social relations
[d] = plane of subjectivity of the agent

there are pluralities of ideas and methods that can (and must) be used in LIS to ensure that progressive knowledge is possible. The limitations that guided quests for laws, continuities, and regularities obscured, among other things, the conjunction of the subject (we the practitioners) from practice, and emphasized the individualist-atomistic conception of society (see Bhaskar 1993, 228–29). He explains the crucial character:

Negativity embraces the *dual* senses of the (evaluatively neutral) *absence* and the (pejorative) *ill*, united in dialectical critical realist explanatory critique, the aim of which is precisely to *absent ills*, underlying which is the metatheorem that *ills*. Which can always be seen as *absences*, are *constraints*, and that *to change is to cause is to absent* (that is, that changes are absenting), and which forms the backbone of the . . . real definition of dialectic as absenting constraints on absenting ills (or absences)—or, in effect, *the axiology of freedom* (238).

The passage is not simple, but it is explicable. Negativity necessarily includes a destructive character; dialectical critical realism guides negativity to what, in particular, is to be rendered absent. In LIS terms, negativity makes possible (or perhaps made possible at a point in time) the creation of a *collection* of works that were selected in preference to other works. In librarianship the absence of some works was symbolic of the *inclusion* of other works; that is, the collection was intended to be representative and not complete. LIS services also embrace negativity as a component of the value of freedom. What is retrieved by a user is an admission of the absence of what is not retrieved; more importantly, what is read as relevant to a user's needs is a further admission of the absence of the irrelevant. The character of services such as retrieval, reference, and reader's advisory embrace the critical dynamism of the negativity; what is absent at one moment can be present in the next—intentionally. He (2002) adds a warning to dialectic and absence: "if we leave out social structures, or if we only have social structures and we leave out nature or inter-personal relations, then we are in a situation of absence, dialectically erroneous absence" (74).

SUMMARY

Bhaskar, in clarifying an important difference between the natural and the social sciences states in several places that inquiry in the social sciences might not be able to achieve the irreducible positivist goal of prediction (see Wikgren 2005). The human aspect of dialectic critical realism is an explanation for the lack of predictability; the confluence of presence and absence requires deep and thoroughgoing research to reach understanding. Wikgren does explain the challenge: "In this respect realism differs from empiricism (the view that knowledge derives from experience of the world), and also from idealism (positing thought and language over matter). In social studies this distinction conditions our analysis: how real is social reality, and how can we best study, for example, the complex social events with information seeking and use" (12)? The potential is not limited to those topics of inquiry; the breadth of LIS could benefit from the critical-realist eye. In particular, Bhaskar's work provides a sound theoretical grounding for a critical appraisal of existing underlying (historical) assumptions that have contributed to the present state of LIS.

In a more specific vein, Bhaskar's idea of dialectic provides a framework—or perhaps a lens—through which inquiry and praxis in librarianship can be examined. His books offer a progressively well-developed idea of the need to envision the social sciences generally as encompassing the two forms of reality. Unlike some theorists, Bhaskar does not advocate subsuming social science under the method or epistemology of the natural sciences; his stance is that there are varying ontological existences that must be accounted for, that human relations cannot be reified as though they were intransitive objects of knowledge. Moreover, the very concept of information can be revisited in light of the dialectic that Bhaskar details. To situate his framework in bold terms, Bhaskar provides a corrective for an abundance of information seeking and information retrieval work that has been done to date, which has been heavily influenced by information-processing cognitive inquiry. Once one comprehends that the informational objects are in fact transitive objects, then one can engage them discursively, epistemologically, and in their own ontological context.

REFERENCES

Archer, M. S. 1995. *Realist Social Theory: The Morphogenetic Approach.* Cambridge: Cambridge University Press.

Bhaskar, R. 1993. *Dialectic: The Pulse of Freedom.* London: Verso.

Bhaskar, R. 1994. *Plato, etc.* London: Verso.

Bhaskar, R. 1997 [1975]. *A Realist Theory of Science.* 2nd ed. London: Verso.

Bhaskar, R. 1998a [1979]. *The Possibility of Naturalism: A Philosophical Critique of the Contemporary Human Sciences.* 3rd ed. London: Routledge

Bhaskar, R. 1998b. General introduction. In *Critical Realism: Essential Readings,* ed. by M. Archer, R. Bhaskar, A. Collier, T. Lawson, and A. Norrie. London: Routledge.

Bhaskar, R. 1998c. Philosophy and scientific realism. In *Critical Realism: Essential Readings,* ed. by M. Archer, R. Bhaskar, A. Collier, T. Lawson, and A. Norrie. London: Routledge.

Bhaskar, R. 2002. *From Science to Emancipation.* New Delhi: Sage.

Golinski, J. 1998. *Making Natural Knowledge: Constructivism and the History of Science.* Cambridge: Cambridge University Press.

Wikgren, M. 2005. "Critical Realism as a Philosophy and Social Theory in Information Science?" *Journal of Documentation 61,* no. 1: 11–22.

Winch, P. 1958. *The Idea of a Social Science and Its Relation to Philosophy.* London: Routledge and Kegan Paul.

4

Social Capital, Symbolic Violence, and Fields of Cultural Production: Pierre Bourdieu and Library and Information Science

Lisa Hussey
Simmons College, USA

BIOGRAPHICAL OVERVIEW

Pierre Bourdieu (1930–2002) was a French sociologist whose work focused on the influence of an individual's position in society on his or her decisions and actions in life. Bourdieu was born in Denguin, a rural community in the Pyrenees in Southwest France. After attending the École Normale Supérieure in Paris in the 1950s intending to study philosophy, a prestigious field at the time in France, Bourdieu served in the French military and was stationed in Algiers, where he remained after the completion of his military service to teach and conduct research. It was this experience, concomitant with conducting research in his native region of Béarn that moved him to the field of sociology from philosophy. His own background provided examples of his theories, such as habitus and the role of cultural and symbolic capital, which he analyzed in his work. He felt he held a unique position of being from a rural, working-class background and holding a respected and influential position in academia.

Although never entirely comfortable with being an intellectual, Bourdieu spent most of his professional higher education holding positions at the University of Algiers (1958–60), the University of Paris (1960–64), the École des Hautes Éstudes en Science Sociales (1964–82) and the Collège de France (1982–2002), where he served as the Chair of Sociology, a position he held until his retirement shortly before his death from cancer. Bourdieu liked to take the marginal view and often took controversial political stances in France (Reed-Danahay 2004, 2). However, Bourdieu did try to maintain a position outside of the political arena because he felt it was the proper place for sociologist to be involved (Grenfell 2004, 2).

Bourdieu's theories focus on the construction and presentation of the social world. He does this, generally using French social structures as an example and explaining how the classes are structured, both in relation to other classes and within each class. In this sense, Bourdieu is not simply looking at European views of class structure based on aristocracy because his work considers what makes a dominant class dominant and what makes it accepted as dominant by other classes regardless of the setting. Bourdieu's theories and concepts developed from his research in Algeria, his native region of Béarn, and Paris. His work, however, was not without critics who focused on his "alleged lack of analysis" (Baert 1998) or his dependence on his own origins to support his research and conclusions. In spite of this, his hierarchical construction of the social world is transferable to many different social settings or societies because of his analysis of the process and practices that influence individual development and help to construct social structures, rather than simply focus only on the distinct classes that compose the social structures.

MAJOR WORKS AND THEORIES

Bourdieu's vast amount of writing and presentations center on the concept of a general theory of practice, of how we, as individuals and as members of society, function every day; how we know what to do; how we make decisions—especially those we make unconsciously; how we know how to speak and what to say. All of this stems from an individual's view of the world, which according to Bourdieu, is shaped through his or her position in society and the structure of that society. In other words, one's history, including family, education, interactions with other classes, language and rituals, all contribute to how one approaches decisions, asks questions, and collects and filters data and information from the world.

However, Bourdieu did not limit himself to analyzing individuals and their outlook on the world. He also considered society and the hierarchy of class structure through discussions and analysis of the construction of the social world, the tools and process in place to provide support, and how all of it is balanced in order to maintain the configuration of power and domination of culture. Using the concepts of habitus, symbolic power, and fields of production, Bourdieu provides a view of the social world where individuals and groups with shared interests (social, economic, education, gender, ethnicity) create society and its structure through processes, practices, and rules and restrictions, both implicit and explicit, that help to create a shared, unspoken understanding of the uses of power, capital, and education. This power and capital are used to negotiate the various fields of production that help shape and influence the structure of the social world, including terms and conditions of social mobility. All of this is done with the implied approval and unconscious complicity at all levels of the social hierarchy. In fact, it is the implicit, unspoken, and unconscious that dominates Bourdieu's analysis of the social world, which is based on the concept of habitus.

Habitus

Habitus is Bourdieu's central theory, the one that underlies everything he wrote and the concept that drives his analysis of social structures and interactions among and between classes, regardless of location. Habitus is the process of how individuals shape their views of themselves, the wider society, and their place in the social world through subtle, often unconscious, inculcation of the family, the education system, local and regional society, and interactions within and outside of their social class. In *Outline of a Theory of Practice* (1977), Bourdieu defines habitus as:

The structures constitutive of a particular type of environment produce habitus, systems of durable, transposable dispositions, structured structures predisposed to function as structuring structures, that is, as principles of the generation and structuring of practices and representations which can be objectively "regulated" and "regular" without in any way being the product of obedience to rules (Bourdieu 1977, 72).

In other words, habitus is how individuals create their worldviews, generally through the unconscious recognition of patterns, rules, and expectations based on one's social class, family history, gender, education, and interactions with others at all levels within society. It is the "embodied feelings and thoughts connected to commonsense understandings of the world (doxa) and arising from particular social positions, including those of class, gender, nationality and ethnicity" (Reed-Danahay 2004, 2); a feel for the game; an understanding of how the world works and how ones fits within this working. Habitus is built upon doxa, the unconscious and unstated knowledge of the natural world. Doxa are those concepts and principles that are left unsaid, often because they came without being said; those ideas that one simple *knows* rather than being told, recognized only through missteps or mistakes that lead to questions regarding the assumption or practice. Habitus influences every aspect of how individuals choose to configure their lives and guides every decision, including those regarding education, career, marriage, entertainment, manners, and speech. However, it is not a voluntary or conscious process. Individuals rarely recognized how habitus influences decisions and actions.

Habitus, however, is not simply individual process, but one that is conducted in concert with others. Other members of the social world at all levels of the social hierarchy also contribute to development of habitus. Bourdieu (1977) sees social classes "defined as much by its *being-perceived* and by its *being*" (4). In other words, class structure is dependent not only on what is presented as reality, but also on individuals' perception of that reality. For example, an individual is defined as middle class or petit bourgeois by fulfilling the expectations of this class through economic and cultural means, as well as his or her own perception of having the economic and cultural means. This perception provides a common view of the social structure and allows those at the top of the social hierarchy, the dominant classes, help to inculcate habitus through the establishment of the legitimate, which may include educational opportunities, formal language usage, widely acceptable cultural pursuits, requirements for career paths, and the potential for social mobility—both upward and downward. Once a legitimate goal, pursuit, or action is established, it is accepted or rejected into the other classes, or the dominated classes, based on the habitus of the social class.

An individual's actions and choices reveal his or her habitus, which then identifies social standing or social class. Each class has its own rules regarding concepts such as gift giving, entertaining, and serving dinner. Each class acts to stay ahead of the class directly beneath it while simultaneously working to achieve the status of the class above it. This is reflected in the choices made based on the current position within the social structure and the desired position within the social structure. In *Distinction* (1984), Bourdieu uses the concept of taste, or cultural distinctions, as an illustration of how social class, regardless of location in the social hierarchy, defines what is expected and acceptable.

Taste is *amor fati*, the choice of destiny, but a forced choice, produced by conditions of existence which rule out all alternatives as mere daydreams and leave no choice but the taste for the necessary (178).

Taste is an identifier of class in the "manner in which culture has been acquired" (2) and is reflected in the way it is used. The simple act of serving dinner provides abundant illustrations of the habitus of the different classes that range from "substance and function to form and manner" (196). Whether it is lean and healthy foods for the dominant or bourgeois or substantive and fatty foods for the working class, the *tastes* associated with the particular class are defined by the needs to reach certain expectations. For example, members of the petite bourgeoisie or middle class will try to show their difference from the working class and reflect their desire to become bourgeois by always serving a formal dinner in a formal dining room rather than the relaxed (vulgar) meals of the working class served in kitchens. Outsiders in certain social situations are easily identified by missteps, such as using the wrong dinner fork or expecting individual courses to be presented.

Power and Capital

Just as habitus creates an understanding of the social world and how one fits within it, the concept of power provides the mechanism for maintaining, or losing, the structure and status of classes in the social world. According to Bourdieu, power is built upon the concepts of capital, which is often formed through economic and cultural resources. Individuals may also acquire capital through educational means, although this is often dependent on the type of education, social influence, and the rarity of certifications or degrees or through symbolic capital that is acquired through "a reputation for competence and an image of respectability and honorability" (1984, 291). Both educational capital and symbolic capital are often included as part of cultural capital, but are differentiated by social standing and class habitus. Each form of capital carries a different weight and significance depending on social class and location within the social class. All of these work together to create a complex hierarchical structure of classes and to identify divisions within the individual classes. Where one resides in the social hierarchy is based on capital, both economic and cultural and on how one is able to translate this capital into power. Economic capital depends on the economic resources of an individual. However, cultural capital can be more complicated. While it requires a certain knowledge base, to have rich cultural capital requires more than just an education or a reputation, but also the comprehension and competence expected from the dominant class. As a result, an individual from a middle-class or working-class background may achieve a certain level of educational capital or symbolic capital without gaining cultural capital. For example, members of the petite bourgeoisie or the middle class often make choices based on creating a perception of upward mobility while at the same time implementing certain economic practices to maintain this lifestyle, such as to buy art or cultural artifacts that are unusual, but not rare; affordable, but not inexpensive; almost good enough, but not quite. This is done based on a promise of a future that probably will never come. The dominant class does not surrender power, nor does it accept newcomers easily. They maintain their position in the hierarchy by changing the rules as the situation changes. As more people actually achieve a goal—an educational degree, a summer vacation destination, art pieces, and so on—the more that item is devalued. Drawn from economic and cultural capital, power establishes the basis to structure the social into distinct classes and to establish and reinforce habitus.

When Bourdieu speaks of power, he is referring to the concept of symbolic power, or power that is derived from the impression of the significance of economic and cultural capital. Symbolic power provides the dominant class, the bourgeois for Bourdieu, the influence and authority to construct established norms and values and to define legitimate standards and culture. As with habitus, this is accomplished without conscious recognition by the dominant or dominated classes.

Symbolic power is that invisible power which can be exercised only with the complicity of those who do not want to know that they are subject to it or even that they themselves exercise it (Bourdieu 1991, 164).

For effective control and power, both economic capital and cultural capital are required. How much of each type of capital depends on the importance placed on the type of capital within each social class. Once symbolic power is given, individuals or specific classes are able to exert control over members of other classes, or dominated members of their own class. Those who are willing to surrender power to others must also acknowledge the particular capital as legitimate. This again refers back to the concept of habitus, which provides the basis for legitimizing particular forms of capital.

Symbolic power also provides the means and justification for the dominant class, or dominant members of social classes, to create new positions and requirements in order to maintain their status and power. Bourdieu recognizes the importance of the rare in relation to education and cultural capital. When something is rare or limited to a select number of individuals, such as an educational degree or cultural artifact, it has effective symbolic capital and provides the holder with a degree of symbolic power. However, as more and more individuals are able to attain degrees and certificates in higher education, the value and application of those degrees decreases. Hence, what was once sufficient for a career changes as the number of qualified individuals increases, which leads to revisions of requirement, many of which can be found in the habitus of the dominated classes.

Social Structures and Field of Production

The construction of the social world, in Bourdieu's analysis, is not limited to class structure, or at least class structure as a simple hierarchy of social and economic status. It also includes fields of production or power. These are the social spaces where members are differentiated based on habitus and capital, both of which provide different levels of power. Members of the same classes may be divided within a particular field of production, such as the cultural or economic fields. Divisions may also be based on educational attainment, such as the contrast between degreed individuals and or autodidacts; based on economic resources, such as the contrast between old money and the nouveau riche; or based on social capital built on reputation, such as the contract between established art galleries and the avant-garde art community. Each field is shaped by the struggles of competing views, each fighting for the right to define legitimate. "A field or a market may be seen as a structured space of positions in which the positions and their interrelations are determined by the distributions of different kinds of... capital" (Bourdieu 1991,14). The fields are not distinct, but rather overlap and influence the structure and space of each field. They are the "site of struggles in which individuals seek to maintain or alter the distribution of the forms of capital specific to it" (14). The constant struggles define the form and the spaces within the fields with participants in the struggle working to gain as much space within the field as possible.

This struggle is most clear in the fields of cultural production where art, both high and low, is produced for specific audiences based on cultural, economic, and educational background. In the *Field of Cultural Production* (1993) Bourdieu provides an analysis of the arts and culture, specifically how culture both influences and is influenced society; and how the "practice of culture...within a social system...not only reproduces itself but also legitimizes itself" (Huhn 1996, 88). Rather than simply focus on only the structures, methods, schools, or political and social repercussions, Bourdieu explains how each factor impacts and changes the production, definition, and acceptance of art and how the hierarchical structure of the art word, and society as a whole, controls the fields of cultural production. "To socially recognize hierarchy of the arts, and within each of them, genres, schools or periods, corresponds a social hierarchy of consumers" (Bourdieu 1984, 1). In other words, the social habitus is used to help create and structure the different fields or markets within the fields of cultural production to satisfy the diverse needs and desires from the various economic fields.

The field of cultural production, as with the social world, is presented as a society that is dominated by one class and the "ways in which culture contributes to this structure" (Bourdieu 1993, 21). Habitus and power help to ensure the acceptance of this as the legitimate view of reality. Within the art world, this structure and domination is even more pronounced due to the established definitions and identification of art, the hierarchization of groups and subgroups, and the positions and position-taking present in the field.

Within the fields of cultural production, Bourdieu identifies two significant forms of capital, economic and symbolic, which in turn create two subdivisions: the field of large-scale cultural production and the field of restricted production. The field of large-scale production is more concerned with profit and is "organized with a view to the production of cultural goods destined for non-producers of cultural goods, 'the public at large'" (Bourdieu 1993, 115). The majority of artists and artistic works fall within this field that is generally defined by commercial success. Despite economic gains, however, many in this category still cling to the accepted view of art. This can be seen in the defensive or apologetic positions successful artists adopt to justify their work.

The field of restricted production, on the other hand, focuses on symbolic capital and creating art for art's sake. Symbolic capital is earned through rejecting commercial works. The more disinterested an artist is in economics, the more symbolic capital is acquired. Commercial success and economic gains are seen as a debasement of culture, a rejection of true or pure art. It is through the field of restricted production that changes to the accepted paradigms are instituted because the artists have the power to question and reject the ideas of the dominant class. This is a smaller and more elite field that is "defined by its own criteria for the production and evaluation of its products" (Bourdieu 1993, 115).

The accepted notion of art is created and perpetuated by an official source, such as the government, the educational system, museums, or members of the art world. In order to change the accepted definition of art, to cause a revolution in thinking, an individual or group must be able to exist or to produce legitimate work outside of the establishment. Bourdieu makes this clear when he discusses the idea of the artist attempting to establish himself by being different.

On one side are the dominant figures, who want continuity, identity, reproduction; on the other, the newcomers, who seek discontinuity, rupture, difference, revolution. To 'make' one's name means making one's mark, achieving recognition (in both senses) of one's difference from other producers...it means creating a new position beyond the positions presently occupied, ahead of them (1993, 106).

The artist attempts to find a way to force others to see and to accept an alternative view or definition of art. Dominants, however, fight any attempt to introduce new ideas and preserve their views. "Those in dominant positions operate essentially defensive strategies, designed to perpetuate the status quo by maintaining themselves and the principles on which their dominance is based" (83). One method is making the normal and everyday rare by focusing on the form rather than the content. This is how an artist claims the ownership of a work of art. It is not the subject of the painting, it is the technique used that makes it unique. However, this can status can only be achieved with enough cultural capital to give legitimacy to the position and economic capital to ignore the market. In other words, symbolic power through habitus and social standing acts as a basis for creating or discovering a new art form within the context of established standard of legitimate art.

It is interesting to note that rejection of or rebellion against a legitimate course does not weaken it, because it is not possible to rebel or reject the legitimate without first recognizing that it is legitimate. The act of rebellion reinforces the dominant by acknowledging its role and its power. The act of refuting or refusing cultural norms, educational degrees, and/or manners and graces reinforces the legitimacy of these concepts because they are being rebelled against.

The struggle in the fields of cultural production is not limited to art and other cultural artifacts. The use of language is another important tool for creating and maintaining social structures and the accepted concept of legitimate culture. Speech is a clear identifier of social position and habitus. "Language is a body technique, and specifically linguistic, especially phonetic, competence is a dimension of bodily hexis in which one's whole relation to the social world, and one's whole socially informed relation to the world, are expressed" (Bourdieu 1991, 86). Speech is influenced from the beginning by those who speak to us and is regulated by the expectation of correct usage based on the setting and the habitus of social position. Each discourse is formed on the relationship between habitus and the field or market of cultural production.

The use of language, the manner as much as the substance of discourse, depends on the social position of the speaker, which governs the access he can have to the language of...official, orthodox and legitimate speech (109).

Members of the dominant class, because they have the power to influence, know the correct language and words to use in formal and informal situations or, if they do not know, have the confidence and knowledge based on their habitus to be able to express their lack of knowledge without expressing ignorance, or to put it another way, to be able to not know something without being judged. "All linguistic practices are measured against the legitimate practices, i.e. the practices of those who are dominant" (53). Bourdieu refers to this domination of language as symbolic violence.

Symbolic violence is a form of violence because those with the most cultural capital and symbolic power force, usually though subtle and unconscious means, the official and accepted meanings of words and symbols onto the dominated classes. In other words, the standards of language are established and enforced, through education and official institutions, by those whose language and speech carry the most power. This often reveals itself in the practice of anticipated censorship or self-censorship, based on the social situation, the cue and codes communicated, and an understanding of what can and cannot be said.

BOURDIEU AND LIS

Although Bourdieu's work focuses on sociology and the social world, it has many interdisciplinary applications. In his work, he looked beyond his profession "to literary and art criticism to offer critiques of sociology and anthropology" (Reed-Danahay 2004, 3). He was often critical of the restrictive nature of objective anthropology and philosophy as neither field allows researchers to fully explore the social world and to question the practices and assumptions that contribute to and create the structure of classes and classes within classes, starting with the assumptions and world views of researchers. This need to recognize one's habitus is as important to library and information science (LIS) as other professions in the social sciences. Although we try to be objective, it is important to recognize that we are not unbiased. Our own worldviews influence how we approach information, be it in a book, a database, or a cultural artifact, and how we as professionals present the information to society.

Bourdieu's work provides several concepts relevant to the LIS professions: habitus, capital, symbolic power and the use of language, and the fields of cultural production. Several scholars in LIS have used Bourdieu's frameworks of symbolic power and cultural capital to analyze practices in the profession. Blaise Cronin and Debra Shaw (2002) used Bourdieu's definition of citations as an objective indicator of symbolic power (1267) in their examination of the relationship of symbolic capital and scholarly distinction. In LIS programs, faculty are expected to publish, and the perception of prestige attached to certain journals provides a level of cultural capital and symbolic power that can be used to earn tenure within a specific institution and to secure various levels of capital within the profession. John Budd and Lynn S. Connaway (1998) also used Bourdieu's concepts to frame their analysis of the relationship between content and power in LIS education. The article recognized the symbolic power attached to educational content and the lack of consistency across curriculums. The lack of consistency reflects a struggle among LIS organizations within certain fields of production in order to define the future direction of LIS education. While focused on different aspects of LIS education, both works looked at the role of language as a form of symbolic power within the profession, which influences the construction and delivery of educational content.

Symbolic power and cultural capital, while significant in education, have a much broader application to the LIS professions. At its core, LIS is a service profession. Many libraries, museums, and information centers focus on providing information services to the larger community. In most Western societies, this includes diverse communities with different orientations to culture, to learning, and to official or government organizations. With an understanding of habitus and how it influences worldviews, LIS can better prepare to serve these communities.

However, how LIS professionals deliver services can act as a tool for reinforcing and strengthening existing social structures, including coercive practices and inequities. In her article "The Meaning of Service," France Bouthillier (2000) uses Bourdieu's theories, along with Anthony Giddens' work, to create a framework for studying the systems of meanings used by service providers in their interactions with users. The purpose of the research was to "offer a framework for studying service practices in relation to social and historical issues" (243). In other words, the research reviewed the role of habitus and cultural capital in the delivery of LIS services; it explored how these services help to reinforce and reproduce social structures and order by providing them within a system of meaning in such a way that they are perceived as legitimate (246). Hence, the use of symbolic power and cultural capital acts as an enforcement mechanism in the dominance of social classes and structures.

Service is not the only tool used to build symbolic power and cultural capital. Libraries and information centers play a significant role in the field of cultural production, acting as facilitators and as preservation agents and/or repositories of culture. As a part of governmental or educational institutions, LIS often acts as a legitimizing agent for cultural artifacts. Libraries are the place to go to find the latest books for reading and to research good information, which gives the impression of acceptability of the materials provided. Archives select which historical artifacts are deemed important or legitimate enough for preservation. Museums display only those cultural artifacts deemed important to society, for all to appreciate. As such, it is important to understand the construction of the field, the power struggles, the capital needed for influence, the positions of both the dominant and the dominated classes, and the position and contribution of libraries and information centers in the struggle.

John Budd (2003) and Anne Goulding (2008) both look at the role of libraries as institutionalized producers and disseminators of cultural capital and symbolic power, or to put it another way, identify the means through which libraries act in the process of acquiring culture. In her analysis, Goulding views library use as "an indicator of cultural capital, suggesting that libraries can be regarded as sites for the production, dissemination and appropriation of cultural capital" (236). In contrast, Budd considers the unconscious or unacknowledged use of symbolic power in their policies and practices, which results in a lack of consideration of interpretive ethical social action. Despite their differing viewpoints, both authors provide a strong analysis of the libraries and their role in the reproduction of cultural mores through the perception of libraries as prominent figures in the fields of cultural production. The question is not whether the library acts as a disseminator of cultural capital, but rather to what degree and to which social groups. The next step from these articles might be to look at collection development polices and the creation of programs in libraries in relation to social structures, cultural and educational capital, and habitus of those involved in the process and the expected recipients of the services.

The information professions extend well beyond libraries and include concepts such as information behaviors and domain knowledge. In this area of research, Denise M. Nascimento and Regina M. Marteleto (2008) reviewed the role of social fields and domain knowledge in relation to Bourdieu's sociology of culture by researching the information practices of members in the architecture discipline. The purpose of the research was to "understand the information phenomena through means of information practice—the way of acting that gives identity to a group" (397). The authors concluded that particular disciplines create their own habitus based on the information structure of a discipline and the domain knowledge of the researcher. This in turns acts as influence on information seeking behaviors and the accumulation of symbolic power and cultural capital and establishes their position within the field of cultural production.

CONSIDERATIONS FOR FUTURE RESEARCH

There are many topics and issues in LIS that could benefit from Bourdieu's theories, including educational programs, services to underserved groups, information behaviors and class structure, and the continued critical analysis of the role of habitus in the information professions. When considering the role of symbolic capital and educational degrees, one may want to look at the respect or significance given to the traditional LIS master's degree (MLIS) in comparison to other information related degrees, such as master's in information science (MIS). In recent history, there has been a growing friction between what are seen as traditional library programs and those that focus on the field of information. While this provides a rich conversation about the evolving nature of information and the role of information professionals, is this debate also weakening the symbolic capital of the various educational degrees? In other words, as more programs and degrees focus on the study of information and its uses, do the values of these degrees decrease as the number of graduates increase? Which programs and degrees have the most educational capital, economic capital, and/or cultural capital and how is this translated into symbolic power in LIS?

The discussion of LIS education can further benefit from a frank and critical analysis of the role of habitus and social capital in LIS education. There is a growing body of literature concerning the state of diversity in LIS. Using Bourdieu's habitus and cultural capital as a framework, researchers can look beyond curriculum issues and address the question of how our backgrounds—made up of a majority of educated, white, middle class individuals—are influencing our teaching. Are topics such as diversity, underserved populations, or gender focused issues seen as more fringe ideas, or are they given prominence in LIS educational programs, and who makes this decision?

As a profession, we may also want to consider the fact that in LIS there is not a set core or even a set definition of librarian or information professional by a major professional organization, the American Library Association (ALA), which is responsible for the accreditation of LIS educational programs. Considering this lack, why is this accreditation process in place? Is it as an educational tool or is it a mechanism of educational capital? Does this stem from the pressures of other professional groups (ABA, AMA) or our own attempt at gaining cultural capital?

Bourdieu's theories can be used in research reaching beyond LIS education and focusing on service and programs offered. For example, the concepts of symbolic power and symbolic violence can be used to analyze the presentation of the libraries and other information centers to underserved groups. This includes the consideration of power and cultural capital in how we, as a profession, present the library and how, as an institution, it is viewed by the wider social community based on social position and educational capital.

This can also be taken a step further to analyze the role of symbolic violence in creating programs for groups perceived as outside of the social norms to attempt to answer questions such as: Are these programs put together based on the stated needs of these groups or are they constructed based on the LIS professional's perception of need? In the delivery of these programs, are LIS institutions reaching out to these communities, or instead furthering social domination through subtle and unconscious means by imposing the official and accepted meanings of words and symbols onto the dominated classes?

CONCLUSION

As the definition and capital of information changes, the concept of symbolic power is very important when it comes to being recognized as information professionals in the social world, especially by those with the most economic and cultural capital—those that create the new positions in society. For LIS, that means the need to have sufficient cultural capital, including educational capital, as well as economic capital to be an accepted authority in the information society. Hence, unless those outside of the profession recognize our degrees as legitimate for handling and locating information, the profession will have limited power in the information society.

REFERENCES

Baert, Patrick. 1998. Bourdieu, Pierre. In *Routledge Encyclopedia of Philosophy*, ed. E. Craig. London: Routledge. Available at http://www.rep.routledge.com.library.simons.edu/article/R044.

Bourdieu, Pierre. 1977. *Outline of a Theory of Practice*. Cambridge: Cambridge University Press.

Bourdieu, Pierre. 1984. *Distinction: A Social Critique of the Judgement of Taste*. Cambridge, MA: Harvard University Press.

Bourdieu, Pierre. 1993. *The Field of Cultural Production*. New York: Columbia University Press.

Bourdieu, Pierre. 1991. *Language and Symbolic Power*. Cambridge, MA: Harvard University Press.

Bourdieu, Pierre. 1998. *Practical Reason*. Stanford, CA: Stanford University Press.

Bouthillier, France. 2000. "The Meaning of Service: Ambiguities and Dilemmas for Public Service Library Providers." *Library & Information Science Research* 22:243–72.

Budd, John. 2003. "The Library, Praxis, and Symbolic Power." *Library Quarterly* 73 (1): 19–23.

Budd, John, and Lynn S. Connaway. 1998. "Discursive Content and Discursive Power in U.S. Library and Information Service Education." *Libri* 48 (3): 140–52.

Cronin, Blaise, and Debora Shaw. 2002. "Banking (on) Different Forms of Symbolic Capital." *Journal of the American Society for Information Science and Technology* 53 (14): 1267–70.

Goulding, Anne. 2008. "Libraries and Cultural Capital." *Journal of Librarianship and Information Science* 40 (4): 235–37.

Grenfell, Michael J. 2004. *Pierre Bourdieu: Agent Provocateur*. London: Continuum.

Huhn, Thomas. 1996. Review of *The Field of Cultural Production*, by Pierre Bourdieu. *Journal of Aesthetics and Art Criticism* 54 (1): 88–90.

Nascimento, Denise M., and Regina M. Marteleto. 2008. "Social Field, Domains of Knowledge and Informational Practice." *Journal of Documentation* 64 (3): 397–412.

Reed-Danahay, Deborah. 2004. *Locating Bourdieu*. Bloomington, IN: Indiana University Press.

5

Beyond a Signpost for Resistance: The Promise of Michel de Certeau's Practices of Everyday Life for LIS Scholarship

Paulette Rothbauer
University of Western Ontario, Canada

A BRIEF BIOGRAPHY

French cultural theorist, Michel de Certeau was born in 1925 and died in 1986. Although his work really only found wide notice among English language readers after his death, as Natalie Zemon Davis (2008) tells us, de Certeau was seen as a kind of celebrity thinker in France, where he was openly mourned by the public. De Certeau was ordained as a Jesuit priest in 1956 (Ahearne 1995, 2) and throughout his scholarly career he maintained what one critic called an "unwavering religiosity" (Buchanan 2000, 2). Much of de Certeau's scholarly output was concerned with early modern religions, particularly with his study of 17th-century Christian mystics (see Ahearne 1995; Giard 1997, ix; Davis 2008). Profoundly affected by the student and worker protests culminating in the general strike of May 1968 in France (Giard 1997), de Certeau collected his commentary and reflections on these events in a pamphlet entitled, *La prise de parole*[1] that was published later in the same year (Highmore 2006, 75). Some see these writings as representative of an important turning point in de Certeau's oeuvre, marking a shift away from the strictures of the institutional discourses in which his religious studies were performed. Other analysts insist that there is a strong and coherent thread of thematic and methodological interests that runs through de Certeau's entire body of work (for example, Buchanan 2000; Highmore 2002). De Certeau also conducted ethnographic studies among native communities in the Latin American countries of Brazil, Chile, and Argentina (Ahearne 1995, 70; Highmore 2006, 8). After 1968 and until his death, he worked consistently as a cultural policy analyst and public intellectual, working with colleagues on various projects for the Ministry of Culture in France (Highmore 2006, 154). De Certeau also pursued intellectual interests in psychoanalysis and was also a founding member of Jacques Lacan's École Freudienne established in 1964 (Ahearne 1995, 2; Highmore 2006, 51). He held several academic positions in France and from 1978–84 he was a professor of French and comparative literature at the University of California at San Diego. He was appointed director of studies at the *École des Hautes Études en Sciences Sociales* in Paris the year before his death.[2]

Apparently, de Certeau identified primarily as an historian (Ahearne 1995, 194; Davis 2008), and he has made significant contributions to the history of early modern religious experience (see *The Possession at Loudon*) as well as to the writing of history and historiography (see *The Writing of History*). He brought to all of his writing the influences of his Jesuit training, his interests in psychoanalysis, and his concern to honour the perspectives of marginalized and invisible voices whether this was "of seventeenth-century 'Christians without a church,'" of the Amerindians crushed by colonizers since the Renaissance, and of the "man without qualities," (sic) our contemporary human beings who are submerged—even in the secrecy of their dreams—by mass consumerism" (Giard 1997, ix). However, most commentators on de Certeau's oeuvre also point out his remarkably wide-ranging intellectual contributions to fields such as cultural and media studies, consumer and leisure studies, cultural anthropology, and literary studies, as well as to social and political thought and psychoanalysis. And, as many analysts have pointed out, Michel de Certeau's work seems truly interdisciplinary in his quest to understand and articulate the practices of everyday life while privileging perspectives that have been silenced and invisible in other accounts. This serious, ethical insistence on the interrelated connections among disciplined ways of knowing may resonate the most with researchers and writers who work on the problematics of everyday life and marginalized voices and perspectives. For this reason (and due to the necessary editorial limits imposed for this chapter), it is primarily de Certeau's ideas about the practices of everyday life that will be covered here, although references will be made to his diverse works as appropriate.[3]

PRACTICES OF EVERYDAY LIFE

In earlier work I sketched a framework for the analysis of everyday life information-seeking behaviour that drew from Michel de Certeau's rubric of everyday life practices (Rothbauer 2005). In this chapter, I elaborate this framework making further reference to de Certeau's ideas about the everyday as an "ensemble of practices" (Highmore 2002, 151).

It is important to emphasize that de Certeau's "practices of everyday life" do not constitute anything like a fully formed theoretical formulation. He begins by informing the reader that the aim of the collected essays published in *The Practice of Everyday Life* (1984) is "by means of inquiries and hypotheses, to indicate pathways for further research" (xi; see also 18). His project was to foreground the practices of everyday life, or the ways that ordinary people "made do" within networks of institutions like education, the military, the media, big business, and the church that comprised the disciplinary (or dominating) forces of society. The question at the center of his inquiries was, as Highmore writes, not how to overthrow networks of power, but rather how society resists being determined by "the grid of discipline" (2002, 159). De Certeau's analytical lens, therefore, focuses on "ways of operating" or on what he described as "the clandestine forms taken by the dispersed, tactical, and make-shift creativity of groups or individuals already caught in the nets of 'discipline'" (xiv–xv). He is interested to uncover the "poetics" of everyday cultural production: how people invent or create everyday life while using the products supplied by the expansionist systems of sociocultural production (Highmore 2002, 148). De Certeau writes,

The purpose of this work is to make explicit the systems of operational combination (*les combinatoires d'opérations*) which also compose a "culture," and to bring to light the models of action characteristic of users whose status the dominated element in society (a status that does not mean that they are either passive or docile) is concealed by the euphemistic term "consumers." Everyday life invents itself by *poaching* in countless ways on the property of others (1984, xi–xii).

De Certeau employs a distinct vocabulary to describe the ensemble of everyday practices from the ubiquitously cited "strategies" and "tactics," to "ways of operating," "poaching," and "making do" along with recurrent binary pairs such as "reading and writing," "consumption and production," and "space and place." An understanding of these terms provides an important key to de Certeau's overall formulation of everyday life practices. It is also important to recognize that for de Certeau the locus of analysis in his study of the marginalized and dominated was situated at the level of activities, procedures and practices, those that are quotidian, taken-for-granted, and massively predominant across all of society. He tells us right away that the individual is not the unit of analysis, but rather the social relations between individuals and ways of operating in everyday life (1984, xi).

His central metaphor for conceiving of the practices of everyday life is borrowed from military operations, encompassed by his use of the terms "strategies" and "tactics" now so widely cited across the disciplines. Given the freight of these two terms, it seems necessary to revisit the meaning that de Certeau explicitly gives to them:

I call a *strategy* the calculation (or manipulation) of power relationships that becomes possible as soon as a subject with will and power (a business, an army, a city, a scientific institution) can be isolated. It postulates a *place* that can be delimited as its *own* and serve as the base from which relations with an *exteriority* composed of targets or threats (customers or competitors, enemies, the country surrounding the city, objectives and objects of research, etc.) can be managed (1984, 35–36).

I call a "tactic" on the other hand, a calculus which cannot count on a "proper" (a spatial or institutional localization), nor thus on a borderline distinguishing the other as a visible totality. The place of a tactic belongs to the other. A tactic insinuates itself into the other's place, fragmentarily, without taking it over in its entirety, without being able to keep it at a distance. It has at its disposal no base where it can capitalize on its advantages, prepare its expansions, and secure independence with respect to circumstances. The "proper" is a victory of space over time. On the contrary, because it does not have a place, a tactic depends on time—it is always on the watch for opportunities that must be seized "on the wing" ... Many everyday practices (talking, reading, moving about, shopping, cooking, etc.) are tactical in character. And so are, more generally, many "ways of operating" (1984, xix).

Strategies establish a place and are proprietorial, suggesting what appropriate activity is, and what accepted conventions are within or for that place (Highmore 2002, 158). Strategies are defined, in part, by a regulatory imperative to govern how a place is constructed and used. Strategies are deployed by the institutions that comprise the grid of discipline to continue to produce the network of disciplinary apparatuses and to produce a regulatory effect through distribution of its "products" to the "consumers." Stable places are produced through strategic operations. According to de Certeau (1984, 36) the effects of strategies are threefold: to produce a "triumph of place over time" by creating a place that resists the erosion of time; to make a "panoptic presence" possible by producing a "mastery of places through sight" (so, a place is recognized and made visible as an institution, as site of power); and to provide "oneself with one's own place" (or to produce regulations and laws that give credibility, visibility and power to an institution).

Such strategies are relentlessly expansionist in de Certeau's vision of everyday life, but what interests him is the creative capacity of individuals (of consumers, of readers) to move within this system. Rather than this "rationalized, expansionist, centralized, spectacular and clamourous production" (1984, 31) de Certeau focuses on the "quasi-invisibility" of consumer production—invisible because it shows itself not in actual products, but through "ways of using" or "making do" within this "calculus of force-relationships" (1984, xix).

The operations of everyday life are characterized for de Certeau by what he termed "tactics" which, in turn, are defined by the concepts of "escaping without leaving" and "poaching." Tactics operate inside the grid of discipline, inside the system—there is no other possibility—individuals dominated by networks of power must necessarily operate alongside the logics of the strategies of such systems. De Certeau attempted to give weight to this idea of tactical operations within the system by invoking the concept of *la perruque* (translated from the French as "the wig") as an everyday procedure of making do. *La perruque* is when a worker uses company time to conduct personal business, in this way resisting the logic of the assembly line (1984, 25, 29–30). While this concept has been critiqued as having no power to disrupt unequal dynamics of social power (see Morris 1990), Ben Highmore provides a strong corrective to the interpretation of de Certeau's notion of resistance as "opposition," claiming that for de Certeau, resistance is "closer to the use of the term in electronics and psychoanalysis: it is what hinders and dissipates the energy flow of domination, it is what resists representation... [it] is as much an activity born of inertia as it is a result of inventive forms of appropriation" (2002, 152). Seen this way, *la perruque* provides massive evidence of the failure of the grid of discipline to wholly determine the contours of everyday life.

By looking at de Certeau's analyses of everyday life we can learn more about how he envisioned the interplay of strategies and tactics. He provides an elaboration of the operations of everyday life in several chapters of *The Practice of Everyday Life* but it is his writing on the relationship between reading and writing and his ideas on place and space that we will be concerned with here.[4]

De Certeau brings the activities of reading and writing together as similar everyday cultural operations: he sees both as practices of creative and active production of readers and writers (de Certeau 1997b, 145; and as cited in Highmore 2002, 155). However, in what de Certeau calls a "scriptural economy" (1984), writing is privileged because it is more visible than reading and such visibility continually reifies its place in our society. Reading is an "inevitable" starting point in de Certeau's work as he saw it as "the "exorbitant" focus of contemporary culture and its consumption" (1984, xxi). He creates a parallel between the binaries of writing-reading and production-consumption. In one of his most famous passages, he debunks the supposed passivity of readers by rejecting the ideology that posits readers, consumers, and users of cultural products as victims who witlessly absorb the values and beliefs provided by the systems of production. He explicitly critiques the ideology of "informing through books" when he describes its logic as rendering consumption as "something done by sheep progressively immobilized and 'handled'... The only freedom supposed to be left to the masses is that of grazing on the ration of simulacra the system distributes to each individual" (1984, 165–66). In place of this ideology, de Certeau posits an idea of the reader (i.e., the consumer of texts) as a poacher and as a silent producer who, through the process of reading a text, creates "a different world (the reader's) [that] slips into the author's place" (1984, xxi). Reading then, for de Certeau, is tactical resistance par excellence, since the reader necessarily has to make do with what the author and the publisher (i.e., the producer) provide. The text in this formulation represents the place of strategies, what de Certeau terms the "readable space," while the "actuality" of reading is a tactical way of operating within the systems of production of cultural texts (1984, 169). Furthermore, for de Certeau the only way to understand this silent production was to look at ways of using; he asked of "[t]he thousands of people who buy a health magazine, the customers of newspaper stories and legends—what do they make of what they 'absorb,' receive, and pay for? What do they do with it?" (1984, 31). The everyday practice of reading, in de Certeau's framework, "eludes the law of information," disrupting the ideology that sees a passive reader receiving wholesale messages from cultural texts. However, reading also illustrates how tactics do not necessarily oppose the strategies of the dominant, but do, rather, work alongside them: to read a text you need to work within it as a frame of reference.

De Certeau provides some elaboration of his notions of place and space. As his definitions of these terms indicate, "place" is seen to be a recognizable, stable, distinct site of power in the context of changing social-cultural-political relations. The "law of the 'proper' rules in the place" and defines it and makes it impossible for some other complex of relations to be in the same place at the same time. As is illustrated by the case of reading, places must also contain tactical ways of operating. Space is characterized by movement and "mobile elements" and is "produced by the operations that orient it, situate it, temporalize it, and make it function in a polyvalent unity of conflictual programs." So, again, rather than seeing the production of space in conflict or opposition to place, de Certeau declares that "space is practiced place" (1984, 117), just as reading is a spatial operation that relies on the text as a "place." As Highmore writes, de Certeau provides a picture of the production of everyday life that holds in abeyance the "binary logic that infects the analysis of the social" (2002, 151) and further, that a focus on the resistance of everyday, tactical ways of operating "offers a different and pluralized account of powers" (152).

LIS RESEARCH AND MICHEL DE CERTEAU: SUPPORT FOR RESISTANCE

Michel de Certeau has been cited very little in the published literature of Library and Information Science (LIS), and when he is cited it is exclusively to the 1984 English language edition (translated by Stephen Rendall) of his book *The Practice of Everyday Life*. Most citations to de Certeau rely on one general application of his work: to posit active or resistant agency of research participants or subjects (e.g., Adams; Chopin; Davenport, Higgins and Somerville; McKechnie et al.; Mehra, Merkel and Bishop; Wyatt et al.). While it is difficult to locate many examples of in-depth treatment of de Certeau's ideas in the published LIS literature, notable use of his ideas is evident in the work of a handful of LIS scholars.

In the late 1990s, Wayne Wiegand and Christine Pawley were the first LIS researchers to cite de Certeau in their respective work. In the published version of his 1997 address to the Library of Congress, Wiegand (1999) used de Certeau to support his analysis of the gaps in information science research when it came to conceptualizing the "personal information economy" of ordinary people. Specifically, Wiegand uses de Certeau to support the idea that people do not passively receive information from a variety of media, information tools or people and that the ways in which they "appropriate that information in efforts to make sense of the world around them in their everyday lives" remained invisible in the information science discourse (24).

Christine Pawley (1998) uses de Certeau's work as a framework to discuss various instances of ideological resistance to hegemonic strategies at work within LIS. She cites de Certeau's ideas about tactical resistance to remind us that the dominated classes in society exercise agency to "create space for themselves to exercise choice and control" and that such practices, if taken far enough, according to de Certeau "compose the network of an anti-discipline" (de Certeau, cited in Pawley 1998, 128). Pawley picks up this thread again later in the article when she discusses the tactical practices performed both by librarians who resisted official policies of censorship during the First World War and the McCarthy era, and LIS faculty who disrupted LIS curricula by offering courses on marginalized and invisible user groups (139–40).

Pawley (2003) introduces two different aspects of de Certeau's work in a later paper on the contradiction among conceptualizations of information literacy as, on one hand, a set of practices with emancipatory and democratic potential, and on the other hand, as systematic control that undermines such liberatory effects. First, Pawley indirectly cites de Certeau's notion of the "scriptural economy" as she links the concept of information with Enlightenment ideas of being informed and improved through reading (428). Second, Pawley uses de Certeau's work on reading as poaching to define a line of scholarly inquiry into readers and texts that complicates the relationship between information and users (437). Pawley (2009) revisits the resistance framework provided by de Certeau's formulation of the strategies and tactics of everyday life when she interrogates the strength of its explanatory power beyond an understanding of the daily appropriations and personal resistances of individual readers (78–80).

Pawley develops her own approach for the history of reading scholarship (focused on making reading institutions the unit of analysis) by strategically critiquing de Certeau's resistance model of reading. Another researcher, David Patterson (2009), maps his inquiry regarding the use of new literary theories as a way to investigate information literacy instruction among undergraduate and college students to de Certeau's notion of the creative agency of reading acts. He suggests that community college librarians recast students as active "creators of knowledge" in all stages of the research act (353). However, in an overview of models of reading in the context of public libraries and pleasure reading, Catherine Sheldrick Ross (2009) provides the most expansive articulation of the resistance model of reading informed by de Certeau (647–49). Ross illustrates how de Certeau, especially his writing in his chapter on reading as poaching in *The Practice of Everyday Life,* helps reading researchers to posit a "meaning-producing poacher reader" (648) that undermines "the notion of the compliant reader as a receptacle for meanings produced by others" (649).

In my own work I have used de Certeau's concepts of spatial tactics to theorize the role of the public library in my understanding of the reading and information seeking practices of library users and readers (Rothbauer 2007). Specifically, I explore de Certeau's insistence on the power of readers to grab hold of what the system provides to find or produce a space in the grid of discipline that imposes social control or in response to what Pawley (1998) calls "hegemonic strategies" in her analysis of LIS curricula. Using de Certeau's formulation of the practices of everyday life as a framework for a study of libraries and reading permits the library to be positioned as a site and source of information for the creation of ideological space that potentially supports the social and personal identities of people who claim alternative sexual identities as lesbian, gay, bisexual, or queer (LGBQ). Rather than simply making claims for resistant readers, using de Certeau's ideas on the practices of everyday life, I attempt to theorize both an ideological space and an actual social place for the library that allows for a negotiation of the tension between professional LIS practice and user perceptions and behaviour. The ethical imperatives in LIS to create ordered access to information for a variety of users who are institutionally categorized by various identity markers, including those that describe sexual identities and orientations (in other words, the library's own grid of discipline), paradoxically, provides the ground and the ideological resources that are appropriated by users in their tactical use of the place of the library. As they make their way through various imposed systems—information, library, and publishing—they find personally relevant reading materials that resonate with their sense of themselves as readers and as people belonging to a larger community of sexual minority citizens. The common litany offered in empirical studies of the information practices of LGBQ library patrons that the library does not yield much useful, relevant, or current information or materials to their searches, does not spell out a complete failure. Such activities and reflections on the same provide a point of commonality among all such users that could be seen in terms of an information practice that corresponds to a ritual coming-out narrative ("I went to look for books at the library but they didn't have what I wanted, or all they had was this" (i.e., old, out-dated, irrelevant titles).

De Certeau's conceptualization of tactics and strategies of everyday life allows us to see that it is not just a matter of escaping dominant systems that treat all consumers and users as dupes, nor on the other hand, is it simply a matter of positing an active agent who nevertheless, exerts no real power to change the system. Everyday tactics are iterative, wily, and difficult to reify into stable and lasting representations, but this does not render them meaningless or trivial—in many ways it is this plurality and heterogeneity that grants power to everyday ways of operating.

THE PROMISE OF PRACTICES OF EVERYDAY LIFE FOR LIS

While it is beyond the scope of this paper to discuss other areas of Michel de Certeau's oeuvre that are rich with possibility for LIS, it would be remiss to fail to mention them at all. His critique of traditional modes of historiography (1988) along with his work that insists on the plurality of voices and meanings for an understanding of social practices and relations among the dominated and the powerful (1986) will be of interest to certain LIS researchers. For those who reject the thesis of social control that pins individuals onto the grid of discipline with their every movement determined by powerful sociopolitical forces, Michel de Certeau offers an approach to the study of culture that privileges multiple modes of operating among a plurality of voices that contributes to an understanding of social and cultural phenomena. Readers are also directed to Ben Highmore's book published in 2006, entitled, *Michel de Certeau: Analysing Culture* for an analysis of de Certeau's "methodological imagination" as read against and with prominent social theorists and writers such as Spivak, Bahktin, and Foucault. In particular, de Certeau's conception of an ethical ethnography should be of interest to LIS researchers working in this tradition.

As discussed in the previous section, the practices of everyday life as formulated by de Certeau have found fertile ground in a handful of LIS studies. His work has predominantly been used to support research on readers and reading but has been cited much less in research concerned with how people use information resources and navigate information systems. It would seem that this field of research is wide open in terms of an application of de Certeau's work. After a brief discussion of the field of everyday life information studies, I briefly provide three specific examples of research problems that could be informed by de Certeau's practices of everyday life, moving an application of his work beyond resistance models of use and consumption to interrogate more deeply the overlapping relations between strategic and tactical operations.

Inquiries regarding the information behaviour of people in everyday life constitute a growing field of study in LIS (Fisher and Julien 2009, 325–26). Although researchers have been examining information seeking, use, and sharing by ordinary people in the context of everyday needs for information at least since the 1960s (Savolainen 2008, 6, 37–38), it is in recent years that serious attention has been given to the study of information practices as central to people's daily lives.[5] One of the key questions in this area concerns the relationship between sociocultural factors and quotidian information practices associated with identifying personal needs for information and relevant or convenient sources of information. A consistent finding is that daily routine and convenience often determine the assessment of reliability and quality as well as the degree of use of information and information resources (see Savolainen 2008, 203–4). De Certeau's work has the potential to enrich our understanding of the meaning of both everyday contexts and mundane information practices, in particular, in studies of marginalized or nonelite populations. For example, how do daily, taken-for-granted information practices (such as those related to media use like reading the newspaper or browsing the Internet) lend stability or disrupt the place of the family or the household? De Certeau gives us a lens by which to see and framework with which to privilege banal and, often, invisible daily information practices.

Given de Certeau's reliance on travel metaphors as well as his insistence on the capacity of users to create an "indefinite plurality of meanings" as they wander through "an imposed system" (1984, 169), it seems that his work could be productively used in studies of the information practices of library users. For example, de Certeau's ideas could frame an analysis of the strategies of database producers who create and market particular information products, along with those of academic librarians in their efforts to impart literature searching and research skills to students. Such a study would ask questions of what students make of the products of these strategies: how do they navigate the database structures, what do they make of tutorial exercises and handouts? Add to their voices those of other users, other producers (for example, reviewers or information technology workers), to gain access to the plurality and polyvalence that de Certeau's framework demands.

More work could be done in LIS on the place of the public library using de Certeau's sense of place and space. How does the library continue to exert social power to stabilize its place in society? What are the explicit strategies to issue from such a place that permits a continuing "triumph of place over time"? How do users exert tactical resistance using library policies, programs and services as overlapping frames of reference?

A similar framework could be brought to the study of some of our enduring library associations. What kinds of self-defining and self-supporting strategies permit the establishment and continuance of associations that span more than one hundred years? In this case, how do librarians and other library workers use the products of their associations? What are the "mobile elements" in such consumption?

It is my hope that readers will be inspired to explore de Certeau's work to find their own questions (and answers) informed by the record of de Certeau's thought. The bottom line for LIS researchers interested in using de Certeau's ideas about everyday life practice is that they need to be prepared to explore, creatively, the spaces in between comforting binaries such as production-consumption, reading-writing, and space-place. De Certeau does not give us a theory that can be applied to our data, to our findings, but does give us analytical tools and methods for thinking about our research, pushing it into new and exciting directions, that allow us to enunciate taken-for-granted, understudied, marginalized, or invisible information practices.

REFERENCES

Adams, Katherine C. 2000. "Loveless Frump as Hip and Sexy Party Girl: A Reevaluation of the Old-Maid Stereotype." *Library Quarterly* 70 (3): 287–301.

Ahearne, Jeremy. 1995. *Michel de Certeau: Interpretation and Its Other.* Stanford: University of California Press.

Buchanan, Ian. 2000. *Michel de Certeau: Cultural Theorist.* London: Sage Publications.

Chopin, Kimberly. 2008. "Finding Communities: Alternative Viewpoints through Weblogs and Tagging." *Journal of Documentation* 64 (4): 552–75.

Davenport, Elisabeth, Martin Higgins, and Ian Somerville. 2000. "Narratives of New Media in Scottish Households: The Evolution of a Framework of Inquiry." *Journal of the American Society for Information Science* 51 (10): 900–912.

Davis, Natalie Zemon. 2008. "The Quest of Michel de Certeau." *New York Review of Books* 55, no. 8 (May 15). Available at http://www.nybooks.com/articles/21375. Accessed August 7, 2009.

de Certeau, Michel. 1997a. *The Capture of Speech and Other Political Writings.* Tom Conley. Minneapolis: University of Minnesota.

de Certeau, Michel. 1997b. *Culture in the Plural.* Trans. Tom Conley. Minneapolis: University of Minnesota Press.

de Certeau, Michel. 1986. *Heterologies: Discourse on the Other.* Trans. Brian Massumi. Minneapolis: University of Minnesota Press.

de Certeau, Michel. 1984. *The Practice of Everyday Life.* Trans. Steven Rendell. Berkeley: University of California Press.

de Certeau, Michel. 1988. *The Writing of History.* Trans. Tom Conley. New York: Columbia University Press.

de Certeau, Michel, Luce Giard, and Pierre Mayol. 1998. *The Practice of Everyday Life, Volume 2: Living and Cooking.* Trans. Timothy J. Tomasik. Minneapolis: University of Minnesota Press.

Fisher, Karen E., and Heidi Julien. 2009. "Information Behavior." *Annual Review of Information Science & Technology* 43: 317–58. Ed. Blaise Cronin. Medford, NJ: Information Today.

Giard, Luce. 1997. "Introduction: How Tomorrow Is Already Being Born." In *The Capture of Speech and Other Political Writings,* by Michel de Certeau, vii–xix. Minneapolis: University of Minnesota Press.

Giard, Luce. 1987. "Biobibliographie." In *Michel de Certeau,* ed. Luce Giard, 245–53. Paris: Editions du Centre Pompidou.

Highmore, Ben. 2002. *Everyday Life and Cultural Theory: An Introduction.* London: Routledge.

Highmore, Ben. 2002. "Michel de Certeau's Poetics of Everyday Life." In *Everyday Life and Cultural Theory: An Introduction,* 145–78. London: Routledge.

Highmore, Ben. 2006. *Michel de Certeau: Analysing Culture.* London: Continuum.

McKechnie, Lynne (E. F.), Christopher M. Dixon, Jana Fear, and Angela Pollak. 2006. "Rules of (Mis)conduct: User Behaviour in Public Libraries." In *Information Science Revisited: Approaches to Innovation,* ed. Haidar Moukdad. Proceedings of the 34th Annual Conference of the Canadian Association for Information Science, June 1–3, York University, Toronto, ON, Canada.

Mehra, Bharat, Cecilia Merkel, and Ann Peterson Bishop. 2004. "The Internet for Empowerment of Minority and Marginalized Users." *New Media & Society* 6 (6): 781–802.

Morris, Meaghan. 1990. "Banality in Cultural Studies." In *Logics of Television: Essays in Cultural Criticism,* ed. Patricia Mellencamp, 14–43. Bloomington: Indiana University.

Patterson, David. 2009. "Information Literacy and Community College Students: Using New Approaches to Literacy Theory to Produce Equity." *Library Quarterly* 79 (3): 343–61.

Pawley, Christine. 1998. "Hegemony's Handmaid? The Library and Information Science Curriculum from a Class Perspective." *Library Quarterly* 68 (2): 123–44.

Pawley, Christine. 2003. "Information Literacy: A Contradictory Coupling." *Library Quarterly* 73 (4): 422–52.

Pawley, Christine. 2009. "Beyond Market Models and Resistance: Organizations as a Middle Layer in the History of Reading." *Library Quarterly* 79 (1): 73–93.

Ross, Catherine Sheldrick. 2009. "Reader on Top: Public Libraries, Pleasure Reading and Models of Reading." *Library Trends* 57 (4): 632–56.

Rothbauer, Paulette M. 2005. "The Practice of Everyday Life." In *Theories of Information Behavior: A Researcher's Guide,* ed. Karen Fisher, Sanda Erdelez, and Lynne (E. F.) McKechnie, 284–88. Medford, NJ: ASIST, Information Today.

Rothbauer, Paulette M. 2007. "Locating the Library as Place among Lesbian, Gay, Bisexual and Queer Patrons." In *The Library as Place: History, Community, and Culture.* Ed. John E. Buschman and Gloria J. Leckie, 101–15. Westport, CT: Libraries Unlimited.

Savolainen, Reijo. 2008. *Everyday Information Practices: A Social Phenomenological Perspective.* Lanham, MD: Scarecrow Press.

Wiegand, Wayne. 1999. "Tunnel Vision and Blind Spots: What the Past Tells Us about the Present: Reflections on the Twentieth-Century History of American Librarianship." *Library Quarterly* 69 (1): 1–32.

Wyatt, Sally, Flis Henwood, Angie Hart, and Julie Smith. 2005. "The Digital Divide, Health Information and Everyday Life." *New Media & Society* 7 (2): 199–218.

NOTES

1. A reprint of this pamphlet, translated into English by Tom Conley, is found in Michel de Certeau's (1997a) *The Capture of Speech and Other Political Writings.*

2. As noted on the inside jacket cover of de Certeau's *Heterologies* (1986).

3. For a complete bibliography of de Certeau's works, see Giard 1987. For a sustained analysis of de Certeau alongside other cultural theorists of everyday life, see Highmore 2002.

4. Readers are also encouraged to examine *The Practice of Everyday Life, Volume 2: Living and Cooking,* ed Michel de Certeau, Luce Giard and Pierre Mayol (1998) as it provides research narratives based on empirical studies of "living" and "cooking" that illustrate some of the more theoretical formulations found in the first volume.

5. See Savolainen's *Everyday Information Practices: A Social Phenomenological Perspective,* published in 2008, for an exhaustive review of the development of this area of study.

6

Michel Foucault: Discourse, Power/ Knowledge, and the Battle for Truth

Michael R. Olsson
University of Technology, Sydney, Australia

INTRODUCTION

The French philosopher and historian Michel Foucault has been described as "the central figure in the most noteworthy flowering of oppositional intellectual life in the twentieth century West" (Said in Radford 1992, 416). His work been highly influential across a broad range of disciplines, from history and sociology to gender studies and literary criticism, and for some years he has been the most highly cited author in the humanities and social sciences. A Google search on his name reveals an impressive 5,200,000 hits! Foucault is widely regarded as central figure in the development of postmodernism, although this was a label he himself rejected. Ironically, this is an excellent example of one of Foucault's own key ideas—"death of the author."

Despite this prominence—and despite some use of his work by authors in the field as long ago as the early 1990s—Foucault remains a largely unfamiliar and underutilised figure in contemporary library and information science (LIS) research. Even today, LIS can be seen as a discipline largely dominated by American and, to a lesser extent, British voices, leading, as a number of critics have pointed out (e.g., Frohmann 1994; Talja 1997; Olsson 1999, 2004), to a focus on the searching behaviour and mental processes of the individual information seeker to the virtual exclusion of social factors. This research paradigm, with its positivist tendencies, is very far removed from the Continental, post-Marxian tradition in which Foucault's work developed. One consequence of this is that the focus, language use, assumed knowledge, and so on of Foucault's work are unfamiliar to most LIS researchers and practitioners, and consequently Foucault is difficult to interpret and appreciate within LIS.

Yet with the emergence, described by Savolainen (2007), of an "information practices" paradigm based on "a more sociologically and contextually oriented line of research" (Talja 2005, 123) and with a growing body of LIS research drawing on social constructivist and discourse analytic approaches (e.g., Talja 2001; McKenzie 2003; Given 2003), the time may be ripe for a wider appreciation of the significance of

Foucault's work in the LIS community and a greater application of his ideas in LIS research. It is hoped the present chapter might encourage others to begin exploring what his work may offer their research and professional practice. In doing so they may find a conceptual framework that allows them to address a range of ongoing criticisms of prevailing approaches in LIS research.

BIOGRAPHY: MAJOR WORKS

Foucault, the son of an eminent surgeon and originally named Paul-Michel Foucault, was born on October 15, 1926, in Poitiers, the son of an eminent surgeon. After the Second World War, Foucault attended the prestigious École Normale Supérieure in Paris, where he earned degrees in both psychology and philosophy. In 1950, at the behest of his mentor, Marxist philosopher Louis Althusser, he joined the French Communist Party, but became disillusioned with both the politics and the philosophy of the party and left in 1953. Foucault's work would be characterised by an increasingly critical stance towards Marxian theories and assumptions.

After periods at universities in Sweden, Poland, and Germany, Foucault returned to France in 1960 to complete his doctorate at the University of Clermont-Ferrand. This formed the basis of his first major work, *Madness and Civilization,* published in 1961. This book examined the impact of Enlightenment ideas such as Reason, and the birth of "scientific" and "humanitarian" approaches, on how Western society came to define and medicalize mental illness and to institutionalise its sufferers. This was an important first step in Foucault's ongoing project to historicize scientific objectivism—to point out that, despite its universalist claims about itself, it is the product of discourse, an Enlightenment reinvention of aspects of classical traditions in philosophy and rhetoric. This was followed up in Foucault's next book, *The Birth of the Clinic* in 1963, written whilst Foucault was teaching at the University of Tunis, which examined the birth of the medical professions and the advent of the "medical gaze."

Foucault developed his theories further in *The Order of Things,* first published in 1965, where he argued that all historical periods have developed different discursive traditions that determine what constitutes "truth" at that point in space and time. His ideas on discourse and the development of his methodology came to full flowering in *The Archaeology of Knowledge,* published in 1969. Here he sought to examine the network of discursive rules that underpin the discursive construction of knowledge and power.

After a brief and controversial stint as head of the philosophy department at the new experimental university, Paris VIII in Vincennes, in 1970 Foucault was elected to the prestigious Collège de France, as Professor of the History of Systems of Thought. During this time, he helped found Groupe d'Information sur les Prisons (GIP) to provide a voice for the concerns of prisoners, as well as writing *Discipline and Punish,* first published in 1975, which examined the birth of modern constructions of crime and punishment.

After this, as Foucault spent more time in the United States, he embarked on his last major work, *The History of Sexuality,* of which the first three volumes were completed before his death of an AIDS-related illness in 1984. Many saw this work, with its focus on the subject, as a departure from Foucault's earlier work. Foucault's response to this was characteristic:

Well, you thought this a few years ago and now you say something else, my answer is … [laughs] Well, do you think I have worked hard all those years to say the same thing and not to be changed? … The main interest in life and work is to become someone else that you were not in the beginning (Gauntlet 2002).

Foucault consistently resisted attempts to label his work—as structuralist, Marxist, postmodern, or any such term—nor, he claimed, did he wish his work to be seen as a consistent teleology. Rather he desired his books "to be a kind of tool-box which others can rummage through to find a tool which they can use however they wish in their own area … I don't write for an audience, I write for users, not readers" (Foucault, 1974).

With this in mind, the present chapter seeks to provide an introduction to some of the key conceptual tools that my own rummaging in the Foucauldian toolbox (although I will not claim to have plumbed its depths) suggest are likely to prove useful to information researchers and practitioners. Reading Foucault's major works can be a daunting task for those unfamiliar with the traditions of Continental philosophy. Those seeking a gentler introduction might be well advised to start with *The Foucault Reader* edited by Rabinow, or one of the many works designed to assist the Foucauldian neophyte, such as McHoul and Grace (1993).

FOUCAULT AND DISCOURSE

Foucault's work can be seen as part of, and instrumental to, the "linguistic turn" in the humanities and social sciences in the latter part of the 20th century and his approach certainly has its roots in, and draws some of its terminology from, linguistics. However, the focus and intent of his discourse analysis are quite different from the type of discourse analysis focussing on conversation developed by, for example, Potter and Wetherill (1987) and introduced into LIS research by Tuominen and Savolainen (1997). Foucault's approach is broader, more macro-sociological and historical in its scope. His work both draws on and is a reaction against both the Marxian and Structuralist traditions, so central to intellectual life in mid-20th-century Europe.

Foucault's discourse analysis therefore focuses not on conversation between individuals but rather on the specialised language developed by a particular community (whether cultural, professional, artistic or academic) at a particular point in space and time. Although discourse, in Foucault's sense, has been broadly equated with the concept of a discipline (e.g., McHoul and Grace 1993), its application has not been solely confined to scholarly fields, nor do discourses necessarily confine themselves to the boundaries of disciplines as they have traditionally been defined. Some discourses span multiple academic and professional fields—Foucauldian discourse analysis is itself an example of this—and some disciplines may engage with multiple discourses; Frohmann (1994), for example, has suggested LIS is one such multi-discursive discipline.

In Foucault's conception of it, discourse is more than just a way of talking—rather it is seen as a complex network of relationships between individuals, texts, ideas, and institutions, with each "node" impacting, to varying degrees, on other nodes, and on the dynamics of the discourse as a whole. While discourse, like paradigm, can all too easily be conceptualised as an abstract, theoretical construction, Foucault emphasised that any discourse is inextricably tied to its particular sociohistorical context and cannot be studied or understood if divorced from this context: "*For Foucault there is … no universal understanding that is beyond history and society*" (Rabinow 1984, 4).

For Foucault, knowledge/truth is neither based on a perceived correspondence with an "objective" reality, as in the positivist/Aristotelean tradition that has dominated Western thinking since the Enlightenment, nor is it wholly subjective, as in existentialist philosophy. Rather, it is intersubjective—a product of the shared meanings, conventions, and social practices operating within and between discourses, and to which an individual's sense-making processes are inextricably linked.

Foucault argues that a discourse community—people who, at least in the context of a particular role, share a recognized body of "truth statements" (Racevskis 1983)—will not accept that a given statement is true in a random or ad hoc way. Rather, its members will have a set of conventions or "discursive rules"—either formal or implicit, but widely recognized within the community—by which a truth statement can be evaluated and validated or repudiated:

the set of rules which at a given period and for a definite society defined:

1. the limits and forms of *expressibility*...
2. the limits and forms of *conservation*...
3. the limits and forms of *memory*...
4. the limits and forms of *reactivation*... (Foucault, 1978, 14–15).

These discursive rules shape not only the form that a valid truth statement can take in that discourse but also, more fundamentally, they dictate what can be said in the context of that discourse—a statement (or truth claim) that does not comply with the recognised discursive rules, will be literally meaningless. Thus a researcher operating in a "scientific" discourse—one that values objectivist, quantitative data—will reject the results of a qualitative study as "unscientific," "imprecise," "not a replicable, controlled experiment," and so forth in exactly the same way they would reject a study written in iambic pentameter or claiming to be based on divine revelation. Foucault's work offers a conceptual lens to examine the historical development of such discursive rules and the ways they operate in different professions, academic disciplines, and cultural contexts.

Whereas bibliographic classification, archival professional practice and even the more recent development of metadata schemas have been dominated by an "essentialist" discourse—one that aims to "capture" the intrinsic meaning of a document or artefact—Foucault's notion of the "archive" (Foucault 1972) is radically different. Foucault emphasises that members of a discourse community are connected not only by a shared engagement with a collection of texts, but also by a set of interpretations of these texts, based on the established discursive rules, which the discourse legitimate as valid or "true". A single text, the Bible being a useful example, may have hundreds of different "identities" for different discourse communities, each of them legitimate in the context of their own point in space and time.

Foucault's own work focussed on printed texts—they are, after all, virtually all that is left to us as artefacts of the discourses of the Enlightenment, the classical world, and so on, which were the focus of his analysis—and early adopters of Foucault's ideas in an LIS context, such as Frohmann and the Radfords, also focussed on formal texts. However, it is important to note that Foucault's writings make clear that a "text" in this sense need not be a formally published document, but could take any form that the particular discourse community recognised as legitimate (Foucault 1972, 1978). Thus, in the study of a contemporary academic discourse, such as my own doctoral research (Olsson, 2005a, 2005b, 2007), a journal article, a lecture by a visiting professor, a seminar or workshop (whether taken or taught), e-mail correspondence with an overseas colleague, and even informal conversations with colleagues could all be considered as discursively validated texts.

KNOWLEDGE/POWER—THE DYNAMICS OF DISCOURSE

Writers such as Dervin (1989, 1999) have criticised LIS research for largely ignoring issues of societal inequity and power relations. Furthermore, Frohmann (1992) argues that prevailing theoretical approaches such as cognitivism, with their focus on the individual information seeker, actually provide no basis for theorising about or studying their influence on information behaviours and practices—in Foucauldian terms, they are excluded from mainstream LIS discourse. Thus, another potentially important feature of Foucault's work for LIS researchers and practitioners is his exploration of the relationship between knowledge and power. Indeed, for Foucault knowledge and power are not seen as separate entities, but as conjoined products of the same social processes—power/knowledge (*pouvoir/savoir*):

We should admit...that power produces knowledge (and not simply by encouraging it because it serves power or by applying it because it is useful); that power and knowledge directly imply one another; that there is no power relation without the correlative constitution of a field of knowledge, nor any knowledge that does not presuppose and constitute at the same time power relations (Foucault 1977, 27).

In Foucault's view, discourses are never static. Rather, the ongoing relations between people, institutions and texts generate regimes of both meaning and authority (power/knowledge) simultaneously. In this view, the creation and dissemination of texts, the "weighting" of one text more than another, involves a series of dynamic power relations. These relations are constantly re-inventing and re-affirming themselves through the process of applying the discursive rules to examine new "texts" and re-examine existing ones:

There is a battle 'for truth' or at least 'around truth'—it being understood again that by truth I do not mean the 'ensemble of truths which are to be discovered and accepted,' but rather 'the ensemble of rules according to which the true and the false are separated and specific effects of power attached to the true' (Foucault, in Rabinow, ed. 1984, 418).

Thus, in contrast to earlier, top-down conceptions (such as Marx) that construct power as something to be "held" and "imposed," Foucault argues that in contemporary discourse constructs knowledge/power operates in an inductive, rather than a coercive, way:

Power is everywhere; not because it embraces everything but because it comes from everywhere....Power comes from below; that is there is no binary and all encompassing opposition between ruler and ruled at the root of power relations...no such duality extending from the top down (Foucault 1979, 93–94).

If a discourse community holds a given statement to be true, this acceptance imbues it with a certain power in the context of that discourse. This power will also, to a degree, flow on to the author as an "authoritative speaker." Looking at information in terms of power relations is something we all do in everyday speech, when we say that a book or article is authoritative, or that a particular university has a strong reputation in a particular field.

So in contrast to more traditional LIS approaches, whose theorizings focus on an individual information seeker's ability—or as Talja (1997) and Julien (1999) would suggest, inability—to recognise and "correctly" interpret the information "in" a system or document, Foucault's ideas describe a very different sense-making process. They point out that individual behaviour cannot be seen in isolation, divorced from its discursive context. An individual's constructions of meaning are not idiosyncratic but are inextricably linked to existing discursive networks of power/knowledge: his/her understanding of the discursive rules that apply in a given context, recognition of the established authority of certain authors, ideas, practices, and so on in a given discourse, as we see, for example, when an academic researcher values texts by authors with established reputations in their field more highly than those by unknown authors.

Further, discourses are not conceived of as closed systems: power relations occur between discourses as well as within them. Discourses themselves form part of a broader network of power relations—the "episteme" (Foucault 1978). "Stronger" discourses will be more widely influential outside the boundaries of their own discipline, while "weaker" ones may seek to bolster their own position by adopting theories and methodologies from "stronger" discourses. It is difficult not to see the long established propensity in certain areas of LIS, such as information behaviour research (Hewins 1990; Jarvelin and Vakkari 1990), to adopt theoretical and methodological approaches from other "stronger" disciplines, such as communication and artificial intelligence, as an example of this!

DEATH OF THE AUTHOR

The Foucauldian discourse analytic approach also calls for a reconceptualisation of the relationship between the author, the text, and the reader. Foucault, in his essay, "What Is an Author?" (in Rabinow 1984, 101–20), echoes Barthes (1988) in talking of the "death of the author"—a phrase that has become a standard slogan of postmodernism. While Barthes is contesting the authority and domination of the author, Foucault is challenging that idea by reducing the author to a function in a discursive formation.

Traditionally, information research and professional practice has been largely influenced by the information transfer model (Tuominen, Talja, and Savolainen 2003), in which authors, texts, and readers are constructed as separate entities. Texts are the vehicles by which "chunks" of information are transferred from the author to the reader. In this model, authors are seen as the creators of information, and readers as passive recipients. Discourse analysis argues instead that readers, individually and collectively, are actively involved in the construction of meaning: that meaning making is a complex sociolinguistic process involving the reader, the text, and their social context. This has strong implications for the construction of the relationship between authors, texts, and readers:

So why does Foucault say the author is "dead"? It's his way of saying that the author is decentered, shown to be only a part of the structure, a subject position, and not the center. In the humanist view, . . . authors were the source and origin of texts . . . and were also thus beyond texts—hence authors were "centers" . . . By declaring the death of the author, Foucault is "deconstructing" the idea that the author is the origin of something original, and replacing it with the idea that the "author" is the product or function of writing, of the text (Klages 2001).

This theory, then, has two key features—both of them with important implications for information research. Firstly, that the meaning ("knowledge," "truth") of a work is not something governed or determined by the author, but rather is a social construct created (and constantly re-created) by the reader/s at a particular point in space and time. Secondly, authors, as the originators of a body of work, are themselves the products of social construction within and between discourses.

In this conception, published texts have no single absolute meaning or truth, but only a socially constructed and located "truth" or "truths." Nor is this "truth" something that can be predetermined by the author. Rather, the established social practices and conventions within a community and the interactions of its members determine the meaning, significance and authority of a work in the context of that particular community. The essentially social nature of knowledge therefore means that the meaning/knowledge-claims/truth of any work are constantly being questioned, reexamined, and reinterpreted. For example, each time a member of a research community evaluates, critiques, cites or re-interprets a work, or draws parallels between one work and another in his/her own publications, teaching, or research practices, that researcher is contributing to the ongoing interpretation of the work's meaning.

Nor need the meaning that a community draws from a work necessarily have any relation to the author's original intended meaning—hence "death of the author." Rather, the meaning/significance of a work is determined by a particular community (which may or may not include the author) and will reflect the concerns, beliefs, and sociopolitical context of that community. Thus, works may be seen as having many different meanings and containing widely different "truths" by different communities, and this process can continue for centuries, even millennia, after the death of the author—for example, the ongoing use of the works of Aristotle or Sun Tzu in contemporary fields as diverse as philosophy, strategic studies, history, and marketing.

An extreme example of the potential divergence between authorial intent and modern interpretation would be the 1850 photographic study of African-born slaves in the American South by Louis Agassiz. Agassiz's intent was to demonstrate that Africans were a separate, less "evolved" species than whites, an absurd and repugnant theory to most modern sensibilities. Nonetheless, modern anthropologists and historians of slavery and the cultural origins of African Americans find his study an invaluable resource (Ward 1992).

Similarly, just as a community may be divorced in time from a work's original author, communities may reinterpret works from other disciplines to suit their own interests and concerns. A good example of this in the context of contemporary information science is the work of Kuhn. Kuhn is quite widely cited in the literature of information science, generally as the originator of the notion of "paradigm." Yet the way in which paradigm is used/constructed by information scientists differs quite markedly from that of Kuhn himself. Indeed, its use by Dervin and others to describe information science directly contradicts Kuhn's proscription that paradigms occur only in the hard sciences, the social sciences being "innately pre-paradigmatic" (Kuhn, 1970). An author-centric approach would lead us to regard such use of Kuhn's work as "wrong"; the discourse analytic perspective would see this as the inevitable consequence of a community reinterpreting Kuhn's work in the context of its members' own interests and concerns.

This is also a good example of how the dynamics of communities can lead to the social construction not only of individual works, but also of authors themselves. In the context of a particular discourse, an author is not primarily a living, breathing human being (after all, as we have seen, they may be long dead) but rather a social construct derived from the community's interpretation of the significance (truth) of their body of work. Thus Kuhn as an author-construct in information science may well be a very different figure, with a very different significance, from Kuhn as an author-construct in the sociology of knowledge or the history of science. Small's (1978) notion of documents as "standard symbols" might therefore usefully be extended to include author-constructs as well, with certain authors coming to represent/symbolise particular ideas/theories/standpoints in the eyes of a particular community or communities.

Since, in the Foucauldian framework, knowledge and power are inextricably linked (the one automatically generates the other), one needs to consider the role of the power and influence that become attached to author-constructs by particular communities, and the impact of this power upon the behaviours/perceptions of members of that community. Author-constructs can therefore act as "Dead Germans" for a community (icons of the core "truths" of a discourse) or, as the contextual terrain shifts, as "Dead White Males" (symbols of what is "wrong" with the established order—the focus of resistance).

PANOPTICISM

Panopticism is a concept developed by Foucault in *Discipline and Punish*. It is grounded in a description of the change in attitude towards crime and punishment that emerged from the Enlightenment—the development of a new discourse focussing on the idea of rehabilitating prisoners, as opposed to earlier discourses based on the idea of execution and torture as both a punishment of the individual criminal and a deterrent to others. One outcome of this is the development of a new kind of disciplinary institution, the Panopticon, as designed by the Enlightenment thinker Jeremy Bentham. Foucault uses the Panopticon as a metaphor for the role of surveillance and self-discipline in contemporary society.

Bentham's Panopticon is circular with a central guard tower. Thus, the prisoners are isolated and may be subject to 24-hour surveillance but cannot themselves see their guards. In this, it is a model of the Enlightenment ideal of efficiency:

If the inmates are convicts, there is no danger of a plot, an attempt at collective escape, the planning of new crimes for the future, bad reciprocal influences; if they are patients, there is no danger of contagion; if they are madmen there is no risk of their committing violence upon one another; if they are schoolchildren, there is no copying, no noise, no chatter, no waste of time; if they are workers, there are no disorders, no theft, no coalitions, none of those distractions that slow down the rate of work, make it less perfect or cause accidents (Foucault 1977, 201).

But this new form of institutionalised surveillance, Foucault argues, has an even more important consequence: that the awareness of potential unseen surveillance forces those subject to it to discipline themselves—to, in effect, become their own guard. This self-discipline, Foucault argues, has become a central feature of contemporary Western society.

In light of recent developments, from ubiquitous CCTV, through government computer-assisted monitoring of e-mail and phone calls in the search for potential terrorists, to the efforts of software giants like Google and Facebook to monitor our online behaviour for their commercial benefit, panopticism seems to be a concept with even greater application now than when Foucault coined it in the mid-1970s. Its application to LIS research, however, remains largely unexplored.

FOUCAULT IN LIS

LIS researchers have been quite late in adopting Foucault, and as yet his impact on the field has been relatively slight when compared to his prominence in the humanities and social science as a whole. Nonetheless, from the 1990s onwards a number of LIS writers have utilised Foucault's work as a lens to analyse and critique LIS institutions and research, as well as a conceptual framework for undertaking information behaviour research.

Amongst the earliest prominent uses of Foucault in an LIS context was the work of Gary Radford. Beginning in 1992, he wrote a series of articles (subsequently in partnership with Marie Radford) seeking to use Foucault's ideas to interrogate and radically reconceptualise our understanding of the library as a social institution, and librarianship as a profession:

The evolving library environment will not be served by a dominant preconception that characterizes the library as an institution for housing particular texts that contain specific facts and the librarian as an impersonal, source-oriented intermediary whose function is to locate them. Following Foucault, the library can be a place of fantasia as well as facts, of creation as well as acquisition. As the positivist version of scientific knowledge gradually loses its dominance... so the positivist foundations of the library experience also must be seriously reconsidered. (Radford 1992, 420)

Another important use of Foucault in an LIS context also appeared in 1992, with Bernd Frohmann's "The Power of Images: A Discourse Analysis of the Cognitive Viewpoint." Frohmann uses Foucauldian discourse analysis to characterise and critique the dominant cognitivist discourse in LIS research, arguing that its natural science philosophy and "mentalist" construction of the individual information seekers have led to:

(a) universality of theory, (b) referentiality and a reification of "images", (c) internalisation of representations, (d) radical individualism and erasure of the social dimensions of theory, (e) insistence upon knowledge, (f) constitution of the information scientist as an expert in image negotiation, and (g) instrumental reason, ruled by efficiency, standardisation, predictability and determination of effects (Frohmann 1992, 365).

Frohmann argues that the cognitivist discourse, by excluding the social, offers no framework for examining issues of political subterfuge or societal inequity, and thus reinforces the status quo and "performs ideological labour for modern capitalist image markets" (1992, 365). Frohmann's subsequent work (e.g., 1994) has also frequently used Foucauldian discourse analysis to analyse and critique prevailing approaches to LIS research.

The *Information Seeking in Context* conferences played an important role in bringing discourse analytic ideas and approaches to the attention of information behaviour researchers. The first conference, held in 1996 in Tampere, Finland, included a ground-breaking paper by Sanna Talja presenting "the discourse analytic perspective, the "theory of knowledge structures" as an alternative to the cognitive viewpoint, "the information man theory" (1997, 67). This was followed at the second conference in 1998 in Sheffield, United Kingdom, by my paper written proposing Foucauldian discourse analysis as a "theoretical framework for examining the information behaviour of groups" and arguing that:

> prevailing approaches can be broadly divided into those that describe rather than theorise about information behaviour and those that seek to explain information behaviour by focussing their theoretical attention on the individual information user.... while many prevailing approaches... conceive of information users, information systems and their social context as discrete entities... discourse is a more holistic approach that sees all these elements as nodes in a network of power relationships (Olsson 1999, 136–37).

Whilst Frohmann's analysis can be seen as adopting an "externalist" stance, critiquing information behaviour research from the "outside," both Talja's and my own approach is different, instead endeavouring to adapt tools from Foucault's toolbox for use within the field of information behaviour research. This can be seen in our subsequent use of Foucault's ideas as a conceptual framework for interview based studies (e.g., Talja 2001; Olsson 2005a, 2005b, 2007). With a growing number of researchers in the area adopting discourse analytic approaches, Foucault's ideas can be seen as an important influence on the emergence of "information practice" as an alternative to the more individually oriented information behaviour discourse.

In an LIS context, where social constructivist theories and approaches are growing in acceptance as researchers and practitioners seek to find new conceptual tools to meet the challenges posed by a rapidly changing cultural, technological and economic landscape, many of Foucault's concepts, such as power/knowledge and panopticism, appear to be more relevant than ever. As more people within LIS become willing to explore the contents of Foucault's toolbox, however strange they may seem at first acquaintance, we may see his work become as influential in our own field as he already is in others.

REFERENCES

Dervin, Brenda. 1999. "On Studying Information Seeking and Use Methodologically: The Implications of Connecting Metatheory to Method. *Information Processing & Management* 35:727–50.

Foucault, Michel. 1970. *The Order of Things: An Archaeology of the Human Sciences*. London: Tavistock.

Foucault, Michel. 1972. *The Archaeology of Knowledge*. London: Tavistock.

Foucault, Michel. 1973. *The Birth of the Clinic: An Archaeology of Medical Perception*. London: Tavistock.

Foucault, Michel. 1977. *Discipline and Punish: The Birth of the Prison*. London: Allen Lane.

Foucault, Michel. 1978. "Politics and the Study of Discourse." *Ideology and Consciousness* 3:7–26.

Foucault, Michel. 1979. *The History of Sexuality, Volume One: An Introduction*. London: Allen Lane.

Foucault, Michel. 1988. *Madness and Civilization: A History of Insanity in the Age of Reason.* New York: Vintage Books.

Foucault, Michel. 1994. *Dits et Ecrits.* Paris: Gallimard.

Frohmann, Bernd. 1992. "The Power of Images: A Discourse Analysis of the Cognitive Viewpoint." *Journal of Documentation* 48:365–86.

Frohmann, Bernd. 1994. "Discourse Analysis as a Research Method in Library and Information Science." *Library and Information Science Research* 16 (2): 119–38.

Gauntlett, David. 2002 *Media, Gender and Identity.* London: Routledge.

Given, Lisa. 2003. "Discursive Constructions in the University Context: Social Positioning Theory and Nature of Undergraduates' Information Behaviours." *New Review of Information Behaviour Research* 3:127–42.

Hewins, E. T. 1990. "Information Needs and Use Studies." *Annual Review of Information Science and Technology* 25:145–72.

Jarvelin, Kalervo, and Pertti Vakkari. 1990. "Content Analysis of Research Articles in Library and Information Science." *Library and Information Science Research* 12:395–421.

Julien H. 1999. "Constructing 'Users' in Library and Information Science." *Aslib Proceedings* 51 (6): 206–209.

Klages, Mary. 2001. *Foucault, "What Is an Author?"* University of Colorado Department of English. http://www.colorado.edu/English/courses/ENGL2012Klages/foucault.html.

Kuhn, Thomas Samuel. 1970. *The Structure of Scientific Revolutions.* Chicago: University of Chicago Press.

McHoul, Alec, and Wendy Grace. 1993. *A Foucault Primer.* Melbourne: Melbourne University Press.

McKenzie, Pamela J. 2003. "Connecting with Information Sources: How Accounts of Information Seeking Take Discursive Action." *New Review of Information Behaviour Research* 3:161–74.

Olsson, Michael. 1999. "Discourse: A New Theoretical Framework for Examining Information Behaviour in Its Social Context." In *Exploring the Contexts of Information Behaviour: Proceedings of the 2nd Information Seeking in Context Conference, Sheffield, UK,* ed. Tom Wilson and David Allen, 136–49. London: Taylor Graham.

Olsson, Michael. 2004. "Understanding Users: Context, Communication and Construction." Paper presented at the *ALIA 2004 Biennial Conference*, Gold Coast Convention and Exhibition Centre, Queensland, Australia, September 21–24.

Olsson, Michael. 2005a. "Meaning and Authority: The Social Construction of an 'Author' among Information Behaviour Researchers." *Information Research* 10(2) paper 219, *http://informationr.net/ir/10–2/paper219.html.*

Olsson, Michael. 2005b. "Making Sense of Sense-Making: Information Behavior Researchers Construct an 'Author.'" *Canadian Journal of Information & Library Science* 29 (3): 315–34.

Olsson, Michael. 2007. "Power/Knowledge: The Discursive Construction of an Author." *Library Quarterly* 77 (2): 219–40.

Potter, Jonathan, and Margaret Wetherell. 1987. *Discourse and Social Psychology: Beyond Attitudes and Behaviour.* London: Sage.

Rabinow, Paul. 1984 *The Foucault Reader.* Harmondsworth, UK: Peregrine Books.

Racevskis, Karlis. 1983. *Michel Foucault and the Subversion of the Intellect.* Ithaca, NY: Cornell University Press.

Radford, Gary P. 1992. "Positivism, Foucault, and the Fantasia of the Library: Conceptions of Knowledge and the Modern Library Experience. *Library Quarterly* 62 (4): 408–24.

Radford, G. P. 1993. "A Foucauldian Perspective of the Relationship between Communication and Information." In *Between Communication and Information. Information and Behavior:* Volume 4., ed. J. R. Schement and B. D. Ruben, 115–36. New Brunswick, NJ: Transaction.

Radford, Gary P., and Marie L. Radford. 2001. "Libraries, Librarians, and the Discourse of Fear." *Library Quarterly* 71 (3): 299–329.

Radford, Marie L., and Gary. P. Radford. 1997. "Power, Knowledge and Fear: Feminism, Foucault, and the Stereotype of the Female Librarian." *Library Quarterly* 67 (3): 250–66.

Small, H. 1978. "Cited Documents as Concept Symbols." *Social Studies of Science* 8:327–40.

Talja, Sanna. 1997. "Constituting 'Information' and 'User' as Research Objects: A Theory of Knowledge Formations as an Alternative to the Information-Man Theory." In *Information Seeking in Context: Proceedings of an International Conference on Research in Information Needs, Seeking and Use in Different Contexts, August 14–16, 1996,* ed. Pertti Vakkari, Reijo Savolainen, and Brenda Dervin, 67–80. London: Taylor Graham.

Talja, Sanna. 2001. *Music, Culture and the Library: An Analysis of Discourses.* Lanham, MD: Scarecrow Press.

Talja, Sanna. 2005. "The Domain Analytic Approach to Scholars' Information Practices." In *Theories of Information Behavior,* ed. Karen Fisher, Sanda Erdelez, and Lynne (E. F.) McKechnie, 123–27. Medford, NJ: Information Today.

Tuominen, K., and R. A. Savolainen. 1996. "A Social Constructionist Approach to the Study of Information Use as Discursive Action." In *Information Seeking in Context: Proceedings of an International Conference on Research in Information Needs, Seeking and Use in Different Contexts, August 14–16, 1996,* ed. Pertti Vakkari, Reijo Savolainen, and Brenda Dervin, 81–98. London: Taylor Graham.

Tuominen, Kimmo, Sanna Talja, and Reijo Savolainen. 2003. "Multiperspective Digital Libraries: The Implications of Constructionism for the Development of Digital Libraries." *Journal of the American Society for Information Science and Technology* 54 (2003): 561–69.

Ward, Geoffrey C. 1992. *The Civil War.* London: Pimlico.

7

Deconstructing the Library with Jacques Derrida: Creating Space for the "Other" in Bibliographic Description and Classification

Joseph Deodato
College of Staten Island

DERRIDA'S LIFE AND WORK

Jacques Derrida was a French philosopher whose name is most commonly associated with the concept of deconstruction. His work, along with that of other theorists such as Roland Barthes and Michel Foucault, played a central role in shaping the poststructuralist movement that emerged in the 1960s and 1970s. Poststructuralism rejected Enlightenment and structuralist claims regarding absolute truths and universality, emphasizing instead the instability and plurality of meaning. Derrida's theories have been both highly influential and hotly contested throughout much of late-20th-century academia (Brothman 1999, 65).

Derrida was born in 1930 to middle-class Jewish parents living in French-governed Algeria. He grew up under the anti-Semitic policies of the Vichy government, which sought to bar Jews from professional and intellectual life. At the age of 10, Derrida was expelled from school after quotas were instituted limiting the number of Jewish students. Continued discrimination and harassment forced him to drop out of his next school. Some scholars (including Derrida himself) have suggested that his early experiences with discrimination were influential in shaping his sensitivity to the theme of the "Other," which would come to play a major role in his philosophical thought.

In 1949 Derrida left for Paris and studied at the École Normale Supérieure, where he later taught from 1964 to 1984. During the 1960s, he wrote for the avant-garde journal *Tel Quel*, a leftist publication of literary and critical theory concerned with the intersection of art and politics. In 1966, Derrida broke into the U.S. intellectual scene with his groundbreaking lecture at John Hopkins University entitled, "Structure, Sign and Play in the Discourse of the Human Sciences." The following year, he published three books (*Of Grammatology*, *Speech and Phenomena*, and *Writing and Difference*) that helped secure a prominent place for him among the century's most influential philosophers. Derrida continued to publish and lecture extensively in Europe and the United States until his death in 2004.

The reception of Derrida's work has ranged from high praise to bitter denunciation. Supporters endorse it as a productive method for generating alternative readings of texts and unraveling social and cultural constructs embedded within dominant discourses. Concerned with the repression of "otherness," deconstruction has found particularly fruitful application in analyses of race, class, gender, and sexuality. However, its influence has been felt in academic disciplines as diverse as architecture, literary theory, law, and management science. Critics of deconstruction complain of its lack of intellectual resolution, positive conclusions, and practical recommendations. And opponents on all sides of the political spectrum have found his philosophy to be opaque, ethically hollow, and hopelessly relativistic.

Perhaps the greatest barrier to Derrida's work lies in the difficulty of reading it. His work is often characterized by abstraction, metaphor, and ambiguity. But for Derrida, these are the characteristics of language itself. Absolute statements and unequivocal conclusions merely obscure the nature of their own construction and reflect the repression that inevitably occurs in all linguistic expression. All attempts to represent meaning and fix it in time and space are necessarily repressive; acts of exclusionary "violence." What Derrida attempts to show, both through deconstruction and his writing, is the play of differences at work within language that prevent the arrival of final and stable meaning. It is perhaps this inseparability between writing style and philosophy that makes Derrida's work so challenging.

DERRIDA'S THEORETICAL CONTRIBUTIONS

Condensing the body of Derrida's work into an easy-to-digest summary can be a challenge. This is not simply because of the complexity of his writing style, his distinct penchant for wordplay and ambiguity, or the litany of neologisms he has coined over the years, but also because his arguments have always been inextricably intertwined with the particular authors and texts he has sought to deconstruct. Many of Derrida's key (non)concepts (*différance,* supplement, trace, *pharmakon,* etc.) vary depending on the specific work with which he engaged. In addition to this, Derrida relished the notion of "undecidability" and explicitly disavowed the possibility of immutable, fixed meanings. In place of truth, identity, and universality, deconstruction celebrates ambiguity, plurality, and multivocality. To further complicate matters, Derrida himself famously stated: "All sentences of the type 'deconstruction is X' or 'deconstruction is not x' *a priori* miss the point," because deconstruction is not reducible to an essential feature, task, or style. To do so would be to revert to the metaphysical realm of absolute meaning. Like any word, *deconstruction* "acquires its value from its inscription in a chain of possible substitutions" (Derrida 1991, 275). In other words, it is determined by its context. Discussing these concepts or themes out of context necessarily runs the risk of oversimplifying or essentializing them. All caveats aside, however, there are several overarching themes within Derrida's work that, taken together, offer a general overview of his theoretical contributions to the intellectual world. The following overview singles out those themes deemed especially useful for theories of library and information science.

Metaphysics of Presence

Derrida took as his starting point the examination of what he saw as a fundamentally flawed premise of the Western philosophical tradition, namely the notion of a "center," or an original, stable foundation of meaning. Since as far back as ancient Greece, Western philosophy has been based on what Derrida referred to as the "metaphysics of presence," or "the determination of Being as *presence*" (Derrida 1978, 279). All foundational principles in philosophical discourse—Truth, Essence, God, Ideal Form, and so forth—have always been defined as some form of pure presence; that which *just is*. The notion of presence is essential to metaphysics because it guarantees the truth of foundational propositions on which the structure of an argument can be built. Thus, the metaphysics of presence relies on belief in a central and absolute Cause or Origin that underlies philosophical thought and guarantees its meaning.

Logocentrism/Phonocentrism

If truth is that which reveals its presence to one's consciousness through reflection, then the object of philosophy is the communication of this truth through language, and therein lies the rub for, as Derrida pointed out, "the very idea of truth" depends on its ability to stand alone, before and outside any means of representing it (Derrida 1976, 20). Indeed, Western philosophy is permeated by what Derrida called "logocentrism," or the assumption that there is a realm of truth that exists prior to and independent of its representation in language. *Logos* is derived from the Greek term for "word" or "reason," but was often used to signify some form of transcendent truth or meaning: what Derrida referred to as the "transcendental signified."

According to Derrida, logocentrism is linked to another important characteristic of Western philosophy that he called "phonocentrism." Phonocentrism refers to the privileging of speech over writing as a more authentic bearer of truth by virtue of its proximity to thought. Speech was considered to be a "natural" or perfect expression of thought; of that which is immediately present to one's consciousness. Furthermore, the presence of the speaker to the listener guaranteed the meaning of what is spoken. Writing, on the other hand, was considered less immediate and therefore inferior to speech because its reception occurs in the absence of the author, which increases the likelihood of misrepresentation and misunderstanding. Conceived of as "written-down speech," writing was deemed to be derivative of speech and therefore twice removed from the source of meaning.

For Derrida, the claim that speech was capable of providing transparent access to meaning amounted to nothing less than "the absolute effacement of the signifier" (Derrida 1976, 20). It was the condition of the logocentric belief that truth can exist without mediation. As Niall Lucy has suggested, the object of phonocentrism was not the protection of the purity of speech as such, but what might be called "a certain ideal of the purity of purity. The idea that *there just is* purity, authenticity, truth, and so on—prior to and independent of any system of writing, outside any need to express, convey, argue for or otherwise represent the 'self-reliance' of the pure, the authentic, the original, etc." (Lucy 2004, 119). In other words, it was a metaphysical requirement that speech come before writing since, in order for speech to be attributed the status of "nonrepresentational" truth, it had to be opposed to writing as mere representation.

Deconstruction

Western thought has been traditionally rooted in a quest for centers, origins, and essences. The problem with centers, in Derrida's view, is that they attempt to exclude, repress, or marginalize others ("the Other"). This is an inherent characteristic of metaphysics, which Derrida defined as:

The enterprise of returning "strategically," "ideally" to an origin or to a priority thought to be simple, intact, normal, pure, standard, self-identical, in order then to think in terms of derivation, complication, deterioration, accident, etc. All metaphysicians, from Plato to Rousseau, Descartes to Husserl, have proceeded in this way, conceiving good to be before evil, the positive before the negative, the pure before the impure...etc. And this is not just one metaphysical gesture among others, it is the metaphysical exigency, that which has been most constant, most profound and most potent (Derrida 1998, 236).

According to Derrida, then, metaphysics necessarily depends on the creation of binary oppositions (good/evil, mind/body, nature/culture, etc.) in which one member of the opposition is considered primary while the other is made secondary. The order of metaphysical succession requires the idea of an undisputed first or original instance, the identity of which is independent of whatever might come after it. So, for example, "good" is primary while "evil" (defined as the absence of good) is secondary. But this succession is not simply linear; it is also hierarchical for, in every case, what is considered secondary is defined in terms of the lack of presence. Good both comes before evil and is privileged over it. Derrida, however, argued that a concept like good could not be defined without recourse to evil. Far from being grounded in presence, the identity of a thing is derived from the play of differences within signification—a play of presences and absences. The "interior presence" of good cannot be established in and of itself but depends on a relationship with the "exterior absence" of evil (Lucy 2004, 102). By ignoring this relationship, metaphysical thought attempts freeze the play of binary opposites by placing one term of the binary at the center while marginalizing the other.

If metaphysics relies on centers to order and fix the play of binary opposites, then deconstruction is a process of *decentering* aimed at releasing the free play of nonhierarchical, nonstable meanings within a text. Christopher Norris described deconstruction as "the dismantling of conceptual oppositions, the taking apart of hierarchical systems of thought which can then be *reinscribed* within a different order of textual signification" (Norris 1987, 19). This new order is not merely the inversion of the previous hierarchy, but the replacement of the hierarchy itself by blurring the boundary on which it depends.

Deconstruction can be summarized as a three-step process. The first step involves identifying the binary oppositions that structure a text and the hierarchical relation that defines one term as central and the other as marginal. The next step is to reverse this hierarchical relationship by placing the marginal term at the center. This has the effect of showing the original relationship to be constructed and produces an alternative reading of the text. However, as Derrida consistently pointed out, the goal of deconstruction is not merely to replace one hierarchy or reading with another but to demonstrate that both (and many others) are equally possible. Thus, the final step of deconstruction requires the formulation of a more fluid and less coercive conceptual organization of terms that transcends the binary logic and acknowledges the mutual interdependence of both terms.

Différance

The key feature of language that makes deconstruction possible is what Derrida called "*différance*." *Différance* refers to the systematic play of differences within signification that govern the production of meaning. *Différance* undercuts the logocentric notion that language can be used to directly express truth—that which is present to one's consciousness. Instead, it illustrates that language is already caught up in a network of associations that extend far beyond one's self and the present moment.

Like all words, the meaning of *différance* is unstable, suspended between the two French verbs "to differ" and "to defer." The first half of this definition draws on Swiss linguist Ferdinand de Saussure's principle of the arbitrariness of the sign. In his *Course in General Linguistics*, Saussure defined language as a system of signs in which each sign was composed of a signifier (a sound or word) and a signified (a concept or meaning). However, Saussure argued that the relationship between signifier and signified was arbitrary; there was "no natural connexion" between a word and the concept it served to express (Saussure 1983, 69). Saussure's cardinal insight was that language was "a system in which all the elements fit together, and in which the value of any one element depends on the simultaneous existence of all the others" (113). In other words, signs are not linked directly to immediately present objects or meanings, but derive their meaning through their relation to and difference from other signs. Similarly, on the level of meaning, concepts distinguish themselves only from their difference from other concepts. Thus, Derrida concluded:

The signified concept is never present in and of itself, in sufficient presence that would refer only to itself. Essentially and lawfully, every concept is inscribed in a chain or in a system within which it refers to the other, to other concepts, by means of the systematic play of differences (Derrida 1982, 11).

There are no positive elements within language—no element that can be called simply "itself." A word only becomes "itself" depending on its relationship to other words in the system. Its meaning depends upon its relationship to what it is not—its difference from something else. Binary oppositions are defined by *différance,* that is, through the definition of the dominant by the Other. "White" is defined in relation to "black," "male" in relation to "female," and so on. The implication of this play of differences is that identity and meaning always owes its existence, in part, to something that is absent—to what it lacks. Neither member of the binary structure ever entirely succeeds in eradicating the presence of the absent other. According to Derrida, a "trace" of the other always remains within its midst.

Derrida further argued that the meaning of a word is never fully present at the time of its utterance but is always deferred, delayed, put off to interpretation. By its very nature, a signifier points to a meaning that lies beyond itself. The meaning of a given word depends on its context and is delayed until the interpreter crosses the time and space that separates that word from the other words in the text that give it meaning. Sometimes, even the context can fail to produce meaning, in which case one might turn to a dictionary to locate the meaning of a word. However, rather than arriving at a meaning, what one finds is actually another string of words. Thus, in Derrida's view, every sign is merely the sign of another sign. They are not grounded in real referents but float freely in a groundless play with other signs. The differences, traces, and deferrals that permeate language create disturbances within meaning that are revealed in the process of deconstruction.

Arche-writing

The primary focus of Derrida's work was the deconstruction of the binary opposition between speech and writing. As mentioned previously, Derrida observed a distinct phonocentrism within the Western philosophic tradition, which valorized speech over writing as a more authentic form of language because spoken words were believed to be a direct expression of thought. Moreover, the intention and meaning of the speaker were alleged to be immediately present, whereas in writing they were considered more remote or absent and thus more liable to misunderstanding. Conceived of as "written-down speech," writing is considered as derivative of speech and therefore twice removed from the source of meaning.

Derrida noted that the characteristics ascribed to writing were equally true of speech insofar as both are signs subject to differential play of meaning within language. He suggested that speech's priority over writing could only be granted by limiting writing to its phonetic form (as written-down speech). In contrast, Derrida argued that writing is in fact a precondition of language and must be conceived prior to speech. By this he did not mean that the invention of writing as technical means of inscription historically preceded the development of speech. Rather, Derrida argued for a more expansive conception of writing: what he called "arche-writing." In Derrida's use, writing, or arche-writing, refers to "the 'free play' or element of undecidability within every language system...Writing is the endless displacement of meaning which both governs language and places it forever beyond the reach of stable, self-authenticating knowledge" (Norris 1982, 29). Redefined in this way, speech already belongs to this generalized conception of writing and neither speech nor writing contains a presence of meaning, only its infinite deferral.

In Derrida's most renowned work, *Of Grammatology* (1967), he set out to deconstruct the binary opposition between speech and writing in the history of Western thought. In his reading of the work of Saussure, for example, Derrida argued that the valorization of speech lay in Saussure's phonocentric conception of writing as being limited to the phonetic-alphabetical script. On the one hand, Saussure claimed that there was a natural bond between sound and meaning since meaning is present in speech. However, he also argued that this correlation was arbitrary. To demonstrate how language represents a system of differences, Saussure employed writing as an example to illustrate how written markings mean nothing in and of themselves but gain their identity only through their difference from other markings in the system. Derrida's deconstructive reading seized on this to show how writing could be seen as central within Saussure's own argument and within the system of language in general. He went on to argue that neither the word *writing* nor the word *speech* is adequate to describe the more abstract play of differences that are common to both. To address this, he formulated a new phrase capable of expressing that speaking and writing are simply two different forms of the same thing: the play of difference within language, or what Derrida referred to as "arche-writing" (Powell 1997, 48).

Textuality and Dissemination

In Derrida's view, all knowledge is textual. It is composed not just of concepts, but of words. And words can suggest different meanings. Derrida refused to grant philosophy the privileged status it had historically claimed as the sovereign dispenser of reason, a claim that went hand in hand with the privileged position accorded to logic over rhetoric and to philosophy over literature. He argued that philosophy had been able to impose its systems of thought only by suppressing the disruptive effects of language, by repressing its own textuality. As Christopher Norris put it, deconstruction works to "undo the idea—the ruling illusion of Western metaphysics—that reason can somehow dispense with language and arrive at a pure, self-authenticating truth" (Norris 1982, 19). Deconstruction zeros in on and exploits the "semantic slippages" that occur within elements of metaphor and other figurative devices found in philosophical texts in order to demonstrate the impossibility of grounding knowledge and truth in the idea of authentic, self-present meaning. As Derrida famously proclaimed, "there is nothing outside of the text"—no signifieds that escape the play of signifiers (Derrida 1976, 158).

By highlighting the textuality of philosophical discourse, deconstruction works to achieve what Derrida called the "dissemination" or dispersal of meaning. The principle of dissemination suggests that there are in fact no limits to what may be relevant in understanding a text. The three essays that make up *Dissemination* (1983) play upon the theme of textuality and dissemination while blurring the distinction between philosophy and literature. In "Plato's Pharmacy," for example, Derrida offered a deconstructive reading of the *Phaedrus*. In the *Phaedrus*, Plato used the myth of Theuth to illustrate the superiority of speech over writing, which he referred to as a *pharmakon*—a dangerous drug or poison. Derrida's reading seized upon the double meaning of the term *pharmakon*, which can also be used to mean the exact opposite—remedy or cure. In so doing, he produced a radically different reading of the text that emphasized its fundamental undecidability. In the deconstructed version, writing becomes both poison and cure, thereby undermining its previously binary logic and revealing the infinite play of differences. Another technique, such as that used in "The Double Session" and *Glas* (1974), is the juxtaposition of literary and philosophical texts to illustrate the effects of intertextuality and the ways in which writing cannot be contained within the limits of a single work or self-enclosed system of meaning.

IMPLICATIONS FOR LIBRARY AND INFORMATION SCIENCE

Derrida's work stands as a critique of the fundamental principles of Western metaphysics and its associated notions of truth, knowledge, meaning, and objectivity. Theories and practices of library and information science (LIS) have been traditionally grounded on many of these same principles. Thus, Derrida poses a challenge to the ways in which librarians conceptualize and carry out their work. This section highlights two areas in particular that could benefit from Derrida's insights, namely bibliographic description and classification.

As we have seen, Derrida refuted the notion that there exists some stable foundation of meaning resting on a correspondence between sign and object. In contrast, he argued that meaning is generated by the play of differences among signs. Meanings are never fixed but always contingent on shifting and arbitrary systems of relationships. From a poststructuralist perspective then, there is no way to assure the correspondence between a text and its meaning. LIS has historically addressed the need to create stable contexts for the correspondence of meaning through what is referred to as "knowledge organization." Tools such as classification schedules, cataloging rules, controlled vocabularies, hierarchical subject trees, and a variety of indexing schemes have been created to "impose patterns on the potential chaos of human knowledge" (Radford and Radford 2005, 75). Such tools have traditionally operated on an "exact match," or "conduit," model of meaning that posits a direct correspondence between text and meaning, signifier and signified. This meaningful organization consists in the assignment of each item in a collection to a unique identifier (i.e., classification number) and a limited number of subject access points (i.e., subject headings). However, as Gary and Marie Radford have suggested, "there is no fixed reality to which any classification system can correspond" (Radford and Radford 2005, 76). Indeed, the only "reality" that exists is that which is created by these very patterns and structures of organization. That is to say, the way libraries order and describe materials has a formidable impact on how those materials will be interpreted by users. In deciding what about a text accounts for its meaning, determining its classification and placement within the collection, and assigning names and access points, libraries shape they way those texts will be understood and used by researchers. Libraries, therefore, do not just organize knowledge, they construct it.

One of the primary ways that libraries seek to assign meaning to texts is through the assignment of standardized subject headings in bibliographic description. The inherent instability of meaning within language is overcome by the imposition of controlled vocabulary. By mandating the use of predefined, authorized terms for bibliographic description, libraries seek to reduce the kind of inherent ambiguity and polysemy found in "natural" language. However, controlled vocabularies are, by definition, limited systems for the representation of information. Books and other informational objects are complex entities capable of encompassing a variety of different subjects, only a few of which are selected for bibliographic description. Furthermore, the subject(s) of a book may not always find corresponding expression within the scheme of standardized subject headings. As Ronald Day has noted, texts, like other linguistic signs, "have a degree of semantic surplus or excess intrinsic to them; restrictions of this excess give rise to more restrictive economies of meaning production…where certain elements and relations are allowed to be expressed and others not" (Day 2004, 595).

The "elements and relations" that wind up getting excluding from systems of bibliographic representation generally reflect the biases of the cultures in which they are created. Since at least the 1970s, there has been a small but vocal opposition to this bias in bibliographic description. Although not poststructuralist in orientation, Sanford Berman's life-long and pioneering work on uncovering the inherent bias of Library of Congress Subject Headings (LCSH) could be viewed as a first tentative step toward a deconstructive analysis of information organization insofar as it examines the limits of expression in controlled vocabularies and reveals the systematic exclusion of the Other. In his 1971 *Prejudices and Antipathies*, Berman highlighted a litany of subject headings demonstrating clear biases on the basis of race, gender, sexuality, ethnicity, class, and religion. For example, the separate treatment given to women in occupational subject headings—such as "Women as accountants," "Women as architects," or "Women as astronauts"—argued Berman, implied that it was unusual and perhaps even inappropriate for women to hold these occupations. Conversely, the absence of similarly distinct occupational headings for men indicated that it was presumed natural for men to have these roles (Berman 1971, 145). Thanks in large part to Berman's tireless efforts, some of the more egregious examples of bias have been removed from LCSH, although later studies have suggested that a significant amount still remains (see Knowlton 2005).

The exclusionary bias within standardized subject headings relates not just to its selected terminology but to its structural aspects as well. The hierarchical structure of subject headings and classifications not only limits terms for naming information but further limits the interpretation of these terms by defining their relations to each other. Cross references direct users from the terms not chosen to express a given concept to the authoritative term for that concept. Relational references indicate hierarchical relationships and establish context. In his study, Berman noted a number of questionable relationships within LCSH that tended to endorse a particular perspective. For example, the cross-referencing of the subject headings "Gipsies" with "Rouges and vagabonds," "Homosexuality" with "Sexual Perversion," "Anarchism" with "Terrorism," and "Abortion" with "Offenses against the person," he argued, shaped the meanings of those terms in very specific ways. Thus, the syndetic structures of controlled vocabularies such as LCSH can be said to create an interpretive context that circumscribes the meaning of subject headings by limiting the play of differences within language.

Similar biases can be said to exist in library classification schemes. Like subject headings, classification schemes tend to construct information in ways that reflect the biases of the cultures that produce them. The primary object of a classification system is to gather similar information together and place it in proximity to related information. Because relationships between concepts can be drawn in a variety of ways, classifications privilege some concepts over others. Furthermore, classification tends to reflect the most mainstream version of these relationships with the result of marginalizing those outside the mainstream (Olson 1998, 235).

Classifications are also closed systems in that they represent some concepts and not others. As a matter of practicality, no classification can ever be all inclusive; they inevitably have limits. According to Hope Olson, "a system of any kind is defined by what it is not and, because systems tend to be dynamic, the definition of a system's limits is always deferred." Thus, classifications are characterized by Derrida's notion of *différance* insofar as "their limits are constructed by their exclusions and are in a state of constant flux because they are socially constructed" (Olson 1998, 235).

Deconstructive analyses conducted by Hope Olson have suggested that theories of knowledge organization are underwritten by a universality/diversity binary opposition. Examining major foundational texts within LIS, Olson noted that universality was considered necessary in order to tame the subjectivity of language, while diversity was deemed to cause communication failure. Using the technique of iteration, Olson revealed how the presumption of universality within knowledge organization depends upon the systematic exclusion of the Other. She argued that the "universal" is taken to be the "white, ethnically European, bourgeois, Christian, heterosexual, able-bodied, male (WEBCHAM) presence" from which all else is deviation (Olson 2001a, 4).

Such biases become clear in the unacknowledged assumptions underlying "user-centered" cataloging. Indeed, the common rebuttal to charges of bias in subject headings has traditionally been premised on the needs of the user. LC, for instance, claims that it does not establish usage, it merely follows it. Accordingly, the Library of Congress' 1951 *Subject Headings: A Practical Guide* instructed catalogers that "the heading... should be that which the reader will seek in the catalog" (Haykin 1951, 7). Thus, LC merely uses the language that users are most familiar with. The problem, as noted by critics like Olson, becomes the identity of "the user." While the underlying philosophy is to keep the user in focus, the assumption is that the user is white, Christian, male, and heterosexual. Olson suggested that such cataloging practices can be described as "user-centered" only if one considers users in a narrow sense (Olson 1999, 244). "Universality," it seems, is permeated by its opposite: specificity. By utilizing the presumed language and perspective of a particular group of users, descriptive practices marginalize the perspectives of other users and create the impression that certain points of view are normal and others unusual.

Olson's deconstructive analyses often seize on common metaphors used in LIS literature to seek out those moments of self-contradiction that allow an oppositional reading of the text. For example, both Charles Cutter and Melville Dewey used military metaphors to describe how their systems of classification provide rational, efficient means of organizing information from an unruly mob into a "wel [sic] disciplined army." Olson noted, however, that an army "also causes perturbation, agitation, and disturbance . . . to those outside of its imposed order: the victims of its violence. The organization of a mob into an army . . . always causes violence by imposing a marginalizing and exclusionary order" (Olson 2001b, 649). By choosing Arabic numerals for notation, for instance, Dewey created an arbitrary limit of ten divisions of the universe of knowledge. These ten divisions do bring order to those subjects it includes but perpetrates violence against those it excludes. Leftover subjects are grouped merely as "Other," usually numbered 9. For example, the 800 class of literature allots eight classes for Western literature but all non-Western literature is grouped into one class (890).

Elsewhere, Olson discussed the metaphor of mapping used by Berwick Sayers and B. C. Brookes in their respective works. Sayers' and Brookes' conception of classification as a "map of knowledge" suggested that, like maps, classifications are accurate and objective relational representations of knowledge or information. Olson found the comparison apt but not for the reasons suggested by its authors. In contrast, Olson suggested that neither classifications nor maps accurately or objectively reflect the complexity of the entities they serve to represent. Maps are just as culturally biased as classifications. Traditional map projections presented a Eurocentric worldview that disproportionately enlarged the size of Europe and North America relative to the rest of the world much in the same way that traditional classifications have allocated more space to Western topics and marginalized others. Furthermore, classifications, much like the two-dimensional representations of three-dimensional geographic entities, necessarily "distort all knowledge in its infinite multidimensionality into a linear arrangement suitable for creating a browsable list or locations on shelves" (Olson 1998, 240). Thus, by reworking the rhetoric of LIS texts, Olson overturns their binary logic to produce a counterreading that reveals the opposite of what their authors intended, namely, the exclusions and biases that are hidden under the guise of their apparent universality and neutrality.

How is it that these biases have been allowed to seep into standards of description and classification that were intended to be neutral, objective representations of the world's knowledge? According to Derrida, these biases are inevitable, a result of time's effects on language's retention of persistent meaning. The movement of time disrupts all attempts to fix meaning. This is what Saussure failed to fully acknowledge in his theory of structural linguistics. Much like classification theorists, Saussure believed that the whole domain of meaning could be systematically mapped by understanding the underlying rules that structure the language system. However, this could only be accomplished by neglecting the realities of language usage and the manner in which language and meaning shift and change over time. In order to view language as a closed and complete system, Saussure was forced to study the state of language at a particular moment, that is, synchronically rather than diachronically. According to Derrida, however, the understanding of language at any particular moment will always be one of interpretation since final meaning is always endlessly deferred, always contingent upon the state of the language at a particular moment, and, therefore, always changing over time. As Brian Brothman has pointed out:

Time's relentless motility disrupts and delays the achievement of a perfectly coordinated and stable language system, a population of peacefully co-existing meanings, an authoritative repository of commonly shared terms. System—a condition outside of time—and the workings of time exist together in unavoidable tension (Brothman 1999, 72).

Controlled vocabularies and classification schemes are language systems for the representation of knowledge or information. As such, they are subject to the disruptive forces of time that prevent the stabilization of meaning. It was no accident, for example, that Berman's initial critique of racial, gender, and other biases within LCSH appeared in the wake of a decade of social protest and activism aimed at redressing these very issues. The discourse on these topics had begun to change, but LC's language system and its associated structures had failed to change with it. As with all signs, the meaning of a text changes over time as a result of its relationship to and difference from other texts—other signs—within the system. A text that was once considered seminal in its field becomes obsolete with the addition of newer texts. A text that was once thought to mean one thing comes to mean something else. This condition is a fundamental aspect of textuality and Derrida's idea of dissemination, both of which complicate traditional notions of a book or informational object as a self-enclosed entity. Unlike the concept of a book, text is "an undisciplined and undisciplinable object," an object without borders in constant relation and dialogue with other texts (Brothman 1999, 77). According to Douglas Raber and John Budd, "this changing relation between text and content, and between signifier and signified constitutes a change in the meaning of the informative object, as new meanings are assigned to existing objects" (Raber and Budd 2003, 512). As a result, languages for indexing and classification must necessarily change over time in order to adapt to the way that information changes.

The notion that biases within standards of description and classification are an inevitable result of time's effect on language should not be taken to suggest that these matters are unavoidable and, therefore, beyond our control. Nor should it be taken to suggest that librarians or catalogers are essentially evil or malicious for injecting biases into the practices of knowledge organization. What it does suggest is that librarians must be made aware of the ways in which their work shapes and constructs knowledge. As a result, librarians have what Hope Olson referred to as an ethical "responsibility to otherness"—a responsibility to create space for the expression of other identities, other values, and other perspectives within structures of knowledge organization (Olson 1993, 111).

According to Olson, creating space for the voices the Other entails developing "techniques for making the limits of our existing information systems permeable" (Olson 2001a, 20). Rather than simply replacing one standard with another, a true deconstructive approach involves breaching the limits of the dominant standard so that other voices can be heard. Olson offered a number of suggestions for accomplishing this. One suggestion, which has already made some headway in libraries, involves allowing users to construct their own descriptions of and relationships between documents and share them with other users. Social bookmarking and tagging is a way for librarians to relinquish some of their control over the construction of knowledge and empower users—especially marginalized users—to create their own structures of knowledge organization. Another suggestion involves adapting technology such as that developed for the MultiLIS integrated system, which allows for the use of parallel subject headings in different languages. Olson suggested that this same technology could be adapted to allow alternative headings for traditionally marginalized topics. Olson also suggested the creation of an adaptive interface that could map the terminology of a marginalized knowledge domain to a mainstream classification. Her own work in mapping *A Women's Thesaurus*, a feminist vocabulary for women's studies materials, to the Dewey Decimal Classification serves as an example. Such practices allow the construction of what Olson called "paradoxical spaces" by permitting "existence on both sides of a limit simultaneously or alternately. It is both inside and outside, center and margins. In this way it does not put a new structure in place of the old but puts a different spin on existing concepts that come to coexist with concepts from the margins" (Olson 1998, 242). The same approach can be adapted for other perspectives and cultures, thereby providing a way of linking marginal discourses to the center and making the boundaries between both permeable.

CONCLUSION

The project of metaphysics speaks to what seems like a fundamental human need to establish a reliable basis for access to stable, enduring knowledge and meaning. To name, define, explain, and understand reality is the process by which humans have historically sought to control it. Derrida himself acknowledged the practical necessity of this and indeed stressed the impossibility of truly overcoming metaphysics. However, what he did try to point out was that this process of naming reality is, in effect, also its construction. The object of deconstruction is to highlight the unacknowledged assumptions that govern descriptions of reality and denaturalize them. Deconstruction harbors a distinct political interest insofar it seeks to give voice to the Other—to that which remains marginalized or excluded from dominant discourses of reality.

Libraries in some sense represent an institutionalized form of metaphysics insofar as they seek to describe, order, and arrange information or knowledge about the world. In the process, they also play a role in constructing knowledge and defining what is knowable about the world. As we have seen these constructions often privilege certain conceptions of the world at the expense of others. Derrida's lesson for libraries is not necessarily that they can overcome this condition but rather to show how ostensibly neutral or objective practices of organizing information implicate these practices in the perpetuation of dominant discourses and to highlight the ethical responsibilities libraries have as arbiters of knowledge and meaning.

REFERENCES

Berman, Sanford. 1971. *Prejudices and Antipathies: A Tract on the LC Subject Heads Concerning People.* Metuchen, NJ: Scarecrow Press.

Brothman, Brian. 1999. "Declining Derrida: Integrity, Tensegrity, and the Preservation of Archives from Deconstruction." *Archivaria* 48:64–88.

Day, Ronald E. 2004. "Poststructuralism and Information Studies." *Annual Review of Information Science and Technology* 39:575–609.

Derrida, Jacques. 1976. *Of Grammatology.* Baltimore: Johns Hopkins University Press.

Derrida, Jacques. 1978. *Writing and Difference.* Chicago: University of Chicago Press.

Derrida, Jacques. 1982. *Margins of Philosophy.* Chicago: University of Chicago Press.

Derrida, Jacques. 1991. "Letter to a Japanese Friend." In *A Derrida Reader: Between the Blinds,* ed. Peggy Kamuf, 269–76. New York: Columbia University Press.

Derrida, Jacques. 1998. *Limited, Inc. Perspectives in Continental Philosophy.* Evanston: Northwestern University Press.

Haykin, David J. 1951. *Subject Headings: A Practical Guide.* Washington: U.S. Government Printing Office.

Knowlton, Steven A. 2005. "Three Decades since Prejudices and Antipathies: A Study of Changes in the Library of Congress Subject Headings." *Cataloging & Classification Quarterly* 40 (2): 123–45.

Lucy, Niall. 2004. *A Derrida Dictionary.* Malden, MA: Blackwell Publishing.

Norris, Christopher. 1982. *Deconstruction: Theory and Practice.* New York: Routledge.

Norris, Christopher. 1987. *Derrida.* Cambridge, MA: Harvard University Press.

Olson, Hope A. 1993. "Assumptions of Naming in Information Storage and Retrieval: A Deconstruction." In *Information as a Global Commodity: Communication, Processing and Use, CAIS/ACSI '93. St. Francis Xavier University, July 11–14, 1993,* 110–19. Antigonish, NS: Canadian Association for Information Science.

Olson, Hope A. 1998. "Mapping beyond Dewey's Boundaries: Constructing Classificatory Space for Marginalized Knowledge Domains." *Library Trends* 47 (2): 233–54.

Olson, Hope A. 1999. "Bias in Subject Access Standards: A Content Analysis of the Critical Literature." In *Information Science: Where Has it Been, Where Is it Going? Proceedings of the 27th Annual Conference of the Canadian Association for Information Science, Université de Sherbrooke, June 9–11, 1999,* ed. James Turner, 236–47. Montréal: CAIS/ACSI.

Olson, Hope A. 2001a. "Patriarchal Structures of Subject Access and Subversive Techniques for Change." *Canadian Journal of Information & Library Sciences* 26 (2): 1–29.

Olson, Hope A. 2001b. "The Power to Name: Representation in Library Catalogs." *Signs: Journal of Women in Culture & Society* 26 (3): 639–68.

Powell, Jim. 1997. *Derrida for Beginners.* New York, NY: Writers and Readers.

Raber, Douglas, and John M. Budd. 2003. "Information as Sign: Semiotics and Information Science." *Journal of Documentation* 59 (5): 507–522.

Radford, Gary P., and Marie L. Radford. 2005. "Structuralism, Post-Structuralism, and the Library: De Saussure and Foucault." *Journal of Documentation* 61 (1): 60–78.

Saussure, Ferdinand de. 1983. *Course in General Linguistics.* Chicago: Open Court Classics.

8

Transformative Library Pedagogy and Community-Based Libraries: A Freirean Perspective

Martina Riedler
Canakkale Onsekiz Mart University, Turkey

Mustafa Yunus Eryaman
Canakkale Onsekiz Mart University, Turkey

INTRODUCTION: A BRIEF BIOGRAPHY OF PAULO FREIRE

Brazilian educator Paulo Freire (1921–97), one of the most influential educational theorists and practitioners of the late 20th century, dedicated his life to helping oppressed communities become aware of their collective power and consequently create new conditions in overcoming oppression (Coben 1998). Freire was born on September 19, 1921, in Recife, a port city on Brazil's northeastern coast. Although his family was a middle-class family, they were severely affected by the Great Depression. His experiences of hunger and poverty shaped his concerns for the poor and helped to construct his particular educational viewpoint. In 1943 he enrolled in the Faculty of Law at the University of Recife, where he also studied philosophy and the psychology of language. Freire almost never practiced law but instead worked as a secondary-school language teacher, teaching Portuguese. He earned his doctorate in 1959 and served as the first director of the Department of Cultural Extension at the University of Recife, bringing literary programs to the rural poor. Because of his success in the literary programs, he was appointed as the president of the National Commission on Popular Culture in 1963 (Gerhardt 1993).

During a military coup in 1964, Freire was imprisoned for 70 days by the military for his educational work among the rural poor, and then exiled to Chile. During his prison time, Freire began his first major educational work, *Education as the Practice of Freedom,* a text he finished while in exile in Chile. In 1968 his most famous book, *Pedagogy of the Oppressed,* was first published in Portuguese. In 1969 he received a letter of invitation to lecture for two years at Harvard University. He worked as a professor at the Center for the Study of Development and Social Change at the university. In 1970 the first English translation of *Pedagogy of the Oppressed* was published. Half a year later, Freire left Harvard University and began to serve as consultant and eventually as assistant secretary of education for the World Council of Churches in Switzerland. He traveled all over the world lecturing and assisting educational programs of newly independent countries in Asia and Africa (Gerhardt 1993).

In 1979 Freire was invited by the Brazilian government to return from his 15 years of exile. In 1988 he was appointed as minister of education for the city of São Paulo. With the position, he had the opportunity of guiding school reform in two-thirds of the nation's schools. At the age of 75, Freire died of heart failure in Rio de Janeiro on May 2, 1997, leaving behind a legacy of love and hope for oppressed people throughout the world.

Paulo Freire published a vast collection of books that have been translated into many different languages. Indeed, a number of Freire's important contributions to educational theory have had a considerable impact on the development of critical pedagogy and revolutionary educational practice. Particularly important among these are his elabora-tion of a dialogic basis for critical pedagogy and radical politics (McLaren and Leonard 1993; McLaren 2000), his idea of developing a pedagogy of the oppressed or a pedagogy of hope (Elias 1994; Gadotti 1994), his concern with praxis or informed ethical prac-tice (Darder 2002), his pedagogical concept of conscientization—consciousness with the power to transform reality (McLaren 2000), and his notion of libertarian pedagogy as the political basis for a radical transformation of education and society (Allman 1999).

FREIRE, CRITICAL THEORY, AND COMMUNICATIVE ACTION

Traditionally, libraries in the modern era have been tasked with discovery and consultation and dissemination of knowledge that is fixed, authoritative, discipline bound, and constructed for individual access. These institutions have thus identified themselves as separate from the mundane world—as standing for purer, more elevated values—and acted as universal archives for transferring or transmitting information based on higher values and objectified knowledge (Wisner 2000; Bruce and Kapitzke 2006; Bruce 2008). This positivist model still dominates many public and school lib-raries, and many people continue to think of libraries as repositories of information and librarians as the caretakers of those resources. However, although acting as reposito-ries has been a central role for libraries from their inception, many factors—including postmodern conceptions of the nature of knowledge in the information age, the democ-ratization of knowledge production and dissemination, the emphasis on community-based lifelong learning, and the move toward collaborative and transformative notions of teaching and learning—have incited libraries to move beyond the traditional care-taker role (Wisner 2000; Bruce and Kapitzke 2006; Bruce 2008).

To address this shift, we explore an alternative view that differs markedly from the more traditional notions of library in its vision of community-based and trans-formative libraries, institutions that do not merely provide opportunities for dis-covery and consultation but create opportunities for community empowerment and transformation. First, after outlining the ongoing debates in areas related to library pedagogy, communicative action, critical pedagogy, community-based learning, and critical theory, we identify problems in the present notions of public libraries and li-brary pedagogy by comparing the dialogic community-based perspective on library and library pedagogy with the traditional static viewpoint. We then challenge the lat-ter's prevalent conceptions of libraries as repositories of information and librarians as caretakers of these resources. Next, to encourage further reconstruction of the the-ory and practice of library pedagogy, we formulate a critical framework based on

Paulo Freire's critical pedagogy—particularly, his concepts of dialogue, praxis, and conscientization—through which we identify the characteristics of a transformative and community-based library (TCBL). Finally, we propose an alternative conceptualization of library pedagogy as a dialogic accomplishment.

TRADITIONAL VERSUS TRANSFORMATIVE LIBRARIES: FREIRE, CRITICAL PEDAGOGY, AND COMMUNITY-BASED LEARNING

Until recently, modern librarians worked in remote offices with opaque windows as if to conceal themselves from those unworthy of professional assistance. Today, however, librarians have moved into the public view, although in many cases, they still wait for information seekers to come to them. Nonetheless, whether engaging in the traditional task of collection building or developing new models for information provision, librarians should become more open to serving multiple audiences. This goal can be achieved by discarding the positivist view of libraries as neutral sites and rethinking them as sites of situated social action, in which library pedagogy is constituted through diverse conversations about different ideas and values that shape library formation and functioning.

At the same time, contemporary theorists of library and information sciences have been increasingly recognizing the importance of making libraries relevant to local communities. Accordingly, they are now discussing the importance of encouraging community members to make their own decisions, actively participate in library activities, and interpret and critically reflect on what the library has to offer (Bruce and Kapitzke 2006; Bruce 2008). Most particularly, these theorists see the main purpose of libraries in democratic societies as enabling learners not only to learn better on their own but also to teach one another within a community of learners. If libraries are so identified as primarily transformative educational sites, then reaching a broader audience can be more accurately—and more meaningfully—understood as reaching a broader cross-section of learners. Hence, making libraries relevant means understanding learner and community needs, developing more supportive and engaging learning scenarios, and creating more inclusive learning communities. To date, however, in the field of library education, much of the time devoted to group learning has targeted young learners enrolled in public or private school systems.

What is crucial and revolutionary about alternative library pedagogy is that it is a method of learning throughout life—beginning with daily life itself and the experiential moments it contains—and thus balances theory and practice. Above all, critical library pedagogy recognizes that learner and community experiences are central to the education process, meaning that the role of the transformative library and its staff is to facilitate the production of knowledge rather than its transmission. That is, through a range of pedagogical methods, concepts and theories emerge naturally in the process of confronting learners' experiences to produce what Freire (1972) terms a libertarian pedagogy or problem-posing education based on a democratic relationship between learner and teacher.

LIBERTARIAN LIBRARY PEDAGOGY AND COMMUNITY-BASED LIBRARIES: A FREIREAN PERSPECTIVE

Freire (1972) supports his argument for a libertarian education and criticized traditional education using the metaphor of a banking education model, one synonymous with the domination that isolates learners from the content and process of education.

Most particularly, such a model assumes that the teacher knows everything, the students nothing (Giroux and McLaren 1987; McLaren 1994; Mayo 1999, 2008; Eryaman and Riedler 2009). Hence, teachers narrate, prescribe, and deposit information, which the students must then mechanically receive, memorize, and repeat. As expert consultants, teachers thus possess the knowledge, and their role is simply to deposit as much of it as possible within the students, filling them as if they were objects not humans.

In modern libraries, librarians are still commonly perceived as expert consultants who possess a special set of tools and competencies by which they can transmit a particular kind of service to library visitors. Many libraries therefore sustain a view of learning in which learners should passively listen while the librarian tells them what they need to know and should have no input on how or what they learn. Such a scenario exemplifies Freire's notion of a banking education that fails to recognize the importance of learners' different backgrounds, the distinctive ways in which they process information, and the fact that learners can learn more efficiently from participatory and dialogic methods of learning. In contrast, Freire's libertarian education, with its informed ethical practice or praxis, is based on a dialogic process in which both teacher and student construct knowledge together. That is, the teacher poses a problem and encourages students to ask questions about and inquire into the problem in a reciprocal dialogue in which the teacher also expresses opinions. Hence, whereas banking education merely allows the acceptance of knowledge, libertarian education facilitates knowledge production, thereby humanizing the students and promoting critical thinking (Roberts 2000; Morrow and Torres 2002).

From the perspective of a libertarian pedagogy, learning in libraries becomes a dialogic process that acknowledges the noncausal, social, moral, and political nature of inquiry, making it a practical and interpretive accomplishment rather than a mere technical or technological activity. In this libertarian view, the most important issue for librarians is not simply technical and procedural evaluation of the efficacy of knowledge transmission but the potential social and practical value of what they do. That is, for the proponents of the libertarian view, learning is more than the simple application of strategies or techniques to bring about predetermined ends: there is always the question of the social, moral, and political value of such techniques and the specificity of particular contexts in which problems must be addressed (Eryaman and Riedler 2009). In addition, learning in a libertarian pedagogy aims to promote conscientization (Freire 1972), the development of a critical consciousness (Freire 1995) or reflexive thoughts and values that reject the oppressive beliefs of the dominant conscience. Such a process can liberate both students and teachers alike. Freire thus encourages dialogic consciousness-raising learning communities in which students not only become aware of their communities and the ideologies therein but also how to become critical of them (Taylor 1993; Rossatto 2005).

Most particularly, the pedagogical dynamics of Freirean critical pedagogy could inspire the development of a transformative and community-based library (TCBL) model in which libraries become democratic spaces for Freire's dialogic conscientization rather than the mechanical and wholly judicious institutions of the traditional static model. For instance, recognizing that communities are but people with similar or divergent stories that mediate their social interaction and progression, libraries could encourage and celebrate a concept that deserves to be reexamined and embraced—that of collectivity. Indeed, within such a framework, libraries could serve significant political and social functions, not only by providing a common democratic bond that allows learners to think of themselves as part of a community, but, in these times of global change, by shaping the tensions between neoliberal individualization and contemporary adaptation to new paradigms like cultural diversity, community-based learning, and democratic participation.

Overall, the TCBL model identifies libraries as democratic and educational sites for a community of learners who construct library practices as an interactive process between the present and the future of the community. It therefore encourages library visitors to reflect critically on the information provided, not simply as individual learners but as politically aware members of a community. It also provides opportunities for the learning community to move beyond the particularistic politics of class, ethnicity, race, and gender to develop a democratic community empowerment that stresses difference within unity. Central to such empowerment is a notion of community developed around a shared conception of social justice, rights, and equality. As a result, there has been a renewed focus in library research on community building, social inclusion, and community informatics, particularly the active exploration of community history, cultural traditions, and the democratic citizenship of students (Bruce 2008; Bruce and Kapitzke 2006).

The TCBL model based on a Freirean framework thus provides a holistic approach to understanding the social role of library learning in the wider social arena in which the dimensions of social inclusion encompass economic, social, political, and cultural concerns. However, the implementation of socially inclusive strategies requires a rethinking of the organization's purpose and practice, a process particular to the unique circumstances of different institutions, the communities they aim to reach, and the communities that aim to represent themselves through these institutions. As a result, the role of libraries as potentially inclusive learning sites is to inform, challenge stereotypes and discrimination, promote tolerance, and contribute to the creation of inclusive communities. Such a model also requires acknowledgment of certain terminology used by librarians to describe what socially inclusive work actually means: community capacity building, community involvement, community learning strategies, lifelong learning, and local regeneration.

In sum, the TCBL model is a hopeful concept capable of providing the community with a needed communicative space in which to encourage socially driven discussions that engage members in a consciousness of their own location in the global arena, as well as their (dis-)connection to others. The community model also changes how people envision learning by encouraging learners to see learning as a socially responsible and ethical course of action—what Freire (1972) terms praxis. However, if facilities and policies are to be developed that make the library a welcoming, comfortable place that supports collaborative research activities and enables individuals to work together effectively, this conversion to a dialogic library pedagogy requires an exploration of the diverse technological and social purposes of the library space. Hence, even while recognizing the TCBL model's potential to turn (traditional) libraries into social and transformative spaces for the development of community member consciousness, we must also consider what prevents such development, particularly the barriers that exist for underrepresented groups, including digital divide; social and political exclusion from democratic participation; and individual, institutional, and structural inequalities of allocation and distribution of public resources.

The TCBL model is one potential means of removing such barriers in that, rather than urging underrepresented groups to reproduce existing knowledge structures, it provides space for learning and growth. More important, it engages young people in the democratic creation in their own communities of public actions that are not simply instrumental or a means to an end but constitutive of a vibrant, flourishing democracy (Boyte and Kari 1996; Putnam 2000). Understanding these spaces and minority experiences within them, then, become crucial to gaining a greater sense of the ways in which young people become active citizens who create and sustain democracy. Nonetheless, this view of democracy and citizenship demands a framework that makes transparent the processes by which minorities can (or cannot) be creative democratic agents in both public libraries and the broader world.

LEARNING AS A COMMUNITY OF PRACTICE IN THE TCBL

In recent decades, conceptions of learning have undergone fundamental changes as the focus has shifted to learners' understanding and application of knowledge rather than "drill and practice" (Bransford et al. 1999). One central part of this change has been the acknowledgment that participation in social practice is a fundamental aspect of learning, particularly when understood as identity change. This aspect is emphasized by the application of Freirean theory to learning in the TCBL, which, in contrast to traditional individual-based understandings, places learning in the context of lived experience and participation in the world (Freire 1972; Lave 1991; Wenger 1998). Most particularly, Freirian thought emphasizes that "learning, thinking, and knowing are relations among people engaged in activity in, with, and arising from the socially and culturally structured world" (Lave 1991, 67). Hence, knowledge and skill become situated products of the context, activity, and interaction in which they are developed and used. Indeed, for Freire, knowledge and skills are simply tools that can only be fully understood through practice in a specific community or culture (Brown et al. 1989).

More specifically, Freire places participation and social belonging within specific contexts, pointing particularly to the community-centered nature of effective learning environments. For him, learning happens best when it takes place within a community with strong norms around learning, one that offers opportunities for interaction and feedback. Like Freire, Lave (1991) and Wenger (1998) stress the notion of "communities of practice," formal and informal communities that cohere around mutual engagement in a common activity. This concept of communities of practice broadens the scope of learning settings by emphasizing not institutional boundaries or definitions like school or workplace but rather the lived character of learning. Nonetheless, although communities of practice can grow anywhere (Wenger 1998), not all communities are learning communities. Rather, communities of practice that support learning are distinguishable from other types of communities by the presence of (1) mutual engagement; (2) joint enterprise; and (3) shared repertoires of words, actions, or concepts (Wenger 1998). Fundamental to these communities is their dynamic, negotiated nature; that is, communities of practice engage multiple perspectives in the negotiation of meaning, requiring that both participants and the community affect and be affected. From this perspective, traditional libraries cannot then be classified as communities of practice: learners are rarely engaged in negotiating library learning, and, for example, librarians and learners are seldom collaborators in joint work.

In contrast, the TCBL aims to provide settings in which learning takes on meaning for participants. It thus aims to give newcomers the opportunity to see and experience practice in its complexity, thereby giving them a broader sense of what the community is about rather than engaging them in particular tasks (Lave 1991). Most particularly, the TCBL model highlights the importance of participation in and the relationships played out through mutual engagement in practice. Above all, the TCBL as a learning community pays attention to and builds on the knowledge, skills, beliefs, and attitudes that learners bring with them. It is therefore "culturally responsive, appropriate, and relevant" in its attempts to help learners make connections between previous knowledge and current activity (Bransford et al. 1999). Hence, in comparison to conventional models of library learning, the TCBL model offers a radically different approach, an understanding of learning as praxis that is particularly relevant to library visitors' transformation into powerful public actors. Indeed, for young people from marginalized backgrounds, the development of praxis may be a critical first step to breaking out of old patterns of marginalization and nonparticipation, although it may first be necessary for individuals to see themselves as "participators" before they can struggle against structures that work to prevent participation in the public realm. When conceived of in this manner, participation becomes something broader than mere engagement in an activity: being linked to identity, it is not something that can be turned on and off (Wenger 1998).

Thinking of learning as praxis directs our focus toward both spaces for learning and the processes that take place within them. That is, if learning involves the ability to negotiate new meanings and become a new person, it requires a space, a community, a counter public within which learners can engage with others in joint practice. At the same time, the TCBL is capable of engendering further thought about the features and processes within such spaces that make transformations of understanding, identity, knowledge, and skills possible. Hence, in the belief that the purpose of library learning is to provide opportunities, through communities of practice, for learners to explore who they are, are not, or could be, the TCBL discourages standardized or uniform library curricula. Instead, it urges examination of something both organic and evolving—the content of learning communities as an integral part of practice. It thus directs attention to patterns of participation and interaction, as well as to curriculum and pedagogy: the what and the how. This approach is particularly appropriate for working with marginalized populations because "focusing on an institutionalized curriculum without addressing issues of identity...runs the risk of serving only those who already have that identity of participation" (Wenger 1998, 269).

CIVIC ENGAGEMENT AS PRAXIS IN THE TCBL

Policy makers and researchers looking to address the problem of declining minority civic engagement typically turn to formal and informal learning spaces including libraries, one of the major learning institutions for young people. However, researchers indicate that a variety of structural, curricular and pedagogical, and environmental factors obstruct minorities' opportunities to experience participatory citizenship in public institutions (Leppard 1993; Seigel and Rockwood 1993; Levine and Lopez 2004). Particularly challenging are the authoritarian and hierarchical structures, curricula that present limited and passive conceptions of citizenship, pedagogy with an insufficient focus on participation, and the broader sociopolitical culture surrounding libraries. For example, while transmitting narrow and passive definitions of democracy and citizenship, the narrowly focused curricula of many public and school libraries reflect an ideologically conservative conception of citizenship. Indeed, Parker (1996) maintains that in presenting politics and governance as neutral, current citizenship curricula raise tensions about the range of differences and dissent allowable in a democracy and reflect an assimilationist ideology that is inappropriate in a pluralistic society. Likewise, narrow library curricula serve to alienate learners from richer, more participatory or active meanings of citizenship, instilling instead what Benne (1987) terms the "minimal meanings" of democracy. Too often, when libraries are most concerned with rote exercise and "right and wrong" information, minorities see no connection between what they are learning and "real life." Hence, the pedagogy practiced in many public and school libraries not only falls short of engaging students in participatory or democratic practices but denies underrepresented groups the opportunity to experience democracy and become active citizens in the present.

In addition to these structural, curricular, and pedagogical concerns, factors in the broader sociopolitical context of libraries affect their ability to provide rich and empowering participatory experiences for disadvantaged groups. One particularly troublesome aspect is the lack of meaningful opportunities for engagement in public libraries where organizational structures, goals, and mandates often exist in direct conflict with minority people's needs, including the need for empowering democratic experiences. Instead, the emphasis on hierarchical control and order, limited and abstract conceptions of citizenship, and a pedagogy that relies on informing and "right and wrong" answers, as well as on accountability policies, present major obstacles to creating meaningful opportunities for these populations. As a result, such structures and practices do little to foster the critical thinking and reflection needed by democratic citizens. Hence, to find examples of meaningful citizenship experiences for disadvantaged groups, it may be necessary to look outside libraries to settings that have the potential to educate and empower these groups through democratic action.

The TCBL, with its Freirean framework, can encourage participatory civic engagement for minorities and underrepresented groups by both enlarging the opportunities for participation and enhancing people's ability to participate in the public world. Most particularly, it can play an important role in transforming marginalized urban youth into powerful democratic actors. Indeed, disadvantaged groups, marginalized by the broader society, may need to carve out their own spaces in libraries and other public institutions free of any assumption that they are deficient, invisible, or hypervisible (Weis and Fine 2000). Also critical to the development of a framework for exploring disadvantaged groups' democratic experiences and the organizations in which they occur is the recognition that women of color, individuals with special needs, and minority youth, particularly, tend to have a "uniquely disempowered status" in society (Roche 1997; Baksh-Soodeen 2001).

CONCLUSION

Because of the new forces emerging globally in this information and communication age, the very nature and functions of libraries, including their content and policies, are continually changing and will most certainly continue to do so (Bruce and Kapitzke 2006; Bruce 2008). Hence, future conceptions of libraries will be very different from those of today (Wisner 2000; Bruce and Kapitze 2006; Bruce 2008). Although it is unrealistic to assume that the TCBL model will inject a happily-ever-after narrative into library theory, Freirean approaches to library pedagogy promise fresh perspectives on the issues of democratic participation and public representation. Above all, the TCBL can engage learners in a challenging adventure during which—with guidance—individuals can learn how to empower themselves and their communities by writing their own narratives of conscientization and praxis.

This theoretical overview has several important implications for the educational role of libraries in contemporary society, implications that suggest certain key recommendations for librarians and researchers:

- Because public and school libraries have the potential to develop into discursive spaces in which community members can debate and define meaning by drawing on their experiential base, it is important for librarians to develop programs based on an understanding of visitors' differentiated needs;
- In-depth qualitative case and action research studies, because they promote a democratic inquiry and community empowerment, can help identify various ways in which library curricula and policies can communicate with learners and local cultural communities;
- Developing a framework for integrating library programs more fully into school curricula and designing them for an adult learning community may best be achieved through collaborative planning between librarians, school teachers, and students, as well as community organizations. It is also crucial that such practitioners take advantage of library learning to broaden the existing educational environment while maintaining a certain degree of flexibility so that the library's identity is not sacrificed;
- Libraries wishing to spearhead a community-based education approach might devise outreach programs by bringing library activities and resources to the various community institutions and agencies, including hospitals, nurseries, detention centers, eldercare centers, and other agencies serving those with special needs.

Overall, because libraries have the potential to develop into discursive spaces for empowering communities through knowledge building, the theoretical principles outlined in this exploration of Freirean critical pedagogy can help TCBLs chart the future direction of both their nature and their pedagogy. Furthermore, the principles can promote the improvement of the librarian practice and library research through enabling professional librarians and researchers in LIS to reflect on their practice and critical issues in LIS and their community, create a research agenda with a focus on social justice and transformation, and engage in a work environment that will help them to develop skills in critical inquiry in order to generate strategies to transform information services in a multicultural society.

REFERENCES

Allman, Paula. 1999. *Revolutionary Social Transformation: Democratic Hopes, Political Possibilities and Critical Education.* Westport, CT: Bergin and Garvey.

Baksh-Soodeen, R. 2001. "Lessons from the Gender Movement: Building a Discipline to Support Practice." *CYD Journal* 2 (2): 61–64.

Benne, Kenneth D. 1987. "The Meanings of Democracy in a Collective World." In *Society as Educator in an Age of Transition,* ed. K. D. Benne and Steven Tozer, 1–23. Chicago: University of Chicago.

Boyte, Harry C., and Nancy N. Kari. 1996. *Building America: The Democratic Promise of Public Work.* Philadelphia: Temple University Press.

Bransford, John D., Anne L. Brown, and Rodney. R. Cocking, eds. 1999. *How People Learn: Brain, Mind, Experience, and School.* Washington, DC: National Academy.

Brown, John S., Allan Collins, and Paul Duguid. 1989. "Situated Cognition and the Culture of Learning." *Educational Researcher* 18 (1): 32–34.

Bruce, Bertram C. 2008. "From Hull House to Paseo Boricua: The Theory and Practice of Community Inquiry." In *Philosophy of Pragmatism (II): Salient Inquiries*, ed. B. Dicher and A. Ludusan, 181–98. Cluj-Napoca, Romania: Editura Fundatiei pentru Studii Europene (European Studies Foundation Publishing House).

Bruce, Bertram C., and Cushla Kapitzke. 2006. *Libraries: Changing Information Space and Practice.* Mahwah, NJ: Lawrence Erlbaum.

Coben, Diana. 1998. *Radical Heroes: Gramsci, Freire and the Politics of Adult Education.* New York: Garland Press.

Darder, Antonia. 2002. *Reinventing Paulo Freire: A Pedagogy of Love.* Boulder, CO: Westview.

Elias, John. 1994. *Paulo Freire: Pedagogue of Liberation.* Malabar, FL: Krieger.

Eryaman, Mustafa Y., and Martina Riedler. 2009. "From Interpretive Progressivism to Radical Progressiveism in Teacher Education: Teaching as Praxis." In *Peter McLaren, Education, and the Struggle for Liberation*, ed. M. Y. Eryaman, 203–24. Cresskill, NJ: Hampton Press.

Freire, Paulo. 1972. *Pedagogy of the Oppressed.* Harmondsworth, UK: Penguin.

Freire, Paulo. 1993. *Education for Critical Consciousness.* New York: Continuum.

Freire, Paulo. 1995. *Pedagogy of Hope: Reviving Pedagogy of the Oppressed.* Trans. Robert R. Barr. New York: Continuum.

Gadotti, Moacir. 1994. *Reading Paulo Freire: His Life and Work.* Albany, NY: SUNY Press.

Gerhardt, Heinz-Peter. 1993. "Paulo Freire." *Prospects: the Quarterly Review of Comparative Education* XXIII (3/4): 439–58.

Giroux, Henry, and Peter McLaren. 1987. "Teacher Education and the Politics of Engagement: The Case for Democratic Schooling." In *Teaching, Teachers and Teacher Education*, ed. M. Okazawa-Ray, J. Anderson, and R. Traver, 157–82. Cambridge, MA: Harvard Educational Review.

Lave, J. 1991. "Situating Learning in Communities of Practice." In *Perspectives on Socially Shared Cognition*, ed. Lauren B. Resnick, John M. Levine, and S. D. Teasley, 63–83. Pittsburgh: American Psychological Association.

Leppard, L. J. 1993. "Discovering a Democratic Tradition and Educating for Public Politics." *Social Education* 57 (1): 23–26.

Levine, Peter, and Mark H. Lopez. 2004. *Themes Emphasized in Social Studies and Civics Classes: New Evidence.* College Park, MD: Center for Information and Research on Civic Learning and Engagement.

Mayo, Peter. 1999. *Gramsci, Freire and Adult Education: Possibilities for Transformative Action.* London and New York: Zed Books.

Mayo, Peter. 2008. *Liberating Praxis: Paulo Freire's Legacy for Radical Education and Politics.* Westport, CT: Praeger.

McLaren, Peter. 2000. *Che Guevara, Paulo Freire and the Pedagogy of Revolution.* Lanham, MD: Rowman and Littlefield.

McLaren, Peter. 1994. "Postmodernism and the Death of Politics: A Brazilian Reprieve." In *Politics of Liberation: Paths from Freire*, ed. Peter McLaren and Colin Lankshear, 193–215. London and New York: Routledge.

McLaren, Peter, and Peter Leonard, eds. 1993. *Paulo Freire: A Critical Encounter*. London and New York: Routledge.

Morrow, Raymond A., and Carlos A. Torres. 2002. *Reading Freire and Habermas: Critical Pedagogy and Transformative Social Change*. New York: Teachers College.

Parker, W. C. 1996. "'Advanced' Ideas about Democracy: Toward a Pluralist Conception of Citizen Education." *Teachers College Record* 98 (1): 104–125.

Putnam, Robert. 2000. *Bowling Alone: The Collapse and Revival of American Community*. New York: Simon and Schuster.

Roberts, Peter. 2000. *Education, Literacy, and Humanization: Exploring in the Work of Paulo Freire*. Westport, CT: Bergin and Garvey.

Roche, Jeremy. 1997. "Children's Rights: Participation and Dialogue." In *Youth in Society*, ed. J. Roche and S. Tucker, 49–58. London: Sage.

Rossatto, Cesar A. 2005. *Engaging Paulo Freire's Pedagogy of Possibility: From Blind to Transformative Optimism*. Lanham, MD: Rowman and Littlefield.

Seigel, S., and V. Rockwood. 1993. "Democratic Education, Student Empowerment, and Community Service: Theory and Practice." *Equity and Excellence in Education* 26 (2): 65–70.

Taylor, Paul V. 1993. *The Texts of Paulo Freire*. Buckingham, PA: Open University.

Weis, Lois, and Michelle Fine, eds. 2000. *Construction Sites: Excavating Race, Class, and Gender among Urban Youth*. New York: Teachers College.

Wenger, Etienne. 1998. *Communities of Practice: Learning, Meaning, and Identity*. Cambridge: Cambridge University.

Wisner, William. 2000. *Whither the Postmodern Library? Libraries, Technology, and Education in the Information Age*. Jefferson, NC: McFarland.

9

Psychoanalysis as Critique in the Works of Freud, Lacan, and Deleuze and Guattari

Ronald E. Day
Indiana University, USA

Andrew J. Lau
University of California at Los Angeles, USA

INTRODUCTION

The topic of psychoanalysis is important in this book on the critical theory of Library and Information Science (LIS) for three reasons: first, it is important to account for the prevalence and possible roles and issues involved with personal psychology and social psychology as cornerstone perspectives in LIS (vis-à-vis the cognitive turn and information seeking behavior, respectively); second, to account for the prevalence and importance of psychoanalysis in some of the French theorists who are of concern in this book; and third, to suggest, through a discussion of psychoanalysis, the overall importance of discursive psychological accounts in LIS. Discursive psychological accounts contain a model of formal causality that allows us to understand human identity, intention, and signification or meaning (in events such as information or knowledge) as constructed emergences and expressions that are achieved through cultural forms acting as affordances[1] in social situations. In LIS, such a framework does away with the metaphysics of viewing information as empirical or pseudoempirical objects (i.e., the realist conception of information [see Frohmann 2004]). It challenges cognitive psychology and philosophies of mind based on such a metaphysics and its corresponding epistemologies and methods (cf. Harré and Secord 1972). Psychoanalysis is probably one of the earliest, and certainly, one of the most famous examples of discursive psychology in the history of modern psychology. The cornerstone of its theory of mind is that of the developmental acquisition of experiences, from childhood on, as affordances for the subject's expressions, and its clinical activities aim toward the positioning of the subject's desire and personal drives issuing from these (particularly, traumatic) experiences within sociocultural norms of expressive possibility, particularly through language.

In this chapter, we will discuss important concepts in the works of Sigmund Freud, Jacques Lacan, and Gilles Deleuze and Félix Guattari. If space were to allow it, we could extend this discussion to the place of psychoanalysis in the work of Jacques Derrida, on the one hand, and, on the other hand, the relation of psychoanalysis to discursive psychology, proper. Unfortunately, we do not have space for these discussions, but what we will do is to present some essential concepts in the writings of the above authors and suggest ways in which these concepts can critique and/or aid LIS theory and practice. Our chosen authors consist of the founder of psychoanalysis and three more radical interpreters of psychoanalysis in the French tradition.

Psychoanalysis contrasts most strongly with the psychological emphasis in LIS during the past 30 years termed the cognitive approach, associated with the works of Nicholas Belkin, Peter Ingwersen, and others. In contrast to the cognitive approach, psychoanalysis understands the psychological subject to be culturally and socially constructed at various levels of determination. This understanding, however, makes psychoanalysis a theory that is allied with discursive psychology, proper, positioning theory, and other psychological approaches that emphasize language as a cultural and social formal affordance for action, rather than as either a container or conduit of meaning or as representational material for so-called "cognitive processing."

THE COGNITIVE TURN IN LIS

Nick Belkin, Peter Ingwersen—and with an emphasis on traditional concepts of emotions, the work of Carol Kuhlthau—and others gave a psychological emphasis to LIS with their cognitive approach. This approach differed from the earlier work in information retrieval, often traced to the Cranfield experiments of the late 1950s, in that it attempted to take into account mental models and other psychological elements and events in those subjects that are commonly referred to in the LIS literature as information users. More recent research trends in LIS have involved information seeking behavior which, as it has often been said, has taken such studies out of the laboratory and into other social contexts, thus expanding the concept of information to include events that stand outside of information retrieval, proper. A recent book by Ingwersen and Järvelin (2005) has attempted to reconcile these two approaches.

The core assumptions of Belkin's cognitive approach in his theory of Anomalous States of Knowledge (ASK) follow two metaphors: first, that information is transmitted from a "generator" to a receiver (qua person) and, second, that information is some sort of quasi-empirical entity (traditionally called *qualia* in the philosophy of mind—short for qualitative feelings) that fills in knowledge gaps in a user's mental "state" (Belkin 1977, 1990). ASK, as part of an Information Retrieval (IR) theory, understands information as something contained in documents and as something transmitted to minds. These two governing metaphors, respectively, are the conduit or transmission metaphor of information and communication, and, the form-content metaphor for how meaning is embedded in documents and in people's minds (i.e., information understood as "epistemic content," as Frohmann [2004] calls it). Here, LIS's cognitive approach follows earlier cognitive psychology in its modeling of the mind as an information processing mechanism.

It is not possible within the short span of this chapter to critique the two metaphors operating in ASK (for such, see Frohmann 1992, 2004; Day 2005, 2007). We should mention, however, that despite appearing to support the above epistemology in the first chapter of his 1992 work Ingwersen then writes in the next chapter of that book that this is not how the cognitive approach should be understood: rather, information should be understood as the effects of stimuli upon a person so that his or her cognitive state changes.

The latter part of this observation, that external stimuli have a possible bearing upon the present or future behavior of an organism, whether limited or not to IR situations, is common sense, and it is dubious whether such an observation is in need of a theoretical statement or that such phenomena, when encountered in other than enigmatic events, are in need of scientific methods or even conceptual analysis. In contrast, our interest in psychoanalysis will be, in part, with how 'external stimuli' and 'internal mental states' and processing may be theorized in ways that problematize the internal/external divide that is often assumed throughout the LIS tradition. In this, psychoanalysis largely shares with other types of discursive psychology the assumption that the cause of personal expressions—that is, the activities that we associate with the term *mind*—are to be sought in a person's use of the tools of cultural forms and in a person's learned social actions performed in social situations, rather than in private mental events, which in the LIS/Information Science cognitivist traditions are characterized as being caused by brain activities or symbol processing. To those who object to this view of mind by arguing that thought is not expressive, we suggest that what is often called thought is simply auto-affective expression by means of subvocalization, dreams, and so forth, and therefore, 'thought,' too, must be considered as expression by the processes that we have outlined. The subvocalization of language in reading is a demonstration of this.

SIGMUND FREUD

Sigmund Freud's name is so well known world wide that he needs little introduction. In Anglo-American countries, orthodox Freudian psychoanalysis largely has been supplanted by mixed methods (discursive, behavioral, and psycho-pharmaceutical) in clinical activities. Our concern here, however, is largely with understanding psychoanalysis as a theory of culturally and socially constructed subjectivity.

The most important of the psychoanalytical premises is that the forces that direct our psychological functions are not directly observable and must be inferred from the evidence of a person's behavior, foremost, from their language expressions. In the Freudian corpus, these forces are located in the unconscious (*das Unbewusste*), which is the core function or faculty in the Freudian understanding of mind. Following Laplanche and Pontalis (1973, 449–53), we will propose that the Freudian corpus may best be dealt with as historically divided by two "topographies"—two geographies of envisioning the mind. The first, dating from *The Interpretation of Dreams* (1900; Freud 1960a) through the early 1920s (though having earlier precedent in Freud's psycho-physiological ruminations in his correspondence with his fellow physician Wilhelm Fleiss at the end of the 19th century), is a psychodynamic theory of the unconscious, whereby the mind is envisioned as a product of cultural forms and social forces.

By the time of the publication of Freud's *The Ego and the Id* in 1923 (Freud 1962), this topography had been replaced by the second topography, that of the Ego (*das Ich*—literally, "the I"), the Id (*das Es*—literally, "the it"), and the Super-Ego (*das Über-Ich*—literally, the "Over-I"). While these three concepts can still be understood dynamically, in the second topography as compared to the first topography, there is (1) a greater emphasis placed upon conceiving of the unconscious as a product of infantile life-forces; and (2) a greater emphasis placed upon describing the mind in terms of quasi-anatomical psychological faculties. From the viewpoint of a discursive psychology, this shift toward the triadic topography is problematic, but it also is more closely aligned with the development of psychology after Freud in that it sought to locate psychological functions in quasi-anatomical faculties, analogous to, or sometimes said to originate in, particular brain regions.

Whether understood largely as a dynamic product of social and cultural forces or as a product of social and cultural forces mixed with strong primitive infantile drives organized into distinct mental faculties, the Freudian concept of the unconscious involves several concepts that clearly distinguish it from later cognitivist models of mental functions and which pose challenges to the cognitive approach in LIS.

First, is the notion of deferred action (*Nachträglichkeit*). The Freudian concept of the unconscious stresses that the unconscious is fully (primary repression) or partially (secondary repression) composed of social impacts or traumas that later form for the person his or her core cultural forms and social rules for expression and agency, as well as form the preconscious screens that then allow for additional learning and socialization in certain directions of development rather than others (Freud 2003).

In Freud's writings, deferred action seems to be understood as operating in two temporal directions. In the first, core experiences are remembered and then latter reinvested in understanding new stimuli. This is a developmental analogue to the Kantian notion of formal conditions for the understanding. In the second, past experiences are reworked according to present experiences (though the degree that this is possible differs as to whether the past experiences are subject to primary or secondary repression).

The Freudian concept of the unconscious and its accompanying concepts muddy any simple understanding of information as some sort of immediately understood stimuli. According to psychoanalysis, meaningful events are products of faculties and frames of understanding based on earlier experiences, some of which may be understood by asking a person why he understands something or by watching what he does when he understands something. In the psychoanalytic session, however, where the subject's thought is assumed to be less logical than normal—involving greater use of symbolic condensation (what in Lacan's work is understood as metaphor) and displacement (what in Lacan's work is understood as metonymy)—the subject's discourse is assumed to require some degree of analysis in order to return it to a logically consistent language. If the historical origins of cognitive psychology are to be found in those attempts to see the mind as a rational processing mechanism made up of logical operations, the Freudian model states that though a rational function of the mind may be optimal, it is far from normal, particularly so in early life. Further, the cognitive division between supposed external stimuli and supposed internal processing is greatly muddied in the Freudian account of the unconscious, wherein stimuli are said to form the basis for the self and its action. Other Freudian concepts, such as identification and object-cathexis, based on mimetic relations to persons and fetishistic relations to objects, further challenge a naïve realist or naïve empiricist concept of information.

Thus, the assumption that information is then incorporated into 'knowledge states' as a part is absorbed into a whole—as in Belkin's ASK—might be seen as a rather crude and simplistic understanding of cognition in contrast to Freud's theoretical toolkit (we might say the same about LIS's famous data-information-knowledge-wisdom pyramid). If we were to object that Belkin and Ingwersen's theories were limited to describing the formation of mental models involved in information retrieval situations, we would then have to ask if the psychoanalytic description of mental processes could be excluded from these situations. In Freud's works, needs are functions of desires and drives and cannot be easily separated from those desires and drives.

The Freudian model was a radical break from earlier psychological behaviorism in so far as it stressed the importance of scripts, narratives, and the topographies of mentality in the formation of what some would call "information" for the subject. In distinction to LIS's cognitive model, it suggests an understanding of information and information seeking that recognizes the retroactive and revisionary nature of thought and it recognizes that thought processes are not always rational. The Freudian model also recognizes that needs are situated within larger desires, whose logic may not be immediately recognized or reportable, or for Freud, consciously accessible. The psychoanalytic therapeutic situation is, indeed, the site of the working out of how the logic of needs can reflect the irrationality of desires. Finally, the Freudian model challenges any easy distinction between internal mental states and external stimuli. In both the first and the second topographies, the unconscious and its expressions are a product of experience. The Freudian model is, foremost, a model of developmental psychology.

As Tuominen (1997), suggests, most information situations, such as reference interviews, do not need the therapeutic model that has been offered in LIS. Thus, the contribution of psychoanalysis to LIS may be seen not in furthering a misplaced therapeutic practice, but rather, in its critique of the empiricist and cognitivist conceptions of information in LIS's cognitive and information seeking behavior theories. In the next two sections we will briefly survey the possible contributions to LIS theory and practice of the works of three other psychoanalytical theorists, those being Jacques Lacan, and Gilles Deleuze and Félix Guattari.

JACQUES LACAN

Lacan was born in 1901 and, like Freud, was a physician by training. Though he was a colorful and controversial character and a rather eclectic scholar, he had a great influence on French psychoanalysis, both advocating a return to Freud and representing a challenge to the orthodox institutions and interpretations of psychoanalysis that formed after Freud's death. Lacan's interpretation of psychoanalysis was influenced by both structural linguistics and by his studies of Hegel from the lectures of Alexandre Kojève.

For Lacan, the unconscious is not part of a topographical structure hidden away in a faculty of a subject's mind, but rather, it is the totality of the "Other." "Other" (*Autre* in French) is the social whole, particularly as embodied in language, rather than any one person, particularly as a reflection of the ego (an "other" with a small "o" or in French, the *petit a* [*autre*]).[2] In this, Lacan returns more to the dynamic theories of Freud's first topography rather than the faculty psychology of Freud's second topography. Further, the goal of Lacanian analysis is not to discover the drives of primitive instincts as they are manifested in individual desires, but rather, to understand the relation between the patient's desires and normative sociocultural actions and forms of expression, that is, to understand one's subjectivity within what in Lacan's oeuvre is termed "the symbolic order."

In Lacan's work, the concept of the drive loses much of its Freudian biological intonations. For Lacan, drives are functions of desires, which, in turn, must pass through cultural and social mediations. For example, in as much as the patient is stuck in a rather infantile mode of narcissistic behavior—what in Lacan's oeuvre is characterized as "the mirror stage," dominated by the imaginary order—the patient's imagination of himself or herself and the world as a reflection of the ego is, however, still mediated by language, though a relatively private language. In other words, using Lacan's terminology, the imaginary order is not completely separable from the symbolic order. In this way, Lacan's reading of Freud distanced psychoanalysis from the latter's biological reductionism. By understanding the mind as a linguistic and communicative product and agent, Lacan's work, even more than Freud's, provides theoretical tools for understanding 'information phenomena' as products of society and culture.

The concept of desire is important in Lacan's work, and it influenced theoretical French psychoanalysis and the work of Deleuze and Guattari. (We will soon examine the work of the latter theorists.) The French translation (*désir*) of Freud's term *Wunsch* (wish) is shaped in Lacan's work by the influence of Hegel's dialectic, which in turn, is part of the German idealist philosophical tradition—a tradition that understands human life in terms of drives (*Trieb*). (Lacan's interpretation of drive as life force, rather than as (biological) instinct, thus pushed a close French variation of this important term in the German intellectual tradition against the prevalent interpretation in English-dominated orthodox psychoanalysis, in whose texts Freud's terms *Instinkt* and *Trieb* are interchangeably translated.) Desire is the force between the subject and the object by which the subject then comes to realize him- or herself. Whereas Freud's German term has a sense of the subject's own fantasy, the French term emphasizes the concept of a force that binds the subject to the object and, through the object, to its own development or becoming. In Lacan's work, desire is a product of dialectic and it constitutes the subject through his or her experiences in the world.

Maturation, for Lacan, means being aware that others are not just different than one's self, but that they are constituted by an alterity—not only as other, but as Other—that cannot be brought within the self's control. This same Otherness also makes the self something other than an ego. *Désir* conceives of the subject as constructed by social relations and cultural forms—most importantly, through language. It is because Lacan conceives the subject to be constituted by means of the social and cultural whole that Lacan could famously state that, "the unconscious is the discourse of the Other" (2006a). Otherness (with a capital "O") speaks, in a sense, to the subject so that the subject may reply, and therefore, speak.

For Lacan, a subject's desire is demonstrated by the chain of signification in his or her speech, showing the unconscious in the discourse of language through the formulation of the relationship S/s (Signifier over signified—reversing Saussure's formulation of the signified over the signifier since, for Lacan, it is the chain of signification that produces the signified).[3] Visually, this formula depicts the signified beneath the bar, the latter of which represents the unconscious. The figurative depiction represents the relationship between Signifier and signified, while also noting the critical separation between them. In this sense, the chain of signification is demonstrative of the subject's desire in that the Signifier implies another Signifier, which in turn implies another and so forth, in a potentially endless movement of deferment, thereby forming the chain of signification (Evans 1996; Lacan 2006b).

The understanding of the subject's relationship to the object though desire is not only indebted to dialectics, but also derives from the psychoanalytic notion of the part-object, wherein parts of an object come to substitute for the whole of that object.[4] The part-object plays the role of functioning as a lure for the subject's desire. One of the classic psychoanalytic part-objects is the mother's breast, but the term more generally refers to any secondary object that becomes the object of desire. In Lacan, the object of desire is always partial, first, because as it is held within the domain of desire its meaning is constituted as a function of desire (that is, its ontology is partially symbolic and imaginary, in addition to being constituted by whatever physical properties the object might have if it is other than a semantic object), and second, because, as it still remains an object proper, it never allows for the completion of desire, but instead, institutes the logic within the subject of desire-desiring-desire, which means that in the subject his or her own desire is a life force only as it is partially suppressed and ultimately unfulfilled. (The subject's desire, thus, can be self-suppressing—most fully charging itself, in a sense, via its own partial self-denial, that is, the subject giving to him- or herself an impossible object of desire.) In this, the part-object—increasingly understood by Lacan in his works as the *objet petit a*—is similar because of its symbolic and imaginary constitution to the Marxist concept of the commodity, in as much as commodities are lures into possibilities of being and action, but are ultimately, in a sense, unfulfilling. The *objet petit a* is shared, and links, the three orders that Lacan calls the imaginary, the symbolic, and the real: it is a function of the imaginary to the extent that we desire someone, something, or some situation like what we imagine we are or should be; it is a function of the symbolic insofar as it carries us through different symbolic worlds; and it marks the presence of the real in as much as it shows itself as that which cannot represent our desire (in the dual sense that Lacan uses the term *the real* in his works: as an empirical reality that exceeds the subject's desire and as the primal trauma and its drives that anchor the subject's desire to empirical reality [see Žižek 1989]).

These formulations imply a great deal for LIS, and for Information Science (IS), as well. For Lacan, speech is, above all, a reply to language—a reply that comes to orient the speech, or more generally, the expression of the subject. The problem of the neurotic, and even more, the psychotic, is that his or her speech is largely a reply to a relatively private language—an imaginary or hallucinatory realm, rather than what is publicly understandable. LIS's cognitive model and many of its information seeking epistemologies begin with the concept of a subject's needs and fulfilling those needs in document retrieval or information seeking behavior. What is not addressed at all or fully enough by such views is that "needs" are not mental states, nor are they fully subjective states, but rather, they are pragmatic events involving the subject's social and cultural positions, predominantly in terms of language, and the types and availability of materials that codetermine with the subject the means for expressions to take place. This suggests that the primary interest of information science is not 'information' per se, but rather, language in social actions and as cultural forms, as such codetermine subjects and objects. What might be considered to be information—as well as what might be considered to be the information seeker (or perhaps we should say in the psychoanalytic context, the information subject)—are functions of these affordances (not the least being the limitations of the social institutions and languages of the LIS cognitive and information seeking traditions). Lacanian psychoanalysis recognizes individual needs in desires, but it further recognizes that desires are drives that are formed and fulfilled by the subject's position in the symbolic.

From this perspective, the task of a librarian would be that of helping the subject to locate him- or herself in the orders of knowledge that make up the library and its languages and systems, and perhaps more importantly in the future, the universes of recorded information that extend beyond the locus of the library. In the most farsighted view of librarians as agents in the knowledge domain of what is sometimes called cyberspace, the librarian's task would become that of helping the subject to extend into and negotiate different communicational domains constituted by heterogeneous languages and cultures, and in this manner, to help the subject become the singular person that he or she is driven to be, as far as such is possible. (Such a concept of life, as that of becoming who one potentially is, reaches back into the earliest philosophical concepts of the drive [in German, *Trieb*], in German idealist philosophy, such as the works of Fichte, Schelling, and Hegel.) While the former concept of the librarian's task represents a more conservative reading of Lacan's project in application to the practical library and information professions, the latter represents a more liberal reading of Lacan's project, allied with Deleuze and Guattari's understandings of radical psychoanalysis.

There is one, very direct, critical application of Lacanian theory to an LIS model, and that is to Belkin's ASK model. Belkin's model characterizes the needs of the user in terms of a lack in relation to his or her knowledge (Belkin 1977, 1990). From a Lacanian perspective, this need would be understood as a lack in relation to a symbolic order. The critical problem occurs in regard to ASK and related cognitivist discourses when these posit the so-called information need as something that (1) originates in the subject's mind, and (2) can be fulfilled by the correspondence of the subject's needs and the information object's 'content.' From a Lacanian perspective, the subject's needs arise from the situated nature of a person in the symbolic order. The subject must position his or her desires within a symbolic universe so that he or she can then accomplish some movement or task in a way that is not just narcissistic, but, at least potentially, practically understandable. The task of Lacanian psychoanalysis is, thus, tactical, not strategic; it does not seek to map the subject's supposed inner knowledge and to find its lacks so that these may then be fulfilled by the information supplied by the analyst or found in documents. Need requires, first of all, that the subject's desire be correctly positioned in the symbolic universe that it wishes to work within so that it may be expressed. This is to say that need is a function of the symbolic. One can only have a need that can be expressed.[5]

What the analyst provides is help for the subject in the subject's finding the materials that would act as affordances for a general desire of expression (the particular expressions—the needs—require the symbolic field to be present in order to even be expressed).[6] Analogously, indirect and direct information in libraries help the user in expressing him- or herself within a symbolic field—first of all, the language of library structures (subject classifications, subject headings, call numbers, etc.), and second, the field of knowledge that the user is trying to work through. The belief that either texts or persons have empirically locatable content would be, for Lacan, based on a misunderstanding of the phenomena of meaning and the concept of language. Texts must be read in order to say that they are meaningful. The knowledge that we say that a person has is understood by a performance; previous to this, such knowledge is hypothetical.[7]

In a sense, for Lacan, the nature of being human is that of always being in 'anomalous states.' The fulfillment of a lack is always a provisional and practical affair. However, it corresponds with the fundamental ontological lack that Lacan premises as the logical basis for desire and, thus, for human life understood according to desire. In Lacanian psychoanalysis, the ultimate task of psychoanalysis for the neurotic patient is to show him or her that the fulfillment of lack is always temporary, that one's life is the force of desire.

GILLES DELEUZE AND FÉLIX GUATTARI

In contrast to Lacan's work, for the philosopher Gilles Deleuze and the radical psychoanalyst Félix Guattari, especially in their joint works, the object or other (no matter its ontological composition) is an "entranceway and exit" (Deleuze and Guattari 1987, 21) for the subject's desire, which the subject passes through in his or her historical events or what Deleuze and Guattari in their oeuvre term "becomings." Furthermore, the possibilities and potentialities for these investments and self-transformations come from sociocultural fields of semiotic and physical materials. Through sociocultural fields, as well as the physical properties of objects and beings, the subject invents him or herself.

How is it possible to pass through an *other* as an entranceway and exit, whether the other is a human being, another type of living being, or even an inanimate object (including technological objects)? Classically in orthodox psychoanalysis, identification, epitomized in Lacan's mirror stage, is the means by which one becomes through another. However, in Lacan, human maturation involves a greater involvement in symbolic, rather than specular, relations (that is, to use Lacan's terminology, greater involvement in the symbolic rather than the imaginary order). In Lacanian psychoanalysis, the neurotic is often seen as someone who misrecognizes the other as one's self (in the sense that the self is misunderstood to begin with: as a representation, rather than as hypothetical and real sets, respectively, of potential and actualized powers). In psychoanalysis, and particularly in Lacan's work, self-awareness is that of knowing that one's self is always mediated not only by other people, but by symbolic fields.

Rather than leaving the concept of the self at the doorstep of an ontologically split sense of self-identity and an ultimately futile sense of knowing the other as Other, however, Deleuze and Guattari see the self not as a being, but as a becoming, and they view the other as a means for this.[8] In this, they work out Lacan's ontological commitments further than, perhaps, Lacan did. Having already rejected the Cartesian self as part of an erroneous metaphysical tradition (extending, as they see it, through Hegel) that valorizes being over becoming, Deleuze and Guattari's works understand being as always provisional and derivative upon becomings. In other words, for Deleuze and Guattari, becoming is the nature of life, and becoming is always that of processes of becoming through others. Despite this provisional nature of the self, however, maturity in Deleuze and Guattari is not a question of progressing from becomings to beings, but rather, of possessing the skills and opportunities to have greater choices in choosing types of becomings that may occur. While the self may be always already ontologically provisional, this doesn't make it any less existentially certain. One's potentialities are built from experiences and skills, though they are actualized and expressed only in given situations. Maturation is the ability to ask with more skill the questions, What is an entity for? and How can I make a relation with a person or object an event of personal and, even historical, significance? In contrast to Lacan's writings, the subject in Deleuze and Guattari's works is given much greater historical power, both personally and socially.

What Deleuze critiqued as the "the control society" (1995) is a type of social order that regiments becomings by means of controlling the variety and types of social actions, cultural forms, and even social situations that becomings may occur through, as well as socially marginalizing or demeaning particular objects, forms of subjectivity, and events. Deleuze and Guattari always stressed "transversal" (Deleuze and Guattari 1987) becomings (that is, across, rather than within, normative regimes of identity and knowledge). For Deleuze and Guattari, social control acts, in part, by limiting the transversal relations through which these transversal "lines of flight" (1987) for a subject can occur. Consequently, Deleuze and Guattari's works stress the transformative nature of affects and bodies and stress the pragmatic aspects of those relations and materials for the subject.

Deleuze's works on affects,[9] Guattari's essays contained in *Molecular Revolution: Psychiatry and Politics* (1984), and their coauthored works[10] present an understanding of subjectivity and developmental psychology that see affect (which in LIS is sometimes given the term *information*) as affecting what Deleuze and Guattari term in their oeuvre "molecular" identities of the mind/body. (Deleuze and Guattari's works don't assume a strict mind/body dichotomy.) Their valorization of persons as essentially molecular and mentally shaped by affects according to speeds and intensities (and only gradually becoming what Deleuze and Guattari term in their oeuvre "molar"—that is, the gradual assumption of relatively fixed identities and more individually shaped intentional gestures) presents an intriguing and largely uninvestigated psychological model for clinical and developmental psychologies. As undetermined affect, such an understanding of information (though Deleuze and Guattari don't call it information as such) avoids some of the theoretical problems of positing information-as-affect as quasi-empirical qualia of meaning or potential meaning used in 'mental processing.' It also presents new challenges and opportunities in psychology and information science. For example, music would need to be accounted for as affective information in a broader sense than is possible within the traditional grammars for feelings or emotions used within standard cognitivist, as well as popular, discourses of psychology. And so, too, what was known as group psychology could be understood according to social movements—literally, social movements or affects that shape the mind/body. The mind/body, here, is seen as relatively plastic, relatively more able to engage in mutual "lines of flight" through "transversal becomings" (Deleuze and Guattari 1987) according to the openings to affect that a mind/body allows. The propensity of mature people toward representation and the propensity of children and adolescences toward affective states of moods and music are, in Deleuze and Guattari's works, given ontological and social explanations—explanations that as of now are still untapped resources for clinical and developmental psychologies, as well as for a philosophy of mind and, possibly, a new area of research in information science.

For Deleuze and Guattari's works, as for parts of Foucault's works, the English term *power* is a translation of two very different French terms: power understood as an expressive or emergent force (*puissance*), and, power understood as a repressive, institutionally structured force (*pouvoir*). Allied to Foucault's works, their critique of the cultural and institutional repressive powers of orthodox psychoanalysis (particularly in *Anti-Oedipus* [Deleuze and Guattari 1977]) aims at critiquing not only its macro-institutions of repressive power, but its support and reification of the micro-fascisms of sociocultural actions and expressions that prevent transversal movements and personal and social revolutions. Their critiques of the control society and the manner of its inscription upon individual psyches and bodies (not the least beginning with public information, knowledge structures, and education) opens up a vast critique of information and politics at the level of public institutions *and* everyday life that LIS has barely touched upon in its political amnesia, not least in regard to public information (which seems to be regarded by LIS institutions as the domain of journalism).

Due to space constraints we cannot discuss more fully the political aspects of Deleuze and Guattari's works.[11] However, Deleuze and Guattari's works stand apart from Lacan's in this regard by taking a much more radical stance toward the personally and socially constructive possibilities of subjectivity than Lacan's works did. Correspondingly, the task of the information provider within this view, for example, may be seen as a political task to foster personal and social change by challenging what may or may not be considered to be information today, a challenge that might result in changing the trajectories and forms of political, social, and cultural subjects. In this, the information provider's job would be as transformational as the Deleuzian philosopher's job: not so much to literally preserve knowledge, but to transform it; not to simply repeat concepts, but to reinvent and invent them (see Gerolami 2009).

PSYCHOANALYSIS AND NEW MEDIA

Psychoanalysis as a theoretical and interpretive framework may elucidate the psychic and psychological underpinnings of the exponential growth and adoption of new media and information and communications technologies (ICTs), which are demonstrably of great interest to the field of LIS. As a framework, it may provide insight into how information is sought, accessed, and used, but also how information contributes to and is contributed to by particular information ecologies and circulates within them as informational communications.

According to Lacan, "The sender receives his own message from the receiver in an inverted form" (2006a). Critic Lorenzo Chiesa (2006) interprets Lacan's claim to be an expression of the movement in Lacan's oeuvre from a focus on the imaginary construction of identity within the individual (as exemplified in Lacan's mirror stage), toward a *transindividual* signification of identity through language (41). The inversion of the message, according to Chiesa, occurs in two forms: an *intersubjective* form, in which the speaker situates him or herself in relation to *another subject* that is the receiver of the message (he or she who is not I), and an *intrasubjective* inversion in which the receiver relays the message back to the sender who then receives it.

With regards to the Web 2.0 movement (and its various iterations), the critical point around which such developments revolve is the notion of interactivity: not only are individuals information seekers or users, but they are also contributors and responders through multiplied manners, expressing greater amounts of information. For example, the National Archives of the United Kingdom and a number of partner cultural institutions organized a Web-based resource in 2007 called *Moving Here: 200 Years of Migration to England* to highlight the history of immigration in the United Kingdom. In addition to online exhibitions of digitized archival materials, the resource also provides a means by which individuals can contribute their own personal histories and narrative experiences of migration. In doing so, a number of individuals contributing their testimonies noted that they were reminded of their own experiences in reading others' testimonies. Furthermore, this example also highlights the relationship between the subject and the Other, the latter in this case being marked through the symbolic significations of individuals' experiences. These experiences, constructed through signification in digital form online, speak to the subject, to which the subject replies. Such a framework may prove applicable to a number of other popular new media and Web 2.0 modes, like blogs and micro-blogs, social networking, and other interactive online resources not yet realized. Psychoanalysis, in stressing the communicative foundations and temporal nature of knowledge and subjectivity, provides a more complete theoretical toolbox for psychologically understanding communicative technologies than cognitivist information theories, which are psychological analogues of an information theory commonly (and often wrongly) used to describe traditional knowledge producers, readers, viewers (and other 'receivers'), and knowledge preserving institutions, such as libraries.

CONCLUSION

What are some of the major theoretical contributions of the psychoanalytic works that we have covered to a critical theory of LIS? Since critical theory is a product of critical philosophy (a term first used by Kant in his rejection of what he characterized as positive, dogmatic, medieval, and naïve empirical philosophies, and his attempt, instead, to articulate the a priori grounds for knowledge, ethical actions, and judgments of taste), the question becomes, following Kant's work and critical theory in the 20th century: *how does psychoanalysis—understood as a critical (rather than as a strictly clinical) discourse—turn us away from current theoretical dogmatisms in LIS and Information Science (IS) and how does it articulate, conceptual problems in these fields in other ways?*

Certainly the chief LIS dogmatism that is brought into *critique* by psychoanalysis is the epistemology of information seeking: namely, that information seeking starts with a subject searching for some type of information object which he or she then uses. The model that psychoanalysis proposes instead, particularly in Lacan and in Deleuze and Guattari's works, is that of a subject and object co-joined by language and other cultural forms, by social forces, and co-located in social situations. Both the subject and the information are mutual products of cultural forms for expressions, social forces, and social situations. The psychoanalytic concept of the object must be seen in terms of drive theories, where drives are understood as products of social forces and cultural forms for expression. The conditions of information 'use,' too, must be viewed in terms of social forces and cultural forms, though at times embedded within teleologically structured actions (what we commonly term tasks). Understanding subjects, objects, and use as co-afforded by social forces, cultural forms, and social situations allows us to understand others' explanations of their intentions and the reasons that they give for acts and actions, and to understand such explanations and reasons as normative, nonnormative, and problematic or not in terms of their likely fulfillment.

In sum, the conduit metaphor as the basis of information theory is critiqued in psychoanalysis by the view that the relation between the subject and object is a function of the subject and the object's position in sociocultural and physical spaces, and by the view that the acts of persons are explained by the cultural forms and social actions that are used by a person and which shape and determine the person's expressions. Among these forms are "information" forms for knowledge and for manners of communicating, and among the tools that are used are what are considered to be information and communication technologies. As any history of these terms shows, their meanings are quite variable. Along with the critique of the conduit metaphor comes a critique of the container metaphor for documentary or informational meaning in both documentary objects and in subjects: that is, a critique that highlights that documentary content is a product of reading and that a person's knowledge can only be hypothesized or indirectly evidenced (by school diplomas, etc.) until it is performed. Knowledge is not a contained substance in a form; for documents it is the performance of reading and for persons it is a performance of certain types of acts that we call knowing or knowledge acts (Day 2005, 2007). *Content is the product of, not the cause for, acts of reading and personal expression.*

Second, the concept of desire in psychoanalysis encompasses the entire social and cultural fields of subjects and objects. Particularly in Lacan's works, the elevation of objects to, at least, some degree of investments of desire means that objects, including information technologies, must be understood, at least in part, as functions of symbolic investments. This is important not only in analyses of the meaning of the terms *informa-tion society* and *information age,* and for understanding the nature of certain technolo-gies privileged in such societies, but it is also important for understanding objects and their historical and social design trajectories according to personal and social dreams and desires (for example, understanding whatever is meant, today, by the class term *computers* according to symbolic investments, rather than according to technological qualities alone).

On the one hand, the Lacanian concept of the symbolic, led by the *objet petit a,* en-compasses both the field of the subject's desire and it allows for the social construction of subjects as groups around common symbolic objects. As we have suggested in an endnote in this chapter, the concept of the *objet petit a,* as a symbolic projection ulti-mately originating in the Other, anticipates what Serres and Latour later termed in their works the "quasi-object." The *objet petit a* is both the cause and the subsequent lure for the subject's desires; it begins at the point of trauma where the real creates the subject through an enigmatic incident that the subject spends a lifetime and his or her drives try-ing to conceptually grasp (for Freud, the pleasure principle is, ultimately, the other side of the death instinct; that is, our lives are spent chasing the enigma of our finitude). On the other hand, in terms of the object, the materiality of objects becomes, in part, the re-sistance that they have to purely imaginative and symbolic investments. In short, much of the discourse on information and information technologies, users, and information use, as well as such tropes as the information society and the information age, beg for an analysis as to their imaginary, symbolic, and real qualities. One may argue that such a project is at the heart of a critical information theory as a type of social informatics.

Third, psychoanalysis proposes a concept of mind made up of personalized ex-pansive cultural forms and learned social actions. This concept of mind gives rise to psychoanalysis's conception of self, as an agent whose present and future actions are in-trinsically afforded by past experience and learning. Parallel to Glenberg and Robertson (1999), Day (2007) has referred to these lattices of cultural forms and learned actions as "indexes" that position the subject in social space and are developmentally extended by analogical learning. Such a model stands against cognitivist models of the mind as an information processing mechanism of symbols or representations.

Fourth, psychoanalysis challenges the temporality of LIS's information seeking model and the ontology of information as presence. It suggests that understanding can be retroactive. It also suggests that what is most informative for the subject is often what is not consciously present. Freud's paradigm examples for this last concept are his notions of the slip of the tongue (1960a) and of jokes as the gateway to the unconscious (1960b). In jokes, for Freud, what is most important is often what is not at first evident, but which later appears—for example, in the punch line of a joke (where the non-expected, com-monly minor, meaning of a term or line of thought suddenly occurs as dominant). In psy-choanalysis, the most important information is not always what the subject thinks that he or she is seeking, but what appears in the midst of the seeking and is often of an opposite value to what is initially being sought. In other words, information in psychoanalysis is often not manifest, but rather latent (this point is highlighted, by Lacan, among other places, in Lacan 2006c, and by Žižek, in, among other places, Žižek 1989.)

Fifth, despite the prominence of subjectivity in psychoanalysis's concept of desire (particularly in points of Lacan's works and certainly in Deleuze and Guattari's joint works), psychoanalysis sometimes shows the possibility of its being a psychological theory based on the "mediation" (Ekbia 2009) of subjects and objects by one another in the establishment of each other's identities. Rather than stressing the identity of the subject or object as in-itself essences, being is developed from out of the in-between, relational, spaces, in and through which subjects and objects create their singularities and from which identities might be subsequently recognized and represented. Such in-between spaces are constructed through social and physical mediation and remediation and, semantically, through the mediation and remediation of cultural forms in such events as conversation. The subject and the object are seen in such a view as mutually afforded (by each other and by the common grounds through which they emerge and interact). Their codetermination leads to their emergences as affected *singularities,* and, when and if they are recognized as certain types of beings or objects, then their represented identities give them their status as *individuals.* Thus, subjects and objects and their relations to one another are to be understood according to determinate (Aristotle: efficient) causes in their interactions, but this is underwritten more fundamentally by formal causes or forms for expression. Subjects and objects are coemergent from out of in-common cultural forms for meaning, meaningful social actions, and social situations (as well, of course, from out of in-common physical affordances if the relation is not purely semiotic). In information environments, as we have suggested, such co-emergence is seen most richly in environments where subjects change each other and change their modes of expression (i.e., their so-called information environments), for example, in some Web 2.0 environments that stress communication, rather than information display and retrieval functions. Deleuze and Guattari's works see the codetermination of subjects and objects by one another through their mutual affects, their shared situations, and their in-common becomings as having consequences reaching into the physical characteristics of beings. Certainly, theirs is a long-term evolutionary view.

In sum, the psychoanalytical works that we have discussed, understood as critical (rather than strictly clinical) discourses, challenge the epistemology of LIS's cognitive models, its information seeking epistemology, its dominant metaphors (the conduit metaphor and the form-content metaphor), its ontological and metaphysical understanding of subjects, and its predominant causal model. It challenges IS's cognitivist theories of mind (as in traditional Artificial Intelligence), its dominant reliance upon determinist causal models for understanding human-technological relations (and the quantitative methods that support them), as well as its neglect in not more clearly addressing information technology as cultural forms that enact symbolic futures. In contrast to both LIS and IS theories of mind, retroactive temporality is accounted for and the term *information* is understood in terms other than that of immediately recognized knowledge or Frohmann's (2004) "epistemic content." The psychoanalytic works that we have discussed offer an understanding of subjects and objects in terms of their mutual constructions and in terms of mutual affordances, they offer a theoretical model that challenges both the mind/body and the inner/outer dichotomies that are prevalent in the Western metaphysical and modern psychological traditions, and they stress a developmental rather an an information processing basis for understanding mind and cognition. In brief, the psychoanalytical discourses that we have examined constitute one set of answers to some of the many a priori, conceptual paradoxes and confusions that plague LIS and IS theory and, consequently, their empirical research and professional practices.

Last, in terms of practical activities involving LIS institutions, perhaps one of the greatest contributions of psychoanalytic discourse is in the theoretical inflection point that attempts to reconceptualize the relationship between the professional field and the varying communities that it aims to serve. Although there may be a tacit, or at least largely unaddressed, recognition that the leveraging of ICTs for information services can be of great benefit for libraries and other information institutions, psychoanalysis gestures toward the intersubjective construction of meaning, identity, and intention, beyond what cognitive psychology and information theories exposit. At the least, for research in this field, psychoanalysis provides a framework by which to critically read information phenomena in manners that move away from the privileged social science perspectives that have pervaded the discipline and the metaphysics of subjectivity that philosophically inform them. Such a framework allows for the excavation of information phenomena in terms that LIS broadly has yet to interrogate.

REFERENCES

Belkin, Nicholas J. 1977. "Internal Knowledge and External Information." In *CC 77: The Cognitive Viewpoint,* ed. M. de Mey, R. Pinxten, M. Poriau, and F. Vandamme, 187–94. Ghent: University of Ghent.

Belkin, Nicholas J. 1990. "The Cognitive Viewpoint in Information Science." *Journal of Information Science* 16:11–15.

Berardi, Franco, Guiseppina Mecchia, and Charles J. Stivale. 2008. *Félix Guattari: Thought, Friendship and Visionary Cartography.* Basingstoke, UK: Palgrave Macmillan.

Chiesa, Lorenzo. 2006. *Subjectivity and Otherness: A Philosophical Reading of Lacan.* Cambridge, MA: MIT Press.

Day, Ronald. E. 2001. *The Modern Invention of Information: Discourse, History, and Power.* Carbondale: University of Southern Illinois Press.

Day, Ronald. E. 2005. "Clearing Up 'Implicit Knowledge': Implications for Knowledge Management, Information Science, Psychology, and Social Epistemology." *Journal of the American Society for Information Science and Technology* 56 (6): 630–63.

Day, Ronald E. 2007. "Knowing and Indexical Psychology." In *Rethinking Knowledge Management: From Knowledge Objects to Knowledge Processes,* ed. Claire R. McInerney and Ronald E. Day, 331–48. New York: Springer.

Deleuze, Gilles. 1991. *Bergsonism.* New York: Zone Books.

Deleuze, Gilles. 2003. *Francis Bacon: The Logic of Sensation.* Minneapolis: University of Minnesota Press.

Deleuze, Gilles. 1995. "Postscript on Control Societies." In *Negotiations: 1972–1990,* by Gilles Deleuze, trans. Martin Joughin, 177–82. New York: Columbia University Press.

Deleuze, Gilles, and Félix Guattari. 1977. *Anti-Oedipus: Capitalism and Schizophrenia.* New York: Viking Press.

Deleuze, Gilles, and Félix Guattari. 1987. *A Thousand Plateaus: Capitalism and Schizophrenia.* Minneapolis: University of Minnesota press.

Deleuze, Gilles, and Félix Guattari. 1994. *What Is Philosophy?* New York: Columbia University Press.

Deleuze, Gilles, and Antonio Negri. 1995. "Control and Becoming: An Interview Between Antonio Negri and Gilles Deleuze." In *Negotiations: 1972–1990,* by Gilles Deleuze, trans. Martin Joughin, 169–76. New York: Columbia University Press.

Dyer-Witheford, Nick. 1999. *Cyber-Marx: Cycles and Circuits of Struggle in High-Technology Capitalism.* Urbana: University of Illinois Press.

Ekbia, Hamid. 2009. "Digital Artifacts as Quasi-Objects: Qualification, Mediation, and Materiality." *Journal of American Society for Information Science and Technology* 60 (12): 2554–66.

Evans, Dylan. 1996. *An Introductory Dictionary of Lacanian Psychoanalysis.* New York: Routledge.

Freud, Sigmund. 1960a. *The Interpretation of Dreams.* New York: Basic Books.

Freud, Sigmund. 1960b. *Jokes and Their Relation to the Unconscious.* New York: Norton.

Freud, Sigmund. 1962. *The Ego and the Id.* London: Hogarth Press.

Freud, Sigmund. 2003. "Screen Memories." In *The Uncanny,* by Nicholas Royle, 1–22. New York: Penguin.

Frohmann, Bernd. 1992. "The Power of Images: A Discourse Analysis of the Cognitive Viewpoint." *Journal of Documentation* 48 (4): 365–86.

Frohmann, Bernd. 2004. *Deflating Information: From Science Studies to Documentation.* Toronto: University of Toronto Press.

Gerolami, Natasha. 2009. "The Library in the Society of Control." *Proceedings of the 37th Annual Conference of the Canadian Association for Information Science.* Available at http://www.cais-acsi.ca/proceedings/2009/Gerolami_2009.pdf. Accessed July 21, 2009.

Glenberg, A. M., and D. A. Robertson. 1999. "Indexical Understanding of Instructions." Indexical *Discourse Processes* 28 (1): 1–26.

Goddard, Michael. n. d. *Félix and Alice in Wonderland: The Encounter Between Guattari and Berardi and the Post-Media Era.* Available at: http://www.generation-online.org/p/fpbifo1.htm. Accessed: July 21, 2009.

Guattari, Félix. 1984. *Molecular Revolution: Psychiatry and Poitics.* New York: Penguin Books.

Guattari, Félix, and Antonio Negri. 1990. *Communists Like Us: New Spaces of Liberty, New Lines of Alliance.* New York: Semiotext(e).

Harré, Rom. 2002. "Material Objects in Social Worlds." *Theory, Culture & Society* 19 (5/6): 23–33.

Harré, Rom. 1989. "The Self as a Theoretical Concept." In *Relativism: Interpretation and Confrontation,* ed. Michael Krausz, 387–417. Notre Dame, IN: University of Notre Dame Press.

Harré, Rom, and Grant Gillett. 1994. *The Discursive Mind.* Thousand Oaks, CA: Sage Publications.

Harré, Rom, and Paul F. Secord. 1972. *The Explanation of Social Behavior.* Totowa, NJ: Rowman and Littlefield.

Ingwersen, Peter. 1992. *Information Retrieval Interaction.* London: Taylor Graham.

Ingwersen, Peter, and Kalervo Järvelin. 2005. *The Turn: Integration of Information Seeking and Retrieval in Context.* Dordrecht: Springer.

Lacan, Jacques. 2006a. "The Function and Field of Speech and Language in Psychoanalysis." In *Écrits,* by Jacques Lacan, 197–268. New York: Norton.

Lacan, Jacques. 2006b. "The Instance of the Letter in the Unconscious or Reason Since Freud." In *Écrits,* by Jacques Lacan, 412–41. New York: Norton.

Lacan, Jacques. 2006c. Seminar on "The Purloined letter." In *Écrits,* by Jacques Lacan, 6–50. New York: Norton.

Laplanche, Jean, and J.-B Pontalis. 1973. *The Language of Psychoanalysis.* New York: Norton.

Negri, Antonio. 1995. "On Gilles Deleuze & Félix Guattari: A Thousand Plateaus." *Graduate Faculty Philosophy Journal* 18 (2): 93–109.

Tuominen, Kimmo. 1997. "User-Centered Discourse: An Analysis of the Subject Positions of the User and the Librarian." *Library Quarterly* 67 (4): 350–71.

Turkle, Sherry. 2007. *Evocative Objects: Things We Think With.* Cambridge, MA: MIT Press.

Wright, Steve. 2001. "Pondering Information and Communication in Contemporary Anti-Capitalist Movements." *Commoner* 1. Available at: http://www.commoner.org.uk/01–7 groundzero.htm. Accessed July 21, 2009.

Wright, Steve. 2006. "There and Back Again: Mapping the Pathways within Autonomist Marxism." Paper presented at the *Immaterial Labour, Multitudes and New Social Subjects: Class Composition in Cognitive Capitalism Conference,* Cambridge, UK, April. Available at: http://libcom.org/library/there-and-back-again-mapping-the-pathways-within-autonomist-marxism-steve-wright. Accessed: July 21, 2009.

Žižek, Slavoj. 1989. "Which Subject of the Real?" In *The Sublime Object of Ideology,* by Slavoj Žižek, 153–99. London: Verso.

NOTES

1. We use the term *affordance* to mean cultural and social materials ("social substances" from Harré 2002) that afford the emergence of meaningful expressions, including those of selves as particular singularities. Primarily, we refer to cultural affordances (such as language), but also to social actions, as well, and when applicable, to physical ("material") affordances. The concept of affordance is related to Aristotle's notion of formal causes (rather than determinate ["efficient"] causes), referring to forms that afford meaningful expressions and emergences by shaping the expressive powers of a substance (including persons). These, latter, too, of course, may be considered to be affordances, but of a physiological or psychological type related to, respectively, empirically recognizable or hypothetical innate powers and dispositions of a substance, rather than what might be seen as those contextual affordances that we have characterized above. Of course, with learned behaviors, contextual affordances play a great role in forming those innate powers and dispositions proper to a person.

Our understanding of this term is greatly shaped by Rom Harré's works where notions of disposition, powers, and more recently, properly, the term affordance are foundational. (See Harré and Secord 1972; Harré and Gillett 1994; and Harré 2002, being only a few of his many works where cultural and social affordances are discussed; many other of his works discuss material affordances in regard to the analysis of natural objects in the physical sciences). The term originates in the works of J. J. Gibson, of course, but Harré has greatly broadened and philosophically deepened it, and we are profoundly indebted to Harré's broad, extensive, and brilliant scholarship. We might note in the context of this chapter in this book that Gilles Deleuze's expressionist philosophy shares with Harré's works a concern with the powers of substances and the cultural, social, and material forms through which substances are expressed, but it is much more general than Harré's more analytical works. Also, Antonio Negri's works, particularly his works on Spinoza's philosophy, take Deleuze's expressionist philosophy in an overtly political direction.

2. Lacan replaces the Freudian topographical mental faculty *structures* (a metaphor borrowed from geography) with topological *functions* (a metaphor borrowed from mathematics). This switch demonstrates Lacan's turn to a functionalist and symbolic basis for psychology and the identity of both subjects and objects, rather than one grounded in faculty psychology. Arguably, this can be seen as somewhat of a return to Freud's earlier, relatively more dynamic topography (from about 1900 to 1923), as compared to the later Freudian faculty psychology of the second topography. For commentary on this, see the entry "topology" in Dylan Evans' reliable *An Introductory Dictionary of Lacanian Psychoanalysis* (1996).

3. In Saussure's works, the word *signifier* refers to words and the word *signified* refers to concepts.

4. A historical account of the trajectory of the concept of the psychoanalytic part-object (particularly explicit in Melanie Klein's works) to Winnicott's "transitional objects" to Lacan's *objet petit a* to what Serres and Latour have termed "quasi-objects" and the role of objects as

"entranceways and exits" for desire in Deleuze and Guattari is given in Day 2001 (chapter 4, particularly page 75 and following), within an account of information and information technology as projected desire and in that chapter, particularly, in regard to Pierre Lévy's misleading appropriation of key concepts in the works of Gilles Deleuze and Félix Guattari. For more on part-objects as quasi-objects, particularly in relation to digital objects, see Ekbia's (2009) engaging analysis. A collection of accounts of information technologies as types of part-objects is given by Sherry Turkle under the term "evocative objects" (Turkle 2007)—we may recall that Turkle's first book was on Lacan.

5. The English grammar of "having" a need misleads us to think that needs precede their forms of expression. Needs, however, are functions of what can be done and expressed. The private language of the schizophrenic or neurotic is only relatively private—there is no strictly private (i.e., personal) language. Wittgenstein, of course, gave exemplary critiques of the grammar of "to have" mental faculties and contents, as well as gave critiques of private language arguments.

6. We shouldn't lose sight that Lacan's psychoanalysis, picking up some strands in Freud's work, remains grounded in a romantic conception of life as a historical drive whose being is worked out by means of actions and events—that is, by becomings. Whether the subject's primal desire is to be understood in terms of a teleological sense of becoming or whether life-as-desire is to be understood as composed of a series of phases or even as the sum total of needs seems to be unresolved in Lacan's works, though the foundational concept of desire as a sort of primary drive certainly suggests the first or second understanding, rather than the last.

7. For more on a relevant, though nonpsychoanalytical explanation of this last point, see Harré 1989.

8. Having rejected Hegel's philosophy, Deleuze and Guattari don't premise an Otherness (in Hegel, Being) as a driving force for the subject's desire (in Hegel, grasped in Absolute Being [i.e., the identity of the particular and the universal] and in Lacan, never graspable). Rather, for Deleuze, Being is immanent—it is a potentiality that is actualized through events, rather than the teleological driver and achievement of personal and historical becoming (as in Hegel's philosophy) or the foundation and ultimate object for desire (as in Lacan's works).

9. Though this theme is important throughout his oeuvre, see particularly Deleuze's, *Francis Bacon: The Logic of Sensation* (2003) and *Bergsonism* (1991).

10. Particularly, *A Thousand Plateaus: Capitalism and Schizophrenia* (Deleuze and Guattari 1987) and *What Is Philosophy?* (Deleuze and Guattari 1994).

11. We should note that Deleuze's and particularly Guattari's political work extended to collaborations with Antonio Negri, Franco Berardi (particularly concerned with new media forms), and others in the Italian *autonomia* ("autonomous Marxism") tradition (see Goddard n.d.; Guattari and Negri 1990; Deleuze and Negri 1995; Negri 1995; Dyer-Witheford 1999; Wright 2001, 2006; Berardi 2008).

10

Anthony Giddens' Influence on Library and Information Science

Howard Rosenbaum
Indiana University, USA

INTRODUCTION

In the intellectual landscape of the sciences, some disciplines are net exporters of theory while others are net importers. Although once a net importer, Information Studies (IS), of which Library and Information Science (LIS) is a part, "has become a much more successful exporter of ideas than in the recent past" while simultaneously becoming "less introverted than before, drawing more heavily on the literature" of cognate disciplines (Cronin and Meho 2008, 563). What is of interest here is a trend in theory importation in the years following Robert Taylor's (1986) and Brenda Dervin and Michael Nilan's (1986) arguments for a user-centered approach to the relationship between people and information systems. LIS scholars subsequently engaged in what Blaise Cronin (2008, 466–67) calls a "sociological turn," although " 'the social' has long been part of our field, either implicitly or explicitly." Some have looked to the work of Bourdieu, Merton, Castells, Latour, Goffman and others; this chapter focuses on the importation of Anthony Giddens' ideas into LIS.

After introducing Giddens and his work, the chapter provides a high level overview of structuration theory, followed by an analysis of the uses of Giddens' work in LIS based on a set of articles that have cited Giddens' work drawn from 13 LIS journals. The main findings are that two main forms of citation to his work are ceremonial and analytic and three main sources from which importation takes place, Giddens, a management scholar, and an LIS researcher. The chapter concludes that Giddens' ideas have greatly informed LIS research, and his work should continue to do so in future.

GIDDENS AND STRUCTURATION

Born in 1938 in London, Anthony Giddens was educated at Hull College (BA,1959), the London School of Economics (MA, 1961), and King's College (PhD, 1974). Giddens began his academic career in 1961 at the University of Leicester and in 1969 moved to the University of Cambridge, becoming a professor of sociology in 1989 (Bryant and Jary 1991). During this time, he developed structuration theory, the focus of this chapter, in a series of books. Between 1997 and 2003, he was the director of the London School of Economics where he is currently a professor. In 2004, Baron Giddens took a seat in the House of Lords with a life peerage.

Giddens' scholarly output is voluminous; since 1971 he has published more than 40 books (mostly sole authored), eight edited collections, and written more than 200 articles, essays, and reviews. He is one of the most widely known and influential living sociologists and his thinking has shaped theory and research in his home discipline and many others, for example, nursing (Hardcastle, Usher, and Holmes 2005), organizational studies (Pozzebon and Pinsonneault 2005) and information systems (Jones and Karsten 2008; Rose 1998). Rob Stones (2005) argues that when considering empirical research, structuration theory has been an

overwhelming success as scores of researchers have found that its concepts have allowed them to gain critical purchase on empirical phenomena in fields as diverse as accounting systems, archaeology, demography, organisational and political culture, the sociology of technology, the management of inter-firm networks, migration studies, the analysis of sport and leisure, and of gender and patriarchy (2).

Lars Kasperson (2000, vi) describes Giddens' work as a " 'global phenomenon,' translated into many languages and read in almost all sociology curricula." During a productive period between 1974 and 1984, he developed structuration theory, its fullest expression presented in *The Constitution of Society: Outline of the Theory of Structuration* (1984). It is difficult to do justice to this complex and wide-ranging theory in this chapter; only a brief description of its main tenets will be provided; those interested in exploring structuration theory are encouraged to read his work (Giddens 1979, 1984).

Given the theme of this book, a question must be answered before beginning an exposition of structuration theory. In what sense can Giddens be considered a critical theorist? Ron Day (2007) describes critical analysis as "that which brings into question established social assumptions and values" (575) and as "a discursive and cultural examination of the construction of meaning and concepts" (578). From the mid 1970s on, Giddens has engaged in a series of critical dialogues with many 19th- and 20th-century social theorists and philosophers whose work shaped has 20th-and 21st-century sociology. Systematically reviewing the work of Durkheim, Weber, Marx, Parsons, Levi-Strauss, Blumer, Schutz, Goffman, Gadamer, and others, he has assessed the strengths and weaknesses of their work, engaging in a "critical appropriation of...key aspects" of their thinking that which would be of enduring value for his project (Giddens 1982, 107). Craig Browne (1993, 145) observes that, Giddens' "typology of intellectual, practical, ideological and moral, as four different meanings of critique, highlights his virtues as a sociological analyst." Further, Giddens argues that "any sociological approach to understanding society is inherently 'critical'" (Hardcastle, Usher, and Holmes 2005, 224).

According to Browne (1993, 138), the "primary intention of...Giddens' writings over the past two decades is that of developing an original perspective and framework which constructively reformulates some of the central assumptions of social theory."

That perspective, structuration theory, is a pervasive and significant contribution to social thought because it addresses in a systematic and rigorous way a fundamental issue in social theory, the relationship between structure and agency. Since sociology emerged as a discipline, the debate over this relationship has been ongoing and divisive, leading to divergent streams of thought that remain in opposition; in fact, " 'action' and 'structure' normally appear in both the sociological and philosophical literature as antimonies" (Giddens 1979, 49). John Thompson (1989, 56) finds the "problem of the relationship between...action and social structure...at the heart of social theory" and is critical of most attempts to come to grips with it because it "is not so much resolved as dissolved, that is, disposed of beneath a philosophical and methodological platform that is already located in one of the camps." Also seen as "macro" and "micro," approaches, in isolation, each is "incomplete and indeterminate in complementary ways...micro- and macro-level explanations must therefore be extended in the direction of the other, if they are to be explanations at all" (Bohman 1991, 156). Baber (1991, 220) points to the difficulty of "providing an adequate theoretical account of the relationship...in any explanation of action." This, however, is precisely Giddens' goal, and structuration theory is his version of an adequate theoretical account of the ways in which the actions of individuals are related to structural features of the societies in which they live.

Structuration theory provides a thoroughgoing and complex explanation of the process by which society and social individuals are created and recreated through ongoing and routine social interactions. It is an example of "grand theory," meaning the attempt to "construct a systematic theory of the nature of man and society." (Skinner 1985, 3). Giddens is seeking to carefully describe the main components of the social world: structure, agency, social structures, agents, and social practices. Of primary interest are the "nature of human action, social institutions and the interrelations between actions and institutions" (Giddens 1991, 201). He wants to understand "what their characteristics are, what sorts of things or entities they are, what features they have and what features they don't have" to develop an explanation of the constitution of the social world "in abstract terms so that the conceptual definitions he settled for would encompass all structures and all agents, the very nature of time and space" (Stones 2005, 7). In this sense the main concepts of structuration theory are ontological because they seek the essences of social phenomena, the "nature of social entities over and beyond any particular empirical manifestation of them in specific social circumstances, time and place" (Stones 2005, 7).

Giddens (1979, 5) begins by criticizing voluntarism and determinism, two main theoretical traditions in sociology, for assuming that the relationship between structure and agency is a dualism. In contrast, he (1984, 2) argues, the relationship is a duality where both are implicated in "social practices ordered across time and space" that are "key mediating moments between" structure and agency (Giddens 1979, 5). Here, Giddens effectively sidesteps the problem of attempting to account for structure and agency from determinist or structural perspectives by providing a new starting point—social practices. Then, to develop the theory, Giddens reinterprets key concepts of agency, structure, systems, and social practices, among others.

Giddens' (1984, 2) radical move is to displace both structure and agency with social practices so that "the basic domain of study...is neither the experience of the individual actor nor the existence of any form of social totality, but social practices ordered across space and time." Social practices are at the core of structuration theory because they are "at the root of both the constitution of subject and object" (Giddens 1984, xxii) and "simultaneously constitute society and individual subjects" (Browne 1993, 138).

Giddens (1984, 376) next introduces the "duality of structure," a concept that accounts for the constitution and reproduction of social practices, institutions and individuals and, in a sense, provides the dynamism of structuration, or "the structuring of social relations across time and space." The essential recursiveness of social life is embedded deeply and fundamentally in the ongoing constitution of society because one of the "main propositions of structuration theory is that the rules and resources drawn upon in the production and reproduction of social action are at the same time the means of system reproduction" (Giddens 1984, 19). The duality here is that structure is simultaneously the medium through which social practices are enacted as people interact and the product of these practices. Structures are "constantly recreated out of the very resources which constitute them" (Giddens 1984, xxiii).

Giddens describes three main components of the duality of structure, modalities of structuration that "clarify the main dimensions of the duality of structure in interaction, relating the knowledgeable capacities of agents to structural features" (1984, 28). Signification refers to meaning and communication structures, domination to structures of power and control, and legitimation to norms and sanctions. We routinely draw upon all three modalities as we interact although in different degrees and with different outcomes depending on the context within which and the others with whom we interact.

Structuration theory involves a conception of structure that departs in significant ways from traditional sociological versions. It is composed of rules and resources "recursively implicated in the reproduction of social interaction and social systems" existing only "as time-space presence, only in its instantiations in such practices and memory traces" that orient conduct and action (Giddens 1984, xxxi, 17). It is a "virtual order of relations, out of time and space," instantiated "in the knowledgeable activities of situated human subjects which reproduce them as structural properties of social systems embedded in spans of time space" (304). Rules of social life are "techniques or generalizable procedures applied in the enactment/reproduction of social practices" that are trans-situational allowing a "methodical continuation of an established sequence" (20–21). They can be constitutive, regulative, or equivalent to habit or routine and structure routine social life through the forming, sustaining, termination, and reforming of social interactions. Resources are media through which people can intervene in the word and, with differing degrees of success, effect change. They are "modes whereby transformative relations are actually incorporated into the production and reproduction of social practices" (17) and are deeply implicated in and necessary components of the exercise of power, which Giddens (176) sees as "profoundly embedded" in taken-for-granted conduct and in "routinized behavior." The two main resources are allocative, command over objects, and authoritative, command over people; both are necessary in the generation of power as people invoke or make use of them differentially in different contexts.

From these basic concepts, structuration theory is expanded to account for the constitution of society and the individual. Social systems are sets of social practices that are reproduced in routine interactions and persist because of the continuity of social practices. They are also composed of structural principles that allow "the binding of time-space in social systems, the properties that make it possible for discernibly similar social practices to exist across time and space and which lend them 'systemic' form" (Giddens 1984, 17). The most deeply embedded of these structural principles are involved in structuring "social totalities" which become institutions when the set of social practices gain the "greatest time-space extension" (17). Organizations are "decision-making units" within which people work together using allocative and authoritative resources to manage "discursively mobilized forms of information flow" (203). Wending his way between determinism and voluntarism, Giddens emphasizes the fact that as we routinely interact, the structures, modalities of structuration, social systems, institutions and organizations within and with which we interact are in every circumstance enabling and constraining.

Moving from the structural and institutional level to the individual level of analysis, Giddens' (1984, xxii) actors are knowledgeable about their social worlds, understand a great deal about what they do in their daily lives and "have an inherent capacity to understand what they are doing while they are doing it." The persistence, routinization, and predictability of social life indicate that most people use the modalities of structuration (especially rules and resources) effectively most of the time. Giddens attributes this to our discursive and, more importantly, practical consciousness; the former is what we can say about what we can do and the latter is what we know about what we do that cannot under normal circumstances be expressed. Practical consciousness "is used in the course of interaction without the actor being able to express in words what he or she knows" (49) and "consists of knowing the rules and the tactics whereby daily social life is constituted across time and space" (90).

According to structuration theory, we routinely engage in situated and contextual interactions where we draw upon structural rules and resources and engage in social practices for a wide variety of purposes. Giddens (1982, 109) explains that "according to the idea of the duality of structure, structure is both medium and outcome of the activities whereby actors knowledgeably reproduce social life in the course of daily social encounters." During the course of these interactions, we intentionally and unintentionally reproduce the structures, social systems, institutions, organizations, and modalities of structuration that make these interactions possible. Many features of these interactions are taken for granted and are invoked and reproduced at the level of practical consciousness "enabling and constraining features of the social system already existing" and leaving open the possibility that social structures can "change as a consequence of people's intentional or unintentional actions" (Hardcastle, Usher, and Holmes 2005, 223). The routinization of much of our social interaction and many of our social practices "is of major significance in binding the fleeting encounters to social reproduction and thus to the seeming fixity of institutions" (Giddens 1984, 72); this is in fact how processes of structuration constitute and reconstitute the social world. Giddens (1982) emphasizes the fact that the distinction between macro and micro levels of social reality is purely analytical and that

to group the connections between the vast lateral extension of human social relations on a world scale, on the one hand, and the transformation of the most personal features of "everyday life," on the other, seems to be a necessary task of social theory (108).

Although structuration theory has been imported into many disciplines, there are challenges when researchers use its concepts as the basis for empirical work. One is quite abstract and is described by Giddens (1984, 284) as the "double hermeneutic," a concept that captures a difference between the natural and the social sciences and is a fundamental condition of inquiry into the social world. While both types of inquiry use a hermeneutic method, the natural scientist investigates a world that is indifferent to her inquiry and does not "answer back." In contrast, "social scientists seek to interpret a pre-interpreted world [and] lay members…routinely reincorporate social science concepts and findings beck into the world they were coined to illuminate or explain" (Giddens 1989, 251). The social scientist's insights and findings enter back into the social world and "disappear" as people adopt and adapt these findings into their routines, setting up a hermeneutic cycle of interpretation and reinterpretation. This implies that social science has an important role to play in the constitution of society and the individual by focusing initially on the analysis of recurrent social practices. It also implies that empirical work that makes use of structuration is difficult because social science researchers are already a part of the world being studied and their theories, concepts, and findings "enter directly into what modern institutions are" (Giddens 1991, 207).

A second challenge is more practical and involves the decision about what to use from structuration theory and how to use it. Giddens (1991, 213) has criticized some who have imported his ideas for doing so uncritically, stating "on the whole I like least those works in which authors have attempted to import structuration theory *in toto* into their given area of study…it is not especially helpful to drag in a large apparatus of abstract concepts." Giddens (1989, 294) sees the concepts of structuration theory as "sensitizing devices," echoing Herbert Blumer's (1954) description of the sensitizing concept, which

Gives the user a general sense of reference and guidance in approaching empirical instances. Whereas definitive concepts provide prescriptions of what to see, sensitizing concepts merely suggest directions along which to look (7).

Despite these challenges, scholars in LIS have embraced Giddens' ideas and many have integrated them enthusiastically into their work.

GIDDENS, STRUCTURATION, AND LIS

One way to assess the extent to which Giddens' work has been imported into LIS and to get a sense of how it has been used is to examine the articles that reference his work. This involves gathering and studying the citations found in these articles and evaluating how they are used in context. The online archives of 13 top LIS journals were searched in April and May 2009 for "Giddens," "structuration" and "duality" (see Table 10.1) yielding a set of 72 articles published between 1984 and 2009. Between 1984 and 1999, 24 articles referencing Giddens, his work or others using his work appeared in these journals. Since 2000, 48 articles have been published, indicating that the importation of his ideas is increasing, with 5 journals accounting for 38 (79%) of these articles (JASIST [8], LQ [89], JIS [8], IR [7], and the JDoc [7]).

A total of 114 citations to any of Giddens' works or that were used in conjunction with the words *structuration* and *duality* were gathered from these articles (1.6 citations per article), examined, and coded. If a citation was to a work not written by Giddens, the cited work was examined to determine its relevance. Sixty-nine (61%) of the citations were to works by Giddens with 27 (24%) to *The Constitution of Society* (Giddens 1984), 7 (4%) to *The Consequences of Modernity* (Giddens 1990), and 5 (3%) to *Central Problems in Social Theory* (Giddens 1979). The first and third books provide the basic statements of structuration theory and account for just fewer than 1/3 of all citations to his works. The second book is an influential analysis of modernity and identity.

Table 10.1
Journals used in the analysis

Journal title	# of articles
Journal of the American Society for Information Science and Technology (JASIST)	18
The Library Quarterly (LQ)	13
Journal of Information Science (JIS)	8
Information Research (IR)	8
Journal of Documentation (JDoC)	7
Information Processing & Management	5
Library & Information Science Research	4
Proceedings of Annual Meeting of the American Society for Information Science and Technology	3
The Journal of Academic Librarianship	2
Archives-and-Manuscripts	1
LIBRI	1
Journal of Librarianship and Information Science	1
Library Resources and Technical Services	1
Total	72

The remaining citations are to 16 other books or articles by Giddens or by Giddens and coauthors. Of the 45 (39%) remaining citations, 32 (28%) were to works by Orlikowski and her coauthors (17 citations, 7 articles) and Rosenbaum (15 citations, 2 articles); 13 (11%) citations were to works by 10 other authors.

This analysis indicates that there have been two main sources for the importation of Giddens' work into LIS since 1984, his monographs and the work of Wanda Orlikowski, a management and information systems scholar who introduced structuration into the information systems literature in the 1990s. Specifically, the source materials include 3 of Giddens' books (1979; 1984; 1990), and 8 articles either by Orlikowski (1991; 1992; 2000) or Orlikowski and coauthors (Orlikowski and Robey, 1991; Yates and Orlikowski 1992; Orlikowski and Gash 1994; Orlikowski and Yates 1994; Yates, Orlikowski and Rennecker 1997). Howard Rosenbaum is within LIS so citations to his works (1993; 1996) are examples of indirect importation of theory; he was one of the first in LIS to use structuration theory and subsequent LIS scholars cite his papers as surrogates for Giddens' work.

There many different reasons for citation; Donald Case and Georgeann Higgins (2000, 641) find a wide range of motivations, among them the assertion that the cited work is a classic, a citation provides legitimacy for an citing author's claim, a citation is negative indicating problems in the cited work, and the cited work has broken new ground. However, in this analysis, 54 percent of the citations to Giddens and structuration are simply citing one or another monograph or article without providing a page number or quoting any text from the cited work. These are ceremonial citations, or:

Conventional means of identifying membership within a particular field and simultaneously signaling at the onset of the article the particular orientation and direction of the research. [Their] distinguishing characteristic…is that the authorities are cited rather than the substantive content of their work (Adatto and Cole 1991, 90).

More than half of the citations simply invoked structuration theory and later developments in Giddens' work as support without referencing specific pages of the work. The same pattern was evident with many of the citations to other authors whose works were referenced as surrogates for Giddens. A harsher take on the role of ceremonial citation is offered by Barbara Via and Deborah Schmidle (2007):

> In some cases, an author may cite a well-known authority in the field, without actually reading the cited work, as a means of asserting that the author is staying current with his or her area of studies. This type of citation is referred to as a ceremonial citation (335).

Less cynically, two more substantive motivations for citing are to make use of specific concepts from a theory or to indicate that the author is developing an argument for which the citations provide support. Forty-five citations (39%) are used to refer to specific concepts from structuration theory or Giddens' analysis of modernity that are used in the citing article or are invoked to support the author's argument or theoretical position. The majority of these occurred after 2000, indicating that LIS scholars are beginning to move beyond ceremonial citations to more substantive uses of his ideas. This is an encouraging trend that demonstrates the positive value of one form of theory importation that involves "taking a concept or theory out of its original social and historical context and using it in another to explain the same or a different social or natural phenomenon" (Murray, Evers, and Janda 1995, 92).

A brief chronological summary of selected works shows the breadth of LIS researchers' uses of structuration theory. Reijo Savolainen (1995) uses "practical consciousness" in an analysis of everyday life information seeking. Rosenbaum (1996) uses "structure" to theoretically ground the concept of the managerial information use environment. Paul Solomon (1997) draws on the "recursiveness of social life" to argue that sense making has individual and social moments. Neil Jacobs (2000) uses "social practices" to identify knowledge communities in public policy development. France Bouthillier (2000) uses structuration to understand the systems of meaning that public librarians bring to service provision work. Richard Fyffe (2002) uses "disembedding" to analyze the relationship between scholarly communication and collection development. Rosenbaum (2000) uses a structurational version of the information use environment to analyze electronic commerce firms. Elizabeth Davenport (2002) invokes structuration to support her analysis of mundane knowledge in organizational learning. Marija Dalbello (2004) uses "institutional change" to analyze information transfer in digital libraries. Eaglestone et al. (2004) use structuration to analyze the adoption of information systems. Zahid Hussain, Andrew Taylor, and Donal Flynn (2004) use "legitimation" to analyze the process by which IT managers get stakeholders to support the use of a new information system. Ragnar Audunson (2005) uses structuration to analyze the public library as meeting place. Savolainen (2006) invokes "ontological security" in a discussion of everyday information seeking. Teresa Harrison et al. (2007) use structuration to explain how social actors' innovative uses of geographic information technologies in the days after September 11, 2001. Casper Rasmussen and Henrik Jochumsen (2007) use "modernity" to analyze the current role and status of public libraries. Finally, Savolainen (2007) uses structuration to comment on the relationship between action and structure and analyze social practices.

CONCLUSION

This chapter has argued that the importation of Giddens' ideas into LIS has been useful and productive. After providing an overview of structuration theory, an analysis showed the extent to which Giddens' work has been cited in a sample of the LIS literature. Setting aside ceremonial citations, the two main uses his work are for the purposes of using specific concepts to address issues in several LIS research domains and to invoke the theory and/or specific concepts to provide support for assertions and claims made by the citing authors. The analysis also showed that there were two main sources to which LIS scholars turn when importing Giddens' work, Giddens and Orlikowski (and her coauthors). A third source, from within LIS, is the work of Rosenbaum.

As mentioned above, because of the complexity of structuration theory and its related concepts, its application in empirical work is not a simple matter. Scholars in many different disciplines, however, have drawn upon the theory and have used it to answer a wide variety of research questions. Despite the preponderance of ceremonial citations to Giddens' work in LIS, there are many scholars who are making substantive use of his theory and related concepts to address important questions in the field.

It is clear that Giddens' influence extends into LIS, and a number of researchers are making use of his ideas to study the social contexts of information seeking and use in social and organizational settings ranging from the private and public sectors to public and digital libraries. They are focusing on the implementation and adoption of different genres of information systems, issues of knowledge management, and a wide range of formal and informal information behaviors. The importation of structuration and related concepts into LIS has been increasing since 2000 as more researchers take the sociological turn noticed by Cronin (2008), and the research is addressing interesting questions and yielding valuable findings. One hopes that this trend continues.

REFERENCES

Adatto, Kiku, and Stephen Cole. 1991. "The Functions of Classical Theory in Contemporary Sociological Research: The Case of Max Weber." In *Max Weber: Critical Assessments (Pt. 1),* ed. P. Hamilton. London: Routledge, 80–100.

Audunson, Ragnar. 2005. "The Public Library as Meeting-Place in a Multicultural and Digital Context: The Necessity of Low-Intensive Meeting-Places." *Journal of Documentation* 61 (3): 429–42.

Baber, Zaheer. 1991. "Beyond the Structure/Agency Dualism: An Evaluation of Giddens' theory of Structuration." *Sociological Inquiry* 61 (2): 219–30.

Blumer, Herbert. 1954. "What Is Wrong with Social Theory?" *American Sociological Review* 18:3–10.

Bohman, James. 1991. *New Philosophy of Social Science: Problems of Indeterminacy.* Cambridge: Polity Press.

Bouthillier, France. 2000. "The Meaning of Service: Ambiguities and Dilemmas for Public Library Service Providers." *Library & Information Science Research* 22 (3): 243–72.

Browne, Craig. 1993. "Central Dilemmas in Giddens' Theory of Structuration." *Thesis Eleven* 36: 138–50.

Bryant, Christopher G. A., and Jary, David. 1991. "Introduction: Coming to Terms with Anthony Giddens. In *Giddens' Theory of Structuration: A Critical Appreciation,* ed. Christopher G. A. Bryant and David Jary, 1–31. London and New York: Routledge.

Case, Donald O., and Georgeann M. Higgins. 2000. "How Can We Investigate Citation Behavior? A Study for Citing Literature in Communication." *Journal of the American Society for Information Science* 51 (7): 635–45.

Cronin, Blaise. 2008. "The Sociological Turn in Information Science." *Journal of Information Science* 34 (4): 465–75.

Cronin, Blaise, and Lokman I. Meho. 2008. "The Shifting Balance of Intellectual Trade in Information Studies." *Journal of the American Society for Information Science and Technology* 59 (4): 551–64.

Dalbello, Marija. 2004. "Institutional Shape of Cultural Memory: Digital Library as Environment for Textual Transmission." *Library Quarterly* 74 (3): 265–98.

Davenport, Elizabeth. 2002. "Mundane Knowledge Management and Microlevel Organizational Learning: An Ethological Approach." *Journal of the American Society for Information Science* 53 (12): 108–24.

Day, Ron. 2007. "Kling and the 'Critical' Social Informatics and Critical Informatics." *Journal of the American Society for Information Science and Technology* 58 (4): 575–82.

Dervin, Brenda, and Michael Nilan. 1986. "Information Needs and Uses." In *Annual Review of Information Science and Technology* 21, ed. M. Williams, 3–33. White Plains, NY: Knowledge Industry Publications.

Eaglestone, Barry, Angela Lin, Miguel Baptista Nunes, and Fenio Annansingh. 2003. "Intention and Effect of IS Solutions: Does Risk Management Stifle Creativity?" *Journal of Information Science* 29 (4): 269–78.

Fyffe, Richard. 2002. "Technological Change and the Scholarly Communications Reform Movement: Reflections on Castells and Giddens." *Library Resources and Technical Services* 46:50 61.

Giddens, Anthony. 1979. *Central Problems in Social Theory.* London: Macmillan.

Giddens, Anthony. 1982. "A Reply to My Critics." *Theory Culture Society* 1:107–15.

Giddens, Anthony. 1984. *The Constitution of Society.* Cambridge: Polity Press.

Giddens, Anthony. 1989. "A Reply to My Critics." In *Social Theory of Modern Societies: Anthony Giddens and His Critics,* ed. D. Held and J. B. Thompson, 249–301. Cambridge: Cambridge University Press.

Giddens, Anthony. 1990. *The Consequences of Modernity.* Stanford, CA: Stanford University Press.

Giddens, Anthony. 1991. "Structuration Theory: Past, Present and Future." In *Giddens' Theory of Structuration: A Critical Appreciation,* ed. Christopher Bryant and David Jary, 201–21. London: Routledge.

Hardcastle, Mary-Ann R., Kim J. Usher, and Colin A. Holmes. 2005. "An Overview of Structuration Theory and Its Usefulness for Nursing Research." *Nursing Philosophy* 6:223–34.

Harrison, Teresa M., Theresa A. Pardo, José Ramón Gil-Garcia, Fiona Thompson, and Dubravka Juraga. 2007. "Geographic Information Technologies, Structuration Theory, and the World Trade Center Crisis." *Journal of the American Society for Information Science* 58 (14): 2240–54.

Hussain, Zahid, W. Andrew Taylor, and Donal J. Flynn. (2004). "A Case Study of the Process of Achieving Legitimation in Information Systems Development." *Journal of Information Science* 30 (5): 408–17.

Jacobs, Neil O. 2002. "Co-Term Network Analysis as a Means of Describing the Information Landscapes of Knowledge Communities across Sectors." *Journal of Documentation* 58 (5): 548–62.

Jones, Matthew R., and Helena Karsten. 2008. "Giddens' Structuration Theory and Information Systems Research." *Management Information Systems Quarterly* 32 (1): 127–57.

Kasperson, Lars Bo. 2000. *Anthony Giddens: An Introduction to a Social Theorist.* Malden, MA: Blackwell Publishers.

Murray, Jeff B., Deborah J. Evers, and Swinder Janda. 1995. "Marketing, Theory Borrowing and Critical Reflection." *Journal of Macromarketing* 15:92–106.

Orlikowski, Wanda J. 1991. "Integrated Information Environment or Matrix of Control? The Contradictory Implications of Information Technology." *Accounting, Management, and Information Technology* 1 (1): 4–9.

Orlikowski, Wanda J. 1992. "The Duality of Technology: Rethinking the Concept of Technology in Organizations." *Organization Science* 3 (3): 298–327.

Orlikowski, Wanda J. 2000. "Using Technology and Constituting Structures: A Practice Lens for Studying Technology in Organizations." *Organization Science* 11 (4): 404–28.

Orlikowski, Wanda J., and Debra C. Gash. 1994. "Technological Frames: Making Sense of Information Technology in Organizations." *ACM Transactions on Information Systems* 12: 174–207.

Orlikowski, Wanda J., and Daniel Robey. 1991. "Information Technology and the Structuring of Organizations." *Information Systems Research* 2 (2): 143–69.

Orlikowski, Wanda J., and JoAnne Yates. 1994b. "Genre Repertoire: The Structuring of Communicative Practices in Organizations." *Administrative Science Quarterly* 39:541–74.

Pozzebon, Marlei, and Alain Pinsonneault. 2005. "Challenges in Conducting Empirical Work Using Structuration Theory: Learning from IT Research." *Organization Studies* 26 (9): 1353–76.

Rasmussen, Casper H., and Henrik Jochumsen. 2007. "Problems and Possibilities: The Public Library in the Borderline between Modernity and Late Modernity." *Library Quarterly* 77 (1): 45–59.

Rose, Jeremy. 1998. "Evaluating the Contribution of Structuration Theory to the Information Systems Discipline." In *6th European Conference on Information Systems,* ed. W.R.J. Baets, 910–24. Aix-en-Provence: Euro-Arab Management School.

Rosenbaum, Howard. 1993. "Information Use Environments and Structuration: Towards an Integration of Taylor and Giddens." *Proceedings of the 56th ASIS annual meeting, 1993,* ed. Susan Bonzi, 235–45. Medford, NJ: American Society for Information Science and Learned Information, Inc.

Rosenbaum, Howard. 1996. "Structure and Action: Towards a New Concept of the Information Use Environment." *Proceedings of the 59th Annual Meeting of the American Society for Information Science,* ed. S. Hardin, 152–57. Medford, NJ: Information Today, Inc.

Rosenbaum, Howard. 2000. "The Information Environment of Electronic Commerce: Information Imperatives for the Firm." *Journal of Information Science* 26 (3): 161–71.

Savolainen, Reijo. 1995. "Everyday Life Information Seeking: Approaching Information Seeking in the Context of 'Way of Life.'" *Library & Information Science Research* 17 (3): 259–94.

Savolainen, Reijo. 2006. "Time as a Context for Information Seeking." *Library & Information Science Research* 28 (1): 110–27.

Savolainen, Reijo. 2007. "Information Behavior and Information Practice: Reviewing the 'Umbrella Concepts' of Information-Seeking Studies." *Library Quarterly* 77 (2): 109–32.

Skinner, Quentin, ed. 1985. *The Return of Grand Theory in the Human Sciences.* Cambridge: Cambridge University Press.

Solomon, Paul. 1997. "Discovering Information Behavior in Sense Making. I. Time and Timing." *Journal of the American Society for Information Science* 48 (12): 1097–1108.

Stones, Rob. 2005. *Structuration Theory.* Hampshire, UK: Palgrave McMillan.

Taylor, Robert S. 1986. *Value-Added Processes in Information Systems.* Norwood, NJ: Ablex.

Thompson, John. 1989. "Theories of Structuration." In *Social Theory of Modern Societies: Anthony Giddens and His Critics,* ed. D. Held and J. Thompson, 56–75. Cambridge: Cambridge University Press.

Via, Barbara J., and Deborah J. Schmidle. 2007. "Investing Wisely: Citation Rankings as a Measure of Quality in Library and Information Science Journals." *Portal: Libraries and the Academy* 7 (3): 333–73.

Yates, JoAnne, and Wanda J. Orlikowski. 1992. "Genres of Organizational Communication: A Structurational Approach to Studying Communication and Media." *Academy of Management Review* 17 (2): 299–326.

Yates, JoAnne, Wanda J. Orlikowski, and Julie Rennecker. 1997. "Collaborative Genres for Collaboration: Genre Systems in Digital Media." In *Proceedings of the Thirtieth Hawaii International Conference on System Sciences (HICSS-30) (vol. VI). Digital Documents Track,* 50–59. Los Alamitos, CA: IEEE Computer Society Press.

11

The Public Library as a Space for Democratic Empowerment: Henry Giroux, Radical Democracy, and Border Pedagogy

Mustafa Yunus Eryaman
Canakkale Onsekiz Mart University, Turkey

A BIOGRAPHY OF HENRY GIROUX

Henry Giroux, born September 18, 1943, in Providence, Rhode Island, is one of the leading theorists and educators associated with the Critical Theory tradition in education. He began his teaching career as a history teacher at a local secondary school in Barrington, Rhode Island. He earned his doctorate at Carnegie-Mellon University in Pittsburgh, Pennsylvania in 1977. Giroux then became an education professor at Boston University. In 1983, he took the position of professor of education at Miami University in Oxford, Ohio where he also served as director at the Center for Education and Cultural Studies. In 1992, Giroux took up the Waterbury Chair Professorship at Penn State University, also serving as the director of the Waterbury Forum in Education and Cultural Studies. In 2005, Henry Giroux was appointed as the Global Television Network Chair in Communications in the Faculty of Humanities at McMaster University in Canada.

Whereas the early work of leading critical pedagogy scholar Henry Giroux focused on the development of a critical pedagogy for radical democracy, by the early 1990s Giroux's theoretical orientation had shifted toward postmodern, feminist, and postcolonial theories to better address such issues as gender, race, ethnicity, and sexual orientation (Giroux 1991; Giroux and McLaren 1992). This shift incorporated the theoretical discourses of poststructuralism and postmodernism, cultural studies, and the politics of identity and difference. Although Giroux (1993) criticizes several elements of modernity, such as the emphasis on universality and the unified subject, because they "represent the worst legacies of the Enlightenment tradition" (39), he defends modernist elements like democracy, liberation, and social justice because they contribute to democratization and equality. Most particularly, Giroux explains postmodernism in relation to the recovery of modernism; therefore, his theory demonstrates the rich interplay between modernist concepts and postmodern possibilities.

More recently, Giroux (2003) generated an interdisciplinary approach to education theory that crosses the boundaries of disciplines like education, cultural studies, media studies, and social theory. As part of this border pedagogy, Giroux (1993) developed "border politics" in which individuals cross the barriers that divide them and struggle together to fight against domination and promote social change. Hence, Giroux's theoretical concepts (Giroux 1991; Giroux and McLaren 1992), which share similarities with those of Paulo Freire, are framed by the experiences, politics, and cultures of the postmodern information age.

HENRY GIROUX, RADICAL DEMOCRACY, AND BORDER PEDAGOGY

Democratic citizenship, the development of a public identity and the availability of opportunities to perform that identity in collective democratic processes, is an important concept in a participatory democracy whose members see themselves as creators of the public world and active agents of society. From this perspective, marginalization is that which limits the ability of citizens to become public actors engaged in the process of contributing to and making a difference in society. Such marginalization is linked to oppression, which Freire (1972) defined as the denial of an individual or group's capacity to be "self-defining subjects creating history and culture" (Glass 2001, 16). Hence, the main responsibility of a participatory democracy is to empower individuals and underrepresented communities by removing social, cultural, and institutional barriers and strengthening these communities' capacity to see themselves as actors in the process of co-creating democracy.

Although public institutions, including schools, museums, and libraries, can play an important role in this process of democratic transformation and participation, today's schools and libraries cannot be seen as totally successful in providing opportunities for disadvantaged groups and communities. Rather, these public institutions legitimize and promote the class, gender, and race roles that constitute neoliberal capitalism and its inequities. Thus, Henry Giroux (1993), arguing that political and economic power is unequally and unjustly distributed in capitalist society, claims that public pedagogy results from a neoliberalist, market-driven discourse that provides the greatest benefits to powerful social groups. Nonetheless, although such promotion and legitimization has traditionally been the central role for schools, museums, and libraries, many factors—including democratization of knowledge production and dissemination, the emphasis on community empowerment, and the move toward collaborative and transformative notions of teaching and learning—have prompted libraries to move beyond this traditional role (Wisner, 2000; Bruce and Kapitzke 2006; Bruce 2008).

One useful framework for examining this shift is Giroux's theory of radical democracy and its major tenet of border pedagogy, which, in contrast to more traditional library approaches, identifies schools and libraries as institutions that deconstruct the ongoing regime of cultural dominance and its hegemonic structures of regulation and control. Such pedagogy thereby gives voice to the needs and expectations of unrepresented minority groups and local communities. After first outlining the tenets of Giroux's theory as they apply to library education, I discuss the role that border pedagogy can play in addressing issues of democratic participation and community empowerment in public libraries. Specifically, I argue that libraries have the potential to develop into transformative spaces for empowering communities through local knowledge production—the "language of possibility" (Giroux 1993) that provides a sense of vision, a movement toward a more democratic future. I conclude with a discussion of the outcomes and purpose of developing a theoretical and practical framework of border pedagogy for library education.

REDEFINING PUBLIC LIBRARIES IN A RADICAL DEMOCRACY: THE ROLE OF BORDER PEDAGOGY

Information and communication technologies (ICTs)—whose changing forms affect the ways that all people, including librarians, create, collect, organize, store, analyze, distribute, send, and use information—are becoming an essential part of Library and Information Science (LIS). The challenge of such widespread use of ICTs, however, resides in the availability and openness of discourses that create knowledge and serve as sites of power relations. Not only can information be produced and distributed widely, but such distribution can break down metanarratives or create new ones depending on the power relations involved. As Giroux (2002) points out, in the presence of ICTs, power takes new shapes that can be displayed and enacted across borders. Such distribution can in turn result in a solidification of hegemonies, with power networks connecting across borders to endorse modernist values.

Unequal distribution of power and information, in contrast, is a major result of social isolation, inequality, and marginalization. It also plays an important role in determining the democratic experiences, beliefs, and competencies of disadvantaged groups. Thus, Ginwright et al. (2006) argue that the political, economic, and social conditions of disadvantaged groups in urban areas "severely limit the full civic participation of urban youth," meaning that "urban youth's actions cannot be understood in isolation from these factors" (25). Racial, ethnic, and socioeconomic factors further complicate the processes that isolate disadvantaged groups from public participation: "[p]owerful signals...about their value, social legitimacy, and future" often marginalize young people of color, many of whom respond by "distrusting the possibility or desirability of ever becoming part of the broader society" (McLaughlin 1993, 43). For instance, levels of political efficacy and trust among both African American and Latino youth have declined since the late 1960s, when the levels among white and African American youth were similar (Flanagan and Faison 2001). Because this lack of trust frequently extends to public institutions, libraries should promote inclusion and participation in the context of disparities in information infrastructure and dissemination and knowledge generation and management. According to scholars that link trust to participation (Cohen 1999; Warren 1999), these low levels of trust and efficacy among youth of color do not bode well for their civic participation or power. Indeed, a summary of the findings of five surveys on youth participation nationally revealed that minority groups not only had the lowest levels of community involvement but such involvement showed a 10 percent *decrease* from that recorded only a few years earlier (Pittman et al. 2000). These general patterns also held in studies of disadvantaged youth—a group that cuts across racial and ethnic categories (Flanagan and Faison 2001). As regards the reasons for low public involvement among urban youth, research points to both the "non-inclusion and discrimination" experienced by youth of color and youth of lower socioeconomic backgrounds (Conover and Searing 2000). Likewise, in high-poverty urban areas, unequal access to information and technologies at libraries and other public institutions that could provide participatory opportunities results in fewer chances for civic engagement (Hart and Atkins 2002).

Whereas the use of ICTs in libraries, homes, and schools continues to increase among a majority of the population, the groups most affected by the digital divide are those having racial minority and low-income family status (Chisholm and Carey 2002; First and Hart 2002). For example, African American and Hispanic children in the United States (approximately 19% and 16% of the population, respectively) use computers and the Internet at a much lower rate than whites (Swain and Pearson 2003). Low-income families face a similar difficulty. Whereas few students in households with annual incomes equivalent to $35,000 or less have home computers and the Internet at their disposal (20%), most students living in households with annual incomes of $75,000 or more (80%) have computers, the Internet, and a variety of ICTs available for personal use (Lamar 2001). The implications of these statistics are considerable given that some research has identified a direct relationship among children between computer literacy and higher test scores in reading, math, and science (Chisholm and Carey 2002).

As a result, several researchers (van Dijk 2000; Bonfadelli 2002; van Dijk and Hacker, 2003; Jerit et al. 2006; Hargittai and Hinnant 2008) support the position that because of unique characteristics, new communication technologies worsen, rather than close, the existing information gap. Moreover, with the rapid development of new media technologies comes a growing necessity not only for technological skills but for new competencies such as assessing source reliability, searching information purposefully, and interpreting information meaningfully (Bonfadelli 2002; van Dijk and Hacker 2003; Hargittai and Hinnant 2008). It thus seems likely that relevant skills for using new media in meaningful ways are also unevenly distributed across different sections of the population and may create additional differences among user groups, perhaps reinforcing information disparities.

Libraries can play an important role in overcoming this digital divide by promoting the inclusion and participation of disadvantaged groups in the democratic system. At the same time, librarians can teach critical literacy skills to youth of color and of lower socioeconomic backgrounds to help them solve their problems and create alternatives to oppressive situations. Nonetheless, both librarians and educators are faced with the task of responding to the postmodern sensibilities of the information revolution and contemporary material conditions by generating pedagogies that engage students of color and support their active participation in the democratic process.

BORDER PEDAGOGY AND TRANSFORMATIVE LIBRARIES

As the United States, and indeed the world, becomes an ever more pluralistic society, it is increasingly important to understand the complex ways in which democracy works and can become more inclusive. In addressing these issues, Giroux (2002) argues that a radical democracy indicates the need for transformative learning spaces in which disadvantaged groups can gain a sense of themselves as public actors while developing connections to the broader world. Indeed, public libraries as alternative spaces for democratic education and development may be critical to initiating and sustaining public action and social change. That is, public libraries as alternative spaces can become protected spaces in which members of disadvantaged groups can work together—formal and informally—to develop new ideas and creative solutions to collective problems.

Hence, the link between internal participation in a transformative library and action in the broader public realm may be even more important for the disadvantaged because it can provide both providing the impetus for their participation and engender change in the institutional structures that impede their active involvement in the public realm. Connecting alternative library spaces with public action, therefore, becomes the critical mechanism for gaining political relevance, as well as an important first step toward broadening the voices and actors involved in democratic decision-making. In this way, transformative libraries become central to a radical democratic framework.

Giroux's border pedagogy can also play an important role in helping librarians turn libraries into transformative spaces that can assist disadvantaged groups to fully participate in the democratic processes of their societies. Indeed, in his book *Border Crossings,* Giroux (1993) emphasizes the importance, especially in the United States, of border pedagogy as a support for radical democracy:

[A] number of polls indicate that while the youth of Poland, Czechoslovakia, and Germany are extending the frontiers of democracy, American youth are both unconcerned and largely ill-prepared to struggle for and keep democracy alive in the twenty-first century. Rather than being a model of democracy, the United States has become indifferent to the need to struggle for the conditions that make democracy a substantive rather than a lifeless activity (72).

He also links border pedagogy to radical democratic politics in which both teacher and student become agents of transformative change. More specifically, for Giroux, borders that have been created using master narratives must be challengeable and students themselves must become "border crossers" as a means of comprehending alterity. There is also a need for radical pedagogical conditions that "allow students to write, speak, and listen in a language in [which]...meaning becomes multiaccentual and dispersed and resists permanent closure. This is a language in which one speaks with rather than exclusively for others" (Giroux 2002, 29).

Giroux (2003) further suggests that by combining both a modernist approach of reasoned analysis of public life with a postmodernist concern for difference, border pedagogy becomes both transformative and emancipatory. He thus proposes the use of partiality as a basis for recognizing the limitations inherent in all discourses and particularly those "that deny gaps, limits, specificity, and counter-narratives" (Giroux 1993, 29). In this context, students need to learn different cultural codes, experiences, and languages; they need to be challenged through text, according to their "level of schooling," about the complexities of their own histories (30). However, because he sees partiality as a postmodernist rejection of master narratives and grand totalizing discourses, he proposes the specific, the particular, the local, the quotidian that helps articulate the Other and portray the changing limits of the border. Indeed, in his earlier work, Giroux (1993) argues that a border pedagogy would not be a totalizing one but would allow for the reading of different texts, both dominant and subordinate, from the points of view of different audiences. Such a pedagogy would thus take up issues of production, audience, address, and reception. From this perspective, the use of texts that originate in popular culture would not only provide easier textual access for students but would also assist them to define and identify the codes and limits of the dominant culture (Giroux 1993, 2003). Such an approach is inherently postmodern: border pedagogy takes popular culture seriously and thereby confirms the importance of minority culture (Giroux 1993).

TRANSFORMATIVE LIBRARIES FOR COMMUNITY EMPOWERMENT

Within the framework of border pedagogy, public libraries can be identified as "pedagogical cultural borderlands" because they contain subordinate cultures that disturb and permeate the dominant, supposedly homogeneous, culture (Giroux 1993, 26). Hence, border pedagogy envisions libraries as transformative sites in which librarians, like students, should become border crossers, not only to assist in the articulation of Otherness but also as a means of their own reconstruction. Librarians cannot, however, fully represent the Other and must listen to Other voices within the learning environment. Moreover, librarians' own narratives must be situated and examined as discourses that are open, partial, and subject to ongoing debate and revision. Hence, the librarian as transformative intellectual sides with the oppressed and takes part in the learning process in order to help society. Accordingly, transformative libraries are institutions of radical democracy in which

students can learn about the limits of commercial values, address what it means to learn the skills of social citizenship, and learn how to deepen and expand the possibilities of collective agency and democratic life. Defending education at all levels of learning as a vital public sphere and public good rather than merely a private good is necessary to develop and nourish the proper balance between democratic public spheres and commercial power, between identities founded on democratic principles and identities steeped in forms of competitive, self-interested individualism that celebrate selfishness, profit making, and greed (Giroux 1993, 4).

Transformative libraries, then, can provide democratic spaces, what Evans and Boyte (1993) term "free spaces," in which young people can meet, talk about their problems and experiences, reflect on their rights, and work to create change in their communities. Such free spaces, typically community-based public places like voluntary and participatory organizations, allow disadvantaged people—women, people of color, workers' groups, sexual or ethnic minorities, urban youth—to "learn a new self-respect, a deeper and more assertive group identity, public skills, and values of cooperation and civic virtue" (17). Located between private lives and large-scale institutions, these settings provide the conceptual and physical space within which ordinary people can come together to engage in democratic action, to "critique what is, shelter themselves from what has been, redesign what might be, and/or imagine what could be" (Fine et al. 2000, 67).

For individuals, having a space of their own can contribute to a sense of agency and control over the world around. Thus, transformative libraries, grounded in community, can create a bridge for youth between their local experiences and the broader society. As the social, political, and economic contexts surrounding disadvantaged youth contribute to their marginalization as democratic actors, a transformative library can represent a space within which they can work to effect changes in those contexts. Hence, transformative libraries can offer youth experiences in "public work" (Bass 1997), help them establish "public relationships" (Lappe 1998), and involve them in "small group" democracies in which they learn to deal constructively with the inevitable frustrations of working together. In addition, transformative libraries that provide a strategic and systematic focus on democratic education can help youth understand the root causes of problems and work to shape and implement solutions to them. Transformative libraries, then, have the potential to provide youth with opportunities for real and meaningful involvement in the public realm as they simultaneously learn democratic skills and concepts. Indeed, research provides ample evidence that young people engaged in participatory community-based projects to improve their lives and the lives of their communities become catalysts for community action (Boyte and Skelton 1997; Hart and Schwab 1997; Tolman and Pittman 2001). As a result, youth work has shifted its emphasis, pointing to the importance of involving the young in full participation and real problem solving (Pittman et al. 2000). Hence, through democratic participation in transformative libraries, youth can address such issues as economic development, environmental concerns, justice and health.

Researchers have also pinpointed several key factors of this dynamic. For example, in discussing the importance of public libraries for the development of democracy and democratic participation, Byrne (1999) identifies the freedom of access to information and freedom of expression as "fundamental human rights which are vital cornerstones of the mission of libraries to be gateways to knowledge in support of human rights, peace, democracy and development" (3). Likewise, while analyzing the progress in the democratization of library and information services during the post-apartheid era in South Africa, More (2004) suggests that as agents of democracy, librarians should do the following:

- *Assist in creating an informed nation:* Librarians as agents of democracy should prepare citizens for political participation and dialogue, and can make libraries accessible for public engagements in which people can share similar interests and concerns;
- *Offer training:* Besides providing access to information, they should offer information literacy education and assist individuals to identify and evaluate information essential to making decisions that affect the way they live, work, and govern themselves;
- *Bridge the digital divide:* Librarians should make information equity a priority and lobby the government to ensure that all schools and public libraries have electronic access to information;
- *Manage change:* Librarians must embrace change and use it as an opportunity for growth and progress. They should therefore work hand in hand with their governments to initiate initiatives like the national virtual library and resourceful public centers and information services;
- *Promote intellectual freedom:* Librarians are exclusively qualified to endorse intellectual freedom and fight censorship. They should speak up against censorship and repudiate to remove material from their libraries on grounds of ideological or religious perspectives;
- *Conduct advocacy:* Librarians should lobby the government agencies through their library associations to ensure that all communities and schools have access to a library or information resource center. Because libraries are also agents of democracy, they should encourage government to treat them as partners;
- *Provide open access to libraries:* Librarians should open their libraries to everybody irrespective of race, age, gender, religion, or political views, and assume a professional neutrality to ensure that their services are free of interference from their personal beliefs or opinions;
- *Promote a culture of reading:* Librarians should be innovative and build a culture of a reading nation. Hence, "born to read" initiatives should be extended to rural areas, libraries should become "places of healing," and their collections should inspire hope for the future;

- *Build balanced collections:* Librarians can support democracy by building balanced library collections on diverse subject matter to meet diverse needs. They can also foster and encourage open discussion and unrestricted debate, and contribute to preserving cultural heritage;
- *Support research:* Academic and special librarians can support research by facilitating its retrieval and use (5–7).

Although More also explores the challenges faced by librarians—including inadequate funding, facilities, and infrastructure; libraries not being seen as priorities; and a lack of professional training in promoting democracy—she argues that the librarian's primary role and responsibility in a transformative library

touches on the core of librarianship. Librarians are uniquely qualified and placed to promote intellectual freedom and fight censorship. It takes noble, courageous, committed librarians...to function as agents of democracy. It involves standing up and campaigning for the right to read, hear and view. It will sometimes mean challenging the government to protect the principles of democracy namely, "the right to freedom of expression...freedom to hold opinions without interference...And freedom to seek, receive and impart ideas through any media regardless of frontiers....This is the ideal librarians should stand for. (9).

CONCLUSION

One fundamental component of deliberative democracy is the communicative space within which deliberation occurs. The concept of the transformative library as a communicative space for democratic action is particularly important because it addresses how potential learning spaces might function for disadvantaged communities. Such settings, because they allow for creative public action, are not simply instrumental or a means to an end; rather, they are constitutive of a vibrant, flourishing democracy (Evans and Boyte 1993; Putnam 2000). Hence, understanding these spaces and the experiences of disadvantaged communities within them is crucial to gaining a greater sense of how people become active citizens who create and sustain democracy.

This view of democracy and citizenship demands a framework that makes transparent the processes by which disadvantaged communities can—or cannot—be creative democratic agents in both local communities and the broader world. Giroux's border pedagogy provides such a framework for examining the possibilities for societal change toward particular values of radical democracy—equity, justice, and freedom—through transformative libraries. Although it does not explain how to succeed within the existing system, it does explain how the current system came to be and points out its weaknesses in order to propose change. Above all, border pedagogy reveals how material systems are reinforced and legitimized by ideology (values, beliefs, norms, and mores) that is unconsciously accepted as the inevitable status quo by a majority of those involved. It also focuses on successful resistance to oppressive aspects of a society by asking following questions that merit further examination: Why do people and disadvantaged groups resist? What are the forms of this resistance? What is the difference between simple oppositional behavior and transformative resistance? It should also be noted that Giroux distinguishes between a resistance that is self-defeating and disempowering and maintains inequitable and unjust aspects of the status quo, on the one hand, and on the other, resistance that is powerful and effective in transforming public institutions into social institutions that promote connections to transformative knowledge, to learners, and to a community.

Giroux's notion of border pedagogy further sets out a new paradigm of information professionalism and multiple information literacies for the new information age in LIS research. The new paradigm replaces the traditional relationship by which individuals are dependent on, and obedient to, the structures of institutions and professions with postmodern transformative libraries and multiple information literacies working through conversation rather than instruction: co-creation between learners and teachers, rather than delivery; mutual support and critical engagement among learners and library professionals. New professional action and multiple literacies in LIS research grow from practical collaboration between professionals, researchers, and members of the public. The information professionalism is not only about delivering a service, it is about encouraging individuals to acquire the critical literacy skills to understand their lives more effectively. The new professionalism in LIS research emphasizes a positive approach to change, the ability to work in a multidisciplinary environment, a willingness to take personal responsibility for conversation, and an enabling and collaborative approach to working with learners.

Giroux's (2006) multiple information literacies recognize the importance of cultural, social, political, and religious diversities present in our society. By addressing issues of ideology, culture, knowledge, and power, learners identify both the value and the limitations of information literacy skills as they become aware of politics of information and evidence and learn to view information from a critical stance. With the library information literacies and library research, learners and learning communities can be empowered to critically analyze new electronic technologies that shape everyday life through popular media, television, and movies. The multiple information literacies in libraries promote the notion of critical reflexivity not only through the product of ability of detecting biased information, but also how to construct new media as a critical voice to the various information ideologies learners are bombarded with. The literacies combine notions of power, technology, and human relations in new ways allowing for learners, library professionals, and researchers to contextualize and reconfigure media into a self-created identity as social exchange.

Transformative libraries with the multiple information literacies engaged in border pedagogy can involve learners in powerful, participatory democratic experiences that they too rarely encounter in other settings. Border pedagogy in general, being aimed at understanding and transforming students' lives and communities, can help learners critique the ways in which their identities have been constructed by educational and cultural institutions. Transformative library pedagogy specifically must be truly democratic; that is, both librarians and learners must practice democracy and solve problems collectively. Hence, democratic libraries must equalize opportunities for individual self-fulfillment while simultaneously discovering and attending to the collective will. To achieve these ends, library pedagogy must draw on the resources that students bring to the library—their experiences, their language, their values, their hopes. Collective inquiry can in turn uncover the historical origins of particular problems faced by local communities, thereby facilitating the understanding that Freire (1972) terms *conscientization*—the consciousness of identity and its origins.

REFERENCES

Bass, M. 1997. "Citizenship and Young People's Role in Public Life." *National Civic Review* 86 (3): 203–10.

Bonfadelli, H. 2002. "The Internet and Knowledge Gaps: A Theoretical and Empirical Investigation." *European Journal of Communication* 17 (1): 65–84.

Boyte, H. C., and N. Skelton. 1997. "The Legacy of Public Work: Educating for Citizenship." *Educational Leadership* 54 (4): 12–17.

Bruce, Bertram C. 2008. "From Hull House to Paseo Boricua: The Theory and Practice of Community Inquiry." In *Philosophy of Pragmatism (II): Salient Inquiries,* ed. B. Dicher and A. Ludusan 181–98. Cluj-Napoca, Romania: Editura Fundatiei pentru Studii Europene (European Studies Foundation Publishing House).

Bruce, Bertram, and Cushla Kapitzke. 2006. *Libraries: Changing Information Space and Practice.* Mahwah, NJ: Lawrence Erlbaum.

Byrne, Alex. 1999. "Libraries and Democracies." Keynote address delivered at the *Seminar on Libraries and Democracy,* Stockholm, November 4. Available at http://archive.ifla.org/faife/papers/others/byrne3.htm. Accessed June 9, 2009.

Chisholm, I. M., and J. Carey. 2002. "Information Technology Skills for a Pluralistic Society: Is the Playing Field Level?" *Journal of Research on Technology in Education* 35 (1): 58–79.

Cohen, Jean. 1999. "Trust, Voluntary Association and Workable Democracy: The Contemporary American Discourse on Civil Society." In *Democracy and Trust,* ed. M. E. Warren, 208–48. Cambridge: Cambridge University Press.

Conover, Pamela J., and Donald D. Searing, 2000. "A Political Socialization Perspective." In *Rediscovering the Democratic Purposes of Education,* ed. L. M. McDonnell, P. M. Timpane, and R. Benjamin 91–124. Lawrence: University Press of Kansas.

Evans, Sara M., and Harry C. Boyte. 1993. *Free Spaces: The Sources of Democratic Change in America.* Chicago: University of Chicago Press.

Fine, M., L. Weis, C. Centrie, and R. Roberts. 2000. "Education Beyond the Borders of Schooling." *Anthropology and Education Quarterly* 31 (2): 131–51.

First, P. F., and Y. Y. Hart. 2002. "Access to Cyberspace: The New Issue in Educational Justice." *Journal of Law and Education* 31 (4): 385–411.

Flanagan, C. A., and N. Faison. 2001. "Youth Civic Development: Implications of Research for Social Policy and Programs." *Social Policy Report: Giving Child and Youth Development Knowledge Away* 15 (1): 1–15.

Freire, Paulo. 1972. *Pedagogy of the Oppressed.* Harmondsworth, UK: Penguin.

Ginwright, Shawn, Pedro Noguera, and Julio Cammarota, eds. 2006. *Beyond Resistance! Youth Activism and Community Change: New Democratic Possibilities for Practice and Policy for America's Youth.* New York: Routledge.

Giroux, Henry A. 1991. "Modernism, Postmodernism, and Feminism: Rethinking the Boundaries of Educational Discourse." In *Postmodernism, Feminism, and Cultural Politics: Redrawing Educational Boundaries,* ed. H. A. Giroux, 183–96. New York: SUNY State University of New York.

Giroux, Henry A. 1993. *Border Crossings: Cultural Workers and the Politics of Education.* New York: Routledge.

Giroux, Henry A. 2002. *Public Spaces, Private Lives: Beyond the Culture of Cynicism.* Lanham, MD: Rowman and Littlefield Publishers.

Giroux, Henry A. 2003. "Public Pedagogy and the Politics of Resistance: Notes on a Critical Theory of Educational Struggle." *Educational Philosophy and Theory* 35 (1): 5–16.

Giroux, Henry A. 2006. *America on the Edge: Henry Giroux on Politics, Culture, and Education.* Palgrave: New York.

Giroux, Henry A., and Peter McLaren. 1992. "Writing from the Margins: Geographies of Identity, Pedagogy, and Power." *Journal of Education* 174 (1): 7–30.

Glass, R. D. 2001. "On Paulo Freire's Philosophy of Praxis and the Foundations of Liberation Education." *Educational Researcher* 30 (2): 15–25.

Hargittai, E., and A. Hinnant. 2008. "Digital Inequality: Differences in Young Adults' Use of the Internet." *Communication Research* 35 (5): 602–21.

Hart, D., and R. Atkins. 2002. "Civil Competence in Urban Youth." *Applied Developmental Science* 6 (4): 227–36.

Hart, R., and M. Schwab. 1997. "Children's Rights and the Building of Democracy: A Dialogue on the International Movement for Children's Participation." *Social Justice* 24 (3): 177–91.

Jerit, J., J. Barabas, and T. Bolsen. 2006. "Citizens, Knowledge, and the Information Environment." *American Journal of Political Science* 50 (2): 266–82.

Lamar, N. G. 2001. "New Jersey's Solution to the Digital Divide." *T.H.E. Journal* 29 (20): 66–71.

Lappe, F. M. 1998. "Educating for Democracy." *New Designs for Youth Development* 14 (3): 21–25.

McLaughlin, Milbrey W. 1993. "Embedded Identities: Enabling Balance in Urban Contexts." In *Identity and Inner-city Youth: Beyond Ethnicity and Gender,* ed. S. B. Heath and M. W. McLaughlin, 36–68. New York: Teachers College.

More, Rachel. 2004. "Librarians as Agents of Democracy." Paper presented at the Seventh Annual Conference of the Library Information Association of South Africa (LIASA), Pholokwane, South Africa, September 27–October 1.

Pittman, Karen, Thaddeus Ferber, and Merita Irby. 2000. *Youth as Effective Citizens.* Takoma Park, MD: International Youth Foundation–U.S.

Putnam, Robert. 2000. *Bowling Alone: The Collapse and Revival of American Community.* New York: Simon and Schuster.

Swain, C., and T. Pearson. 2003. "Educators and Technology Standards: Influencing the Digital Divide." *Journal of Research on Technology in Education* 34 (3): 326–35.

Tolman, J., and K. Pittman. 2001. *Youth Acts, Community Impacts: Stories of Youth Engagement with Real Results.* Vol. 7. Takoma Park, MD: The Forum for Youth Investment, International Youth Foundation.

van Dijk, Jan. 2000. "Widening Information Gap and Policies of Prevention." In *Digital Democracy,* ed. K. Hacker and J. van Dijk, 166–83. London: Sage.

van Dijk, Jan, and K. Hacker. 2003. "The Digital Divide as a Complex and Dynamic Phenomenon. *Information Society* 19 (4): 315–26.

Warren, Mark E., ed. 1999. *Democracy and Trust.* Cambridge: Cambridge University.

Wisner, William. 2000. *Whither the Postmodern Library? Libraries, Technology, and Education in the Information Age.* Jefferson, NC: McFarland.

12

Hegemony, Historic Blocs, and Capitalism: Antonio Gramsci in Library and Information Science

Douglas Raber
Ferndale Public Library, USA

INTRODUCTION

Of the critical social theorists profiled in this book, only a handful have actually participated in direct political action or party work to change a regime or social order. One can make a case that of the group only Freire and Gramsci were primarily political actors whose theory was derived from the laboratory of informed political practice rather than observation. Perhaps Gramsci is unique in that his practice was conducted and his theory formed completely outside of the established political order. In fact, Antonio Gramsci wrote the main body of his theory not in an office on a university campus but in a prison cell where he was held by Mussolini's Fascist state for his role as a revolutionary and head of the Italian Communist Party (PCI) from 1924 to 1926. Throughout *The Prison Notebooks*, Gramsci (1992, 1975) refers to Marxism as the "the philosophy of praxis" in order to confuse his guards and disguise his purpose. He was afraid that otherwise he might be denied writing materials.

Born in Sardinia in 1891, Gramsci came of age in Turin, one of the points of what later became known in Italy as the Red Triangle (Turin, Milan, and Genoa, Italy). He was actively engaged in the prewar European socialist movement, joining the Italian Socialist Party in 1913. By 1914 he was writing for socialist newspapers and earning a reputation as an effective political journalist. Even at this early stage of his writing Gramsci (1977) displayed the creativity that characterized his integration of theory and practice. His writing took a Leninist direction in the journal *L'Ordine Nuovo* and he was instrumental in the 1921 founding of the Italian Communist Party, which allied itself with the Communist International (Comintern) established by Lenin's Bolsheviks in Moscow two years earlier. In a way, Gramsci can be regarded as an incidental theorist. Even in prison, Gramsci did not intend his writing to be an abstract reflection on political problems but as a direct and practical guide to the hopelessly disorganized Italian left specifically and to Western European revolutionary practice in general.

Gramsci's philosophy of praxis, however scattered it may be across so many different texts written for so many different purposes, offers a surprisingly coherent understanding of how modern capitalism works. His work provides a profound reinterpretation of the relationship between the Marxist concepts of base and superstructure and allows new insights into the relations between the material conditions of human existence and human consciousness as aspects of human history.

GRAMSCI'S MARXISM

Gramsci's Marxism begins with the notions that human being and history are products of human labor, and that human nature is not a fixed quality. The production and reproduction of life, value, and culture constitutes the material foundation for human existence, and all are aspects of the complex of social relations that constitute human nature as phenomenon of "'becoming' (man 'becomes', he changes continuously with the changing of social relations)" (Gramsci 1971, 355). The social relations of production that organize human labor constitute the economic *structure* or *base*. The relations of production are the material conditions under which life is produced and reproduced and they have personal consequences for individuals. Their nature plays a dominant role in determining life outcomes, or as Laswell (1990) put it so well, who gets what, when, and how.

One's relationship to the means of production plays a dominant role in determining one's life possibilities. In capitalist societies, life possibilities depend crucially on whether one is an owner of the means of production or sells one's labor for wages. Class, if not class consciousness, is an objective historical phenomenon related to private property and its ownership. Industrial capitalist societies are characterized by the historical dominance of relations of production by the *bourgeoisie,* the industrial property owning class, and the subordination of the *proletariat,* a class constituted by working men and women who are compelled for their survival to sell their labor, and in effect their lives, to the bourgeoisie at exploitative terms. This relation allows the bourgeoisie to extract *surplus labor* from the proletariat. The proletariat produces greater value than it consumes to sustain its life, and the bourgeoisie appropriates this surplus as private property, a privilege of ownership of the means of production.

Even Marx recognized that by the late 19th century the division of labor within capitalism had created a diversity of different classes whose members bear different kinds of relationships to the means of production. These classes include but are not limited to small business owners, professionals, landowners, and agricultural workers. Their relationship to the means of production can be ambiguous and their actual nature, relative size and influence, and role in organizing a particular society depend upon historical conditions unique to that society. The position of the bourgeoisie as the capital owning class, however, is dominant and the relations of production between the bourgeoisie and other classes are structured by the bourgeoisie to favor its interests and ends as a ruling class. This condition constitutes the essential injustice of capitalist societies. Value is created by the many and appropriated by the few for their private benefit. The final contradiction that drives the history and politics of capitalist societies is the contradiction between the social nature of the production of value, and life, and the nature of its appropriation, control, and use as private property. This contradiction is the source of both the economic crises and social problems that plague capitalist societies.

Relations of production between classes, the economic base, provides the foundation for the social organization of particular capitalist societies and gives rise to particular and unique *superstructures* in particular places and at particular points in human history (Gramsci 1971, 55–90). The superstructure consists of social, political, and cultural practices through which the ruling class exercises its control over society as whole. It includes not only the state and its associated juridical and coercive institutions, but also the social and cultural institutions and practices typically associated with the idea of civil society, including churches, schools, news and entertainment media, social organizations, and libraries. Its role is twofold: to secure the historical reproduction of capitalist relations of production and to reduce or eliminate the need for state coercion to achieve this end by securing the consent of the proletariat and other subordinate classes regarding the legitimacy of the relations of production. The superstructure is an ideological apparatus that is necessary and historically organic to a given structure. It is the glue that keeps capitalist structures from falling apart because of tensions generated by their internal contradictions (Gramsci 1971, 375–77).

The concepts of structure and superstructure arise from Marx's assertion that relations of production constitute "the economic structure of society, the real foundation, on which rises a juridical and political superstructure" (Marx 1973, 503). The ideas that dominate and govern a particular moment in history are the ideas of the class that dominates and governs the means and relations of material production (Marx 1970, 64–65). Given these kinds of statements, it is not difficult to see how some interpreters of Marx arrive at the conclusion that Marxism implies economic determinism, but one must also recall that Marx insists that "[m]en are the producers of their conceptions, ideas, etc.—real, active men, as they are conditioned by a definite development of their productive forces and of the intercourse corresponding to these" (Marx 1970, 47). His point is simply "that circumstances make men just as much as men make circumstances" (59).

Early 20th-century revolutionary theory however, manifest in the International Communist movement led by the Soviet Union, insisted on a determinist interpretation of Marx. Gramsci (1971, 158–68) argued that this approach to understanding capitalism was not truly different from that offered by liberal laissez faire economics and he dismissed both as *economism*. While he credited Lenin, to whom he had to refer as Ilich, with great insight regarding the contemporary practicalities of revolutionary theory, especially the role of the Party as an agent of change, there were two points of theory about which Gramsci was not convinced. The dominant view held that the base is organized by and for the interests of the ruling bourgeoisie and the superstructure is simply the political instrument for class rule. Such parliamentary forms as exist are primarily intended to provide a means for bourgeois fractions to air and resolve their differences, and genuine popular participation is always constrained or even prohibited. Given the political role of the superstructure then, social change depends on revolution at the base by the proletariat and its assumption of its historical role as the class whose rule will end class rule. History awaits the dictatorship of the proletariat to be followed by the end of private property, the dissolution of classes and the withering away of the state.

It was Gramsci's genius to see two things. First, as opposed to the relatively simpler structures of mid- to late-19th century capitalist societies, complex, modern 20th-century capitalism makes class difficult to discern and renders class identity ambiguous. The base and the values of the capitalist relations continue to provide the dominant ideological foundations of capitalist social formations, but class as a social and psychological phenomenon, if not an economic one, becomes indeterminate as individuals become who they will in the context of historically determined class structures. Second, and as a result, superstructures can and do influence real material change in the nature of the capitalist economic base. What people believe and value and how they choose to behave is not entirely or exclusively determined by the dominant relations of production, nor by their objective role in those relations.

Gramsci understood that the superstructure, rather than merely an instrument of domination, is a relatively autonomous historical phenomenon and potentially a site of political conflict whose outcome can alter relations of production. Ideology, rather than being merely an effect of relations of production designed to reproduce those relations, can also serve revolutionary ends by serving as a cause of their change. For Gramsci, the philosophy of praxis identifies the space within which human beings make their own history; it explains the determinants of that history, but does not imply that history is determined. "The claim...," he writes, (1971, 404) "that every fluctuation of politics and ideology can be presented and expounded as an immediate expression of the [economic] structure, must be contested in theory as primitive infantilism, and combated in practice with the actual testimony of Marx."

THE HISTORIC BLOC AND WAR OF POSITION

The concept of the *historic bloc* is central to Gramsci's Marxism. It provides the foundation for his analysis of the *hegemony* exercised by the bourgeoisie over capitalist social formations as well the revolutionary *war of position* that can be conducted against bourgeois hegemony. At any given moment in the life of a social formation there is only one historic bloc. It organizes the base, dominates the superstructure, and manages the relations between them. Its purpose is to reproduce the means and relations of production from which it derives its resources, its political power, and its intellectual/ cultural, or as Gramsci calls it, its ethico-political hegemony. In a very real way, the base provides an historic bloc with its content, and the superstructure gives it form (Gramsci 1971, 377). The historic bloc is constituted by and represents political alliances, but it cannot be reduced to a mere political alliance (Sassoon 1980, 119–25). It is a "complex, contradictory, and discordant *ensemble* of the superstructures [that] is the reflection of the *ensemble* of the social relations of production" (Gramsci 1971, 366). A historic bloc is an ensemble of social groups, intellectual and ideological forces organized around the historic interests of the "fundamental social group" that organizes and leads the bloc (Gramsci 1971, 115–16).

A historic bloc, then, is not merely a structural phenomenon that somehow determines social outcomes. A bloc, in addition to its control of the means of production, depends on ideological principles and political alliances that are subject to constant negotiation, challenge, and change. It is characterized by diverse interests whose particular fortunes and influence will vary as an outcome of political contests both within the bloc, and between the bloc and its historical challengers, including the proletariat. It organizes and asserts its hegemony over society largely by controlling the terms and agenda of political discourse, but its own internal divisions combined with events and behaviors beyond its control can and do create historical imperatives to which it must respond. Hegemony is a concept the Gramsci uses to clarify the nature of historic bloc's power. This power is dominant, but not dominating. It is far from total and it is exercised by setting political agendas rather than dictating political outcomes. Gramsci writes (1971, 57–8) that,

the supremacy of a social group manifests itself in two ways, as "domination" and as "intellectual and moral leadership." A social group dominates antagonistic groups, which it tends to 'liquidate', or to subjugate perhaps even by armed force; it leads kindred and allied groups. A social group can, and indeed must, already exercise "leadership" before winning governmental power (this indeed is one of the principal conditions of winning such power); it subsequently becomes dominant when it exercises power, but even it hold it firmly in its grasp, it must continue to "lead" as well.

In effect, a historical bloc represents a kind of social contract between the bourgeoisie, the social groups it needs to maintain its dominant position, and the subordinate classes. It will exercise coercive power if necessary but that is a risky and costly means of social control. As a result, the situation of the historic bloc is relatively stable but subject to changing economic and political conditions that can lead to renegotiation at any moment.

There will always be positions within social formation from which will arise challenges to the historical bloc. Some will be based on traditional segments of society generally seeking a return to an ideologically constructed mythical past. Others will be based on marginalized and radicalized segments seeking a transformation to a utopian future. Some will arise from within the bloc itself as different interests that constitute it assert different visions of the bloc's future. *Fractions* with different immediate interests exist within historic blocs, and each will seek its own power within the bloc (Poulantzas 1978, 77–85). Contests between fractions can result in a historical instability of the bloc's hegemony, allowing either progressive or reactionary forces to take advantage of the weakness and possibly gain a governing influence over the bloc, even if they cannot alter the relations of production at the base. Some fractions within the historic bloc might actually occupy socially progressive and politically leading positions that challenge the bloc's legitimacy outright despite personal consequences. Alternatively, weaknesses manifest in a bloc's hegemony can also lead to authoritarian and totalitarian solutions to problems of political instability, as for example when the military or powerful charismatic leader steps in to rule on behalf of the bourgeoisie (Marx 1968, 95–180).

The key to Gramsci's thought in this regard lies in his rejection of economic and historical determinism. Rejecting the idea that there are inexorable laws and inevitable outcomes in human affairs, Gramsci (1971, 8–9, 161, 258, 333–34, 366–67) argues that in addition to its economic aspects, human existence is characterized by an ethical-political, or as he frequently refers to it, an "intellectual" reality, manifest in and through superstructures. As alluded to earlier, the historical relations between base and superstructure are dialectically determined. Causes and effects work in both directions, despite the relative predominance of the base. Gramsci writes, "Between the premise (economic structure) and the consequence (political organization), relations are by no means simple and direct: and it is not only by economic facts that the history of a people can be documented. It is a complex and confusing task to unravel causes and in order to do so, a deep and widely diffused study of all spiritual and practical activities is needed" (Gramsci 1958, 280–81).

Recent Marxist theory manifests a controversy over whether base and superstructure should be regarded as inherent categories of historical existence or as cultural and intellectual constructions. This issue turns on another controversy regarding the role of classes as agents of history (Laclau and Mouffe 1985) (Derrida 1994). Both problems are related to the failure to realize a genuine socialist hegemony (Stiglitz 1996), and to the postmodern turn of thought in late capitalism (Jameson 1991). This situation is about much more than merely the collapse of the Soviet Union and the resilience of Western capitalism. By the mid-1970s many Western Marxist scholars and socialist activists, largely because of the influence of Gramsci's thought, had already come to regard the Soviet Union as a practically and theoretically bankrupt historical model, and were searching for a new way to understand the West (Claudin 1975, 598–602).

According to Gramsci, however, the location of a historical subject in a social formation, whether individual or social group, is an objective but not a determinate phenomenon. There are objective, but not necessarily historically determined political interests. Of course, Gramsci asserts that the relations of production have a powerful and dominating material influence on the course of history. This notion is central to Gramsci's concept of hegemony, but he insists that historical subjects are located, and more importantly, willfully locate themselves in the nexus of historically conditioned productive and social relations that constitute a hegemony. Louis Althusser's structuralism (Althusser and Balibar 1970 [1968]) has been criticized for merely substituting an idealist essentialism for economic determinism (Laclau and Mouffe 1985, 97–105), as a result leaving "little room for a revolutionary subject" (Fields 1988, 141) but it seems clear that he was working from Gramsci's ideas when he used the psychoanalytic concept of overdetermination to describe the dialectic moment in which base and superstructure, economic and intellectual reality, interact to create the actual historical location of a subject in a social formation.

The position of a subject, then, depends on objective historical conditions *and* what the subject thinks about those conditions (Althusser 1970, 87–128). A subject's political reality, while ideologically constructed and ordinarily reflecting the ideas of the dominant hegemony, is also the source of the superstructure's power to influence the base and alter if not the relations of production, at least the outcomes of production. A subject's political reality, one the subject actively contributes to and constructs, can provide a possible historical position from which the dominant hegemony and the relations of production which support it can be challenged. Class membership, that is, a subject's location in a social formation with regard to the relations of production between capital and labor, is a fundamental but not determining factor. It plays a large but not exclusive role in the construction of a subject's political interest. People choose their political positions, more or less consciously, but in any case deliberately. Thinking something to be true contains the possibility of making it true. Of course, in this condition also lies the power of the superstructure to engage people in their self-oppression.

In Althusser's language, the relations of production are in the last instance the determinant force within social formations, but it is an instance that usually never fully arrives because of willful, counter-determinant resistance to their logic. The continued dominance of capitalist relations of production is no more assured than is their radical transformation (Schumpeter 1950). The goal of the contest between labor and capital is to alter the relations of production that unnecessarily limit human freedom—to change the social formation at its base in order to realize and take full advantage of the social nature of the production of human values, and thus to transcend the private appropriation and commodification of human labor. The outcome of this contest will be determined by what Gramsci calls the "war of position." This is not a war of violent civil strife. It is necessarily a protracted struggle of ideological and political practice that or-dinarily takes place on the terrain of civil society, but in some instances can occur within the state itself (Gramsci 1971, 108–11, 120, 229–39). The historic bloc of capitalist so-cieties displays ideological and political vulnerabilities that can be identified, exploited and attacked by progressive political forces in the cause of economic and social justice.

The existence of fractions shows that capitalist relations of production can be orga-nized in a variety of ways, and more and less progressive choices are available. Com-bined and uneven development both within and between national social formations means that different peoples will organize themselves in different ways (Lenin 1969) (Trotsky 2008). In other words, not everyone lives in or through exactly the same his-torical moment. As a result, superstructures vary, and some capitalist social formations will be more progressive than others. Politics at the level of the superstructure can be used to effect what Gramsci (1971, 366–67) calls a "catharsis," or "the passage from the purely economic (or egoistic-passional) to the ethico-political moment," and in this moment the base can be "transformed into a means of freedom, an instrument to cre-ate a new ethico-political form and a source of new initiatives." Ideas have power, and the progressive material reform of the relations of production that genuinely improve the life outcomes of the oppressed is possible, even though such change may fall short of revolutionary transformation.

According to Gramsci (1971, 235, 243), the political means of accomplishing these ends lies in challenging capital's hegemony within the "trenches" of the superstructure, particularly in the realm of civil society, as a means to the seizure of state power. This is the terrain of a war of position. He argues that progressive social groups and individu-als must penetrate civil society of the dominant hegemony, seize positions within it, and "turn" its institutions toward progressive and transformative ends. Gramsci writes (1971, 243): "The massive structures of modern democracies, both as State organiza-tions, and as complexes of association in civil society, constitute for the art of politics as it were the 'trenches' and the permanent fortifications of the front in the war of position: they render merely 'partial' the element of the movement which before used to be 'the whole' of war." Gramsci's understanding of the art of politics follows from his under-standing of the dialectical relations between base and superstructure. Change is not a matter of reforming the base so that reform of the superstructure may follow. The art of politics is a matter of reforming base and superstructure simultaneously through politi-cal action that accompanies a change of political consciousness (Gramsci 1975, 1328). The fact that Western capitalism relies on the discourse of democracy to legitimate its hegemony also creates an opening for a politics that demands the meaningful extension of democracy at the level of the base.

PRACTICAL POLITICS

In our time, the historic bloc is one of capitalist democracy. It is characterized by pri-vate ownership of the means of production and wage labor, and ideologically organized by a democratic discourse conducted through institutions of parliamentary and electoral politics that for the most part serve the interest of capitalist production and reproduction. While formally organized by the bourgeoisie at the level of the nation-state, this social formation is a global phenomenon, and with it, the ruling class exercises hegemony rather than direct domination over economic and political relations. (Gramsci 1971, 416–18). Modern, 20th-century capitalism is further characterized by a structure of such

economic complexity and superstructure of such social and political diversity that outright domination of society by a single class is effectively impossible.

Late capitalism offers a complex political situation in which the nexus that conditions the location of historical subjects tends to work against class polarization. There
are wealthy suburbanites who support environmental causes, and rural industrial workers who reject unions. The direct ownership of the means of production typically is
dispersed, and those who own the means of production may not be the same persons
who exercise direct control over these means. Among other consequences that follow
from this condition, the historic bloc of late Western capitalism is not dominated by the
bourgeoisie as a self-conscious, self-identified *class,* and the subject of its dominance is
not exclusively the working class. The modern capitalist state still maintains monopoly
control over the means of coercive violence, including the police and military, but to
maintain its position, the ruling historic bloc relies more on ideological force exercised
through agents constituted by civil society than on coercion exercised directly as state
power.

In fact, the more it relies on ideological persuasion and self-imposed subordination,
and the less on violence, the more likely it is the historic bloc will enjoy political success. The collapse of Soviet state hegemony in Russia, for example, was clearly related
to failures on the part of the historic bloc led by the Communist Party to reconcile contradictions between its claims to ideological leadership and its need to rely on state
coercion to retain power. It is precisely this need to rely on intellectual and moral leadership, however, that opens the historic bloc to a challenge of its legitimacy on its own
terms, and suggests potentially progressive historical roles for various groups, including
intellectuals and professionals, that might otherwise organically serve the historic bloc.
Gramsci saw this conditions as crucial to a war of position.

For some time now, the historic bloc of Western capitalism has employed two broad
legitimation strategies in the effort to solve the problems of protecting and extending
its hegemony and moral authority, and reproducing capitalist relations of production,
including its own position as a privileged historical subject in the social formation. The
first involves grounding the institutions of the state and civil society on a "rational/
legal' basis (Weber 1946, 78–79, 196–209, 293–95). The second is to grant concessions
to popular demands for social and political participation and economic security, if not
equality. Outstanding historical examples of both strategies in action include the governing policies of Franklin Roosevelt's New Deal, and Lyndon Johnson's Great Society.
Both regimes offered a constrained but real membership in the bloc to formerly excluded historical subjects by creating permeable class boundaries for individuals. These
regimes recognized the grievances of historically excluded social groups, and represented themselves symbolically as extensions of a historical discourse of democracy.
They both had lasting consequences for the nature of the American social formation and
contributed to the realization of genuinely progressive economic and political outcomes.
Gramsci (1971, 106–7, 119–20, 222) identifies this strategy as one of "passive revolution." It allows the bourgeois-dominated historic bloc to find ways to further develop the
social formation's productive forces, thus reinforcing its hegemony in response to crisis
and "the relative weakness of the rival progressive force."

These political strategies are overdetermined, driven not just by considerations of
practical politics seeking a social equilibrium and the maintenance of capital's power,
but also by a widespread acceptance of the discourse of democracy's legitimacy, even
among the members of the historic bloc. By granting a legitimate place to the discourse

of democracy in its political strategies, and accepting the idea that this condition implies meaningful participation beyond voting and formal equality of citizenship, the historic bloc brings an "intellectual" reality into play, and finds in persuasion an ideological solution to the frailty of its hegemony. In effect, the historic bloc's own conditions of its rule create the possibility that its superstructure can be penetrated by progressive individuals and groups and turned to the advantage of the subordinate historical subjects. While essential relations of production are not changed, new superstructural arrangements imposed by political action can lead to the redistribution of wealth and privileges, including greater degrees of social participation, recognition of the legitimacy of interests that challenge the hegemony of the historic bloc, and redress of social and economic inequalities.

This kind of thing can also happen in more limited political realms. For example, following the passage of the Telecommunications Act of 1996, we witnessed a significant struggle among fractional telecommunication interests, including incumbent and competitive local exchange carriers, long-distance telephone companies, and cable operators for control of the telecommunications market, within the context of the game defined by that act of legislation. The focus of their contest was relative competitive advantage, and the legitimate interpretation of the rules of the game rather than the nature of the game itself. All of the players accepted without question the need for "liberalization"— deregulation of telecommunication markets.

In the process of this contest, however, the localized hegemony over telecommunication capital became vulnerable to public interest ideologies and groups that "penetrated" the state, most notably the Congress and the Clinton Administration itself. The result was a state political commitment to the provision of "Universal Service" (Raber 2004, 114–22). While universal service remained a moving target of ambiguous meaning, this commitment has since secured a place on the public agenda for meaningful discussion of government support for the distribution of broadband telecommunications service and network neutrality, both of which are at play in the current policies aimed at promoting economic recovery from recent crisis of finance capital and the recession caused by that crisis.

GRAMSCI AND LIS

A search of LIS literature quickly reveals that the work of Antonio Gramsci has had almost no influence on LIS research. In the mid-1980s, Harris (1986, 211–52), using Gramscian theory, examined the role of libraries and librarianship in the construction and maintenance of capitalist hegemony in the United States, particularly with regard to practices that reinforced print culture as an aspect of that hegemony. He located librarianship as a historical subject in an ensemble of institutions, both public and private, constituting the means of sanctioning and distributing public knowledge in a capitalist social formation. In effect, following Gramsci (1971, 3–23) Harris identified librarians as intellectuals organic to the dominant culture of capitalist hegemony. Harris admitted that his work was preliminary, but he did offer a theory about why public libraries are the way they are. He also raised a number of intriguing research questions, including questions about the ambiguities of librarianship's commitment to and use of intellectual freedom, most of which went unexplored. Since there has not been research along these lines it is impossible to tell if Gramsci's thought has influenced library practice, but the odds are good that it has not to any great extent.

As a historian, Harris brought a critical perspective to his own work and perhaps it's not surprising that Gramsci's influence is most apparent in the study of library history. Here too there are more calls for critical research than actual application of Gramsci's theoretical approach. Wiegand (2000), Malone (2003), Rose (2003), and Goedeken (2005) are explorations of library historiography, each in its own way critical of what their authors see as traditional and limited approaches to the study of library history. Weigand sets the tone for these pieces. His examination of 50 years of library history research literature, from the perspective of one who has deeply engaged the record, leads him to conclude that the record of library history has much more to give than library historians have been willing to take from it. Self-imposed "blind spots and tunnel vision" (1999) have prevented library historians from deeper insights the record likely will support and caused them to fail at one of history's primary missions—to help us better understand the present. In an earlier work (2003), I suggest that the lack of vision observed by Wiegand is an effect of librarianship's nature as a profession of "organic intellectuals" (Gramsci 1971, 5–23). Librarians and those who do research about libraries are simply too deeply engaged in the unconscious everyday practice of hegemony to conceive let alone find alternative ways of looking at things. It is possible that at least some librarians are aware of alternatives yet lament the lack of means, including a professional vocabulary, for articulating those alternatives.

Malone notices that library history lacks a serious multicultural perspective, instead offering a top-down approach concentrating on white, male leadership and administration, but Rose warns that historians have to be careful with "theory." In his view, history done to prove a theory can too easily prevent the record from speaking for itself and so lead to the neglect of "actual libraries." In these two articles we can see their authors addressing the effect of the dominant culture on the meanings and interpretations that frame the study of library history, as well as a struggle over those meanings and interpretations. Research can and does serve as a site and a stake in a war of position characterized by ideological conflict over the appropriate way to do history.

Brendan (2007) and Dick (2007) provide recent examples of library history done with the benefit of Gramsci's insight. Brendan, also spinning off of Harris, takes a look at the social/political role of the American Library Association (ALA) during the depression of the 1930s. While contributing to the reestablishment of capitalist hegemony that came under genuine threat from widespread economic collapse, the ALA also played a real and significant role in defeating populist antitax movements that threatened the postdepression welfare state of which libraries have become a part. The issues are complex and not without ambivalence, but Brendan's work shows a progressive aspect of librarianship manifest in a war of position between conservative and progressive fractions of the American bourgeoisie as it coped with the political dislocations caused by the depression. Dick offers a similar kind of analysis of the role played by public libraries during the political contests against the apartheid regime in South Africa during the 1980s. By virtue of their actual use, as well as the active resistance to apartheid by librarians, state institutions that the regime should have been able to count on as instruments of hegemony were turned and instead played an ambivalently progressive role. Gramsci helps both Brendan and Dick look for signs of a political effect the record reveals, if one knows where to look.

The items cited here rely explicitly on Gramsci's work, but other critical library history is being done that within the context of a discursive formation that includes his perspectives. Christine Pawley, Toni Samek, Andrew Werthheimer, James Carmichael, and

Alastair Black have all contributed to a literature that is arguably more concerned with the library in the life of the user than the user in the life of the library (Zweizig 1973; Wiegand 2003).

Beyond library history Gramsci's influence does not show up very often, and when it does the work is not particularly integrated. Strottman (2007) follows Sandy Berman's critical work on subject headings and bibliographic control by using the concept of hegemony to deconstruct the way the LCSH guide manifests regional biases that frustrate catalogers and users of Southwest collections, especially material regarding Hispanics and Native Americans. Willis and Chiasson (2007) use the same concept to explore the way rhetorical devices are used to manufacture consent during the implementation of ERP (enterprise resource planning) with regard to information technology, concluding that the creation of an integral hegemony formed through continuous negotiation and debate across subgroups will result in greater success.

In a piece that has interdisciplinary implications, Frechette (2006) uses a Gramscian approach to examine how the cyber-safety discourse, particularly its focus on children and on pornography as inappropriate content, constitutes a diversion and denial of identity to other forms of Internet discourse that might be also or alternatively be considered as inappropriate. The signifiers *inappropriate, security, safety, and privacy* all carry meanings that are potentially contested. The dominant hegemony, furthering the interest of centers of telecommunication and consumer goods capital has so far controlled these meanings in a way that excludes advertising and marketing communication aimed at children as inappropriate, and according to Frechette, has done so to protect its interest in children as a market to be exploited. This kind of work has tremendous implications for public policy, but it hasn't been very vigorously pursued by LIS or any other discipline for that matter.

AN AGENT OF SOCIAL CHANGE

Despite the lack of research on libraries from a Gramscian perspective, one remarkable fact about the public library stands out. It is an institution grounded on conventional American democratic ideology and predates the welfare state and welfare state politics, yet in at least one way it represents a successful penetration of the capitalist historic bloc's hegemony over popular culture. It may or may not play much of a role as a site and stake in ideological conflict. Harris is generally persuasive, and there is reason to believe that most American public libraries are purveyors of conventional culture, but this does not undermine the reality of the public library as an institution that is deliberately *designed* to decommodify that culture. Public libraries use authoritatively allocated public money to acquire private cultural goods and ICT services, such as books, media, information access; make these goods and services publicly accessible, and provide value-added services associated with their character. By law, these goods and services are universally and equally accessible to all citizens within the taxing jurisdiction of the library and for the most part available free of any charge to their consumers. Public libraries transform private goods into public goods. They represent a deliberate state intervention in the market economy in order to provide a public good.

Public librarians are aware of this condition and have organized themselves independently and through their formal associations to represent the interests of library users and advocate for continued or expanded public support of libraries. This advocacy is deliberate progressive action within a "trench" of the superstructure but it tends to be theorized in terms of traditional interest group politics and liberal notions of the public good. It is rarely justified in terms of welfare state justice or passive revolutionary solutions to problems of distribution arising from the private ownership of the means of communication, let alone in Gramscian terms of counter-hegemony, despite the socialist implications of the service. This volume of readings represents a more conscious and fully theorized action in another trench, that of LIS education and research located in institutions of higher learning. It is an effort to bring together and present introductions to counter-hegemonic social and political theory with the hope that it might inform progressive practices, at least in the realm of LIS teaching and research if not professional practice.

From a Gramscian perspective, both are welcome manifestations of resistance to the dominant hegemony but neither is likely to lead to significant social change. Despite their progressive intentions and challenge to defensive positions within the superstructure, there is some reason to believe that both will actually serve as unintended contributions to passive revolutionary activity—reform that will extend the life of the American capitalist social formation by contributing to the further development of its productive forces. At least one reason for this possibility is that both efforts are uncoordinated and disconnected from any other progressive political action. The advocacy movement in public librarianship and the critical theory movement in LIS, while similar in spirit and aim, are nevertheless independent *social* acts, and neither is in anyway connected to other social acts by other progressive actors in different trenches.

What's missing is the organization required to integrate library advocacy, LIS critical theory, and all such similar movements into an integrated form that will allow them in turn to create and establish a new historic bloc that exercises a new hegemony. What's missing is the Party, or at least an organization that can fill the Party's role. Following his rejection of economism and historical determinism, Gramsci argues that social change does not happen of its own accord. A change agent—a historical actor—is necessary. According to Marxist theory, that actor is the proletariat–the working class. But this class, along with allies that might include librarians, college teachers, and other such intellectuals who have escaped the ideological constraints of their status as "organic" to the dominant historic bloc (Gramsci 1971, 5–14), needs an agent to organize and lead the formation of the new historical bloc that will exercise a hegemony of social justice. In Gramsci's words (1971, 125–205), it needs a *Modern Prince.*

The task of the Modern Prince—the Party—is to organize intellectual/moral reform, to serve as the collective agent capable of historical action, and provide the "'cultural-social' unity through which a multiplicity of dispersed wills, with heterogeneous aims, are welded together with a single aim, on the basis of an equal and common conception of the world" (Gramsci 1971, 132–22, 349). That aim is not to merely seize state power, but to provide the organizational foundation for the integral state—one that reflects a new conception of the world and civil society (Gramsci 1971, 267) and the absorption by civil society of the political realm. The integral state is the manifestation of a new historical bloc exercising hegemony derived from the collective will of a social formation, reflecting unity without uniformity. For Gramsci (1971, 227–29) democracy is mode of politics that abolishes the divisions between rulers and ruled rather than merely a set of rules that allows those divisions to persist. It is a substantive condition rather merely a procedural context. Questions of strategy and tactics cannot be addressed outside of the context of specific social formations and historical circumstances (Sassoon

1980, 193), but for Gramsci (1971, 239), the Party and its actions are central to war of position, which "once won, is decisive definitely."

It is not likely that a political party of the kind Gramsci imagined is necessary for hegemonic change to occur is going to emerge soon in any existing capitalist democracy. Arguably, the development of Gramsci's theory and its application in either practical politics or research confronts a number pressing questions. What kind of political agent or organization can serve the same counter-hegemonic organizing function as the Party? Is such an organization possible under current historical and ideological conditions? Is historical action that might lead to a new hegemony even conceivable, let alone possible? For now, it seems clear that disparate progressive and counter-hegemonic movements are likely to remain disparate and unorganized.

CONCLUSION

Progressive forces and movements, especially those insisting upon a fair and equal distribution to all socially constitutive groups of the rights guaranteed to the bourgeoisie under parliamentary state forms, have caused changes to the superstructure of capitalist societies that have significantly reduced the power of the bourgeoisie and materially changed the relations of production. Twenty-first-century capitalist societies are considerably more inclusive than their 19th-century counterparts, and all can be more or less characterized as welfare states that provide a considerable number and kinds of publicly funded state services to address social inequalities generated by capitalist economies.

In Gramsci's view, modern capitalist social reality must be understood as the material outcome of a dialectical relationship between human beings and their circumstances. The existing historic bloc, including the concessions to democracy and social justice it manifests, is an outcome of the struggle for justice that this relationship allows. It is not a historical accident nor simply a generous gesture by a liberal ruling class. It has been fought for and successfully pursued by progressive social forces and political interests. In his explanation of human nature, Gramsci (1971, 360) makes clear that the historic bloc, and the superstructure that represents it, is not merely a determined outcome of certain relations of production:

The measure of freedom enters into the concept of man. That the objective possibilities exist for people not to die of hunger and that people do die of hunger, has its importance, or so one would have thought. But the existence of objective conditions, of possibilities, or of freedom is not yet enough: it is necessary to "know" them, and to know how to use them. And to want to use them. Man, in this sense, is concrete will, that is, the effective application of the abstract will or vital impulses to the concrete means of which realise such a will...Man is to be conceived as an historical bloc of purely individual and subjective elements and of mass and objective or material elements with which the individual is in an active relationship.

This passage reveals the intimate relationships Gramsci theorized between history, social existence, and individual human lives. Individual and social existence can be characterized by the nature of the historic bloc that governs, but to be conditioned by the past is not the same thing as to be determined by it.

Ultimately the political solution we may have to accept is one based on the widespread acceptance of a rather Panglossian observation; that while not perfect, capitalist relations of production when combined with a political superstructure of parliamentary democracy, rational/legal structures of governance and authority, equality before the law, and a guarantee of individual rights, makes for the best of all possible worlds. There is powerful empirical evidence for this claim. Certainly since World War II, the general level of prosperity in the capitalist West has increased. The cultures of Western capitalist democracies manifest a real commitment to human rights, and the nation-states based on these cultures display pluralist polities that represent diverse political interests and compromise among these interests despite evident political partisanship. This view, however, *is* Panglossian and not without its expected irony. Given the persistence of systematic and structural inequalities and exclusions, the relative privileging of property rights over human rights, the dominance of market relations over human relations, and an economy that favors the independence of commodities over that of their producers, the widespread acceptance of this view might be taken as evidence of the effectiveness and success of the capitalist historic bloc's ideological strategy in the war of position. So it goes.

REFERENCES

Althusser, Louis. 1970. "Contradiction and Overdetermination." In *For Marx,* trans. Ben Brewster, 87–160. New York: Vintage Books.

Althusser, Louis, and Etienne Balibar. 1970 [1968]. *Reading Capital.* Trans. Ben Brewster. New York: Pantheon Books.

Brendan, L. 2007. "The ALA, Public Libraries, and the Great Depression." *Library History* 23 (2): 85–96.

Claudin, Fernando. 1975. *The Communist Movement: From Comintern to Cominform. Part Two.* New York: Monthly Review Press.

Derrida, Jacques. 1994. *Specters of Marx: The State of the Debt, the Work of Mourning, and the New International.* New York: Routledge.

Dick, A. L. 2007. "The Books Were Just the Props: Public Libraries and Contested Space in the Cape Flats Townships in the 1980s." *Library Trends* 55 (3): 698–716.

Fields, Belden A. 1988. "In Defense of Political Economy and Systemic Analysis: A Critique of Prevailing Theoretical Approaches to the New Social Movements." In *Marxism and the Interpretation of Culture,* ed. Cary Nelson and Lawrence Grossberg, 141–58. Urbana and Chicago: University of Illinois Press.

Frechette, J. 2005. "Cyber-Democracy of Cyber-Hegemony? Exploring the Political and Economic Structures of the Internet as an Alternative Source of Information." *Library Trends* 53 (4): 555–76.

Goedeken, E. A. 2005. "Assessing What We Wrote: A Review of the Libraries & Culture Literature Reviews, 1967–2002." *Libraries & Culture* 40 (3): 251–67.

Gramsci, Antonio. 1958. *Studi Gramsciani.* Rome: Instituto Gramsci.

Gramsci, Antonio. 1971. *Selections from the Prison Notebooks.* Ed. and trans, Quintin Hoare and Geoffrey N. Smith. New York: International Publishers.

Gramsci, Antonio. 1975. *Quaderni del Carcere.* Vols. 1–4. Ed. Valentino Gerratana. Turin: Einaudi.

Gramsci, Antonio. 1977. *Selections from Political Writings (1910–1920).* Compiled and ed. by Quintin Hoare, trans. John Mathews. New York: International Publishers.

Gramsci, Antonio. 1992. *Prison Notebooks. Vols. 1–3.* Introduced and ed. by Joseph A. Buttigieg, trans. Joseph A. Buttigieg and Antonio Callari. New York: Columbia University Press.

Harris, Michael. 1986. "State, Class and Cultural Reproduction: Toward a Theory of Library Service in the United States." *Advances in Librarianship* 14:211–52. New York: Academic Press.

Jameson, Frederic. 1991. *Postmodernism, or, The Cultural Logic of Late Capitalism.* London: Verso.

Laclau, Ernesto, and Chantal Mouffe. 1985. *Hegemony and Socialist Strategy: Towards a Radical Democratic Politics.* London: Verso.

Lasswell, Harold D. 1990. *Politics, Who Gets What, When, and How.* Gloucester, MA: Peter Smith.

Lenin, V. I. 1969. *Imperialism: The Highest Stage of Capitalism.* New York: International Publishers.

Malone, C. K. 2000. "Toward a Multicultural American Public Library History." *Libraries & Culture* 35 (1): 77–87.

Marx, Karl. 1968. "The Eighteenth Brumaire of Louis Bonaparte." In *Karl Marx and Frederick Engels, Selected Works.* New York: International Publishers.

Marx, Karl.1970. *The German Ideology. Part One.* New York: International Publishers.

Marx, Karl. 1973. "Preface to a Contribution to the Critique of Political Economy." In *Karl Marx and Frederick Engels, Selected Works, Vol. 1.* Moscow: Progress Publishers.

Poulantzas, Nicos. 1978. *Political Power and Social Classes.* London: Verso.

Raber, Douglas. 2003. "Librarians as Organic Intellectuals: A Gramscian Approach to Blind Spots and Tunnel Vision." *Library Quarterly* 73 (1): 33–53.

Raber, Douglas. 2004. "Is Universal Service a Universal Right? A Rawlsian Approach to Universal Service." In *Information Ethics in the Electronic Age: Current Issues in Africa and the World,* ed. Tom Mendina and Johannes J. Britz. Jefferson, NC: McFarland & Co.

Rose, J. 2003. "Alternative Futures for Library History." *Libraries & Culture.* 38 (1): 50–62.

Sassoon, Anne Showstack. 1980. *Gramsci's Politics.* New York: St. Martin's Press.

Schumpeter, Joseph A. 1950. *Capitalism, Socialism, and Democracy.* 3rd ed. New York: Harper.

Stiglitz, Joseph E. 1996. *Whither Socialism?* Cambridge, MA: MIT Press.

Strottman, T. A. 2007. "Some of Our Fifty Are Missing: Library of Congress Subject Headings for Southwestern Cultures and History." *Cataloging & Classification Quarterly* 45 (2): 41–64.

Trotsky, Leon. 2008. *The History of the Russian Revolution.* Chicago: Haymarket Books.

Weber, Max. 1946. *From Max Weber: Essays in Sociology.* Ed. and trans. H. H. Gerth and C. Wright Mills. New York: Oxford University Press.

Wiegand, W. A. 1999. "Tunnel Vision and Blind Spots: What the Past Tells Us about the Present: Reflections on the Twentieth-Century History of American Librarianship." *Library Quarterly* 69:1–32.

Wiegand, W. A. 2000. "American Library History Literature, 1947–1997: Theoretical Perspectives?" *Libraries & Culture* 35 (1): 4–36.

Wiegand, W. A. 2003. "To Reposition a Research Agenda: What American Studies Can Teach the LIS Community about the Library in the Life of the User." *Library Quarterly* 73 (4): 369–82.

Willis, R. and M. Chiasson. 2007. "Do the Ends Justify the Means? A Gramscian Critique of the Processes of Consent during an ERP Implementation." *Information Technology & People* 20 (3): 212–34.

Zweizig, Douglas L. 1973. "Predicting Amount of Public Library Use: An Empirical Study of the Public Library in the Life of the Adult Public." PhD diss., Syracuse University.

SUPPLEMENTAL BIBLIOGRAPHIES

LIBRARY SCIENCE LITERATURE

Brendan, L. 2007. "The ALA, Public Libraries and the Great Depression." *Library History* 23 (2): 85–96.

Dick, A. L. "The Books Were Just the Props: Public Libraries and Contested Space in the Cape Flats Townships in the 1980s." *Library Trends* 55 (3): 698–716.

Frechette, J. 2005. "Cyber-Democracy or Cyber-Hegemony? Exploring the Political and Economic Structures of the Internet as an Alternative Source of Information." *Library Trends* 53 (4): 555–76.

Goedeken, E. A. 2005. "Assessing What We Wrote: A Review of the Libraries & Culture Literature Reviews, 1967–2002." *Libraries & Culture* 40 (3): 251–67.

Harris, Michael. 1986. "State, Class and Cultural Reproduction: Toward a Theory of Library Service in the United States." *Advances in Librarianship,* vol. 14, 211–52. New York: Academic Press.

Malone, C. K. 2000. "Toward a Multicultural American Public Library History." *Libraries & Culture* 35 (1): 77–87.

Raber, Douglas. 2003. "Librarians as Organic Intellectuals: A Gramscian Approach to Blind Spots and Tunnel Vision." *Library Quarterly* 73 (1): 33–53.

Rose, J. 2003. "Alternative Futures for Library History." *Libraries & Culture.* 38 (1): 50–62.

Strottman, T. A. 2007. "Some of Our Fifty Are Missing: Library of Congress Subject Headings for Southwestern Cultures and History." *Cataloging & Classification Quarterly* 45 (2): 41–64.

Wiegand, W. A. 1999. "Tunnel Vision and Blind Spots: What the Past Tells Us about the Present: Reflections on the Twentieth-Century History of American Librarianship." *Library Quarterly* 69:1–32.

Wiegand, W. A. 2000. "American Library History Literature, 1947–1997: Theoretical Perspectives?" *Libraries & Culture* 35 (1): 4–36.

Wiegand, W. A. 2003. "To Reposition a Research Agenda: What American Studies Can Teach the LIS Community about the Library in the Life of the User." *Library Quarterly* 73 (4): 369–82.

Willis, R., and M. Chiasson. 2007. "Do the Ends Justify the Means? A Gramscian Critique of the Processes of Consent during an ERP Implementation." *Information Technology & People* 20 (3): 212–34.

Zweizig, Douglas L. 1973. "Predicting Amount of Public Library Use: An Empirical Study of the Public Library in the Life of the Adult Public." PhD diss., Syracuse University.

SELECT WORKS BY ANTONIO GRAMSCI

Gramsci, Antonio. 1957. *The Modern Prince and Other Writings by Antonio Gramsci,* Trans. and introduced by Louis Marks. London: Lawrence and Wishart.

Gramsci, Antonio. 1971. *Selections from the Prison Notebooks of Antonio Gramsci,* Ed. and trans. Q. Hoare and G. Nowell-Smith. London: Lawrence and Wishart.

Gramsci, Antonio. 1984. *Notes on Language.* Selected and ed. by Steven Mansfield, trans. Steven Mansfield and Livio Alchini. *Telos.* 59: 127–50.

Gramsci, Antonio. 1985. *Selections From Cultural Writings.* Ed. and introduced by David Forgacs and Geoffrey Nowell-Smith, trans. William Boelhower. London and Cambridge, MA: Lawrence and Wishart; Harvard University Press.

Gramsci, Antonio. 1989. *An Antonio Gramsci Reader: Selected Writings, 1916–1935*. Ed. and introduced by David Forgacs. London: Lawrence and Wishart, 1988. Reprint, New York: Schocken Books.

Gramsci, Antonio. 1990. *Selections from Political Writings (1910–1920)*. Selected, ed., and introduced by Quintin Hoare, trans. John Mathews. London and New York: Lawrence and Wishart; International Publishers, 1977. Reprint, Minneapolis: University of Minnesota Press.

Gramsci, Antonio. 1990. *Selections from Political Writings (1921–1926)*. Ed., trans., and introduced by Quintin Hoare. London and New York: Lawrence and Wishart; International Publishers, 1978. Reprint, Minneapolis: University of Minnesota Press.

Gramsci, Antonio. 1992–2007. *Prison Notebooks*. Vols. 1–3. Ed. and introduced by Joseph A. Buttigieg.; trans. Joseph A. Buttigieg and Antonio Callari. New York : Columbia University Press.

Gramsci, Antonio. 1994. *Letters from Prison. Ed. and introduced by* Frank Rosengarten, trans. Raymond Rosenthal. New York: Columbia University Press.

Gramsci, Antonio. 1994. *Pre-Prison Writings*. Ed. and introduced by Richard Bellamy, trans. Virginia Cox. New York: Cambridge University Press.

Gramsci, Antonio. 1995. *Further Selections from the Prison Notebooks*. Trans. and ed. Derek Boothman, with general introduction by Derek Boothman. London: Lawrence and Wishart, 1995. Reprint, Minneapolis: University of Minnesota Press.

SELECT WEB SITES

Marxists Internet Archive Library http://www.marxists.org/archive/index.htm

Marxists Internet Archive Library: Antonio Gramsci http://www.marxists.org/archive/gramsci/

theory.org.uk: Media/Gender/Identity Resources: Antonio Gramsci http://www.theory.org.uk/ctr-gram.htm

International Gramsci Society http://www.internationalgramscisociety.org/

International Gramsci Journal http://www.uow.edu.au/arts/research/gramsci-journal/

Gramsci Links Archive http://www.victoryiscertain.com/gramsci/

SELECT BIBLIOGRAPHY

Adamson, Walter L. 1980. *Hegemony and Revolution: A Study of Antonio Gramsci's Political and Cultural Theory.* Berkeley: University of California Press.

Ayers, Alison J., ed. 2008. *Gramsci, Political Economy, and International Relations Theory: Modern Princes and Naked Emperors.* New York: Palgrave Macmillan.

Bellia, Carmelo. 1978. *The Social Economics of Antonio Gramsci.* New York: New York University.

Bozzini, Gabriella. 1985. *Antonio Gramsci and Popular Culture: From Subordination to Contestation.* Berkeley: University of California at Berkeley.

Buci-Glucksmann, Christine. 1979. *Gramsci and the State.* Trans. David Fernbach. London: Lawrence and Wishart.

Clark, Martin. 1977. *Antonio Gramsci and the Revolution that Failed.* New Haven: Yale University Press.

Coben, Diana. 1998. *Radical Heroes: Gramsci, Freire, and the Politics of Adult Education.* London: Taylor and Francis.

Davidson, Alastair. 1977. *Antonio Gramsci: Towards an Intellectual Biography.* Atlantic Highlands, NJ: Humanities Press.

Finocchiaro, Maurice A. 2002. *Gramsci and the History of Dialectical Thought.* Cambridge: Cambridge University Press.

Fiori, Giuseppe. 1990. *Antonio Gramsci: Life of a Revolutionary.* Trans. Tom Nairn. London: Verso.

Germino, Dante L. 1990. *Antonio Gramsci: Architect of a New Politics.* Baton Rouge, LA: LSU Press.

Hill, Deb J. 2007. *Hegemony and Education: Gramsci, Post-Marxism, and Radical Democracy Revisited.* Lanham, MD: Rowman and Littlefield.

Holub, Renate. 1992. *Antonio Gramsci: Beyond Marxism and Postmodernism.* London: Routledge.

Ives, Peter. 2004. *Language and Hegemony in Gramsci.* London: Pluto Press.

Joll, James. 1978. *Antonio Gramsci.* London: Penguin Books.

Jones, Steve. 2006. *Antonio Gramsci.* London: Routledge.

Mayo, Peter. 1999. *Gramsci, Freire and Adult Education: Possibilities for Transformative Action.* New York: St. Martin's Press.

Morton, Adam David. 2007. *Unravelling Gramsci: Hegemony and Passive Revolution in the Global Political Economy.* London: Pluto Press.

Mouffe, Chantal, ed. 1979. *Gramsci and Marxist Theory: Essays.* London: Routledge.

Ransome, Paul. 1992. *Antonio Gramsci: A New Introduction.* Hertfordshire, UK: Harvester Wheatsheaf, Hemel Hempstead.

Saccarelli, Emanuele. 2007. *Gramsci and Trotsky in the Shadow of Stalinism: The Political Theory and Practice of Opposition.* London: Routledge.

Sassoon, Anne Showstack. 1987. *Gramsci's Politics.* 2nd ed. Minneapolis: University of Minnesota Press.

Sassoon, Anne Showstack. 2000. *Gramsci and Contemporary Politics: Beyond Pessimism of the Intellect.* London: Routledge.

Simon, Roger. 1991. *Gramsci's Political Thought: An Introduction.* London: Lawrence and Wishart.

Williams, Gwyn A. 1975. *Proletarian Order: Antonio Gramsci, Factory Councils and the Origins of Italian Communism, 1911–1921.* London: Pluto Press.

13

The Social as Fundamental and a Source of the Critical: Jürgen Habermas

John E. Buschman
Georgetown University Library, USA

INTRODUCTION

Born in 1929 in Dusseldorf, Germany, Jürgen Habermas is consistently described as among the most influential of recent public intellectuals, philosophers, and social theorists. The immediate aftermath of World War II and the revelations of the criminal and pathological nature of the German regime were searing experiences and led to his work in social theory, philosophy, and democratic theory. Habermas attended university in Göttingen and Zurich studying philosophy—though he was not Marxist or a radical at that time. After immersing himself in the work of Heidegger, Habermas came to be disillusioned with him over his evasiveness concerning his activities during the war. He had a parallel issue with the papering-over of the past by the West German (Adenauer) government in the war's aftermath. His 1953 public confrontation with Heidegger over his support of the Nazis during the 1930s marked the point of his specific move away from German traditions toward Anglo-American democratic experiences, and in 1954 he earned his PhD from the University of Bonn. Habermas thereafter became Theodor Adorno's research assistant at the Institute for Social Research at the University of Frankfurt (The Frankfurt School). This marked his turn to more radical approaches, and the cause of subsequent conflict with the Frankfurt School's other prominent scholar, Max Horkheimer. He left for the University of Marburg in 1958, and then went on to be appointed to the post of professor of philosophy and sociology back at the University of Frankfurt in 1964 after Horkheimer's departure. He was director at the Max Planck Institute in Starnberg from 1971–83 and returned to Frankfurt in 1983.

Habermas first came to public notice with *Strukturwandel der Offentlichkeit* in 1962 (*Structural Transformation of the Public Sphere,* published in English in 1989) and his two-volume magnum opus *Theory of Communicative Action* (1984; 1987b) cemented his place as one of the foremost thinkers across a wide range of fields. The public sphere thesis was long known in Anglo-American circles largely via a précis he wrote in 1964—itself translated and published in English only 10 years later (Habermas

1974) along with a translated excursus by another scholar (Hohendahl 1974). Habermas intellectually combines the Frankfurt School, Hegel, Marx, communication theory, hermeneutics, and debates in epistemology, to name some of the major scholarly areas he synthesizes. "[T]wo leading, and massive, themes recur throughout...and give his works their continuity. One is a concern with metatheoretical problems in social theory, especially with respect to the relation between theory and critique. The other is the objective of placing such a critique in the context of an interpretation of the main trends of development in Western capitalism (Giddens 1982, 82–83). The essential importance of the "lifelong project of establishing the preconditions of open and free communication" (Webster 2003, 162) should be added to this. His intellectual project has been frequently described as rescuing the unrealized rational and democratic potential of modernity and the Enlightenment (Peters 1993). Habermas is considered the continuation of the tradition of the Frankfurt School (Held 1980), and has served in a variety of additional distinguished academic posts beyond those in Germany (the New School for Social Research, Cambridge University, and Northwestern University). Habermas engaged with German political issues like unification, democratization in light of the historical legacy of the Holocaust, Green Party politics, and a unified Europe. He "retired" from the University of Frankfurt in 1994, but his work continues and spans well over four decades (for general biographical background see Palmisano 2001; Habermas 2004; Finlayson 2005; for a fuller bibliography of writings beyond the selection in this chapter and also for useful additional sources, see Bohman and Rehg 2007).

Richard Bernstein (1983, 9) encapsulates the dilemma Habermas is attempting to move beyond: when there are philosophical claims to "clear and distinct criteria or foolproof transcendental arguments to support" them, the inevitable counterargument is that "close examination reveals that there is something fraudulent and ingenuous about such claims" (Bernstein 1983, 9). In turn, the counter-counterargument is that the debunking thesis is "self-referentially inconsistent and paradoxical" because despite arguing against truth, the argument implicitly assumes its proofs are true (Bernstein 1983, 9). Bernstein notes we've been at just this dead end for some time, and he cites Habermas as one of the foremost thinkers in working through (actually working beyond) this aporia. Yet while his work is well known, it is not known well within library and information science (LIS) theory. It would be fair to characterize LIS's use of Habermas as partial (despite claims to the contrary).

Any presentation of Habermas' work is by definition selective and this attempt will not escape that shortcoming either. This review will tend to focus on some of Habermas' earlier ideas. Those ideas still percolate through the increasingly subtle and abstract refinements of his later work responding to critics (White 1995). For our brief purposes here, we will review the emancipatory interest in knowledge, the theory of knowledge as social theory, communicative action, and the public sphere. Habermas' work is highly interrelated, but these categories—and their somewhat-arbitrary arrangement—give some notion to the sweep and depth of his thinking.

THE EMANCIPATORY INTEREST IN KNOWLEDGE

Habermas' response to Marx, positivism, Kant, Hegel, Freud, and Husserl cannot be recounted in full here (for summary treatments see Habermas 1971a, 301–17; McCarthy 1978, 75–91). However, as a starting point, Habermas, like many critical theorists, finds positivism problematic, especially as manifested in the sciences. We are in the thrall of "scientivism," by which he means "science's faith in itself, the conviction that science must no longer be regarded as one form of possible cognition, but that cognition must be identified with science" (Habermas 1971b, 650).

The problems with positivism are threefold. First, the "objectivity" and "neutrality" of the sciences is a mask of their situated and interest-laden nature: "it mistakenly disregards fundamental interests to which it owes not only its impulse, but also the very condition that makes [scientific] objectivity possible" (Habermas 1966, 295). The second is that positivism as exemplified in a scientific and technocratic society (in which the social sciences ape the "hard" sciences) "removes the total social framework of interests... from the scope of reflection and rational reconstruction." That is, technocratic or purposive-rational systems are set up with *given* set of aims built in, unreflected upon and beyond democratic control (Habermas 1970, 82; Habermas 1976b; Held 1980, 300–307). Third, science and social science-intensive modern technocratic capitalistic societies have undergone periodic crises of legitimation and upheaval that represent the failures of these very systems (the Depression, the 21st-century financial crisis, the Vietnam War, and Civil Rights struggles, Middle Eastern wars, pollution, Love Canal, Three Mile Island, and global warming to name several specific examples in the United States and beyond). As a result, the state must intervene: high-level government designations and funding to help clean up the toxic effects of science and technology harnessed for economically productive (but socially and/or environmentally destructive) purposes; the underwriting of the financial sector and/or the welfare state to smooth out the dislocations and distortions of the market and/or smoothing out the dislocations of war (Habermas 1970, 1998a, 2003).

This results in the state—to compensate for the technocratic failures outlined—utilizing techniques of persuasion like advertising to maintain the legitimacy of the system: "the structuring of attention by directing it to certain thematic areas and by playing down uncomfortable themes, problems, and arguments.... [T]he political system assumes the task of *planning ideologies.*" There is no such thing as *"administrative creation of meaning,* only ideological retailing of cultural values." (Habermas 1976a, 377; italics in original). This then, is "systematically distorted communication"—situations that "maintain their legitimacy despite the fact that they could not be validated if subjected to rational discourse" (Schroyer quoted in Held 1980, 256; see also Habermas 2003). Knowledge (in Habermas' sense of the word) is critical reflection on this masking and distortion, and it has an inherent emancipatory interest (Held 1980, 256). "The interest-bound character of knowledge in general" does not prevent critique for normative purposes, the goal of which is "the liberation of human beings from their domination by forces constraining their rational autonomy of action" (Giddens 1982, 88–89). It follows that social entities which aid in the iterative unmasking of distortion and/or further rational discourse have a positive role in this line of thinking—like the press, social movements, educative institutions, and libraries (Habermas 1981a, Giroux 1984; Buschman 2003). It also follows that these entities are, like the sciences, not neutral in their content or actions in relationship to society and its content. So far here, Habermas is not far from the main currents of the Frankfurt School's critical theory (Brosio 1980), but is providing a social-communicative variation on some important themes. It is also notable that this essential approach has proven durable enough to survive as a nonteleological justification in circumstances where plurality and pluralism have become paramount (White 2004). However, there are within these concepts two key arguments that are explored in the next sections.

THE THEORY OF KNOWLEDGE (EPISTEMOLOGY)
AS SOCIAL THEORY

Habermas makes a crucial link between the historical/social and epistemological realms when he argues that Marx was right and wrong at the same time. To correct Hegel's idealism, Marx argued that "the subject of world constitution is not transcendental consciousness in general but the concrete human species" (Habermas 1971a, 27). In other words, history is and was more than pure thought and understanding. Utilizing Hegel's dialectic and the "self generation of man as a process" (Marx quoted in Habermas 1971a, 43), Marx grounded that process in the social and economic world and "the dimension of power relations that regulate men's interaction among themselves" (Habermas 1971a, 51). Thus Marx arrived at his analysis of historical development and his critique of capitalism—"a social form that no longer institutionalizes class antagonism [via] immediate political domination and social force; instead, it stabilizes it in the legal institution of the free labor contract, which congeals productive activity into the commodity form" (Habermas 1971a, 59). However, he argues that Marx unwittingly adopted an epistemology in the process: "an instrumentalist translation of [the] philosophy of absolute reflection [by positing] the self-constitution of the species through labor." The materialist critique of philosophy was conceived by Marx as a form of natural science (Habermas 1971a, 62–63).

Turning Hegel on his head was highly reductive, and in the end "Marxism merge[d] with the rising tide of positivistic philosophy" (Giddens 1982, 85). Habermas notes that Marx's scientific materialism contained within it the problems of positivist epistemology: masking a theory of knowledge and validating the claims of the "unchained universal" of scientific, instrumental reasoning. Even under Marxism, science and purposive-rational reasoning is no longer one possible form of knowing, but the radically reductive (in terms of human freedom) definition of knowledge itself (Habermas 1971a, 63). For Habermas, knowledge constitution is social and it "take[s] form in the medium of work, language, and power" (Habermas 1971a, 312–13; see also McCarthy 1978, 59). In other words, epistemology is a social product, and his analysis of Marx firmly established for Habermas that social and historical theories have built-in epistemologies (whether explicitly recognized or not). Those epistemologies in turn have built-in normative assumptions about society and history, and normative claims can be made on both. In sum, "the nature and basis of human knowledge can only be pursued as a social investigation. Epistemology ... can only be pursued as social theory (Young 1990, 31), and the "critique of knowledge is possible only as social theory" (Habermas 1971a, vii; see also Held 1980, 296–300). Questions of the theory of knowledge (epistemology) are not remote from, but rather are key to normative critique and historical analysis. This continues to be a key point of contention in LIS exchanges over epistemology (see the bibliographies in Buschman 2006; Buschman 2007b).

COMMUNICATIVE ACTION

Though a disclaimer was given before, it must be repeated here: the theory of communicative action is a deep and complex thesis that can in no way be fully conveyed in this chapter. His goal is a "philosophical ethics not restricted to metaethical statements ... and [that is] possible today only if we can reconstruct general presuppositions of communication and procedures for justifying norms and values" (Habermas 1979, 97). This makes perfect sense if understood in light of the prior sections: he is attempting to provide a nonfoundational social-communicative epistemology, which is itself connected to normative claims, critique, and history. Communication is conceptualized by Habermas *as* social action:

If we assume that the human species maintains itself through the socially coordinated activities of its members and that this coordination is established through communication—and in certain spheres of life, through communication aimed at reaching agreement—then the reproduction of the species also requires satisfying the conditions of a rationality inherent in communicative action (Habermas 1984, 397).

Sentences are not, in his thinking, isolated from their social context and "taken into the philosopher's 'laboratory' and dissected [as] a string of mere words" (Young 1990, 99). Rather, there are rational presuppositions behind sentences within functioning, multi-layered social contexts developed over time. "Sentences and the signs that make them up are not isolated elements but take their meaning...from a publicly available and shared language system" (Young 1990, 100). That shared system is the lifeworld, which Habermas characterizes as a "culturally transmitted and linguistically organized stock of interpretive patterns" constructed through communicative action (Habermas 1984, xxiv).

In constructing his epistemology, Habermas is concerned with "the task of seeking out the rationality embedded in everyday communicative practice and reconstructing a comprehensive concept of rationality from the validity basis of speech" (Habermas 1983, 176). In so doing Habermas explores three concepts as a rational truth-basis:

conditions of validity (which are fulfilled when an utterance holds good), validity-claims (which speakers raise with their utterances, for their validity), and redemption of a validity-claim (in the framework of a discourse which is sufficiently close to the conditions of an ideal speech situation for the consensus aimed at by the participants to be brought about solely through the force of the better argument, and in this sense to be "rationally motivated").... When claims to truth or justice become really obstinately problematic, there are no neat deductions... which could enforce an immediate decision for or against. Rather a play of argumentation is required, in which motivating reasons take the place of the unavailable knock-down arguments. [T]he fulfillment or non-fulfillment of conditions of validity, in problematic cases, can only be ascertained by means of the argumentative redemption of the corresponding validity-claims. [D]iscourse theory...only claims to reconstruct an intuitive knowledge of the meaning of universal validity-claims which every competent speaker has at his or her disposal [and it] provides only an explication of meaning, it does not provide a criterion (Habermas 1985, 85–86).

Though this chapter has tended to focus on earlier, basic building-block concepts, it is worth noting that Habermas does not solely rely on the *ideal speech situation* of un-fettered, rational communication and he later engaged its messier social and political context (Habermas 1998b). Further, he need not argue that words have independent inherent Augustinian connections to things by which we know reality, nor does he feel the need to deeply defend the internal logic of syntax. Rather, he points to cumulative social (public) meanings, the agreements upon those meanings generated over time, the process of coming to those agreements, and the practical everyday social integration as the philosophical grounding of rationality and linguistically constructed knowledge:

[O]ur ability to communicate has a universal core—basic structures and fundamental rules that all subjects master in learning to speak a language [and] in speaking we relate to the world about us, to other subjects, to our own intentions, feelings and desires. In each of these dimensions we are constantly making claims, even if usually only implicitly, concerning the validity of what we are saying. [C]laims of these sorts can be contested and criticized, defended and revised [and while] there are a number of ways of settling disputed claims—for example by appeal to authority, to tradition or to brute force the giving of reasons-for and reasons-against [is] fundamental to the idea of rationality (McCarthy in Habermas 1984, x).

His epistemology

permit[s] a progressive radicalization of the argument; there must be the freedom to move from a given level of discourse to increasingly reflected levels.... At the most radical level there must be the freedom to reflect on... conceptual systems in an attempt to reconstruct the progress of knowledge (critique of knowledge) and to reflect on... cognitive-political will-formation (McCarthy 1976, 482–83).

This operates, in Habermas' analysis and system of thought, not only via philosophical/epistemological theory, but through an analysis of historical processes, the basis of/reasons for historical change, and the resulting social structures which still bear the imprint of those processes, as will be seen in the next section. For now, the important point of Habermas' epistemology of communicative action is that it contains a defense of rationality and knowing as a social product while accounting for the linguistic construction of knowledge, and it can be normatively grounded.

THE PUBLIC SPHERE

Habermas' public sphere thesis could arguably be called communicative action in action. The public sphere concept has been much explored, questioned, defended, and revised, and still maintains a central place in debate and conceptions of democratic theory after more than forty five years. With it, he sought to answer a series of questions concerning larger historical processes which historians' limitations usually do not allow them to tackle: we know roughly when and where notions of democratic self-government initially developed, and we know they largely coincided with the growth of mercantile and then market capitalism, but we don't know *how* or *why*. At its most basic, Habermas' thesis is that democracy began in discourse: "I wish to conceive of the democratic procedure as the legal institutionalization of those forms of communication necessary for rational political will formation" (Habermas in Flyvbjerg 1998, 214). That will-formation is not merely a selection among elites, but fundamentally "the horizontal, communicative relation among equal citizens" (Cohen 1999, 388). Working backward from that language, one can see the foundational importance of epistemology, communicative action, and the emancipatory interest in knowledge: norms, knowledge and truth are grounded in the linguistic processes of argumentation and reaching intersubjective understanding, eventually leading to democracy.

Habermas identifies that this process began in the development of a distinction in what we now take for granted: the difference between public and private. Previous epochs did not conceptualize such a division: "there is no indication European society of the high Middle Ages possessed a public sphere as a unique realm distinct from the private sphere" (Habermas 1974, 50; Manchester 1992, 21–23 provides a clear description of this phenomenon). The public and private realms were fused. The ubiquitous and anonymous medieval peasant lived with his animals and family (and guests) all together in close quarters, all sharing sleeping spaces; clothing was superfluous in warm weather (Manchester 1992, 22, 51–54). The best political example higher on the other end of the social scale was kingly splendor: there was no essential division between the private "person" of the monarch, the associated public symbols of power (the crown and religio-state ceremony), and state authority. The monarch and the nobility "'were' the country and not just its representatives. . . . [T]heir lordship [was] not for but 'before' the people" (Habermas 1989, 7–8; Habermas 1974). Power was absolute and fused to the divine in the person—the body—of the sovereign, who could legitimately say "I am the state/the state is me."

Greatly simplified, Habermas locates the transformation initially in the nobility's self interest, their gradual independence from the king's court, combined with a nascent humanism developed during the Renaissance. The resulting sociability and "society" apart from the court represented an early form of separate public and private realms. In the further interests of its own independence, the nobility formed alliances with towns and merchants, in turn leading gradually to *their* further independence and the growth in the importance of their markets. While these new social relationships were highly influenced by traditional forms of power and authority, "a far-reaching network of horizontal economic dependencies emerged that . . . could no longer be accommodated by the vertical relationships of dependence [and] domination in an estate system based upon a self-contained household economy." Gradually the interests of the mercantile class came in conflict with unregulated feudal power of government and "the genuine domain of private autonomy stood opposed to the state" (Habermas 1989, 12–19). Habermas then locates the crucial transformation in the historical circumstances of the 18th-century Enlightenment furthering nascent intellectual and economic trends:

Public discussion emerged as a response to growing opportunities and responsibilities for commerce [and] three conditions favored the emergence of the public sphere: work outside the home, reading publics facilitated by the development of printing and newspapers, and the rise of the bourgeoisie whose interests were best served by heeding "the force of the better argument" (Goodnight 1992, 245).

The public sphere was self-constituted in the split between the public and the private and through rational argumentation: "discoursing private persons who critically negate political norms of the state and its monopoly on interpretation. . . . Public opinion institutionalizes itself with the goal of replacing . . . secret politics with a form . . . that is legitimated by means of rational consensus" (Hohendal 1979, 92–93). This radically altered the concept of governmental authority, subjecting it to the principle of "supervision . . . which demands that proceedings be made public" in order to be legitimate. The corresponding development of a catalog of democratic rights and constitutional limitations on power "were a perfect image of the . . . public sphere" based as they were on both a reconceptualization of authority and the "presuppositions of free commodity exchange" (Habermas 1974, 52–53). In critical and increasingly unfettered discursive public exchange over government action and policy in the economic sphere, we find a new source of legitimation of democratic power and the creation of the public sphere.

Habermas' critique of the transformation of the public sphere has focused on the market colonization of private life and the transformation the public sphere and communicative reasoning into something antithetical to democracy (Kellner 2000) The media have been transformed into a means of stimulating mass consumption and administering a public sphere taken over by corporations and elites in service to economic ends (these ideas were referred to earlier). It is the illusion of democracy—consumer choice, public opinion, and the rituals of voting and elections—that they now serve:

The world fashioned by the mass media is a public sphere in appearance only. [C]ritical discussion…tends to give way to 'exchanges about tastes and preferences' between consumers [and] the mass media today strip away the…husks from…self-interpretation and utilize them as marketable forms for the public services provided in a culture of consumers [and] the original meaning is reversed (Habermas 1989, 171).

Corporations conflate the idea of consumption decisions with citizenship, and in a feedback loop "the state has to 'address' its citizens like consumers" (Habermas 1989, 195) and political decision-making becomes an exchange of symbols, "a stylized show" (205–6) and a spectacle of "managed integration" (207). The public sphere is undercut in the form of a "post-literary" false public fed on "canned [cultural] goods"—essentially harmless in their critical content, and the "relentless publicist barrage and propagandist manipulation by the media to which consumers are exposed" (245–46).

The new function of politics is as a "field for the competition of interests" which obviates rational political will formation (Habermas 1974, 54), and is itself an idea that fundamentally roots politics in consumerism (Kelly 1979, 31). Mass communications in combination with the need to manage democracy and the economy has *refeudalized* the public sphere—substituting consumption, spectacle, and pseudo-debate for formal pomp and display of medieval kingly splendor (Habermas 1974; Habermas 1989; Peters 1993). Public opinion is a "mood-dependent preference" (Habermas 1989, 237) in democracies, not rational will-formation and self-determination, but Habermas maintains the need to subject the exercise of power "to the mandate of democratic publicity" and his work remains an enormously powerful and suggestive framework (Habermas 1989, 244). There are few better formulations of the centrality of free communication to democracy and a just society:

[O]nly in an emancipated society, which had realized the autonomy of its members, would communication have developed into that free dialogue of all with all which we always hold up as the very paradigm of a mutually formed self-identity, as well as the ideal of true consensus. To this extent the truth of statements is based on the anticipation of a life without repression (Habermas 1966, 297).

CONCLUSION: HABERMAS AND LIS

Thomas McCarthy summed up Habermas' work as a quest to "reduce the context dependency of understanding and leave room for both quasi-causal explanation and critique" (McCarthy 1991, 127). That is, Habermas wishes to overcome the totalizing dead end and aporia of postmodernism and its consequent sense of capering play as the only sensible response to postmodern capitalist culture (Habermas 1987a). He does this via a theory of communication which gets at the "'universal-pragmatic infrastructure' of speech and action"; a theory of socialization as the "acquisition of communicative competence"; a theory of social systems which gets at "objective interconnections going beyond what was subjectively intended" or its cultural context; and a theory of social evolution enabling enough historical understanding to interpret and critique the situation (McCarthy 1991, 127). It is worth noting again that this perspective has survived as a non-teleological, pragmatic approach at critique (White 2004). Habermas' (see 1998a; 1998b) recent work has tended to focus on democratic theory, but these four ideas, again significantly refined over the years, still stand in back of much of his recent theory.

Within this large context, LIS has made only partial use of Habermas' work and insights. These tend to fall into three categories. The first and most productive of these is the use of his work to analyze, situate and make normative and democratic claims on LIS and librarianship. This tends to be a vein of research which seeks to situate and/ or critique LIS research or library practices in relationship to democratic practices in a number of ways and shares with the education field the search for normative foundations tied to justifications for social support and the fact that social integration and the communicative public sphere have moved beyond political institutions out into other arenas (Habermas 1981b; Habermas 1989; Buschman 2003; Buschman, 2006; Carleheden 2006; Englund, 2006; Buschman 2007a). Flowing from this perspective on Habermas are considerations of social inclusion in the field (Williamson 2000), the role of libraries as spaces in public discourse (Alstad and Curry 2003; Leckie and Buschman 2007) and the parallel potential role of the Internet (Cooke 2007). This understanding of Habermas has also been used as a lens to evaluate information resources and information literacy discourse (Andersen 2005; Andersen 2006).

There is a second, related line of work that engages the Habermas-Foucault relationship and debates (Buschman 2007b; Stahl 2006; Anderson and Skouvig 2006; Stahl 2004). Here, Habermas is joined to a thinker who has made some inroads into LIS research and there are areas of common focus and productive (and prodigious) disagreements between them. Habermas believes Foucault is a serious thinker, but his ideas tend toward nihilistic and various contradictory conclusions and irrationality (Habermas 1987a). The third and final area of research concerns those studies that seek in some way to instrumentalize Habermas' insights in order to make technical systems (of analysis or technologies) more responsive and/or efficient (Benoit 2001; Benoit 2002; Ng 2002; Petric 2006; Yetim 2008; Asif and Klein 2009). To these three categories should be added a mention of two books by John Budd (2001; 2008). Budd does not write exclusively—or even extensively—on Habermas, but he tends to situate him in a constellation of thinkers, issues, or exchanges and points toward some of the valuable insights within those contexts he is exploring. All of these references and categories do not claim to capture all of the work in LIS utilizing Habermas, but they give a broad notion of what scholars have thus far found productive in his work. In focusing on discourse, democracy, normative values (like justice, inclusion, and fairness), and new arenas of the playing-out of the public sphere, Habermas is a thinker that should "speak" to the LIS and librarianship deeply, and help to situate its research and practices.

REFERENCES

Alstad, Colleen, and Ann Curry. 2003. "Public Space, Public Discourse, and Public Libraries." *LIBRES* 13 (1). Available at http://libres.curtin.edu.au/libres13n1/.

Andersen, Jack. 2005. "Information Criticism: Where Is It?" *Progressive Librarian* (25, Summer): 12–22.

Andersen, Jack. 2006. "The Public Sphere and Discursive Activities: Information Literacy as Sociopolitical Skills." *Journal of Documentation* 62 (2): 213–88.

Andersen, Jack, and Laura Skouvig. 2006. "Knowledge Organization: A Sociohistorical Analysis and Critique." *Library Quarterly* 76 (3): 300–322.

Asif, Zaheeruddin, and Heinz K. Klein. 2009. "Open and Free Deliberation: A Prerequisite for Positive Design." *Information & Organization* 19 (3): 186–97.

Benoit, Gerald. 2001. "Critical Theory as a Foundation for Pragmatic Information Systems Design." *Information Research* 6 (2). Available at http://informationr.net/lr/6–2/paper98.html.

Benoit, Gerald. 2002. "Toward a Critical Theoretic Perspective in Information Systems." *Library Quarterly* 72 (4): 441.

Bernstein, Richard J. 1983. *Beyond Objectivism and Relativism: Science, Hermeneutics, and Praxis.* Philadelphia: University Of Pennsylvania Press.

Bohman, James, and William Rehg. Habermas, Jürgen. In The *Stanford Encyclopedia Of Philosophy* [Electronic Resource]. Stanford University [Database Online]. Stanford, CA, Fall 1997–2009]. http://plato.stanford.edu/entries/habermas.

Brosio, Richard A. 1980. *The Frankfurt School: An Analysis of the Contradictions and Crises of Liberal Capitalist Societies.* Muncie, IN: Ball State University.

Budd, John. 2001. *Knowledge and Knowing in Library and Information Science: A Philosophical Framework.* Lanham, MD: Scarecrow Press.

Budd, John. 2008. *Self-Examination: The Present And Future Of Librarianship.* Westport, CT: Libraries Unlimited.

Buschman, John. 2003. *Dismantling The Public Sphere: Situating and Sustaining Librarianship in the Age of the New Public Philosophy.* Westport, CT: Libraries Unlimited.

Buschman, John. 2006. "The Integrity and Obstinancy of Intellectual Creations: Jürgen Habermas and Librarianship's Theoretical Literature." *Library Quarterly* 76 (3): 270–99.

Buschman, John. 2007a. "Democratic Theory in Library Information Science: Toward an Emendation." *Journal of the American Society for Information Science & Technology* 58 (10): 1483–96.

Buschman, John. 2007b. "Transgression or Stasis? Challenging Foucault in LIS Theory." *Library Quarterly* 77 (1): 21–44.

Carleheden, Mikael. 2006. "Towards Democratic Foundations: A Habermasian Perspective on the Politics of Education." *Journal of Curriculum Studies* 38 (5): 521–43.

Cohen, Joshua. 1999. "Reflections on Habermas on Democracy." *Ratio Juris* 12 (4): 385–416.

Cooke, Louise. 2007. "Controlling the Net: European Approaches to Content and Access Regulation. "*Journal of Information Science* 33 (3): 360–76.

Englund, Tomas. 2006. "Deliberative Communication: A Pragmatist Proposal." *Journal of Curriculum Studies* 38 (5): 503–20.

Finlayson, James G. 2005. *Habermas: A Very Short Introduction.* New York: Oxford University Press.

Flyvbjerg, Bent. 1998. "Habermas and Foucault: Thinkers for Civil Society?" *British Journal of Sociology* 49 (2): 210.

Giddens, Anthony. 1982. *Profiles and Critiques in Social Theory.* Berkeley: University of California Press.

Giroux, Henry A. 1984. "Public Philosophy and the Crisis in Education." *Harvard Educational Review* 54 (2): 186–94.

Goodnight, G. Thomas. 1992. "Habermas, the Public Sphere, and Controversy." *International Journal of Public Opinion Research* 4 (3): 243–55.

Habermas, Jürgen. 1966. "Knowledge and Interest." *Inquiry* 9:285–300.

Habermas, Jürgen. 1970. *Toward a Rational Society: Student Protest, Science, and Politics.* Boston: Beacon Press.

Habermas, Jürgen. 1971a. *Knowledge and Human Interests.* Boston: Beacon Press.

Habermas, Jürgen. 1971b. "Why More Philosophy?" *Social Research* 38 (4): 633–54.

Habermas, Jürgen. 1974. "The Public Sphere: An Encyclopedia Article (1964)." *New German Critique* (3, Fall): 49–55.

Habermas, Jürgen. 1976a. "Systematically Distorted Communication." In *Critical Sociology: Selected Readings,* ed. Paul Connerton, 348–87. New York: Penguin.

Habermas, Jürgen. 1976b. "Theory and Practice in a Scientific Civilization." In *Critical Sociology: Selected Readings,* ed. Paul Connerton, 330–47. New York: Penguin.

Habermas, Jürgen. 1981a. "Modernity versus Postmodernity." *New German Critique* (22): 3–14.

Habermas, Jürgen. 1981b. "New Social Movements." *Telos* (49): 33–37.

Habermas, Jürgen. 1983. "Remarks on the Concept of Communicative Action." In *Social Action,* ed. Gottfried Seebass and Raimo Tuomela, 151–78. Boston: D. Reidel Publishing.

Habermas, Jürgen. 1984. *The Theory of Communicative Action: Reason and the Rationalization of Society.* Boston: Beacon Press.

Habermas, Jürgen. 1985. "A Philosophico-Political Profile." *New Left Review* (151): 75–105.

Habermas, Jürgen. 1987a. *The Philosophical Discourse of Modernity: Twelve Lectures.* Cambridge, MA: MIT Press.

Habermas, Jürgen. 1987b. *The Theory of Communicative Action: Lifeworld and System.* Boston: Beacon Press.

Habermas, Jürgen. 1989. *The Structural Transformation of the Public Sphere: An Inquiry into a Category of Bourgeois Society.* Cambridge, MA: MIT Press.

Habermas, Jürgen. 1998a. "Remarks on Legitimation through Human Rights." *Modern Schoolman* LXXV (January): 87–100.

Habermas, Jürgen. 1998b. *The Inclusion of the Other: Studies in Political Theory.* Cambridge, MA: MIT Press.

Habermas, Jürgen. 2003. "Interpreting the Fall of a Monument." *German Law Journal* 4 (07): 701–8.

Habermas, Jürgen. 2004. "Public Space and the Political Public Sphere—The Biographical Roots of Two Motifs in My Thought." Commemorative lecture for the Kyoto Prize, San Diego, CA, November 11, 2004. Available at http://homepage.mac.com/gedavis/jh/kyoto_lecture_nov_2004.pdf.

Held, David. 1980. *Introduction to Critical Theory: Horkheimer to Habermas.* Berkeley: University Of California Press.

Hohendahl, Peter. 1974. "Jürgen Habermas: 'The Public Sphere' (1964)." *New German Critique* 3 (Autumn): 45–48.

Hohendahl, Peter U. 1979. "Critical Theory, Public Sphere and Culture: Jürgen Habermas and His Critics." *New German Critique* 16: 89–118.

Kellner, Douglas. 2000. "Habermas, the Public Sphere, and Democracy: A Critical Intervention." In *Perspectives on Habermas,* ed. Lewis E. Hahn, 259–87. Chicago: Open Court.

Kelly, George A. 1979. "Who Needs a Theory of Citizenship?" *Daedalus* 108 (4): 21–36.

Leckie, Gloria J., and John Buschman. 2007. "Space, Place, and Libraries: An Introduction." In *The Library as Place: History, Community, and Culture,* ed. John Buschman and Gloria J. Leckie, 3–25. Westport, CT: Libraries Unlimited.

Manchester, William R. 1992. *A World Lit Only by Fire: The Medieval Mind and the Renaissance: Portrait of an Age.* Boston: Little, Brown.

McCarthy, Thomas A. 1976. "A Theory of Communicative Competence." In *Critical Sociology: Selected Readings,* ed. Paul Connerton, 470–97. New York: Penguin.

McCarthy, Thomas A. 1978. *The Critical Theory of Jürgen Habermas.* Cambridge, MA: MIT Press.

McCarthy, Thomas A. 1991. *Ideals And Illusion: On Reconstruction and Deconstruction in Contemporary Critical Theory.* Cambridge, MA: MIT Press.

Ng, Kwong Bor. 2002. "The Applicability of Universal Pragmatics in Information Retrieval Interaction: A Pilot Study." *Information Processing & Management* 38 (2): 237–48.

Palmisano, Joseph M. 2001. *World of Sociology.* Detroit: Gale Group.

Peters, John Durham. 1993. "Distrust or Representation: Habermas on the Public Sphere." *Media, Culture & Society* 15 (October): 541–71.

Petrič , Gregor. 2006. "Conceptualizing and Measuring the Social Uses of the Internet: The Case of Personal Web Sites." *Information Society* 22 (5, Nov.): 291–301.

Stahl, Bernd Carsten. 2004. "Whose Discourse? A Comparison of the Foucauldian and Habermasian Concepts of Discourse in Critical LIS Research. In *Proceedings of the Tenth American Conference on Information Systems, August 6–8, 2004.* New York: Association for Information Systems.

Stahl, Bernd Carsten. 2006. "On the Difference or Equality of Information, Misinformation, and Disinformation: A Critical Research Perspective." *Informing Science* 9 (01): 83–96. Available at http://www.cse.dmu.ac.uk/~bstahl/publications/2004_foucault_habermas_amcis.pdf.

Webster, Frank. 2003. *Theories of the Information Society.* New York: Routledge.

White, Steven K. 1995. "Reason, Modernity, And Democracy." In *The Cambridge Companion to Habermas,* ed. Steven K. White, 3–18. New York: Cambridge University Press.

White, Steven K. 2004. "The Very Idea of a Critical Social Science: A Pragmatist Turn." In *The Cambridge Companion to Critical Theory,* ed. Fred Leland Rush, 310–35. New York: Cambridge University Press.

Williamson, Matthew. 2000. "Social Exclusion and the Public Library: A Habermasian Insight." *Journal of Librarianship and Information Science* 32 (4): 178–86.

Yetim, Fahri. 2008. "Critical Examination of Information: A Discursive Approach and Its Implementations." *Informing Science* 11 (01): 125–46.

Young, R. E. 1990. *A Critical Theory Of Education: Habermas and Our Children's Future.* New York: Teachers College Press.

14

Martin Heidegger's Critique of Informational Modernity

Ronald E. Day
Indiana University, USA

INTRODUCTION

Martin Heidegger (1889–1976) was a German phenomenologist, one of the best-known philosophers of the 20th century. His work was strongly engaged by, and in many ways influenced, the work of Jacques Derrida and allied French thinkers such as Philippe Lacoue-Labarthe and Jean-Luc Nancy, the French literary theorist and novelist Maurice Blanchot,[1] the Italian theorist Giorgio Agamben, and the French psychoanalyst, Jacques Lacan, as well as American theorists, such as Avital Ronell, who wrote one of the earliest contemporary engagements of technology by critical theory (Ronell 1989). He was embraced by Sartre as an existentialist, a position that is repudiated in his "Letter on Humanism" (Heidegger 1977c) and, more broadly, by the division between the ontic and the ontological in his work, beginning with his first published work, *Being and Time.* His works' consideration of method and historical tradition were originally expanded upon by his student, Hans-Georg Gadamer. While Heidegger's work has been maligned by many in the popular press, and even in academe, particularly in the United States, for his assumption of the rectorship at the University of Freiburg during 1933–34 and for statements in his writings during that time regarding the role of the German university in the Nazi state, many of these attacks selectively overemphasize, and even factually distort (that is, the work of Victor Farías), particulars of Heidegger's work and life during this period.[2] However much Heidegger's work at one time gave a conservative turn to the Nietzschean destruction of the metaphysical tradition in philosophy and society, his total oeuvre constitutes a monumental social critique of modernity and philosophy's role in it. Heidegger's explicit call for the destruction of metaphysics in his earliest full-length work, *Being and Time* (1927 [1962]), was a call to move philosophically back to, and beyond, ancient Greek philosophy and its ensuing tradition (particularly as interpreted and destined through Latin philosophy), toward an analysis of human beings that is ontologically prior to the Western philosophical tradition's privileged concepts of subjectivity and representation. His work challenged and still challenges the emerging modern social sciences of his time and today, particularly what he termed their "thesis of the precedence of method," reasserting the need for foundational critical thought prior to the fallacious appropriation of epistemologies and methods borrowed from the physical sciences. The general critical effect of his work is to call into question many popular modes of discussion (e.g., journalism and mass communication), psychology (e.g., ego-centered clinical psychoanalysis and psychiatry and much experimental psychology), and social sciences epistemologies (e.g., the model of causation taken by psychology and sociology from physics) and methods (e.g., the privilege of statistics).

By beginning with "the question of being," Heidegger's work asks, What does it mean to be a being known as a human being in the midst of other beings? His work addresses the most important question of modernity and today: the relation between human knowledge and the existence of all beings, not least of all, the human. The difficulty, as well as both the successes and failures of his rhetorical strategies and politics, must be seen in light of his attempt to critically distance the very social and cultural traditions—and language—that shape our modes of understanding.

In Library and Information Science (LIS) proper, there has been little extended discussion of his work, other than in the works of the present author and Rafael Capurro. There have been use of concepts from *Being and Time* in critiques of artificial intelligence and human computer interaction by Terry Winograd, Phil Agre, Paul Dourish, and others.[3] In this article, I will not be covering much of this secondary literature, which makes fragmentary use of Heidegger's vast oeuvre. Instead, I will be concentrating on the issues of language, technology, identity, and community within the context of Heidegger's critique of the Western metaphysical tradition and modernity in an attempt to show the importance of Heidegger's work as a whole to LIS and to discourses on "the information society." I propose that Heidegger's work has profound and broad implications for LIS and societies now thought of as information societies, both directly and through the work of Derrida and others mentioned above, and that this is best seen by an analysis of some of his central concepts.

In thinking of the relationship between Heidegger's vast work and that of information science and information culture in such a short discussion, we must severely reduce his work to several major issues. In this chapter, I have decided to address the following major themes in his work: (1) Heidegger's project of destroying the metaphysical tradition and his bracketing of the privilege of the subject in such and how this project affects mentalistic and user-centered studies of information in LIS, (2) Heidegger's writings on technology and their relationship to, and critique of, information as a form of epistemic presence, (3) Heidegger's concept of naming in poetics, and (4) Heidegger's conception of being in terms of *Mitsein* (explicitly so in *Being and Time*), and the relation of such to a politics of communication and freedom. In all these themes, I would like to suggest that Heidegger's work poses a massive challenge to LIS to rigorously account for its psychological and technocratic positioning of human knowing and its representational understandings of information, points that, in the busyness of its scientific methods, there have been heretofore few critical engagements.

THE DESTRUCTION OF THE SUBJECT AND THE END OF PHILOSOPHY AND THE TASK OF THINKING

While some have strongly stressed the linguistic turn or *Kehre* in Heidegger's work, marking a distinction between, on the one hand, the ontological analysis of human being as a particular type of being (namely one concerned about its manner of being in terms of existence [human being as *Dasein*[4]]), its relation to other types of beings, and, foremost, its relation to death, and on the other, an analysis of language as the "house of being," there is a social critique of modernity that pervades both these major concerns in Heidegger's work, namely, the problem of technology—the shape of human beings' skillful designs and activities in the world. To arrive at this analysis of technology, however, it is helpful to consider what, for Heidegger, constitutes the metaphysical subject and why it needs to be decentered, and in fact, destroyed, as a social, cultural, and philosophical concept.

Heidegger's task of the destruction of metaphysics and subjectivity is a task inherited from Nietzsche. For Heidegger, Nietzsche's overturning of metaphysics failed because it replaced a metaphysics of being with a metaphysics of becoming. Against the backdrop of Edmund Husserl's phenomenology of consciousness, Heidegger's work attempted a phenomenology that always begins with a step back from consciousness, psychologism, and subjectivity. Phenomenology requires that we start by describing relations of existence. For Heidegger, the study of the nature of being requires that we start by examining the relations of human beings, as he does in *Being and Time*. (In works after *Being and Time*, Heidegger engages language as the primary frame for all human relations.) Heidegger's understanding of human being is primarily concerned with the ontological and only the ontic within that. For example, when intentions are discussed, as in *Being and Time*, they are discussed in terms of relations between beings, that is, as "concerns" with other beings, as well as Dasein's concern for itself. Similarly, as well, in *Being and Time* Heidegger doesn't write about normal and abnormal states of mind, or pathologies, but rather, moods (*Stimmung*)—a word that is etymologically and conceptually related to "attunement" (*Gestimmtheit*) in *Being and Time*. The importance of moods in Heidegger is that they are psychological states that one inhabits, rather than that one "has." The Heideggerian conception of moods suggests a psychology that is based on understanding the relation of beings to their own fears and hopes in regard to their being in the world, rather than in terms of inner states and faculties.

For Heidegger, human beings are singular amidst other beings, as a particular type of being (*Dasein*). Dasein is a type of being that is primarily concerned within its own nature of being. Ontologically, Dasein is distinctive in that it encounters its own existence as a question and engages its historical and sociocultural configurations as narratives and themes in order to choose future actions. Appropriating a concept of radical temporality from Nietzsche[5] and the concept of historical breaks or "caesuras" from the poetics of Friedrich Hölderlin, Heidegger views history in terms of historical traditions punctuated by moments of radical, transfiguring breaks that open history up to other historical possibilities. Such breaks open history and Dasein to freedom, understood as a space of action and historical redirection in the midst of what previously was seen as necessary and inevitable. Such breaks reassert the authenticity of Dasein as a being for whom its own historicity is important. (The occurrence of these breaks can be assisted by philosophical-historiographic critiques [such as those offered by Heidegger's own works].)

Man's historicity is offered in such moments, which constitute genuine "events," distinct from the expected moments in normal times. Like Dasein's encounter with death, in the event[6] the unique ontological character of human being, not covered up by historicism nor by soothing everyday (*Alltäglichkeit*) chitchat, appears. We may say that such authentic historicity is a manner of being responsible (in the sense of being attuned and responding) in an attuned manner to Dasein's being in the world. Historiographic, and moreover, historiological criticality is for Heidegger, thus, part of Dasein's authentic mode of being, as a being not only in time, but *constitutive of time* (see, for example, *Being and Time* section I.6). Such a critical imperative constitutes the heart of the ethics and the politics of Heideggerian philosophy—both in Heidegger's writings and in the writings of Derrida and others influenced by Heidegger.

For Heidegger, the experience of time as temporality is specific to *Dasein's* mode of being. Time is experienced by *Dasein* as an issue, foremost as an issue of finitude. Through its awareness of finitude, *Dasein* knows both the "ek-static" or "thrown" nature of being and the fear of its own extinction in death. But death, for *Dasein,* can only be known by another's death. This concern for itself through another leads to the very important concept of *Mitsein* (being-with) in *Being and Time.* While the existential analytic of *Dasein's* relation to its own death makes for compelling reading in *Being and Time,* arguably it is the concept of *Mitsein* that underlies it and contributes to much of Heidegger's analysis and approach in later work, even if, like *Dasein* the term isn't used after *Being and Time.* The concept of *Mitsein* has, also, been extended to analyzing animals or the universe as a whole by Derrida, Agamben, Lacoue-Labarthe, Nancy, and others, sometimes under the concept of the "in-common." Both *Dasein* and *Mitsein* signify essential properties that are *given* to human beings by the very fact of their being.[7]

The implications of Heidegger's ontic-ontological divide is immense for Library and Information Science (LIS). First of all, the psychological basis for user studies is situated by the Heideggerian analysis as being part of the metaphysical tradition. Cognitivist notions, particularly those of older cognitive psychology as used in Belkin and Brookes' writings in LIS, would be seen as metaphysical expressions since they work within a idealist and Cartesian framework. Critiques of such have previously appeared in LIS (Frohmann 2004; Day 2007), but they remain much in the minority in the field. As a whole, the field contains few explicit critiques of the cognitivist epistemological and psychological assumptions and its metaphysical models in Belkin's very influential ASK model.

Second, as we shall see, below, the modern conception of the term *information* and of information science belongs to a metaphysical understanding of knowledge as representation. This understanding is particularly onerous for Heidegger in its characterization of knowledge as "ready-to-hand" (*zuhanden*) (*Being and Time*).[8] Entities that are ready-to-hand are characterized as objects that are present or have "presence" in the sense that Hegel used the term, as an entity that is "objective" in the sense of being dialectically opposite (*Gegenstand*) man as the thinking subject.[9] For Heidegger, modern science, as part of what he terms the "onto-theological tradition" of Western metaphysics, sees beings as distinct *objects* to be understood and managed by *objective* methods. Particularly in terms of human beings, Heidegger sees this as problematic, not only in the social sciences, but in modern technocratic institutions, treating humans and other beings according to principles and practices of "human management" and "resource management."

In brief, information as a form of presence that is ready-to-hand constitutes, for Heidegger, the fullest extension of metaphysics into the realm of knowledge and, today, social life (and, most astoundingly, into the realm of art [Heidegger 1977b; see Day 2001, 2008]). From this point of view, information in its social, professional, and technical uses as a sense of metaphysical presence requires rigorous critical analysis, and this critical project may be seen as a central task in the destruction of the metaphysical tradition today. In so far as this task is taken up, today, as a discursive-textual mode of critical analysis, we may say that it constitutes (naming such after Derrida's project, which, though, in certain manners redirects and sometimes challenges Heidegger's critique), a task of deconstructing the modern conception of "information." The deconstruction of "information," coming from the Heideggerian "Destruktion" of metaphysics *(Being and Time)*, constitutes a very specific type of textual-historical-cultural task for critical information theory, distinct from any looser use of the term "deconstruction" (Day 2001).[10] It is a task that depends upon an understanding of a metaphysical tradition in Western society and culture, epitomized in certain philosophical texts, but also invested throughout Western culture, society, politics, and particularly, in and through the mass media.[11]

Third, though there have been incorporations of Heidegger's work into LIS via hermeneutics, we need to remember that the discussion of hermeneutics in Heidegger's work was largely that of an ontological hermeneutics, not a textual one or, further, a psychological one. Traditional textual hermeneutics involves analyzing the relation of textual parts to the whole of texts and to their historical contexts. Hermeneutics, proper, is not a traditionally psychological investigation either since, as in the hermeneutic tradition, the personal agent (e.g., the reader) is analyzed as a product of historical context, not as an autonomous agent of cognition. This emphasis upon the historicity of personal agency is a central theme in both Heidegger and Gadamer's works. Heidegger's discussion of the hermeneutic circle in *Being and Time* (the term is conspicuously absent in work after *Being and Time,* even though after Heidgger's "turn" the being of Dasein was discussed almost exclusively in terms of language) is in regard to how Dasein's modes of ontic being obscures or opens up the question of being. (And so, the problem is how psychological investigation, for example, itself obscures a more fundamental ontological investigation into the relation of being and beings [and thus, into the investigation of other beings, other than Dasein, as well—see *Being and Time,* section 32]). In other words, Heidegger's project throughout his oeuvre was ontological—or to be more precise, it was a critique of ontology understood within the Western metaphysical tradition. Ontic discussions take place within the foundations of this project.

Fourth, by viewing "information" as one of the latest and most acute symptoms of the metaphysical tradition, not the least spread through ontic chitchat regarding the value of information in culture and society, the Heideggerian critique challenges the very grammatical blurring of the various meanings of information in information science and it challenges the institutional (both public and commercial) claims and profitability of information society and subsidiary discourses. The Heideggerian critique opens up a rhetorical/discursive critical analysis of the reification of the term *information* and it rejects a positivist philosophy of information (e.g., Floridi), demanding a critique of such in terms of its metaphysical assumptions.

Last, while we will return to the political implications of Heidegger's conception of Mitsein at the end of this essay, here it may be proposed that Dasein must always already be analyzed in the midst of its being among other beings. Such a view challenges a liberal-communicative conception of society as made up of individuals "communicating" their thoughts with one another "reasonably." The notion of a communicative society of reason is problematized in Heidegger's work by a conception of individuality that sees such as constructed by traditions of custom and language that are both blind and insightful toward phenomena. Individuals are historically, socially, and culturally constructed, in addition to their more fundamental ontological manners of being as human beings. Rationality in communication may be variously possible or impossible depending on different social, cultural, and material conditions and on different life experiences. Further, concepts of rationality are products of cultural affordances and their traditions, and so it cannot be used as a transcendental measure for communicative success.

Individual actions resulting in events of freedom, for Heidegger, take place between necessity and potentiality, the latter made possible by rethinking historical traditions—made up of social and cultural forms—toward the founding and construction of the future. Ethical decisions (versus prescriptive moral actions) take place in decision spaces of indeterminate historical results. Such moments of indeterminacy have no certain outcome because normative ontic chains of action are what are being called into account at such moments. Ethics in philosophy takes the form of century-old questions regarding just actions that are replies to real situations and they are characterized most by a lack of answers that morality supplies. The consequences of this view for information ethics would be to place information—rethought as an uncertain form of knowledge (knowledge as "in-formation")—at the center of ethics, rather than to take information ethics as a type of "practical" ethics involving information artifacts and technologies (see Day 2001). *In-formation,* as designated here, is the call to which we reply when the categories of knowledge are not yet adequate. The concept of information as the indeterminate call of being to which we respond outside of traditional frameworks of knowledge is a radical rereading of our modern conception of information as presence, but one that does not lie outside of earlier uses of "information" as incomplete knowledge. It is fundamentally ethical, as well as aesthetic and cognitive concept (Day 2001, chapter 5). It is foundational in a critical theory of information based upon a destructive/deconstructive project acting upon the modern conception of information.

Such a Heideggerian-deconstructive counterreading of "information" and of information science constitutes an important project for a "critical information theory." This task would be a timely and important critical encounter with the Western metaphysical tradition in its philosophical, cultural, and social forms (Heidegger 1977b).

HEIDEGGER, SCIENCE, AND TECHNOLOGY

Heidegger in his lecture, "The Age of the World Picture" (Heidegger 1977a) argued that the sciences are characterized by an etching, tearing out, or de-sign (*reissen*) of an initial frame (*Grundriss*) from phenomena, with certain epistemic commitments and certain ontological commitments that then are not further questioned and within which further research is carried out. Heidegger's understanding of scientific research is that it is characterized by an increasingly reductionist design of knowledge upon phenomena. Heidegger's critique of science extends into the sociology of scholarship, which, for Heidegger, is now characterized by the busyness of researchers doing "empirical" research on established topics setup within the frameworks of established scientific points of views and the institutions, funding, and publishing agents that support them. For Heidegger, critical thought upon the frameworks of such views is lost in such a sociology of knowledge. For Heidegger, the task of philosophy is to provide conceptual critique toward rethinking a Western metaphysical tradition that shows itself in a positivist understanding of science in technological modernity.

Heidegger's critique of science is part of his critique of modernity as the cultural and social triumph of metaphysical reason in modern technology and the technological organization of society. Modern technology for Heidegger involves the causal mechanization of arts (*techne*) within a teleological metaphysics and, ultimately, such extends to the social organization of society. Heidegger's critique of technology in terms of art (both, and variously, understood as craft and as aesthetics) is fairly complex, and I have recounted it elsewhere, particularly in regard to the concept of the work of art (Day 2008). Here, I will provide the most relevant parts of that account for our present purposes.

In "The Origin of the Work of Art" Heidegger (1971c) discusses art as a form of work that explicitly displays creation or expressive emergence ("a work is always a work, which means that it is something worked out, brought about, effected" [Heidegger 1971c, 56]). In a later lecture and then essay, "The Question Regarding Technology" (1977e), Heidegger discusses art's process of creating and bringing about expressive emergence. He does this by returning to the ancient Greek term for art, *techne,* and the use of this term in Aristotle's discussion of four types of causality in Aristotle's *Physics.* In Heidegger's essay (1977e), Aristotle's four causes are reinterpreted from their understanding in Latin and modern philosophy (as *causa*) to what Heidegger claims is their proper context in ancient Greek philosophy (as *aition*), a reading that reinterprets Aristotle's four causes and the meaning of *techne* and *poiesis* according to the four causes' co-responsibility with one another as mutual affordances for a thing's appearance, rather than according to the traditional teleological reading of them (where an ideal "first cause" is understood as an origin that is fulfilled in the final product [the "final cause"] through efficient and material causes). In Heidegger's (1977e) rereading of *causa* by *aition,* Aristotle's first or formal cause (the cultural context, social situation and needs, and the resulting plan for the work), the efficient cause (the craftsperson or other agency for bringing about the work), the material cause (matter), and the final cause (the reception and purpose for which the thing is brought forward) are understood as a total assemblage of concepts, materials, and labor that brings forth a work in an artistic event. For Heidegger, the Greek term *techne* refers to the techniques and activities that work to bring forth (Heidegger: *poiesis*) a work.

The notion of *techne,* here, is close to the traditional notion of the English word *art,* in the sense of craft or skill. It is Heidegger's intention to blur the modern (18th century and later) separation of art and craft, that is, to blur the difference between the fine and the crafted arts, a division that occurred in late-18th-century aesthetic theory, as well as in art practices. In so doing, Heidegger develops a phenomenological understanding of the artwork based on site-specific and time-valued labor and reception. By critiquing the understanding of the work as a symbolic object, which is said to contain or embody meaning in its form, and by asserting an understanding of the work as an event or *work* (constructed by *techne* [context-sensitive technique and method] and whose meaning is afforded by its social and cultural conditions for emergence [*poiesis*]), the fine arts are rejoined to the crafted arts according to pragmatic, functional, and constructivist understandings, rather than those of ideational representation. With this gesture, too, the container-content metaphors for the form-content distinction in aesthetics[12] (and in communication and information, too) are abandoned. Form, instead of being understood as a teleological first cause, is understood as cultural affordances for expression—socially situated and historically specific for the artwork's meaning.

In brief, Heidegger returns to Aristotle's writings on *poiesis* and *techne* in order to recover an understanding of creation that he sees in artworks and which he sees as forgotten in the dominance of modern technological production. This earlier understanding, which Heidegger attempts to recover from the ancient Greek texts, views art as the process of creating an object, responsive in the way of Aristotle's four causes, to the site and time specificity of the context of production.

Heidegger's critique of modern technology is characterized by his criticism of the tendency to technically narrow beings to "useful" elements and then to exploit those elements, regardless of their originating conditions of appearance and existence. (Heidegger [1977e] points, for example, to the exploitation of the Rhine River as a source of hydroelectric power.) The exploitation takes place not simply in terms of technological framing, but in terms of the stringing together of technological elements into a social "machine." The problem is not that of tools, per se, but the stringing together of social and technological tools toward an instrumental rationality and a reduction of human activities to quantifiable labor within systems of production.[13] This is to say that the issue for Heidegger is that of the appropriation of beings within a systemic instrumentality. The central issues, here, are that of the erasure of human historicity and the exploitation of both human and nonhuman beings for instrumental goals. Within this metaphysical tradition, beings are seen as resources for the purpose of short-term exploitation for predetermined ends, a purpose that is often detrimental for beings overall, including human beings in the long run.

It is for this reason that Heidegger (1977e) understands physics, the science of determinate (i.e., Aristotle: "efficient") causal forces, as paradigmatic of modern reason and he understands Aristotle's four causes as having been distorted by a Latin interpretative tradition wherein cause is primarily understood as determinate force, rather than as affordance. Heidegger's criticism is not of physics, per se, but rather, of the inappropriate and misleading overextension of the determinate sense of causation present in Newtonian physics (as causal forces between bodies) to other studies and phenomena, foremost in the social sciences (and not least to communication and information theory), as well as art. The ultimate moment of this overextension of a certain type of determinate causal explanation occurs, for Heidegger, in explanations of art objects in terms of their being viewed as products of the transfer of mental ideas or as the transfer of semantic affects. (Cf., for example, Warren Weaver's discussion of *affects* in dance performances as instances of communication causes and *effects* [Weaver 1949].)

For Heidegger, the artwork, like the natural being, appears as an expression (*poiesis*) of an environment's affordances. Heidegger views *techne* as being the means by which *poiesis* occurs in the hands of humans, rather than "naturally," Thus, for Heidegger (1977e), the "essence of *techne*" is not made up of the privileged values of effectiveness, efficiency, and teleological completion and reproduction in modern technology, but rather, of the mutual affordances—and with this, the site-specificity and time-valuedness—of the poetic or creative.

For Heidegger, a return to site-specific and time-valued manners of analyses and production marks the beginnings of the "task of thinking" (Heidegger 1977b), a task that takes place in critical regard to the metaphysical underpinnings of not only the philosophical tradition, but industrial modernity. Heidegger's task of thinking occurs at the historical end of metaphysics, that is, at the end of the dominance of the metaphysical subject and its humanism as the measure for thinking all beings and the world, including human beings. Art, for Heidegger, is the most obvious entrance into thinking coresponsible emergence and creation—a type of thinking of being that he claims has been forgotten by the Western metaphysical tradition and its foremost expression in the culture of modern technology. Heidegger is arguing for a form of thought that is engaged with thinking the mutual affordances necessary for beings to emerge and to be expressive in co-responsible manners, rather than a form of thought that seeks to understand and condition an environment in terms of what we think beings are and should be for the purpose of engineering their exploitation (and even their creation) for the fulfillment of human needs, which, too, are engineered in a similar fashion. His thought challenges the cultural traditions of technological modernity, the foundations of humanism, the traditional conceptual divisions between human beings and other beings, and the onto-theological underpinnings of philosophy, policy, and production. It opens up to an "ecological" type of thought rooted in thinking beings in terms of co-responsible affordances and emergence. Heidegger's thought on beings begins with thinking the shared being of beings, rather than thinking beings in terms of individual essences.

While Heidegger's critique of science is sometimes too general—or, perhaps it would be better to write, sometimes unclear or lacking in analytic nuance—his investigation into the ancient roots of *techne* provide a powerful social and scientific critique of scientism and the overapplication of determinate causation, particularly in the social sciences and the policy activities and psychological models that issue from these.

In LIS no attention has been paid to theories of causation—and thus, method—in qualitative or quantitative studies. Those studies that have pointed to a misplaced scientism or to sloppy vocabulary in LIS have largely been ignored in the dominant literature and by the major players, and the founding frameworks remain in place with very little crossover into other disciplines. The theorization of technology has largely remained at the level of use or a simplistic dichotomy of "good" versus "bad" technologies. In brief, the Heideggerian theorization of *techne* and his critique of science could give LIS a considerable theoretical toolkit.

HEIDEGGER, POETICS, AND VOCABULARY

Martin Heidegger's lectures and writings on the problem of language, and thus, that of communication and information, are many. Particularly after *Being and Time* Heidegger's focus shifted from ontology proper to viewing language as both the restriction and possibility of ontic being. Heidegger's analysis of language in *Being and Time* largely is an analysis of discourse and its relationship to ontological authenticity. The problem of the relation of language to authenticity is more fully developed, however, in Heidegger's many years of considering poetic works, particularly those of the poet Friedrich Hölderlin. Authenticity in poetry, for Heidegger, occurs in an event of "naming." Naming, for Heidegger, represents an event of truth (understood as *aletheia*—a veiling and unveiling of being—rather than the correspondence of intellect and thing (*adequatio*)—see Heidegger 1977d). In naming, to use Heidegger's words, worlds appear upon the earth. The European documentalist, Suzanne Briet, too had a sense of naming in her understanding of the documentary process, though, unlike Heidegger, her focus was on the further elaboration and continuation of vocabulary and discourse from the primary documents of controlled vocabulary and classes to secondary documents (Briet 2006).

In section 34 of Heidegger's *Being and Time,* we find discourse emphasized as the important element of language, along with the observation that what is important about discourse is that it emerges as an attunement to Dasein's existential being in the world:

In discourse the intelligibility of Being-in-the-world (an intelligibility which goes with a state-of-mind) is articulated according to significations; and discourse is this articulation. The items constitutive for discourse are: what the discourse is about (what is talked about); what is said-in-the-talk, as such; the communication; and the making-known. These are not properties which can just be raked up empirically from language. They are existential characteristics rooted in the state of Dasein's Being (Heidegger 1962, 206).

In Heidegger's later works his analysis shifts from a focus on discourse to a focus on poetry and the word. In this later work, language is seen as the "house of being." For Heidegger, the poetic ("saying" [Heidegger 1971a, 1971e]), similar to the etching out of the world through the work of art (Heidegger 1971c), shows the simultaneous appearance and withdrawal of being as a world begins to appear through language. This appearance of the "world" and the disappearance of the "earth" (Heidegger 1971c) is very different than the language of propositional statements that attempt to correspond to empirical objects and events. Truth as the simultaneous veiling and unveiling of *aletheia* differs from truth as correspondence in so far as the former marks both the possibilities and limits of representation whereas the former takes representation for granted (see, for example, "On the Essence of Truth" [Heidegger 1977d]).

With the poetic word, being is brought into the "Open" where it is both unveiled and veiled. Within the opening of truth (*aletheia*), correspondences of meaning (*veritas*) through representation then take place. For Heidegger, the poetic word most primordially speaks the fact of language, which is ontologically prior to representation. *"Language speaks" to human beings first of all the fact of language* (Heidegger 1971e, 124). For Heidegger, poetic speech is an originating event for discourse.

For Heidegger, information and communication theory hide the facticity of language; that we first of all respond to language rather than to any one speaker. According to Heidegger, the job of information theory is first of all to naturalize the appearance of language as the representation of ideas and as the means for communication between a speaker and a hearer, thus ensuring that language will itself appear only as a means, rather than as the origin, for communication or information. As information, language is characterized as the representation of thoughts or as the representation of empirical events. What is forgotten in this is the foundational role that language has in constructing both the language of, and the means for, being. Within what Heidegger terms "framing" (sometimes translated as "enframing" [*Gestell*]), language operates as representation. With the modern conceptions of information and communication, framing becomes the epistemology within which language is understood:

Within Framing, speaking turns into information [*Das so gestellte Sprechen wird zur Information*]. It informs itself about itself in order to safeguard its own procedures by information theories. Framing—the nature of modern technology holding sway in all directions—commandeers for its purposes a formalized language, the kind of communication which "informs" man uniformly, that is, gives him the form in which he is fitted into the technological-calculative universe, and gradually abandons "natural language"....Formalization, the calculated availability of Saying [i.e., poetic language], is the goal and the norm....Information theory conceives of the natural aspect of language as a lack of formalization (Heidegger 1971e, 132).

For Heidegger, the metaphysical tradition is a tradition of obscuring the social and cultural constructions of normative meanings and representations. Like modern technology, Heidegger views modern communicative practices as producing statements out of previously established statements. Language understood as communication, thus, is dedicated to the reproduction of normative forms for understanding. Ontic discourses, for Heidegger, tend to proceed out of the forgetting of the fact of language as a founding gesture for the very possibility of such discourses' claim to be representational. Poetic language, for Heidegger, returns us to the "house of being" in its reply to the world. In doing so, it must also reply first of all to language as a whole and to the fact of language as a founding gesture of, particularly, human being.

It must be remembered that in Heidegger's work ontic activities are situated in ontological concerns. Heidegger's concern throughout his oeuvre is with what he believes is the philosophical, social, and cultural forgetting of the prior conditions or ontological openings for ontic activities. It is the forgetting and erasure of these more primordial, ontologically prior, modes of being which is the danger. For modern man such a forgetting and erasure of authenticity occurs through what Heidegger terms the "onto-theological tradition" of Western metaphysics. For Heidegger, the danger is that the social, cultural, historical, and material (the four causes discussed in "The Question Concerning Technology" [Heidegger 1977e]) co-affordances for emergence may be forgotten, and thus, the historicity of man's being is forgotten in representations that, transmitted globally through standardized social and cultural forms constitute "world pictures" or representations (*Weltbild*—Heidegger 1977a). Heidegger's concerns about language are, thus, a concern about how language is understood communicationally and informationally and how these understandings forget the constitutive role of language for being.

For LIS, Heidegger's understanding of language challenges representational epistemologies and conduit metaphors for information and communication that still underpin LIS theory and practices. Heidegger's later works forefront the event of poetics in both language and the arts and raise the status of such against normative understandings of "information," today, in both LIS and popular discourses. Last, Heidegger's work attempts to investigate the primordial event of naming. It investigates the ontological nature of naming and what is at stake for human beings and other beings when names enter into discursive systems as informational representations of the true. In brief, Heidegger's work forefronts the central issue of LIS research—vocabulary—in a manner that challenges traditional LIS assumptions that originate out of the metaphysical tradition.

THE POLITICS OF INFORMATION: "POETICALLY MAN DWELLS"

I would like to conclude this article with some considerations of the different models of person and community that Heidegger's writings offer us.

Heidegger's conception of personhood is rooted in an ontological analysis that stresses persons as emergent through mutual, co-determinate relations. Just as technical creation occurs through co-determinate affordances (Aristotle's four causes), so personal poiesis and all other natural events of poiesis must be understood as emergent out of co-determinate affordances. But this emergence also means, for Heidegger, that what emerges constitutes a difference that not only is distinct, but also gathers together all that which it emerged from. In terms of beings, this emerging-from and belong-to is what Heidegger characterizes as a being's "dwelling." Heidegger, in one of his essays commenting on Hölderlin's poetry (entitled after a line—"poetically man dwells"—of a poem attributed to Hölderlin, "In Lovely Blue"), gives a list of manners by which humans do not poetically dwell, beginning with standardized labor (*Arbeit*) and industrial production, characterized by reproduced and reproducible production regardless of local needs (Heidegger 1971d). For Heidegger, poetic emergence is "site-specific" and "time-valued" (to appropriate Barrett Watten's terms—see Day 2008).

For Heidegger, the poetic marks the emergence of site-specific and time-valued singular objects and beings. This emergence in the artwork is that of an originary sketching out (*reissen*), whose technique or art is forgotten in the formation of a founding concept or *Grundriss* that then acts as a frame for methodological (broadly, "scientific") research. The sketch or tear (*Riss*) of re-presentation marks an ontological "dif-ference" (Heidegger 1971b, 202—a concept that, of course, is later taken up by Derrida). That dif-ference is an ontological difference between being and beings, a difference that metaphysics forgets in its cataloging of the universe only in terms of clear and distinct individual types of beings, that is, in terms of representations only. In the language of Heidegger and Derrida: in metaphysics the traces of being are erased, as representation is assumed and presence and *aletheia* gives way to truth as *veritas* or correspondence.

Heidegger's thought of persons, thus, is less that of individuals, and rather more that of emergent singularities from out of in-common cultural, social, and material properties, analogous to the relation of particular types of beings out of being itself. Iteratively, beings emerge in the openness of being. All beings emerge from their *Mitsein* with other beings and they only have their singularities within such *Mitsein*. Likewise, community is, thus, an in-common community, without strict beginning or end, but stabilized in traditions and emergent and guided by those traditions.

CONCLUSION

Martin Heidegger's works constitute a critique of metaphysics as it unfolds from ancient Greek thought through modernity in philosophy, society, and culture. For Heidegger, the latest phase of metaphysics' unfolding is to be found in information theory and information culture, where language and even the arts are understood as the representation and transmission of ideas *qua* messages.

The Heideggerian project repeatedly points to the failure of metaphysics to think the in-commonness of beings, and with this, its failure to think individuals as temporal, emergent singularities. For Heidegger, this failure has catastrophic consequences.[14] In terms of knowledge, knowledge becomes thought in metaphysics as information—self-present, auto-affective, knowledge. The modern sense of information is that of a ready-to-hand knowledge. Information, in this sense, is representational—its meaning is known beforehand. Information is, to use Descartes' terms for true knowledge, "clear and distinct." In terms of persons, persons are understood as a priori identities with set powers, useful or not within technological systems similarly arranged. And the same follows for communities, species and other identities.

A counter-philosophy of in-formation, beginning with a critical theory of information, would be dedicated to thinking the conditions by which in-formation becomes information; how beings emerge into knowledge, particularly, the sense of certain knowledge that the modern conception of information suggests. It would be dedicated to thinking the dif-ference of being in information. In Briet's work (2006), for example, we would need to critically return to the moment of the antelope's cataloging within the system of differences that make up the catalog and we would have to examine the "will-to-catalog" that is part of modern science. (Briet closes that moment down very quickly in the name of the modern "necessity" of—that is to say, the modern will for—documentation.) We would want to account for the conversion of ontological dif-ference to ontic differences (Derrida's *dif-férance* to "difference"). We could then also follow the various secondary documents and examine how they repeat, but also shift, the signifier of the newly discovered "antelope" within their different worlds, and yet how each of these shifts gets erased as being just instances of the same information (i.e., facts about the antelope) and how each of the forms of discourse is reduced to being just different types of documentation (or today, "information"). Within such a project, in-formation would need to be rethought not as the apex of a metaphysicalized form of knowledge, but rather, in a much earlier sense of the term, as an affect that needs to be responded to (Day 2001) and we could read those responses in terms of their idealization of the animal as a type. Such "affects" are not to be thought of as quasi-empirical *qualia* (in the philosophy of mind, short for "qualitative feeling") or stimuli for information processing by the brain, but rather, as calls of being to which also belong the categories of understanding that we bring to bear. In brief, we would need to understand the modern sense of "information" and information science as various types of metaphysical attunements to the world, and we would proceed with a bracketing of that attunement through a rigorous deconstruction of its instances. From a Heideggerian perspective, this would help lead us to a path of thinking beyond the Western metaphysical tradition. From a more recent Derridean perspective, it would be a timely, critical rethinking of our own cultural inscriptions (now no longer confined to what Heidegger thought of as the West), so as to allow us to rethink the political situation and historical direction of identity, community, and knowledge.

Being is given to man, but the Heideggerian questions are, How so, what are the consequences, and above all, what has been forgotten, particularly in a reduction of all beings and knowledge to being information? One may propose that these are the starting questions for any critical theory of information.

REFERENCES

Briet, Suzanne. 2006. *What is Documentation? English Translation of the Classic French Text.* Lanham, MD: Scarecrow Press.

Day, Ronald E. 2001. *The Modern Invention of Information: Discourse, History, and Power.* Carbondale: Southern Illinois University Press.

Day, Ronald E. 2007. "Knowing and Indexical Psychology." In *Rethinking Knowledge Management: From Knowledge Object to Knowledge Processes.* Ed. Claire R. McInerney, Ronald E. Day, 331–48. New York: Springer.

Day, Ronald. E. 2008. "Works and Representation." *Journal of the American Society for Information Science and Technology,* 59 (10): 1644–52.

Derrida, Jacques, and Christie McDonald. 1985. *The Ear of the Other: Otobiography, Transference, Translation: Texts and Discussions with Jacques Derrida.* New York: Schocken Books.

Dourish, Paul. 2001. *Where the Action Is: The Foundations of Embodied Interaction.* Cambridge, MA: MIT Press.

Frohmann, Bernd. 2004. *Deflating Information: From Science Studies to Documentation.* Toronto: University of Toronto Press.

Fynsk, Christopher. 1986. *Heidegger: Thought and Historicity.* Ithaca: Cornell University Press.

Heidegger, Martin. 1962. *Being and Time.* Trans. John Macquarrie and Edward Robinson. New York: Harper and Row.

Heidegger, Martin. 1971a. "The Nature of Language." In *On the Way to Language,* 57–108. New York: Harper and Row.

Heidegger, Martin. 1971b. "Language." In *Poetry, Language, Thought,* 189–210. New York: Harper and Row.

Heidegger, Martin. 1971c. "The Origin of the Work of Art." In *Poetry, Language, Thought,* 17–87. New York: Harper and Row.

Heidegger, Martin. 1971d. "... Poetically man dwells ..." In *Poetry, Language, Thought,* 213–29. New York: Harper and Row.

Heidegger, Martin. 1971e. "The Way to Language." In *On the Way to Language,* 111–36. New York: Harper and Row.

Heidegger, Martin. 1973. "Overcoming Metaphysics." In *The End of Philosophy,* 84–110. Chicago: University of Chicago Press.

Heidegger, Martin. 1977a. "The Age of the World Picture." In *The Question Concerning Technology and Other Essays,* 115–54. New York: Harper.

Heidegger, Martin. 1977b. "The End of Philosophy and the Task of Thinking." In *Basic Writings from Being and Time (1927) to The Task of Thinking (1964),* 373–92. New York: Harper.

Heidegger, Martin. 1977c. "Letter on Humanism." In *Basic Writings from Being and Time (1927) to The Task of Thinking (1964),* 193–242. New York: Harper.

Heidegger, Martin. 1977d. "On the Essence of Truth." In *Basic Writings from Being and Time (1927) to The Task of Thinking (1964),* 117–41. New York: Harper.

Heidegger, Martin. 1977e. "The Question Concerning Technology." In *The Question Concerning Technology and Other Essays,* 3–35. New York: Harper.

Heidegger, Martin. 1996. *Hölderlin's Hymn "The Ister."* Bloomington: Indiana University Press.

Lacoue-Labarthe, Philippe. 1990. *Heidegger, Art, and Politics: The Fiction of the Political.* Oxford, UK: Blackwell.

Rapaport, Herman. 1989. *Heidegger & Derrida: Reflections on Time and Language.* Lincoln: University of Nebraska Press.

Ronell, Avital. 1989. *The Telephone Book: Technology—Schizophrenia—Electric Speech.* Lincoln: University of Nebraska Press.

Weaver, Warren. 1949. "Recent Contributions to the Mathematical Theory of Communication." In *The Mathematical Theory of Communication,* 1–64. Urbana: University of Illinois Press.

NOTES

1. Herman Rapaport's *Heidegger & Derrida: Reflections on Time and Language* (1989) remains an outstanding analysis of the relationship of Heidegger, Blanchot, and Derrida's works. Christopher Fynsk's *Heidegger: Thought and Historicity* (1986) remains an outstanding analysis of Heidegger's works.

2. A useful counterpoint to this is Philippe Lacoue-Labarthe's *Heidegger, Art and Politics* (1990).

3. In "Heideggerian AI." I find this term to be an oxymoron, though, since Heidegger's thought would have found the notion of artificial intelligence to be the height of Western metaphysics.

4. Following the standard convention in the literature, we will leave the term *Dasein* ("existence") untranslated. The term appears in *Being and Time* as a technical term for human being's mode of ontological existence, as a being concerned with its own existence.

5. The notion that persons can change the progress and narratives of history (understood as duration) by means of reinventing the future by mixing present situations with recovered elements of the past (thus, creating two senses of "history"—that of linear duration and that of radical breaks and historical retrieval [Nietzsche's "untimely"]) is a theme that runs through German-French modern theory, though with different variations. For example, Deleuze's concepts of repetition and potentiality (*Difference and Repetition*) and his two forms of time (*Logic of Sense*), Benjamin's notion of messianic history and his concept of *Jetztzeit,* Negri's politics "at the edge of time" (*Kairos, Alma Venus, Multitudo*), and Derrida's concept of iteration in language and identity all stress the power of the agent to revalue the historical order—that is, to use the power of difference in presence (or identity) as an historical space of freedom for historical and political revaluation toward reinventing the future.

6. This notion of "event" is important not only in Heidegger's work, and Nietzsche's before him, but in the work of Jacques Derrida and Gilles Deleuze, as well.

7. Cf. Derrida's analysis of "the gift"—patterned off of the German: *Es gibt,* literally, "there is" (French: *il y a*). Here, the issue is that Dasein's mode of being is something given to it within the universe as a whole.

8. There is a considerable literature in Human-Computer Interaction (HCI) on Heidegger's concepts of "ready-to-hand" (*zuhanden*) and "present-at-hand" (*vorhanden*) entities as applied to transparent and nontransparent HCI design. Since it will take us afield, I will not cover this literature. For more on this distinction, see Dourish 2001.

9. Derrida's critique of presence constitutes a continuation, but also on certain points a pointed critique of Heidegger's critique of metaphysics.

10. On the relation of Heidegger and Derrida's works see, for example, Rapaport (1989).

11. Heidegger's remarks concerning what we now discuss as the media are both scholarly and personal. His discussion of "everyday talk" (*Alltäglichkeit*) in *Being and Time* is important, though other, more fragmentary, remarks can be found throughout his writings and lectures. In this context, his sometimes combative attitude to the interviewer in his famous interview in the German weekly, *Der Spiegel,* in 1966 should not be understood solely as a reaction to the interviewer's biographical inquiries. Heidegger's concerns with the media as a site of chitchat, and not as a site of "authentic" thought or politics, appears off and on throughout his oeuvre. Following a trajectory of a critique of the mass media in terms of its metaphysical inscriptions and projections, we should also note Derrida's revealing remark as to his role as a philosopher and theorist: "As for me, I talk about the philosopher, but I am not simply a philosopher.... I believe that in a given historical, political situation of the university, it is necessary to fight so that something like philosophy remains possible. It is in this strategic context that on occasion I have spoken of philosophy's usefulness in translating or deciphering a certain number of things, such as what goes on in the media, and so on" (Derrida and McDonald 1985, 141). In a similar way, I would propose, philosophy—or beyond the traditional rhetoric and topics of this, what Heidegger called "thought"—must be possible (and urgent) in both popular and specialized studies of "information," particularly during "information ages," of which I have argued that there have been several in modernity (Day 2001).

12. Beginning with Alexander Gottlieb Baumgarten's works and lectures and, later, Immanuel Kant's *Critique of Judgment,* the term *aesthetics* left its ancient Greek roots referring to feelings or affects in general and it came to refer to a certain domain of affects, namely, those that involve the fine arts. Thus, as is well known, aesthetics in the modern sense—meaning the study of art—only emerges at the end of the 18th century and it signals the turn of art from a notion of crafts production and technique to that of being an object of contemplation leading to a feeling (i.e., an aesthetics) of either harmony (the beautiful) or disharmony (the sublime).

13. See, for example, Heidegger's comments in his 1942 lecture on Hölderlin's hymn, "The Ister":

The machine of modern technology is essentially distinct from every kind of "tool" not only insofar as it has its own sequence of effects and its own way of producing energy and is thereby a different means in the hand of human beings....The fascinating side of this process can, especially in conjunction with the discipline pertaining to technology, cover over to a large extent the "misery" into which human beings are thrust by technologization. Perhaps there is no longer any such "misery" for those human beings who are completely technological. Conceived metaphysically, modern machine technology is a specific kind of "truth," in terms of which the essence of the actuality of everything actual is determined. The machine that belongs to such technology is different from a "tool," for technology itself is self-subsistent (Heidegger 1996, 44).

Such remarks on technology are consistent throughout Heidegger's oeuvre. See, for example, Heidegger's lecture, "The Age of the World Picture" (Heidegger 1977a).

14. See, not least of all, these remarks from notes from 1936 to 1946 collected by Heidegger for later publication:

The decline of the truth of beings occurs necessarily, and indeed as the completion of metaphysics....The decline occurs through the collapse of the world characterized by metaphysics, and at the same time, through the desolation of the earth stemming from metaphysics....The decline has already taken place. The consequences of this occurrence are the events of world history in this century. They are merely the course of what has already ended. Its course is ordered historico-technologically in the sense of the last stage of metaphysics....The still hidden truth of Being is withheld from metaphysical humanity. The laboring animal is left to the giddy whirl of its products so that it may tear itself to pieces and annihilate itself in empty nothingness (Heidegger 1973, 86–87).

15

Bruno Latour: Documenting Human and Nonhuman Associations

Will Wheeler
Georgetown University Library, USA

BIOGRAPHY AND INTRODUCTION

Bruno Latour (born June 22, 1947, Beaune, Côte-d'Or) is a French sociologist of science, anthropologist and an influential theorist in the field of Science and Technology Studies (STS). After teaching at the Ecole des Mines de Paris (Centre de Sociologie de l'Innovation) from 1982 to 2006, he is now Professor and vice-president for research at the Institut d'études politiques de Paris (2007), where he is associated with the Centre de sociologie des organisations (CSO). [. . .]

Along with Michel Callon and John Law, Latour is one of the primary developers of actor-network theory (ANT), a constructionist approach influenced by the ethnomethodology of Harold Garfinkel, the generative semiotics of Greimas, and (more recently) the sociology of Durkheim's rival Gabriel Tarde (*Wikipedia, The Free Encyclopedia,* April 2010).

Wikipedia provides a perfectly adequate and accessible quick description of Bruno Latour as above. The somewhat thicker description given here, however, shows that there is quite a bit more going on in Bruno Latour than this excerpt suggests. In fact, it would not be too much to say that Latour demonstrates that evidence from scientific practice controverts entirely both our received understanding of the so-called objective external reality "out there" *and* our received understanding of the so-called subjective internal socially constructed world of our minds "in here." This does not mean that Latour believes there is no reality or that he argues we have no mind nor society. Rather, Latour is repositioning his work outside, beyond, and away from that debate as a useless dead end. Latour stands on *neither* side of the objective/subjective divide, nor is he trying to dialectically mediate; rather he is sidestepping, walking away from, and starting over with new premises based on how we actually work in practice. Latour's work is convincing because he provides detailed evidence and meticulous studies across a wide range of scientific disciplines and because he builds careful, logical arguments. Latour is indispensable to an understanding of humans, technology, and information society.

There are nine essential things to know about Bruno Latour. Although his work is richer and more complex than this reduction, knowing these nine at the beginning will give researchers exploring the social in Library and Information Science (LIS) a sense of what will interest them.

1. Latour is not a critical theorist in the usual sense of that phrase. He does not do deconstruction, nor social construction, nor is he a relativist. But neither is he Cartesian, reductionist, nor part of the hegemony of Science (capital S). He is, in fact, the polar opposite of these, going in exactly the opposite direction to both. He actively denies these names attributed out of ignorance to his work, and names both camps as following the same dead ends.

2. The old object/subject compact of modernity (traceable to Plato) holds an untenable break between an "out there" and an "in here." The untenability is revealed (at least) by the paradoxical ability of Scientists (capital S) to cross this divide to bring back "the truth" to Society (also capital S). Latour demonstrates the fallacy of this thinking through careful study of what scientists (small s) actually do. While this may sound similar to deconstructivist argument, it is actually deconstruction's exact opposite, because, rather than sink into relativism, it instead dismisses the object/subject distinction as simply unusable. Latour is starting over fresh with a relatively known reality that keeps being forged by the work of humans and nonhumans.

3. Science (capital S) is not the process of discovering a reality "out there." The true study of science (and society) shows a completely different picture: a science that is made up of the successive constructions of relatively known states of affairs established through chains of circulating reference that are more or less well articulated.

4. Inscription (various forms of writing, charting, mapping, drawing, compartmentalizing) is *the* key ingredient that accomplishes science (small s). The transportability, durability, and readability of various forms of inscription draws things together in such a way that argument is transformed and the work needed to dispute findings increases.

5. Society (capital S) is misrepresented in the social sciences and should be recalculated as associations and/or collectives of human and nonhuman actors who hold complex networks of changing relationships. The proper study of society (small s), then, has more to do with unraveling and/or tracing these networks of connection and less to do with an amorphous ether-like substance called "Society" or "social forces."

6. All of Latour's work is embedded in careful, detailed on-site case study. The meticulous detail of his tracings of science in practice is as nearly as possible indisputable. However, the detail that proves his case can make it difficult to follow his theory. Because we are generally so embedded in assumptions about the way things really are, the author recommends readers go back to the details periodically to reinforce understanding.

7. Latour's life work can be seen as successive iterations of these discoveries via case studies, simple examples from daily life, and more complex present-day and historical examples in scientific discovery. Throughout his books and through many different sciences, Latour demonstrates these principles and they hold. He really has only one theory that extrapolates to any particular case. The recalculation

of society and the social science, for example, follows from the recalculation of science.

8. The value of Latour's work for LIS is the clarity of his theory and the detail of his practical accounts. His work explores the very challenge we most have, accounting for human and nonhuman interaction (think: technology), the transformations between humans and nonhumans (think: technology), and our worries about the longevity of our electronic inscriptions (think: technology). Consider how valuable a true perspective on technology would be for information science! How valuable a true perspective on durable inscription would be for libraries! Latour's work informs our daily interactions in the information revolution.

9. Latour is fun to read. He doesn't take himself too seriously and presents his work in mild, funny, and self-deprecating ways. It is an invitation to think anew, a motion to come on over and consider this interesting thing that happens when you look at science closely. Placed within this group of essays you must suspend your typical predispositions toward critical theory and allow yourself to consider something different. Bruno Latour starts in a different place and ends up somewhere else than you expect, but you have caught the scenery for the entire trip and you reach your destination together. Latour is a refreshing journey.

Through a combination of detailed case-level examples buttressing a complex revolutionary view of science, society, and the social, Latour has been prolific and consistent: it is possible to look at any of his work and see the elements of his theory and the clear presentation of his case. He continues to try different means to persuade and steer a long tradition of Western thinking in a different direction. In presenting the work of Bruno Latour here, I will focus only on two works that most clearly and comprehensively presents the essential Latour: one, *Pandora's Hope* (1999) where he traces his argument through the study of science, and two, *Reassembling the Social* (2005), where he extends these arguments into social sciences. I will also take a few key points from his most-cited article, "Why Has Critique Run out of Steam?" (2004).

PANDORA'S HOPE

"Do you believe in reality?" This is how Bruno Latour starts out *Pandora's Hope*. Latour's laughing answer is "But of course! What a question!" Latour also notes that the questioner, a scientist, seems relieved not to get the opposite answer, "something like Of course not! Do you think I am that naïve?" (Latour 1999, 1) In this exchange Latour distances himself from the postmodernist dilemma and begins his mission, both to answer how such a question could be asked and to redefine how we should understand reality. As Latour says, science studies "started when we first began to talk about scientific *practice* and thus offered a more realistic account of science-in-the-making, grounding it firmly in laboratory sites, experiments, and groups of colleagues....Facts, we found, were clearly constructed...realism gushed forth...and we began to speak of *nonhumans* that were socialized...and with which scientists and engineers began to swap properties...folding into each other, forming constantly changing collectives" (1999, 15–16).

Latour's argument hinges on the very close observation of what scientists actually do. The argument then cascades down and ripples outward. The discoveries made in that detailed examination of practice call for a series of new understandings that challenge our sense of the world (or rather, the sense we generally have come to believe of a hard and fast "out there" and totally interpretive "in here." This is what Latour calls the "modernist settlement" [1999, 308, 310]). Latour shows this object/subject dichotomy to be false, as well as any dialectic, or compromise. Also false are postmodernist solutions that only continue further down the same path without questioning the initial wrong turn. The following summarizes key points in this cascade, not to prove Latour's case, but to highlight the sequence such that the questioning reader can get a sense of the ripple effects.

What do scientists actually do? This is what Latour is best at tracing. In nearly all of his works, the argument proceeds through a careful observation of actual work in a laboratory, on a research project, through an experiment, or involving a machine. He also carefully studies the sequence of mediations and translations that end up in the words and diagrams of final reports. In *Pandora's Hope,* he follows three kinds of scientists in the field (Boa Vista, Brazil)—a botanist, a pedologist, and a geographer, as they are investigating a section of Brazilian forest and savanna in order to sort out which (the forest or the savanna) might be encroaching on the other. Latour follows them meticulously as they first designate an area to study, discuss what they see as critical evidence (landscape, types of trees, grasses, thinning and mixing of the two over some space), look at site maps together, mark ground into grids, take soil samples, create codes for soil types, discriminate shadings of color to match up with the codes, decide which plant life is telling for the site, collect samplings of plant life, tally their collections, distribute samples on tables and rearrange them, store their collections in numbered and ordered shelves, construct charts and printed tables to represent again the samples in words and symbols, and, eventually, translate all of this into their final report.

What is key, at *every* stage is the ability to trace, backwards, the steps taken. "Like the footnotes used in scholarly works…the specimens will guarantee the text.…We will be able to go from (the) written report to the names of the plants, from these names to the dried and classified specimens[,] [a]nd if there is ever a dispute, we will, with the help of [the] notebooks, be able to go back from these specimens to the marked-out site from which [they] started" (1999, 34). This summarizes what takes Latour more than 40 pages to describe in fine detail. In one case, for instance, he looks carefully at a device for collecting soil samples noting a key point: "the pedocomparator will help us grasp the practical differences between abstract and concrete, sign and furniture…the pedocomparator belongs to 'things.' But in the regularity of its cubes, their disposition in columns and rows, their discrete character, and the possibility of freely substituting one column for another, the pedocomparator belongs to 'signs'" (1999, 48). "Consider this lump of earth. Grasped by Rene's right hand, it retains all the materiality of soil.… Yet as it is placed inside the cardboard cube in Rene's left hand, the earth becomes a sign" (49) Here is an essential move for Latour, crossing object, subject, language, sign, and method, that is, there are entities in between our rigid notions of "objects" and "subjects." In addition, as we shall see later, these entities do work, mediate and get mediated, displace and get displaced, delegate and get delegated. When we bring human and nonhuman entities into the same description, a lot more goes on.

For Latour, there are additional key aspects to this process of scientific practice: "at each stage we have not only reduced, we have also gained or regained, since, with the same work of representation, text, calculation, circulation, and relative universality,… inside the field report, we hold not only all of Boa Vista (to which we can return), but also the explanation of its dynamic. We have been able, at every stage, to extend our link"

(1999, 70–71). In other words, scientific practice *changes* the relationship of understanding, reducing in some sense "all that's there," but also adding features that weren't there before, things we in fact couldn't really see. In the paper, we can "see it all" and see it in a different way than we could in the forest/savanna of Boa Vista. Actually, we *couldn't see it*—it is the paper, by its very reductions, that allows us to see it *now* in *this* way.

From this close observation, Latour develops a concept of "circulating reference": "Our philosophical tradition has been mistaken in wanting to make phenomena the meeting point between things-in-themselves and categories of human understanding... (they) have fought ceaselessly among themselves around this bipolar model. Phenomena, however, are not found at the *meeting point* between things and the forms of the human mind; phenomena are what *circulates* all along the reversible chain of transformations, at each step losing some properties to gain others that render them compatible with already-established centers of calculation" (1999, 71–72). In this case, the kinds of properties lost, for instance, are the tangibility of plant material; the kinds gained, the ability to compare by number, grid, and graph. "It is hardly surprising that philosophers have been unable to reach an understanding on the question of realism and relativism: they have taken two provisional extremities for the entire chain, as if they had tried to understand how a lamp and a switch could 'correspond' to each other after cutting the wire and making the lamp 'gaze out' at the 'external' switch" (72–73).

All of Latour follows from this central concept of circulating reference. If we follow closely the work of scientists, we discover that this circulating reference among entities stabilizes accounts of things. We also see that circulating reference is held in place, translated, and transported via various forms of inscription not limited only to the writing in the final report. The naïve pre-scientist, then, is merely missing the inscriptional forms that allow better and more successive transformations to be held in the chain without breaking the cycle of reference. This is the way that humans are mixed into the world. We are navigating (all of us scientists and others) in a complex of circulating references.

It is always possible to extend this circulating reference in more directions through other connections—historical ones, those from other sciences, what comes in from considering a wider context, and that which politics might add. These, however, rather than "explain," merely open up further aspects of the now multipart chain, such that it is a network of intersecting chains that link and re-link, drop links and add links as both humans and nonhumans enter into reductions, translations, mediations, and innovations in understanding. Close inspection, always and everywhere, reveals chains of circulating references that rely on inscription to translate, carry forward, and provide reference back to a series of intersecting human and nonhuman variables. Truth and belief pass in and out of certainty based on the strength and traceability of the chains.

The next step for Latour is to show how science is mixed up with lots of things beyond "science." The notion of circulating reference changes everything. Reality has more to do now with how scientists (and any other individuals) establish connections than an unalterable reality that out there that exists no matter what we do. "Science studies,...[does] not to state *a priori* that there exists 'some connection' between science and society because *the existence of this connection depends on what the actors have done to establish it.* Science studies merely provides a means of tracing this connection *when it exist*" (1999, 86). In addition, science studies shows that society, politics, and science bound together, are inseparable. As Latour simply and eloquently states, "The social history of the sciences does not say: 'Look for society hidden in, behind, or underneath the sciences.' It merely asks some simple questions: 'In a given period, how long can you follow a policy before having to deal with the detailed content of a science? How long can you examine the reasoning of a scientist before having to get involved with the details of a policy?...All we ask of you is not to cut away the thread when it leads you, through a series of imperceptible transitions, from one type of element to the other" (1999, 86–87). Note here the reasonableness of this demand. Think of any case that comes to mind—emission caps and trade is an easy one—and you will see how quickly science and politics embroil each other. In case after case, Latour shows that there *are* connections that *can* be traced in this way and that these tracings *must* include nonhuman as well as human actors.

We now have a new definition of reality, or what it is that is going on when scientists delineate a state of affairs: "The quality of science reference...depends...on the extent of its transformations, the safety of its connections, the progressive accumulation of its mediations, the numbers of interlocutors it engages, its ability to make nonhumans accessible to words, its capacity to interest and convince others, and its routine institutionalization of these flows.... There do not exist true statements that correspond to a state of affairs and false statements that do not, but only continuous or interrupted reference" (1999, 97). The scientist (and anyone) in "explaining" what's going on is tied to these essential ways of establishing what is going on, and the explanation survives or fails on its ability to hold these factors stable.

What about these so-called nonhumans? According to Latour, rather than think of them as objects "out there," we must consider them part of a collective that gets established when a state of affairs has continuous reference. Latour speaks of humans "socializing" nonhumans into this collective (see 1999, 114). As an example, Latour uses Pasteur's discovery of lactic fermentation. He shows how Pasteur successively moves an unknown partially articulated nonhuman entity into the realm of "fact": "in which the entity is made of floating sense data, taken as a name of action, and then, finally, turned into a plantlike and organized being with a place within a well established taxonomy" (1999, 122). The nonhuman entity and the human (scientist) interact, transforming each other. Latour goes on to discuss how the scientist (in this case Pasteur) helps define the nonhuman through successive displays of its actions—first in the lab, then by description to colleagues, and finally, by attributing independence to the nonhuman.

Latour traces very carefully, in this instance as in others, how scientists work toward a solution, first describing an unknown before some agreement has been reached in terms of what it does or doesn't do in a lab, establishing some stable characteristics under certain tests, then hesitatingly describing it with language like "it appears to be" or "scientist X claims that," and then, voilà, science drops these modifiers, gives a name, and a "fact" is born with language like "as everyone knows," this substance x causes that effect y. In Latour's words, "The accuracy of the statement is not related to a state of affairs out there, but to the traceability of a series of transformations" (1999, 123). So, the experiment is text, but it is tied to a situation where actants undergo trials in a lab, then the scientists is tried by his colleagues, and both the newly articulated entity and the scientist exchange and enhance their properties (124–25). In this case Pasteur doesn't discover an already existing lactic ferment but rather, in Latour's terms, a new chain of reference is established where an entity gains properties and Pasteur gains authority.

Through the explication of the revelation of lactic ferment by Pasteur, Latour illuminates a fundamental contradiction in the modernist settlement: "that on the one hand facts are experimentally made up and never escape their manmade settings, and on the other hand it is essential that facts are *not* made up and something emerges that is *not* manmade" (1999, 125). It can't be both—and here Latour shows, through detail in a specific case of experimentation, how scientists fabricate yet simultaneously deny fabrication. Science studies is about rewriting this contradiction into a more commonsensical and inclusive understanding that finally gets us somewhere beyond the objective/subjective double bind.

Why is this so important? Because *all* are included—every example shows constructions—and you don't have to be persuaded by this one case; Latour is a calling for you to reexamine this for yourself. Latour's model is a workable alternative to the usual one. Latour "would like to establish an entirely different model for the relations between humans and nonhumans [using] the notion of *propositions.* Propositions are not statements, or things, or any sort of intermediary between the two. They are, first of all, actants. Pasteur, the lactic acid, the laboratory are all actants. What distinguishes propositions from one another is not a *single* vertical abyss between words and the world, but *many* differences between them, without anyone knowing *in advance* if these differences are big or small, provisional or definitive, reducible or irreducible. This is precisely what the word 'pro-positions' suggests. They are not positions, things, substances, or essences pertaining to a nature made up of mute objects facing a talkative human mind, but *occasions* given to different entities to enter into contact. These occasions for interaction allow the entities to modify their definitions over the course of an event—in the present case, an experiment" (1999, 41).

Again, rather than establish objects "out there" and subjects "in here" that we discover: "The relation established between propositions is not that of a correspondence across a yawning gap, but what I will call *articulation.* . . . Instead of being a privilege of a human mind surrounded by mute things, articulation becomes a very common property of propositions, in which many entities can participate" (1999, 142). "Our involvement with the things we speak about is at once *more intimate* and much *less direct* than that of the traditional picture: we are allowed to say new, original things when we enter well-articulated settings like good laboratories. Articulation between propositions goes much deeper than speech. We speak *because* the propositions of the world are themselves articulated, not the other way around" (144). According to Latour, we are part of a cluster, a gathering, a collective, and we're engaged, as scientists, humans, in figuring it out. We get new places in knowledge partly on our own, it seems, and partly as moved to by the articulation of other propositions around us. Propositions, then, engage in this circulating reference to come into "existence" outside the subject/object dichotomy. Rather than existence/nonexistence, Latour proposes we distinguish between well-articulated and inarticulate propositions. In addition, every change in the articulation makes a difference in the circulating reference that has been articulated (149–50).

Latour goes on to suggest that this new relationship of articulation means that what we have traditionally taken as kinds of steady (but undiscovered sometimes) existence is rather a continuously upheld state of relationships. That is, lactic ferment didn't exist before Pasteur, rather "we should be able to talk calmly about *relative existence.* . . . Relative existence means that we follow the entities without stretching, framing, squeezing, and cutting them with the four adverbs never, nowhere, always, everywhere. If we use these adverbs, Pouchet's spontaneous generations will *never* have been there *anywhere* in the world; it was an illusion all along; it is not allowed to have been part of the population of entities making up space and time. Pasteur's ferments carried by the air, however, had *always* been there, all along *everywhere,* and were bona fide members of the population of entities making up space and time long before Pasteur" (1999, 156).

Latour offers an alternative picture of the world that is beyond the scope of this essay. Since he is offering a completely different explanation of the world and of reality, he necessarily engages philosophy beyond the needs of LIS. Or rather, if we really want to get it right, enmeshed as we are in technology and society (traditionally defined), we will have to go back farther than we expected. This may be too far for the reader, but it *is* the place we eventually must go. The differences emerging in modern society due to increasing technology have been misunderstood, according to Latour: "Unlike what is held by the traditional distinction, the difference between an ancient or 'primitive' collective and a modern or 'advanced' one is *not* that the former manifests a rich mixture of social and technical culture while the latter exhibits a technology devoid of ties with the social order.... The difference, rather, is that the latter translates, crosses over, enrolls, and mobilizes more elements, which are more intimately connected, with a more finely woven social fabric, than the former does. One finds, of course, longer chains of action in 'modern' collectives, a greater number of nonhumans (machines, automatons, devices) associated with one another, but one must not overlook the *size* of markets, the *number* of people in their orbits, the *amplitude* of the mobilization: more objects, yes, but many more subjects as well. Those who have tried to distinguish these two sorts of collective by attributing 'objectivity' and 'efficiency' to modern technology and 'humanity' to low-tech *poesis* have been deeply mistaken. Objects and subjects are made simultaneously, and an increased number of subjects is directly related to the number of objects stirred—brewed—into the collective. The adjective modern does not describe an *increased distance* between society and technology or their interaction, but a deepened *intimacy,* a more intricate mesh, between the two" (1999, 195).

REASSEMBLING THE SOCIAL

Note that Latour in *Pandora's Hope* has *already* made the leap from science to society, *already* through this close inspection of the doing of science arrived far away and right in the middle of our entire description of what is going on with regard the state of affairs we generally call the world, society, and humanity. In "Why Has Critique Run Out of Steam?" he makes this explicit: "Once you realize that scientific objects cannot be socially explained, then you realize that the so-called weak objects, those that appear to be candidates for the accusation of anti-fetishism, were never mere projections on an empty screen either. They act too, they too do things, they too *make you* do things. It is not only the objects of science that resist, but all the others as well, those that were supposed to have been ground to dust by the powerful teeth of automated reflex-action deconstructors" (Latour 1999, 242–43).

In *Reassembling the Social,* Latour takes the lessons learned from science and applies them to the social sciences. Instead of the social being a specific domain of reality, social is what comes about when entities associate. The concept of associations that constitute society is similar to the idea of circulating references that constitute "facts" among humans and nonhumans in the laboratories of science. In the case of society actors gather, socialize each other (while not in themselves "social") by successive bindings that must remain unbroken in order to keep that particular social intact. That is, the social is constituted by chains of association. "'[S]ocial' is not some glue that could fix everything including what the other glues cannot fix; it is *what* is glued together by many

other types of connectors…[it is] what should be explained by the specific associations provided by economic, linguistic, psychology, management, etc.…it's perfectly
acceptable to designate by the same word a trail of *associations* between heterogeneous
elements…to remain faithful to the original intuitions of the social sciences by redefin-
ing sociology, not as the 'science of the social,' but as the *tracing of associations.*…[T]
he adjective social does not designate a thing among other things…but a *type of connection* between things that are not in themselves social" (Latour 2005, 5).

Interestingly though, social scientists have not been following these bindings as well
as the scientists have, nor have they as carefully inscribed these relationships of references in uninterrupted chains like the scientists have. They have extended the mistaken
notion of Science (capital S) as a hunt for facts, so Latour has to re-inform the proper
way to do their work going back to a time before the modernist settlement. In a way, this
is the reverse of what Latour has done with science studies: whereas with science studies, he follows scientists to show how they actually work in contradiction to how they
say they work, in the case of the social sciences, he follows actants in society in order
to show how social scientists have not been creating the kinds of stable references, connections, and associations that they should. While this might seem to "[dilute] sociology
to mean any type of aggregate from chemical bonds to legal ties, from atomic forces
to corporate bodies, from physiological to political assemblies…this is precisely the
point … as all those heterogeneous elements *might be* assembled anew in some given
state of affairs…this is…the most common experience we have in encountering the
puzzling face of the social. A new vaccine is marketed, a new job description is offered,
a new political movement is being created, a new planetary system is discovered, a new
law is voted, a new catastrophe occurs. In each instance we have to reshuffle our conceptions of what has been associated together because the previous definition has been
made somewhat irrelevant. We are no longer sure about what 'we' means" (2005, 5–6).

Once we make this break from a "thing" called "social" to an array, a collective, a
set of relationships among actants, we are then free to constitute the social by examining the ways the connections are made, maintained, circulate, get disrupted, reassemble,
and reconstitute as new social facts. "In such a view, law, for instance, should not be
seen as what should be explained by 'social structure' in addition to its inner logic; on
the contrary, its inner logic may explain some features of what makes an association
last longer.…Science does not have to be replaced by its 'social framework,' which is
'shaped by social forces' as well as its own objectivity, because its objects themselves
are dislocating any given context through the foreign elements research laboratories are
associating together in unpredictable ways.…Religion does not have to be 'accounted
for' by social forces because in its very definition—indeed its very name—it links together entities which are not part of the social order" (2005, 7).

Latour proposes a number of names for this new sociology, "sociology of associations" "sociology of innovation" and "actant-rhizome ontology," but settles on what it
has come to be known as actor-network theory (ANT). The prior sociology is then the
"sociology of the social" (2005, 9). Latour admits that the former sociology is convenient for many situations, but stipulates that where innovations are occurring and where
change is happening fast, the former sociology is inadequate. He further stipulates that
it must be the actors themselves (humans and nonhumans) who must be granted voice in
order to understand what is happening—*they* are the ones forging the new associations
and social science must trace them, not simply deny their authority by substituting the
catchphrases of the social sciences as if they explained (11). Like science granting to

the objects they study an agency, as Latour argues they should, in this, then, objects and facts, people and society disappear, and what replaces them is circulations of connected tracings that pull things together: "Social is *nowhere* in particular as a thing among other things but may circulate *everywhere* as a movement connecting non-social things" (107). Latour calls this the "sociology of translation" (2005). Paralleling physics, "sociology of the social remains pre-relativist, while our sociology has to be fully 'relativist.' In most ordinary cases, for instance, situations that change slowly, the pre-relativist framework is perfectly fine. But as soon as things accelerate, innovations proliferate, and entities multiply...a relativist solution has to be devised to move between frames and to regain some sort of commensurability between traces coming from frames traveling at very different speeds and accelerations....If physicists at the beginning of the previous century were able to do away with the common sense solution of an absolutely rigid and indefinitely plastic ether, can sociologists discover new traveling possibilities by abandoning the notion of a social substance...?" (12).

Latour goes on to extrapolate in *Reassembling the Social* that this redefinition leads to a set of uncertainties: that groups are not the stable entities social science generally takes them for, that outside agents make us "do things," that objects (nonhumans) have agency too, and that social science should rather investigate "matters of concern" rather than "matters of fact," as mysteries to be explained rather than things taken for granted as "social." Latour also offers that the social science's laboratory is observation, listening closely to actors, and the writing of texts.

Perhaps the most complex, most difficult to understand concept is Latour's notion that distinguishes "matters of concern" from "matters of fact." Here he argues that the social sciences should take "facts" beyond laboratories, look to the controversies generated, across many different planes that we have called "the social," and perhaps *not* be differentiating social science methods, but rather follow *the same* methods Latour has outlined for science studies. Humans and nonhumans, together, co-construct matters of concern that fall in and out of relatively constant production as "objects" or "things" by virtue of an ongoing enterprise of connections, associations, and references. I think the best, most graphic example of what Latour means by this is the account given in "Why Has Critique Run Out of Steam?"

[the] *Columbia* (disaster) in early 2003 offer[s]...a tragic instantiation of...[the]...metamorphosis of an object into a thing....What else would you call this sudden transformation of a completely mastered, perfectly understood, quite forgotten by the media, taken-for-granted, matter-of-factual projectile into a sudden shower of debris falling on the United States, which thousands of people tried to salvage in the mud and rain, collect in a huge hall to serve as so many clues in a judicial scientific investigation? Here, suddenly, in a stroke, an object had become a thing, a matter of fact was considered a matter of great concern....how could there be a better example of this making and unmaking than this catastrophe unfolding all its thousand folds?...

At the very same time...another extraordinarily parallel event was occurring...this time a Thing—with a capital T—was assembled trying to coalesce, to gather in one decision, one object, one projection of force: a military strike against Iraq. Again, it was hard to tell whether this gathering was a tribunal, a parliament, a command-and-control war room, a rich man's club, a scientific congress, or a TV stage. But certainly it was an assembly where matters of great concern were debated and proven—except there was much puzzlement about which type of proofs should be given and how accurate they were. The difference between...(them)...was that while in the case of *Columbia* we had a perfectly mastered object that was suddenly transformed into a shower of burning debris...there, at the United Nations, we had an investigation that tried to coalesce, in one unifying, unanimous, solid, mastered object, masses of people, opinions, and might. In one case the object was metamorphosed into a thing; in the second, the thing was attempting to turn into an object. We could witness, in the one case, the head, in another, the tail of the trajectory through which matters of fact emerge out of matters of concern. In both cases we were offered a unique window into the number of *things* that have to participate in the gathering of an *object* (2004, 235, 236).

Here we see how Latour does not distinguish between the proper study of science and the proper study of society—they are part and parcel of the same set of mechanisms that must be understood to get anywhere with either. People and things and objects, humans and nonhumans, gather, interact, make each other do things, have agency, have historical accounts, go in ever traceable directions such that the explanation must go in widening circles, in multiple directions, following networks of connections. At the heart is the ability of scientists *and* social scientists to leave more (strongly) or less (weakly) articulated accounts. Again: "There do not exist true statements that correspond to a state of affairs and false statements that do not, but only continuous or interrupted reference" (1999, 97). Another point of interest to LIS is the way some, especially social, things circulate via forms. "[A] form is simply something which allows something else to be transported from one site to another.... Such a displacement from ideal to a material can be extended to *information*. To provide a piece of information is the action of putting something into a form. But now the word takes a very mundane, practical meaning; it can be a paper slip, a document, a report, an account, a map, whatever succeeds in the incredible feat of transporting a site into another one without deformation through massive transformations.... Once again, scientific activity offers many privileged cases of transportation through transformations" (Latour 2005, 225). Latour goes on to note the *form*alism of social sciences: "I knew from the beginning that, although those sociologists (of the social) make for awkward social theory, because they interrupt the task of assembling the social, this is just the reason why they are so good at *performing* it, that is at *formatting* the relations between sites.... If the social sciences per-*form* the social, then those forms have to be followed with just as much care as the controversies. ...We can say that the sociology of the social circulates in the same way as physical standards do, or better yet, that social sciences are part of *metrology*" (226–27).

This reference to metrology harkens back to the pedocomparator of *Pandora's Hope*. Latour has come full circle, or rather displays a remarkable consistency across the science/social science divide: science (including social science) is made up of circulating references held together by complex chains that include complex mediators that are neither sign nor object. Here chains are forged with forms and standards, what we saw before as what "renders them compatible with already established centers of calculation" (1999, 71–72). In Latour's words: "Standards and metrology solve practically the question of relativity that seems to intimidate so many people: can we obtain some sort of universal agreement? Of course we can! *Provided* you find a way to hook up your local instrument to one of the many metrological chains whose material network can be fully described, and whose cost can be fully determined. Provided there is no interruption, no break, no gap, and no uncertainty along any point of transmission. Indeed, traceability is precisely what the whole of metrology is all about! No discontinuity allowed, which is just what ANT needs for tracing the social topography. Ours is the social theory that has taken metrology as the paramount example of what it is to expand *locally everywhere,* all the while bypassing the local *as well* as the universal" (Latour 2005, 229). Compare this kind of tracing to the tracings described by Latour, observed in Boa Vista (or any science), and one can see Latour's argument, in both cases, is of the same kind.

Latour sums up: "[T]he question of the social emerges when the ties in which one is entangled begin to unravel; the social is further detected through the surprising movements from one association to the next; those movements can either be suspended or resumed; when they are prematurely suspended, the social as normally construed is bound together with already accepted participants called 'social actors' who are members of 'society'; when the movement toward collection is resumed, it traces the social as associations through many non-social entities might become participants later; if pursued systematically, this tracking may end up in a shared definition of a common world I have called a collective; but if there are no procedures to render it common, it may fail to be assembled; and lastly, sociology is best defined as the discipline where participants explicitly engage in the reassembling of the collective" (2005, 247). This is not a sleight of hand or mere wordplay, but a call to use the proper techniques of science in the social sciences. We then must (if we follow Latour) pay closer attention to what the nonhumans do, not what we imagine they were intended to do, but rather what mediations they cause, how humans and nonhumans cluster in associations, how very close observations reveal ever changing relationships, how following the trails where they lead leads to proper science, more accurate policy, and many other unexpected places. These constantly changing, but traceable interactions mutually bind large numbers of nonsocial entities into a collective association we then call "the social."

CONCLUSIONS FOR LIS

Latour's theories have been used more or less frequently in the LIS literature, depending on whether you count mere citation, what you count as LIS, and what you consider substantive engagement. The ACM Digital Library shows about 30 citations for Latour and Actor Network Theory appears as a keyword entry in only 6 records. These are all relatively recent and cite mostly older works of Latour, such as his 1987 *Laboratory Life*. Many are proceedings papers. I haven't read them all, but Latour does not seem to be central aspect of these works. There are only 4 citations of Latour in LISA (searching in the abstract), one of which cites the more recent *Pandora's Hope*. I could not find any citations of Latour in Wilson's Library Literature and Information Science (neither in the Full Text nor in the Retrospective portions). Science studies could be seen as emerging into LIS—but it remains an uncertain tracing. Since Latour is most likely to be classified closer to science and technology studies, it makes sense that he is cited by the ACM more than by LIS literature. Two relatively well-known figures in our field, Bowker in *Sorting Things Out* and Starr in *How Things Work,* draw substantively on Latour and science studies, but it is not clear how widely their message has been received.

Blaise Cronin in "Receiving the French: a Bibliometric Snapshot of the Impact of "French theory" on Information Science" in *Journal of Information Science* 35:4 (2009), shows that Latour is the most cited of French theorists in a short-list of information science journals, but in reviewing article-by-article a sampling of the most recent in flagship journals like *Information Science* and *JASIS&T,* few made more than passing mention of Latour. There was one interesting article by Lucase Introna and Louise Whittaker, "Power, Cash, and Convenience: Translations in the Political Site of the ATM" (*Information Science* 22 [2006]: 325–40) that explicitly takes actor network theory as a model, but that was only one of two dozen sampled that did so, and I would note the ATM article, while interesting technologically, economically, politically, and sociologically is a thin case of information exchange compared to the complex scholarly communications that many in LIS would reasonable say are closer to the LIS core of interest. Five relatively recent articles in Library Quarterly mention Latour in the context of scholarship and library work, but, again, only cite Latour in passing or only cite his earliest work.

It is not clear that Latour should be lumped with French theorists or any "critical turn" (Cronin, 400) and Cronin himself points this out. Cronin also understands the challenges of citation analysis and Web of Science as the place to do it, so, it is very useful to know that Latour is mentioned by many whom some would call central in information science, but it remains to be seen how carefully they follow Latour, since 207 of 235 articles citing Latour (according to Cronin's study) are citations of Latour's 1979 *Laboratory Life* (108 citations) or his 1986 *Science in* Action (99 citations). It is perhaps that Latour *is* mistakenly lumped with "critical theory" and "French theory" that he has been underutilized. I have tried to show in this article how far he stands in opposition to French critical theory.

Substantive use of Latour as he has refined and expanded his thinking remains tangential to libraries. It is possible that Latour has growing relevance in affiliated disciplines like technology and society studies, and computer-supported cooperative work, but it is not clear they see themselves as part of our field. Cronin speaks a bit to this issue as well in an earlier article "The Sociological Turn in Information Science" *Journal of Information* Science, 34:4 (2008). Placing Latour among the constructivists, he suggests their relativism is unappealing to LIS (471). In looking at the "social" in LIS, he notes a burgeoning literature, but regrets the social sciences have seemed to pay little attention to LIS. I think the problem is, as we see with Latour, that LIS tends not to engage social science theory very deeply and thus do not make enough of a critical mass of scholarship to impinge on critical thinking in other social sciences.

However, if Latour really wants things to change, he'd better be hoping that his theory can be grasped by regular people like librarians and mainstream information scientists as well as philosophers of science. I am not sure we as librarians nor as information scientists fall into Latour's category of scientists who mostly don't bother worrying about this stuff or the social scientists who, influenced by critical theory, endlessly do just that (see *Pandora's Hope*, 19), but I expect we have most likely been moving to the social science camp. There are possibilities in Latour's insights that might revolutionize our understanding of the relationship we have with technology and our associations with it. Practicing his methods and engaging more deeply with his theoretical position might take us places we haven't considered. We could become more articulate about our propositions and the collective in which we find ourselves embedded, especially regarding interactions of humans and computing machinery. He *must* be writing for us, for people in the midst of this change, if he really thinks our sense of reality and society can change. We're allowed to take a stab at it, even imperfectly. It's a shift that could lead us far.

The question remains, What's in it for LIS? Obviously, librarians might like the concept of circulating reference. Clearly there something library-like in the necessity for keeping traces of scholarship in science and there is clear information theory in how meaning circulates. We are part of both of those. Latour points out that the root word underpinning reference is "to bring back" (*Pandora's Hope,* 32) and library reference is clearly of a kind with that reference. Libraries help hold many of the pieces that are circulating between scientists, preserve them, and make them just that much more traceable. In theory, libraries can bring them back whenever they are needed.

More importantly, libraries are in the midst of incredible innovation and change due to machine age, so that is the very place, according to Latour, where we ought to be able to observe shiftings and realignment of actors in their networks of associations. If we think of computing machines as part of this and having their own agency, we might get farther and to a different place in our understanding of what's going on here and now in our libraries and in our scholarship about information society. Surely on academic campuses, and surely throughout the so-called "knowledge industry" we see disruptions, change, and many new boundaries being drawn. Thinking *even simply,* just for libraries, one could point to the emergence of realigned digital resource departments, new media centers, and radically altered organizational charts. Thinking *even simply,* just for libraries, we could point to the changing "nature" of serials and serial publishing. Think of our concept of serial as well: is it "the same object" we have "always" known, or has the e-journal exploded over our heads and we're picking up the pieces to figure out what happened? Are we not, collectively meeting in our own United Nations of LIS trying to make together that new object? These are just simple and basic possibilities—what might we find if we attempt to trace all of the elements that are assembled?

But one might ask what to do with Latour in daily life, tomorrow, could he really help? How would one actually begin to think more carefully using Latour? I suggest it must be with the actors themselves. This leads to an open operational question: who are the actors in our network? Do we even know? Have we even attempted to account for them? And it's not as simple as "the end users" although they are part of it. I would ask all of us to think again to our daily lives with computers, calendar software, online catalogs, librarians, systems offices, scholars, publishers, office software, distributors, interface developers, Web browsers, chat, e-mail, cell phones, keyboards, monitors, databases, search algorithms, classification schemes, and NISO standards. Can we (again, even simply) think of ourselves as "socializing" them into our world, and, conversely, don't *they,* just as much, "make us do things," socializing *us* into *their* collective? Maybe so, maybe enough to take a deeper look. Even so simple an object as the printer asks for more attention than it seems to deserve as a "simple machine." In my reference librarian role, this actant engages me more than any other—it breaks, it refuses to print PDFs, it causes numerous humans to cluster around it cajoling and pleading. I, as a practitioner and decade-long instructor in the top LIS program (and I-school) suggest our I-school colleagues have not given proper attention to these "mundane artifacts." Surely it warrants questioning.

Latour offers a new way of understanding what's going on—it will take time to practice, time to consider the new objects as part of the equation, time to look for all the actors—but clearly we are in an arena of innovation and change that seems, intuitively, even simply, to mimic his accounts. Watching carefully we might be able to trace more articulate chains of reference for ourselves.

REFERENCES

(see Latour's Web site for complete biography and bibliography: http://www.bruno-latour.fr/)

SELECT BOOKS

Latour, Bruno. 1987. *Science in Action: How to Follow Scientists and Engineers through Society.* Cambridge, MA: Harvard University Press.

Latour, Bruno. 1988. *The Pasteurization of France.* Cambridge, MA: Harvard University Press.

Latour, Bruno. 1993. *We Have Never Been Modern.* Trans. Catherine Porter. Cambridge, MA: Harvard University Press.

Latour, Bruno. 1996. *Aramis, or The Love of Technology.* Cambridge, MA: Harvard University Press.

Latour, Bruno. 1999. *Pandora's Hope: Essays on the Reality of Science Studies.* Cambridge, MA: Harvard University Press.

Latour, Bruno. 2004. *Politics of Nature: How to Bring the Sciences into Democracy.* Trans. Catherine Porter. Cambridge, MA: Harvard University Press.

Latour, Bruno. 2005. *Reassembling the Social: An Introduction to Actor-Network Theory.* Oxford and New York: Oxford University Press.

Latour, Bruno, and Steve Woolgar. 1979. *Laboratory Life: The Social Construction of Scientific Facts.* Los Angeles: Sage.

ARTICLES MOST OFTEN CITED IN WEB OF SCIENCE

Latour, Bruno. 2004. "Why Has Critique Run Out of Steam? From Matters of Fact to Matters of Concern." *Critical Inquiry* 30 (2, Winter): 225–48. (cited 83 times)

Latour, Bruno. 2000. "When Things Strike Back: A Possible Contribution of 'Science Studies' to the Social Sciences." *British Journal of Sociology* 51 (1): 107–23. (cited 56 times)

Latour, Bruno. 1990. "Postmodern? No, Simply Amodern! Steps toward an Anthropology of Science Studies." *History and Philosophy of Science* 21 (1): 145–71. (cited 47 times)

Latour, Bruno. 1988. "A Relativistic Account of Einstein's Relativity." *Social Studies of Science* 18 (1): 3–44 (cited 44 times)

Latour, Bruno. 1996. "On Actor-Network Theory—A Few Clarifications." *Soziale Welt-Zeitschrift Fur Socialwissenschftliche Forschung und Praxis,* 47 (4): 369–81 (cited 38 times)

Latour, Bruno. 1999. "For David Bloor . . . and beyond: A Reply to David Bloor's 'Anti-Latour.'" *Studies in History and Philosophy of Science* 30A (1): 113–29 (cited 36 times)

Latour, Bruno. 1994. "Pragmatogonies—A Mythical Account of How Humans and Nonhumans Swap Properties." *American Behavioral Scientist* 37 (6): 791–808 (cited 32 times)

NOTE

All italics within quotations are Latour's. For further reference, Latour provides a useful glossary of key terms he uses with specific meanings in *Pandora's Hope*.

16

Jean Lave's Practice Theory

Sanna Talja
University of Tampere, Finland

INTRODUCTION

Jean Lave's book *Cognition in Practice* (1988) develops the theory of practice as an alternative to cognitivist[1] research. The book is a thorough review and criticism of cognitive research on problem solving and human information processing. Based on several empirical studies on problem solving in mundane settings and everyday activities, Lave argues that cognition is not within the mind but stretches over mind, body, activity, and culturally organized settings—hence always involving other actors. Lave's critical project is in fact twofold. It is criticism of schooling and what Lave (1988) calls the knowledge transfer assumption—the assumption that the skills and knowledge acquired in schools are widely applicable in other arenas of life as well. Second, it is an in-depth analysis and critique of the lack of ecological validity in laboratory-type cognitive research. Lave argues that both schooling practices and laboratory-type cognitive research ignore discontinuities between situations.

This chapter presents the basic ideas and arguments of practice theory as formulated by Lave (1988). The structure of the chapter is as follows: after discussing some of the major differences between practice theory and other social theoretical approaches, I review the differences between Lave's practice theory and theorists who are often cited as also having formulated a theory of practice. Second, I introduce some of the empirical foundations and key findings on which Lave started to formulate her theoretical arguments. Third, I present the main ideas and concepts in Lave's theory of practice. I end by discussing the implications of Lave's theory of practice for information science research.

OVERVIEW OF JEAN LAVE'S RESEARCH

Jean Lave earned her PhD in social anthropology from Harvard University in 1968. She was a professor in education and geography at the University of California,

Berkeley until her retirement. The main body of Lave's research concentrates on the redefinition of learning and knowing in terms of social practice (see a 1977–2002 selection of Lave's works in the bibliography). Lave's best-known scholarly work is the book *Situated Learning: Legitimate Peripheral Participation* (1991), which she wrote together with Etiennne Wenger. Lave and Wenger (1991) coined the concept communities of practice (CoP) to describe the context where learning and knowledge creation take place. The CoP concept underlines that learning is most efficient when it is ubiquitous in ongoing activity and evolves through legitimate peripheral participation, that is, through involvement and participation in authentic work tasks and concrete productive and goal-oriented activities. Lave and Wenger stressed that learning is deeply embedded in authentic work and everyday life settings. They defined communities of practice as groups of people working and acting on a specific activity domain, engaging in joint tasks and projects in pursuit of which they employ common procedures, work with the same tools, and express themselves in a common language.

The CoP theory has had a major influence on advancing the adoption and application of knowledge management (KM) in workplaces. It offered a new paradigm for the management of organizational knowledge and learning in organizations. Within information science, the CoP concept and Lave and Wenger's situated learning theory have been used in studies focusing on knowledge sharing in workplaces (Davenport 2001; Hara 2007) and in studies that have looked at the possibilities of designing of online communities of practice for the purposes of organizational learning and knowledge sharing.[2]

Vann and Bowker (2001) noted that the widespread popularity of the CoP concept has, to a large degree, left Lave's originally profoundly critical project in building a theory of practice in its shadow. Østerlund and Carlile (2005) similarly remarked that most studies applying Lave and Wenger (1991) have focused on communities and ignored the concept of practice. This chapter, in turn, focuses on the foundational ideas of Lave's practice theory.

LAVE'S PRACTICE THEORY AND OTHER SOCIAL THEORETICAL APPROACHES

Lave is usually credited for having started the movement towards the situated cognition and situated learning paradigm. The situated cognition movement was, however, a broader intellectual movement across fields.[3] Important works on situated learning and situated activity were published by, for instance, Yrjö Engeström (1987), Lucy Suchman (1987), John Seely Brown, Allan Collins, and Paul Duguid (1989), and Edwin Hutchins (1991). Situativity theories[4] or situated learning theories thus did not emerge solely in educational research, and, similarly, are not applied only in educational research. Although situated learning theories speak of learning, teaching, and schooling, they are more generally concerned with the issues of how people become informed, how people come to possess something that can be called knowledge, what is the nature of deep expertise, and what explains workers' ability to perform highly complex work tasks.

In addition to learning research, Lave's work draws from the sociology of scientific knowledge (SSK), especially from empirical laboratory studies of scientific practices (Latour 1979; Knorr-Cetina 1981; Lynch 1982; Traweek 1988). These studies were based on close observation of science-in-the-making and approached the manufacture of science and scientific knowledge as a mundane everyday practice (Lave 1988, 82). Laboratory studies foregrounded the way in which the tools and instruments used by scientists are not just devices for reaching results but play a crucial role in the design of experiments and in the formation of scientific hypotheses. Technologies-in-use, theories, and results, are intertwined. Results from experiments can be highly ambiguous, and decisions as to how to interpret them are not taken individually but as part of the mutually learned and shared everyday work practices of a community of scholars. The way that laboratory studies brought into view the mundane hands-on, tool-mediated, and situationally unfolding character of scientific knowledge production has been important for the development of Lave's practice theory (Lave 1993, 8).

In *Cognition in Practice* (1988), Lave herself named Pierre Bourdieu's book *Outline of a Theory of Practice* (1977) and Anthony Giddens' (1979; 1984) works as central influences in the emerging practice theory. Ludwig Wittgenstein (1980) is also often mentioned as an important practice theorist, and Harold Garfinkel (1967) and Alfred Schutz (1964) are, likewise, theorists sometimes linked with practice theory. However, important differences exist between Lave's practice theory and the thinking and interests of Bourdieu, Giddens, Wittgenstein, Garfinkel, and Schutz.[5]

As Thevenot (2001, 66) points out, Bourdieu's idea of social practice "derives from customs, beliefs, symbols, and shared dispositions at the core of a community." Bourdieu's (1984) central concept, habitus, assumes a kind of permanence in dispositions across contexts, and foregrounds repetitive, habitualized types of conduct (Thevenot 2001, 71). In Lave's practice theory, human activity is not viewed as grounded in habits or routines. In Lave's theory, practice has a more emergent, improvisational, and generative, future-creating, character.

Giddens (1979; 1984) in turn emphasizes the general dependence of members of society on the existing repertoire of practices in their society. Practices are governed by rules (norms, codes) and resources that establish the possibilities for actions. In Giddens' theory, the system of practices reproduces itself whenever it is being drawn upon (Barnes 2001, 27). Giddens' notion of social practice differs from Lave's in that it is not concerned with the particularities of situated practices. Giddens discusses the self-actualization of individuals in terms of lifestyles, and sees the continuity of society in practices, customary and routinized ways of behaving (Knorr-Cetina 2001, 175; Thevenot 2001, 72).

Lave, in turn, does not see rules as governing practice, rather, she argues that activity and its values and goals are generated simultaneously. Lave (1990) makes a distinction between two different notions of culture: culture of acquisition and understanding-in-practice. In the first, learning and knowledge are assumed to stem from an already existing pool of knowledge, and result from cultural transmission, which is assumed to lie at the heart of the reproduction of social systems. Acquired or transmitted knowledge is abstracted and decontextualized and not necessarily effectively or actively drawn upon in real-life activity settings. Knowledge resulting from understanding-in-practice is self sustained, context embedded, opportunity based, intuitive, and embodied, based on the situations whose specific characteristics are part of the practice as it unfolds (Lave 1988; 1990).

In Wittgenstein's (1980) philosophy, action is grounded in practices, concrete doings that take place over time. Although the notion of language games is a key concept in Wittgenstein's late philosophy, for Wittgenstein, meanings and interpretations do not determine action. However, also Wittgenstein talks about practice as habitualized rule following. Rule following is something that comes naturally to people acting within a specific situation, in an almost automatic fashion (Bloor 2001).

Ethnomethodologists such as Garfinkel (1967) are sometimes labelled as practice theorists, and some researchers associate practice theory with the social phenomenology of Schutz (1964). For identifying differences between Lave's practice theory and these social theories, Reckwitz's (2002) way of classifying and naming major social theories is useful. He speaks of culturalist mentalism, textualism, intersubjectivism, and practice theory. The differences between the foci and units of analysis among these are presented in Table 16.1.

For Reckwitz (2002, 247), Schutz's social phenomenology represents the prototype of mentalist subjectivism. Lave similarly sees phenomenology as treating social systems only as "epiphenomena of intersubjectively constituted experience" (1988, 193). Many social theories foreground the existence of common frames of understanding rather than pragmatic activities and their performance, and this applies especially for Schutz's social phenomenology.

The difference between ethnomethodology and Lave's practice theory is that although ethnomethodologists are particularly attentive to situated (inter)action, ethnomethodology is not concerned with agents' particular ways of engaging with the material environment. Lave (1988) argues that even though ethnomethodology's partners in conversation and interaction are conceived as corporeal, embodied, and part of time-space loci, interaction itself easily becomes the only context studied. In practice theory, it is the activity setting with its structures and material conditions that entails particular selves, skills, values and sensibilities, and ways of acting and doing things.

The existence of common frames of understanding, systems of meanings, or discourses, is not denied by Lave.[6] Lave (1988) does emphasize that the discourses commonly used in society, for instance, in making sense of schooling or mathematical talent, are learned and shared by most people—teachers, researchers and "jpfs" (just plain folks) alike. For Lave, this is exactly why we cannot rely on interviews alone if we are interested in situated activity. When Lave began to develop the practice theory, she and her colleagues also developed a methodology for observing happenings as they unfold in real-life situations.[7]

In summary, the focus on practice means *not* foregrounding analytic categories such as sense making, meanings, understandings, interpretations, or experiences. A similar distinction must be made with the more traditional sociological concepts of rules,

Table 16.1
Reckwitz's (2002) classification of social theories (modified)

Social theory	Representative(s)	Unit of analysis	Focus
Mentalism	Schutz's phenomenology	Minds, sense making	Subjective acts of mental interpretations
Textualism	Foucault	Discourses	Discursive constructedness of reality
Intersubjectivism	Garfinkel, conversation analysis	Interactions	Situational and interrelational use of language
Practice theory	Lave, Lave and Wenger, Schatzki[8]	Practices	Real-time performance of activities

norms, and values. Shared norms, values, symbols, or *culture* in general, are not the analytic concern in practice theory, but the interconnectedness between material conditions
and resources for activity, persons-acting, and activity settings (Lave 1988).

THE EMPIRICAL FOUNDATIONS OF LAVE'S PRACTICE THEORY

Apprenticeship Learning in Tailor Shops in Liberia

Lave began to develop her theory of practice based on the findings from her extensive
fieldwork on apprenticeship learning of tailors in Liberia. The research involved five
field trips to Monrovia during the period 1973–78. She spent time in the tailor shops in
Tailors' Alley, getting to know Vai and Gola tailors who occupied a poor and marginal
location at the periphery of the business district of the city of Monrovia. She was interested in what the apprentices learned and how they learned in the absence of planned
teaching, and wanted to see the outcomes from the years of apprenticeship (Lave 1990,
21; 1996, 151).

Tailor apprenticeship involved sustained opportunities to observe masters and other
apprentices at work, to learn the full process of producing garments, and to learn about
the pricing and selling of finished products. A kind of curriculum existed in apprenticeship learning in the sense that apprentices first learned to make cheaper clothes (like
underwear and children's garments) and gradually proceeded to making more official
and expensive clothes (like suits) worn by those occupying higher positions in the social hierarchy. Apprentices' learning started from simpler tasks like sewing by hand and
finishing already tailored clothes, and gradually progressed to more demanding tasks
such as cutting out garments from pieces of cloth. The learning process was subdivided
by type of garment, and by type of task, in a way that minimized risks of serious errors
and experiences of failure (Lave 1990, 21). Apprentices' products were not evaluated
by masters or compared, since the ongoing taken-for-granted expectation was equal accomplishment by all learners (Lave 1996). Apprentices would decide themselves when
the garments they had made were good enough to sell, and by selling they learned what
customers were willing to pay for their products (Lave 1996).

Masters were embodied exemplars of what apprentices were becoming. However,
apprentices not only reproduced existing practices or acquired skills of making garments; generating new styles and procedures is a natural part of the craft. For Lave
(1996), an important observation was that apprentices were learning many things at
once: they were learning about major social identities and divisions in the society that
they were in the business of dressing, they were learning how make a living by making
clothes, they were learning to lead a specific kind of life as tailors, and in the process of
becoming practicing tailors they were learning respect for their craft. Thus the success
of learning without teaching is based on that learning is not separated from practice, that
divisions between learning and doing do not exist, that social identity and knowledge
are merged, as are education and occupation, and form and content of learning. When
success is not measured against predefined goals, when there is no fear of failure, when
comparisons among learners are noticeably absent, avoidance of blame is not what mo-
tivates learners and rewards are intrinsic. Lave (1996) stressed that the assumption that
teaching is a necessary prerequisite if learning is to occur cannot be correct. If learning is about people becoming kinds of persons—knowledgeably skilled persons—then
learning is necessarily a context-embedded, situated activity rather than learners being
offered a pool of knowledge to acquire or absorb.

The Adult Math Project

Lave's ethnographic research among the apprentice tailors thus led her to challenge the idea of the transferability of knowledge and skills. The Adult Math Project (AMP, 1978–80) was subsequently designed by Lave and her colleagues Michael Murtaugh and Olivia de la Rocha. During a sabbatical year (1981–82), in the Center for Information Processing, University of California, San Diego, Lave also started to work on a critical review of the literature of cognitive research.

In the AMP project, Lave and her colleagues (Lave, Murtaugh, and de la Rocha 1991) studied the use of mathematics in everyday activities, observing grocery shopping in supermarkets, Weight Watchers' cooking, and money flow management in households. These kinds of mundane activities as observed by Lave and her colleagues have not always been considered as relevant objects for cognitive research, because of its aim of developing general models of human information processing and problem solving. For Lave (1988), looking at mundane practices that are maximally different from the taken-for-granted research settings of schools and laboratories is necessary to gain new insights and to put theories to the test.

The major finding from the Adult Math Project (AMP) was that there exists, in different settings, an infinite number of different types of arithmetics (Lave 1988, 63). Mathematics taught at schools is but one type of arithmetic practice. Lave (1996) argues that everyday math is not an application of informal learning as opposed to formal learning and mathematics but something fundamentally different from school mathematics.

The Adult Math Project involved both observation of arithmetic use of in everyday situations and school-type mathematical tests conducted with the same participants. When the study participants' success in situated arithmetic practices and results from tests in mathematical skills were compared, there was no correspondence in success rates across contexts (1988). Consequently, Lave (1988, 3) formulated her core argument as follows:

Several years of exploration of arithmetic as cognitive practice in everyday contexts has led to a kernel observation … [that] the same people differ in their arithmetic activities in different settings in ways that challenge theoretical boundaries between activity and its settings, between cognitive, bodily, and social forms of activity, between information and value, between problems and solutions.

In cognitivist theorizing, the generative basis of action is inscribed only *in* the person (Lave 1988). Lave argues against the view that the cognitive abilities of individuals are stable and constant across contexts, and are the proper objects for theorizing, and that contexts are too specific and variable to be theorizable. For Lave (1988, 170), persons-acting, activities, and activity settings (domains) are inseparable. Lave (ibid, 180) makes a distinction between *a person* and *the person-acting (within a setting)* as units of analysis. *A person* as the object of study may include consideration of the person's activity and situation, but in fact looks at these only as located within the person, and mainly through the person's representations of them. In practice theory, setting and activity are constitutive for *the person-acting,* and importantly, the action necessarily involves the person's body. If we start from practice, the person-acting on a task may in fact be multiple persons, and the doing may involve multiple bodies, all moving in the same time and at the same time, jointly aware of problems, constituting solutions through action and jointly changing the course of action (one of the best empirical descriptions of distributed cognition is Hutchins' 1991 study on ship navigation).

LAVE'S CRITIQUE OF THE LEARNING TRANSFER ASSUMPTION

In cognitivist research, the cognitive skills that are considered as the most transferable across situations are those of problem handling, problem solving and decision-making. The primary interest is in information processing within the heads of individuals. Lave (1988), in turn, stresses that if we assume that problem solving within ongoing activities is in nature individual, rational (at best) and cognitive, then we do *not* assume that activities are culturally and socially structured, or that problem solving is part of contextualized social experience.

To exemplify the logic of experimental cognitivist laboratory research, let us look at a (randomly selected) study on decision-making. Wilson and Schooler (1991) explored whether and how the quality of decision-making is affected if people are asked to reason about their choices, and whether introspection about the causes for feelings and attitudes enhances the quality of decision-making. College students' preferences for different brands of strawberry jams were compared with an expert panels' rating of the jams. Students who were required to write down the reasons for their strawberry jam preferences agreed less with the opinions of experts than the control group that was not asked to give a detailed account of the reasons for their liking of different jams. Those psychology students who were asked to list their reasons for liking and disliking jams tended to get more negative in their evaluations. In a second experiment, college students' preferences for college courses were compared with expert opinions. Students who were asked to analyze the attributes of courses, as compared to the control group who were not, made choices corresponding less with expert opinion. The study concludes that detailed analysis of possible reasons for choices can focus people's attention on nonoptimal criteria and cause them to base their subsequent choices on these criteria.

Lave's (1988) criticism of laboratory research on human cognition questions the assumption that research based on imposed tasks will give valid results. According to Lave, laboratory experiments ignore how the fact of being tested affects subjects' performance. In the strawberry jam test (Wilson and Schooler 1991, 186), those who were asked just to taste and rate jams were positioned in a less testlike situation than the students who were asked, by the experimenter, to be analytic and to organize their thoughts before giving their evaluations. Lave (1988, 37) argues that experimental tasks foster a static, objectified conceptualization of decision-making and problem-solving processes. Experimenters work on the basis of transferability expectations and disregard the effect of the test-type context on the studied subjects' actions. Context of decision-making and positioning of subjects within that context are not seen as essential factors for subjects' performance, hence, strawberry jam tasting and evaluating college courses form equally good contexts for the study of decision-making. Lave (1988, 62), in turn, argues that "the validity of extrapolation from the experimental to any other situation is doubtful." Success and failure in Lave's theory is a relation among persons-acting and activity settings. At school and in laboratory research, subjects are turned into objects having no control over the given problems and tasks, whereas in mundane activity settings, actors are in control of their own activities and tasks (ibid, 69–70).

Lave (1988) points out that laboratory-type experimental studies on reasoning and decision-making always require a *measure*—expert opinion—as a norm against which subjects' performance is evaluated. This is based on a specific kind of understanding of the nature of knowledge and expertise. It is assumed that knowledge consists of coherent and hierarchically organized discrete chunks "whose boundaries and internal structure exist independently of individuals" (1988, 43). What is not immediately recognizable as the basis of cognitivist theorizing is that it is based on a belief in cultural and cognitive uniformity.

Lave (1988) points out that the organization of schooling, the socialization experiences of people in school, and their theories as alumni of schools, all rely on the belief that there exists a pool of information that can be transmitted from one generation to the next. School subjects and contents are, supposedly, derived from a context-free and value-free body of knowledge—which is a proper yardstick against which to measure performance (ibid, 87, 100). The belief about learning transfer and the assumption of continuity in cognitive activity across settings is especially strong as regards mathematics. It is assumed that arithmetic is learned in school, and then carried away from school to be applied at will in any situation that calls for calculation (1988, 4). According to Lave, empirical evidence does not support the assumption that people who are not successful in school arithmetic algorithms could not be successful in other settings requiring mathematical and logical problem solving as a central aspect of ongoing activity.[9]

The theory of learning that prevails in schooling is that children can be taught general cognitive skills—reading, writing, mathematics, and critical thinking—if and only if these skills are abstracted and disembedded from the routine contexts of their use in everyday life (1988, 8). Verbally transmitted, explicit, general knowledge is seen as the main prerequisite for making cognitive skills transferable across situations (ibid, 14). It is assumed that knowledge acquired in context-free circumstances is available for general application, widely transportable, and relatively impervious to change (ibid). Extraction of knowledge from the particulars of experience in situated activity is seen as the very condition for making knowledge available for general application across situations (41).[10]

Lave (1988) points out that classroom tests only serve as a measure of individuals' out-of-context success. Examinations measuring individual success and failure and depending on memorization are "condensed, symbolic, and ritual ordeals" (1988, 16).[11] Lave argues that internalization is a less important mode of contact with the world than action in the world (1988, 16). For Lave (1988, 14)

knowledge-in-practice, constituted in the settings of practice, is the locus of the most powerful knowledgeability of people in the lived-in-world.

Lave (1988, 184) also argues that in real-world practices, there exist no boundaries between cognitive, bodily and social forms of activity, between information and value, or between problems and solutions. Being knowledgeable is only possible within a specific activity setting, and the knowledge that is important is a matter of value, desire, feeling, and judgment. The activity/practice and values related to it are generated simultaneously. Neither the goals or values or meanings integrated with the practice/activity are given from outside the practice itself.

THE RELATIONSHIP BETWEEN PROBLEMS AND SOLUTIONS

The prime target of research in cognitivist research is problem solving, and Lave argues that problem solving has been given a misleading eminence in cognitive theory. Its theoretical centrality reflects a reduction of cognition to problem solving and failure to see problem-solving activities as parts of practices, ongoing activities in context. Lave (1988) redefines the very nature of problem solving. For Lave, problems and solutions are not separable. Problem-solving activity is activity in context, since knowing how to solve problems, and knowing what one is doing, are only possible within a particular field of action (ibid, 165). Problems are presented to problem solvers by problem givers only in specific activity settings such as formal schooling. Lave (ibid, 19) argues that when problems arise in situated action, problems are not separable from the procedures or means for solving them. We can only define a problem when we have an understanding of its possible solutions—a sense of an answer and a process for bringing it together with its parts (19). The goals of problem-solving activity are also inherent to the constitution of problems. Seeing a problem means that a partial form of solution already has been produced (ibid, 165). Because problem solving means *knowing* the procedures for problem solving and the solution space, if we cannot imagine a solution, and if we do not already have an idea of where a solution will lead, we will not see the existence of a problem to be solved.

Thus, for Lave (1988), problems only have an existence inside situated activity. Problems are not (pre)structured or predefined in nature, and therefore the problem-solving process cannot be adequately described as the application of normative, decontextualized rules, or rational models of good thinking. Lave (1988, 175) defines a problem as "a dilemma to which the problem solver is emotionally engaged." Note that the word *emotionally* in this case does not necessarily entail negative feelings such as anxiety or uncertainty. In Lave's theory, seeing a problem and attempting to solve it means being already engaged in concrete ongoing activity within a setting (domain). Problems are born of values in conflict, and "are themselves actions upon the world" (1988, 156). Finding something problematic is not caused by lack of knowledge but on the contrary subsumes a great deal of knowledge. It is the nature of dilemmas[12] that they require managing contradictory principles and conflicting values (1988, 139). Dilemmas have no factual solutions or correct answers; resolving them is usually a matter of choosing between equally viable alternatives. Yet, when a solution is needed, Lave (1988, 139) writes that "on the basis of experience, people are almost certain to have more than one occasional resolution to a dilemma." Constituting a solution or a method at arriving at one is thus a matter of experience within an activity setting (ibid, 159).

In all models of rational decision-making, evidence should, in principle, precede a decision and provide the motivation for the solution. Within real-life activity-settings, marshaling evidence after the fact of the decision is commonplace (ibid, 157). Multiple relations between evidence and conclusions are characteristics of authentic problem-solving practices, because a problem's parameters are not given but assembled in the process of deciding about procedural possibilities (Lave 1988). Decision-making activity involves first establishing a field for generative action and then the action itself. Lave (1988, 159) stresses that problem solving is an iterative, transformational process. In the course of practical action, problems generated for solution can be abandoned as well as resolved. A problem solver may redefine a problem, or transform it into an entirely different problem. Problems often have no clear or stable solutions, and problems that prove too difficult to be solved are not necessarily the ones that are the most critical or in urgent need of resolution.

STRUCTURING RESOURCES

Lave found that in mundane activity—as in counting calories in food preparation—everyday mathematical problems are in complex ways interconnected with concerns and issues that are not primarily about mathematics. This accounts for the existence of multiple forms of math in practice (ibid, 101). Other aspects of ongoing activity shape the forms of mathematics used, and arithmetic problem solving often had closer ties with these other aspects of the activity than to uses of arithmetic in other contexts. Lave uses the concept of structuring resources to describe how other activities provide structure to an activity (such as doing math, which may experienced be as the same activity in different situations), constituting it and transforming it into a specific form.[13]

In the situated activity of grocery shopping, shoppers did conduct cost per item calculations, but arithmetic in practice was not simply about counting. Shoppers simultaneously took into account multiple concerns: storing space at home, estimated rate of item consumption, nutritional values, family food preferences, and quality concerns. In addition to these multiple concerns, the structure of the setting where activity took place influenced action and the kinds of problems that emerged in practice. Lave and her colleagues saw that shopping decisions were taken in pace with the affordances at the supermarket as shoppers moved through its spaces, encountering and comparing products. Variation in the affordances of the environment also resulted in differently structured activity. The supermarket forms an information-rich environment and a changing arena for shoppers. However, shoppers acted on the basis of the assumption that shopping is routine in character. This was a way to manage and domesticate the information richness of the environment. Shoppers face overwhelming amounts of information, only a small part of which is relevant for making grocery choices (ibid, 154). However, through time, experienced shoppers successfully render the supermarket from an information-rich arena into an information-specific setting, that is, into a personally ordered and edited version of the arena (ibid, 168).

People's social relationships also give structure to activities. The activity of calculating money, for instance, would seem to be an activity that is fairly consistent over situations. Lave and her colleagues discovered, however, that in household money management, money does not have a universal standard value. Money gets divided into special purposes stashes reserved for different aspects of everyday living (ibid, 132). These compartmentalized stashes were incommensurate: differentially valued, handled, and used. The differential values were related to family members' relations with each other, and supported the categories of activities into which families organized their lives (ibid, 132–34).

Lave (1988, 143) points out that although the concept of structuring resources clearly is important, it requires further elaboration. Lave's concept of structuring resources can be related to affordance theory (Gibson 1977),[14] which is applicable for exploring in a more detailed manner how, for instance, a technology's materiality offers constraints and possibilities for use, and how material affordances reconfigure action and agency (Raudaskoski 2009).

INFORMATION SCIENCE RESEARCH AND PRACTICE THEORY

Lave's practice theory is particularly interesting from the viewpoint of information science because of our field's continued effort to build good theories on the nature of information, knowledge, and human-information interaction. Lave's work has much to offer also as regards research on the learning and teaching of information work practices.

Lave's work also helps us to understand the history of information science. One of Lave's central insights is that the specific interests and concerns of cognitivist research implicitly contain a strong faith in the transferability of knowledge and skills. In the mid-1970s, many fields—including education, psychology, and information science—began to look for scientific foundations for their academic enterprises from cognitive science, because cognitive science seemed to offer increasingly sophisticated formal models of language, logic, and problem solving (Lave 1988, 7). Since much of cognitive theory was about information processing, this explains its attractiveness for information science—then a new academic field that chose to organize itself around the concept of information.

Information processing was, in cognitivist research, something that takes place within the individual mind. Culture, society, and nature, in turn, offered a pool of information to be acquired. Knowledge was understood to result from the storing of cultural acquisitions in memory (Lave 1988, 90). Herbert A. Simon (1980), for instance, equated expert knowledge with a well-indexed, easily accessible encyclopedia (1988, 18, 90). Within information science, the understanding of information use as the addition of pieces of information to the knowledge stored in an individual's mind is well established (Savolainen 2006). New information has mostly been seen as something that changes a person's mental model.

Lave's argument that problem solving and decision-making have been given an exaggerated role in cognitive research is particularly relevant from the viewpoint of information science theories. According to Lave (1988, 142), problem solving does not have a broad and fecund role to play in everyday activity in its customary settings. She argues that when studying everyday practice, "it is difficult to detect problems to be solved or conventional scholastic problem-solving activity" (Lave 1988, 141). In information science, the legacy of cognitive science influenced basically all major theories of human information behavior developed between late 1970s and 1990s. Major theories of information behavior are, in essence, theories of problem solving and decision-making. Information behavior theories usually posit a situation where an actor is faced with a problem—a gap in knowledge, or lack of meaning—and visualize enablers and barriers for overcoming the problematic situation through acquisition of information. For instance, Belkin's (1980) ASK model, Dervin's (1983) sense-making theory, Kuhlthau's (1993) Information Search Process (ISP) model, and Wilson's (1981) information behavior model, are all basically models of problem solving activity. Gaps, problems, and uncertainty, have traditionally been considered as key concepts in information science, linked with the concept of information. Most efforts for theory building or modeling relate needs for information to gaps in knowledge or problematic situations, and consequently view information seeking and finding as the core activities to study.

Lave, in turn, sees that expertise and participation in a particular practice entails problem solving and decision-making as part of ongoing activity. Lave's practice theory shifts the research focus from problems encountered in work and everyday life to practices. Building theories around the concept of practice entails at a different understanding of agency, activity settings, and the nature of everyday life. The research focus on situated activity and the related methodologies are already well established in some areas of information science.[15] Recently, researchers have begun to debate whether *information practices* would function better as an anchoring core term than *information behavior* (Information behavior/practice debate 2009). This may reflect an ongoing bigger shift in theoretical and methodological orientations within information science. For bringing such a shift about, Lave's theory of practice has much to offer.

REFERENCES

Anderson, John R., Lynne M. Reder, and Herbert A. Simon. 1996. "Situated Learning and Education." *Educational Researcher* 25 (4): 5–11.

Barnes, Barry. 2001. "Practice as Collective Action." In *The Practice Turn in Contemporary Theory,* ed. Theodore R. Schatzki, Karin Knorr-Cetina, and Eike von Savigny, 17–28. London: Routledge.

Barton, David, and Karin Tusting, eds. 2005. *Beyond Communities of Practice: Language, Power and Social Context.* Cambridge: Cambridge University Press.

Belkin, Nicholas J. 1980. "Anomalous States of Knowledge as a Basis for Information Retrieval." *Canadian Journal of Information Science* 5 (May): 133–43.

Bereiter, Carl. 1997. "Situated Cognition and How to Overcome It." In *Situated Cognition: Social, Semiotic and Psychological Perspectives,* ed. David Kirshner and James A. Whitson, 281–300. Mahwah, NJ: Lawrence Erlbaum Associates.

Bloor, David. 2001. "Wittgenstein and the Priority of Practice." In *The Practice Turn in Contemporary Theory,* ed. Theodore R. Schatzki, Karin Knorr Cetina, and Eike von Savigny, 95–106. London: Routledge.

Bourdieu, Pierre. 1977. *Outline of a Theory of Practice.* Cambridge: Cambridge University Press.

Bourdieu, Pierre. 1984. *Distinction: A Social Critique of the Judgment of Taste.* Cambridge, MA: Harvard University Press.

Brown, John Seely, Allan Collins, and Paul Duguid. 1989. "Situated Cognition and the Culture of Learning." *Educational Researcher* 18 (1): 32–42.

Brown, John Seely, and Paul Duguid. 2001. "Knowledge and Organization: A Social-Practice Perspective." *Organization Science* 12 (2): 198–213.

Clark, Andy. 1989. *Microcognition: Philosophy, Cognitive Science and Parallel Distributed Processing.* Cambridge, MA: MIT Press/Bradford Books.

Davenport, Elisabeth. 2001. "Knowledge Management Issues for Online Organisations: Communities of Practice as an Exploratory Framework." *Journal of Documentation* 57 (1): 61–75.

Dervin, Brenda. 1983. "An Overview of Sense-Making Research: Concepts, Methods, and Results to Date." Paper presented at the Annual Meeting of the International Communication Association, Dallas, Texas. http://www.ideals.illinois.edu/bitstream/handle/2142/2281/Dervin83a.htm;jsessionid=929A76C7FA7CB38193950AA690EB8AE9.

Engeström, Yrjö. 1987. *Learning by Expanding: An Activity-Theoretical Approach to Developmental Research.* Helsinki: Orienta-konsultit.

Engeström, Yrjö, and Michael Cole. 1997. "Situated Cognition in Search of an Agenda" In *Situated Cognition: Social, Semiotic and Psychological Perspectives,* ed. David Kirshner and James A. Whitson, 301–9. Mahwah, NJ: Lawrence Erlbaum Associates.

Garfinkel, Harold. 1967. *Studies in Ethnomethodology.* Englewood Cliffs, NJ: Prentice Hall.

Gee, James Paul. 2004. *Situated Language and Learning: A Critique of Traditional Schooling.* New York: Routledge and Kegan Paul.

Gherardi, Silvia. 2006. *Organizational Knowledge: The Texture of Workplace Learning.* Oxford: Blackwell.

Gibson, James J. 1977. "The Theory of Affordances" In *Perceiving, Acting and Knowing,* ed. Robert Shaw, and John Bransford, 67–82. Hillsdale, NJ: Erlbaum.

Giddens, Anthony. 1979. *Central Problems in Social Theory.* Berkeley: University of California Press.

Giddens, Anthony. 1984. *The Constitution of Society.* Berkeley: University of California Press.

Hara, Noriko. 2007. "IT Support for Communities of Practice: How Public Defenders Learn about Winning and Losing in Court." *Journal of the American Society for Information Science & Technology* 58 (1): 76–87.

Hedman, Jenny, and Anna Lundh, eds. 2009. *Informationskompetenser: Om Lärande i Informationspraktiker och Informationssökning i Lärandepraktiker* [Information Competences: About Learning Within Information Practices and Information Searching Within Learning Practices]. Stockholm: Carlssons.

Hutchins, Edwin. 1991. "The Social Organization of Distributed Cognition" In *Perspectives on Socially Shared Cognition,* ed. Lauren B. Resnick, James M. Levine, and Stephanie D. Teasley, 283–307. Pittsburgh: Learning Research and Development Center, University of Pittsburgh / American Psychological Association.

Information behavior/practice debate: a discussion prompted by Tom Wilson's review of Reijo Savolainen's *Everyday Information Practices: A Social Phenomenological Perspective.* 2009. *Information Research* 14 (2), http://InformationR.net/ir/14–2/paper403.html.

Knorr-Cetina, Karin. 1981. *The Manufacture of Knowledge: An Essay on the Constructivist and Contextual Nature of Science.* Oxford: Pergamon Press.

Knorr-Cetina, Karin. 2001. "Objectual Practice." In *The Practice Turn in Contemporary Theory,* ed. Theodore R. Schatzki, Karin Knorr-Cetina, and Eike von Savigny, 175–88. London: Routledge.

Kuhlthau, Carol C. 1993. *Seeking Meaning: A Process Approach to Library and Information Services.* Westport, CT: Libraries Unlimited.

Latour, Bruno, and Steve Woolgar. 1979. *Laboratory Life: The Social Construction of Scientific Facts.* Beverly Hills, CA: Sage.

Lave, Jean. 1977. "Cognitive Consequences of Traditional Apprenticeship Training in West Africa." *Anthropology and Education Quarterly* 18 (3): 177–80.

Lave, Jean. 1982. "A Comparative Approach to Educational Forms and Learning Processes." *Anthropology and Education Quarterly* 13 (2): 181–87.

Lave, Jean. 1985. "Introduction: Situationally Specific Practice." *Anthropology and Education Quarterly* 16 (3): 171–76.

Lave, Jean. 1988. *Cognition in Practice: Mind, Mathematics and Culture in Everyday Life.* Cambridge: Cambridge University Press.

Lave, Jean.1990. "The Culture of Acquisition and the Practice of Understanding." In *Cultural Psychology: Essays on Comparative Human Development,* ed. James W. Stigler, Richard A. Schweder, and Gilbert Herdt, 309–27. Cambridge: Cambridge University Press.

Lave, Jean. 1991. "Situated Learning in Communities of Practice" In *Perspectives on Socially Shared Cognition,* ed. Lauren B. Resnick, James M. Levine, and Stephanie D. Teasley, 64–82. Pittsburgh: Learning Research and Development Center, University of Pittsburgh / American Psychological Association.

Lave, Jean. 1993. "The Practice of Learning." In *Understanding Practice: Perspectives on Activity and Context,* ed. Seth Chaiklin and Jean Lave, 3–32. Cambridge: Cambridge University Press.

Lave, Jean. 1996. "Teaching, as Learning, in Practice." *Mind, Culture, and Activity* 3 (3): 149–64.

Lave, Jean. 1999. "The Politics of Learning in Everyday Life." ICOS lecture. Ann Arbor: Interdisciplinary Committee on Organizational Studies, University of Michigan. http://www.si.umich.edu/ICOS/Presentations/041699/

Lave, Jean, and Ray McDermott. 2002. "Estranged Learning." *Outlines: Critical Social Studies* 4 (1): 19–48.

Lave, Jean, Michael Murtaugh, and Olivia de la Rocha. 1984. "The Dialectic of Arithmetic in Grocery Shopping." In *Everyday Cognition: Its Development in Social Context,* ed. Barbara Rogoff and Jean Lave, 67–94. Cambridge, MA: Harvard University Press.

Lave, Jean, and Etienne Wenger. 1991. *Situated Learning: Legitimate Peripheral Participation.* Cambridge: Cambridge University Press.

Leontjev, Aleksei. 1978. *Activity, Consciousness, Personality.* Englewood Cliffs, NJ: Prentice Hall.

Lloyd, Annemaree. 2007. "Learning to Put Out the Red Stuff: Becoming Information Literate through Discursive Practice." *Library Quarterly* 77 (2): 181–98.

Lloyd, Annemaree, and Sanna Talja, eds. 2010. *Practicing Information Literacy: Bringing Theories of Learning, Practice and Information Literacy Together.* Wagga Wagga, Australia: Centre for Information Studies.

Lynch, Michael. 1982. *Art and Artefacts in Laboratory Science.* London: Routledge and Kegan Paul.

Østerlund, Carsten, and Paul Carlile. 2005. "Relations in Practice: Sorting through Practice Theories on Knowledge Sharing in Complex Organizations." *Information Society* 21 (2): 91–107.

Raudaskoski, Sanna. 2009. "Tool and Machine: The Affordances of the Mobile Phone." PhD diss. University of Tampere, Finland. Available at http://acta.uta.fi/.

Reckwitz, Andreas. 2002. "Toward a Theory of Social Practices: A Development in Cultural Theorizing." *European Journal of Social Theory* 5 (2): 243–63.

Säljö, Roger. 2002. "My Brain's Running Slow Today—the Preference for 'Things Ontologies' in Research and Everyday Discourse on Human Thinking." *Studies in Philosophy and Education* 21 (4–5): 389–405.

Savolainen, Reijo. 2006. "Information Use as Gap-Bridging: The Viewpoint of Sense-Making Methodology." *Journal of the American Society for Information Science and Technology* 57 (8): 1116–25.

Savolainen, Reijo. 2008. *Everyday Information Practices: A Social Phenomenological Perspective.* Lanham, MD: Scarecrow Press.

Schatzki, Theodore R. 2002. *The Site of the Social: A Philosophical Account of the Constitution of Social Life and Change.* Philadelphia: University of Pennsylvania Press.

Schutz, Alfred. 1964. *Collected Papers II: Studies in Social Theory.* The Hague: Marinus Nijhoff.

Simon, Herbert A. 1980. "Problem Solving and Education." In *Problem Solving and Education: Issues in Teaching and Research,* ed. David T. Tuma and Frederic Reif, 81–96. Hillsdale, NJ: Erlbaum.

Suchman, Lucy. 1987. *Plans and Situated Actions: The Problem of Human-Machine Communication.* New York: Cambridge University Press.

Thevenot, Laurent. 2001. "Pragmatic Regimes Governing the Engagement with the World." In *The Practice Turn in Contemporary Theory,* ed. Theodore R. Schatzki, Karin Knorr-Cetina, and Eike von Savigny, 56–73. London and New York: Routledge.

Traweek, Sharon. 1988. *Beamtimes and Lifetimes: The World of High Energy Physicists.* Cambridge, MA: Harvard University Press.

Vann, Katie, and Geoffrey L. Bowker. 2001. "Instrumentalizing the Truth of Practice." *Social Epistemology* 15 (3): 247–62.

Vygotsky, Lev. 1978. *Mind in Society: The Development of Higher Psychological Processes.* Cambridge, MA: Harvard University Press.

Wenger, Etienne. 1998. *Communities of Practice: Learning, Meaning, and Identity.* Cambridge: Cambridge University Press.

Wenger, Etienne, Richard McDermott, and William M. Snyder. 2002. *Cultivating Communities of Practice: A Guide to Managing Knowledge.* Cambridge: Harvard Business School Press.

Wertsch, James V. 1991. *Voices of the Mind: A Sociocultural Approach to Mediated Action.* Cambridge, MA: Harvard University Press.

Wilson, Thomas D. 1981. "On User Studies and Information Needs." *Journal of Documentation* 37 (1): 3–15.

Wilson, Timothy D., and Jonathan W. Schooler. 1991. "Thinking Too Much: Introspection Can Reduce the Quality of Preferences and Decisions." *Journal of Personality and Social Psychology* 60 (2): 181–92.

Wittgenstein, Ludwig. 1980. *Culture and Value.* Oxford: Blackwell.

NOTES

1. Cognitivism is a theoretical endeavour that developed in tandem with the emergence of computer technology in the 1950s and for which computer technology is a powerful source of inspiration (Säljö 2002). Cognitivist research focuses on individual human beings as processors of information. Theoretical concepts such as mental models and schemas are used to describe information processing within the minds of individuals. Cognitivism is also a term used to distinguish between two different traditions within cognitive science. Theories of situated cognition, socially shared cognition, and distributed cognition, all lean on the notion of situatedness that leads to the primacy of social practice as the unit of analysis (Engeström and Cole 1997). The situated, practice-oriented study of cognition does not focus on the storage, processing, and retrieval of information within individual minds.

2. The question of how to cultivate the formation of CoPs in workplaces is an interest inspired especially by Wenger's (1998, Wenger et al. 2002) later expansion of CoP theory (17–18).

3. Situated cognition and social cognition theories draw from the works of Vygotsky (1978) and Leontjev (1978). The situated cognition movement also incorporates cultural-historical activity theory (CHAT) (Engestrom 1987), sociocultural theory (Wertsch 1991), extended cognition (Clark 1989). and distributed cognition (Hutchins 1991).

4. Situated learning theory is also called theory of situated action, or social learning theory. Sometimes theories of situated action, situated cognition, and situated learning are bundled together as "situativity theories."

5. Later, Lave (1999) came to see Bourdieu's notion of everyday life as problematic, since it is a viewpoint that sheds more light on the everyday life of the cultural elite, and on their relation with culture (with a capital C), which is taught at schools and, at least during the 1970s in France, continued to be something that distinguished classes from one another. Bourdieu (1984) assumes a sort of hierarchy among cultural practices, despite the fact that he sees

the natural aesthetic disposition and way of experiencing as more normal than the learned and trained pure aesthetic gaze of the cultural elite.

6. Lave and Wenger's (1991) work has been criticized by critical discourse analysts for neglecting the critical role of language and interaction in establishing and negotiating identities. Lave's 1993 article discusses the role of language and discourses in a more in-depth manner than her earlier works, however, and in a way that is well in line with textualist social theorizing. Many researchers see that it is possible and necessary to analyze both discourses that operate and are used within a studied activity setting and the hands-on concrete doings in that setting (e.g., Schatzki 2002; Gherardi 2006).

7. The methods Lave and her colleagues used in the Adult Math Project (AMP) included shadowing the study participants in supermarket visits, asking participants to think aloud during shopping, asking questions about what they were thinking and doing, asking participants to keep diaries, and guided tours in households (Lave 1988, 49).

8. Theodore Schatzki (2002) has made considerable effort in developing practice theory. Another key theorist is Silvia Gherardi (2006).

9. Chapter 2 in Lave (1988, 25–44) is a review of learning transfer experiments.

10. As can be expected, the heaviest critiques of Lave's work concern the issue transferability. For instance, Anderson, Reder, and Simon (1996) argue that transferability depends on the degree to which a successive task has components similar to a prior task. According to Bereiter (1997), transfer is possible if the learner consciously focuses on the identification of similarities and differences across situations. He also states, however, that as learning proceeds it tends to get less and less generalizable to other situations. Being smart (or expert) means being attuned to the specific features of a practice to the degree that any problems that arise can be coped with effortlessly (Bereiter 1997).

11. For those interested in pursuing the later development of situated learning theories' critique of schooling, James Gee's (2004) work is especially interesting and relevant.

12. Lave sees dilemmas as an inevitable part of everyday life. However, a frequently voiced criticism of CoP theory is that it does not adequately address the existence of conflicting interests, power struggles, or noncollaboration. The existence of diverse speech communities and conflicting discourses within a single setting or domain is one of the major themes in a volume called *Beyond Communities of Practice: Language, Power and Social Context* (Barton and Karin 2005) that both critiques and extends the CoP theory.

13. Lave's practice theory and CoP theory have both been criticized for focusing on expertise gained on single practices. Gee (2004) introduces the concept of affinity spaces and describes learning as a social journey as a person moves through multiple affinity spaces each having their unique trajectories. Brown and Duguid (2001) similarly argue that learning takes place not only in small, tightly knit communities but also in networks of CoPs that can be called networks of practice. An academic discipline such as information science, for instance, links university departments and research groups from institutions around the world and thus makes up a disciplinary network of practice.

14. The term *affordance* refers to features in social, technological, physical and material tools and environments that enable or restrict our actions (Gibson 1977).

15. Especially, interdisciplinary empirical knowledge management research (organizational learning and knowledge sharing research), and studies on information organization and documentation work in office and home environments lean on practice theory. In information literacy research, situated learning and practice theories are increasingly used as foundations for research efforts (e.g., Hedman and Lundh 2009; Lloyd and Talja 2009).

17

Henri Lefebvre and Spatial Dialectics

Gloria J. Leckie
University of Western Ontario, Canada
Lisa M. Given
University of Alberta, Canada

INTRODUCTION

Henri Lefebvre is, as many argue, one of the greatest French scholars of the 20th century. In his lifetime (1901–91), he produced a large number of major works and continued to do so well into his 70s. Within France, during his career, he was a prominent and publicly-known Marxist scholar, one who was actively involved in the social movements of his day. As his works become available in translation, he continues to have considerable influence, particularly within the Anglo-American academic milieu, on epistemological and theoretical perspectives in philosophy, sociology, cultural studies, geography, urban studies and political economy.

Lefebvre's life is well documented. He was born in Hagetmat, Landes, France and his early years were spent in the city of Navarreaux. He attended the Sorbonne, graduating in 1920 with a degree in philosophy. During the 1920s, Lefebvre was active within a group of radical French philosophical intellectuals and subsequently joined the Communist Party of France in 1928. In 1930, he became a professor of philosophy and was active within the French resistance during the Second World War. He later took a position with Radiodiffusion Française, a radio broadcaster in Toulouse. Lefebvre broke with the Communist Party in 1958 and accepted a position as a philosophy professor at the University of Strasbourg in 1961, moving from there to the university at Nanterre (Université Paris Ouest-Nanterre La Défense) in 1965. He was a highly respected professor and was influential in the Situationist International and the French student unrest of 1968. His contemporaries included Louis Althusser, Roland Barthes, Jacques Lacan, Maurice Merleau-Ponty, and Jean-Paul Sartre.

Lefebvre's scholarly legacy includes a wide range of theoretical discourse, beginning with early writings on Marx and Marxism, Hegel, existentialism, nationalism and other topics. Two of his more famous early works included *Dialectical*

Materialism (translated into English in 1968; first edition published in 1939 as *Le matérialisme dialectique*) and his work *Critique of Everyday Life* (translated in 1991 from *Critique de la vie quotidienne,* which was published as three volumes between 1947 and 1981). Also notable were his later writings on urbanism and the urban condition, some of which are now available in the translated and edited collection *Writings on Cities* (1996). Lefebvre was influential in the development of the thinking of a number of well-known scholars in a variety of disciplines, including Fredric Jameson, Michel de Certeau, Guy Debord, Mark Gottdiener, David Harvey, and Edward Soja, to name a few.

Relatively late in his career (in 1974, when he was 73), Lefebvre published his 57th book, *Production de l'espace,* which began to appear in English translations by the 1980s, although the most notable English translation did not appear until 1991. This work was somewhat of a departure for Lefebvre, who, up to this point, had not written on the topic of space per se (though as Shields (2004, 210) comments, aspects of his thinking on space did appear in some of his earlier works on urbanism). The translation of this particular work into English propelled Lefebvre into prominence in Anglo-American scholarly circles (Shields 1999, 141; Elden 2004, 169; Merrifield 2006, 102); ironically, it was not a book that garnered much academic attention in France, where he was much better known for his writings on Marx and on historical materialism (Schmid 2008, 27). Merrifield (2006, 102) notes that the *Production of Space* (hereafter cited as POS, as per Merrifield) was brought to the attention of the Anglo-American scholarly community by David Harvey, who mentioned it in his influential work *Social Justice and the City* (1973), thereafter making the *Production of Space* Lefebvre's best known academic treatise in English and spawning a "Lefebvrian cottage industry of sociospatial Marxism" (Merrifield 2006, 102). Accordingly, we shall examine POS in detail in this chapter, to provide an overview and shed some light on its importance and usefulness for scholarship in library and information science (LIS).

STARTING TO THINK ABOUT SPACE

The basic elements of Lefebvre's treatise about the nature of space are laid out in the first chapter of POS, entitled *Plan of the Present Work.* Subsequent chapters of the book expand upon many of the ideas presented in the *Plan,* so we shall do a relatively close analysis of this long first chapter, followed by some commentary on the contents of the remaining chapters.

Lefebvre begins by considering how space has been conceived of by previous scholars and scholarly traditions. He notes that there was a shift in the thinking about space from a philosophical viewpoint (e.g., Aristotle's notion that space was a category for analysis of the senses) to a more mathematical perspective (e.g., Cartesian logic). Mathematicians, he declares,

invented spaces—an "indefinity,", so to speak, of spaces: non-Euclidian spaces, curved spaces, x-dimensional spaces....spaces of configuration, abstract spaces, spaces defined by deformation or transformation, by a topology, and so on (POS, 2).

As this mathematical or scientific thinking about space proliferated, a rift developed between "mathematics and reality—physical or social reality" that became increasingly problematic, in Lefebvre's view. He asks, then,

How were transitions to be made from mathematical space (i.e., from the mental capacities of the human species, from logic) to nature in the first place, to practice in the second and thence to the theory of social life—which also presumably must unfold in space? (POS, 3)

Over time, Lefebvre notes, epistemological enquiry positioned space as a "mental thing" or "mental place" (POS, 3) so that it became common to hear about different kinds of spaces, such as literary, ideological, psychoanalytic, and dreamspace, to name a few. To illustrate this tendency, Lefebvre takes on one of his contemporaries, Michel Foucault, commenting that:

Foucault can calmly assert that 'knowledge [savoir] is also the space in which the subject may take up a position and speak of the objects with which he deals in his discourse,... Foucault never explains what space it is that he is referring to, nor how it bridges the gap between the theoretical (epistemological) realm and the practical one, between mental and social, between the space of the philosophers and the space of people who deal with material things (POS, 4).

Similarly, Lefebvre asserts, other major French scholars of the time, including Julia Kristeva, Roland Barthes, and Jacques Derrida, have contributed to the fetishization of space and the dominance of the mental realm over the social and the physical. Theoretical practice produces a *mental space* (italics his) that is purported to be extra-ideological but in reality, reproduces the ideas of the dominant class, "separated from social practice and which sets itself up as the axis, pivot or central reference point of Knowledge" (POS, 6).

All this theorizing has not, in Lefebvre's view, led to any better understanding of space or to any unified thinking about it (i.e., a "science of space," as he calls it, POS, 7). At best, what has been provided are descriptive "fragments" and "cross-sections" of space, which "may supply inventories of what *exists* in space or even generate *discourse on* space, [but] cannot ever give rise to a *knowledge of* space" (POS, 7). He then goes on to examine how semiology, one of the popular theoretical practices of the day, is highly problematic when applied to space. Lefebvre notes that

When codes worked up from literary texts are applied to spaces—to urban spaces, say—we remain...on the purely descriptive level. Any attempt to use such codes as a means of deciphering social space must surely reduce that space itself to the status of a *message,* and the inhabitants of it to the status of a *reading.* This is to evade both history and practice.... Yet did there not at one time...exist a code at once architectural, urbanistic and political, constituting a language common to country people and townspeople, to the authorities and to artists—a code which allowed space not only to be "read" but also to be constructed? (POS, 7)

Like semiology, other specific theoretical domains have generated discourses about numerous specialized spaces, such as those for "leisure, work, play, transportation, public facilities—all are spoken of in spatial terms" (POS, 8). Thus, the intellectual efforts noted previously project the spatial onto the social, in the process separating them from one another. It is at this stage in the chapter that Lefebvre begins to bring in a Marxian analysis. He points out that, under the present (i.e., capitalist) mode of production, intellectual labor, like material labor, is endlessly divisible. The result of this is that we are confronted with a rather chaotic multiplicity of spaces piling up on one another, including "geographical, economic, demographic, sociological, ecological, political, commercial, national, continental, global, not to mention nature's (physical) space..." (POS, 8), with no common understanding or framework to guide us, and no end in sight for the theoretically possible permutations of spaces.

Nonetheless, Lefebvre suggests, there *is* a common framework or science of space, that being the explication of the link between society's mode of production and the construction or production of space. This framework encompasses three aspects, in which space

1) "represents the political (i.e.,...neocapitalist) use of knowledge" (POS, 9). In other words, knowledge is integrated into both the mode of production and the social relations of production;
2) "implies an ideology designed to conceal that use...[which is] indistinguishable from knowledge" (POS, 9);
3) "embodies at best a technological utopia...a sort of computer simulation of the future, or of the possible, within the framework of the real" (POS, 9) (i.e., the existing mode of production). This technological utopia is a feature of the mode of production and permeates many domains of life such as literary, architectural, urban, and social planning.

Lefebvre notes that most people have an understanding that capital and capitalism have an influence on space, evident through buildings and other infrastructure, investments, the distribution of labor and a range of actors such as banks, corporations, governments, and so forth. What is often forgotten, he asserts, is that capitalism is always bound up with hegemony: the ruling class (i.e., the capitalists) exercises its power and control over all aspects of society, including institutions and ideas. Lefebvre then poses, and answers, two key questions: "Is it conceivable that the exercise of hegemony might leave space untouched? Could space be nothing more than the passive locus of social relations, the milieu in which their combination takes on body...?. The answer must be no" (POS, 11).

Returning to the point that the notion of space has been artificially divided by academic and other discourses, Lefebvre suggests that what is needed is a critical, unitary theory that brings together the three fields of space: the physical ("nature, the Cosmos," POS, 11), the mental (such as "logical and formal abstractions," POS, 11), and the social. Lefebvre refers to this as a concern with

logico-epistemological space, the space of social practice, the space occupied by sensory phenomena, including products of the imagination such as projects and projections, symbols and utopias (POS, 12).

The consideration of the "space problematic" was, in Lefebvre's view, started by a number of scholars, including Hegel, Nietzsche, and Marx, but never fully realized. While all three had important things to say (directly or indirectly) about space, none articulated clearly the three realms of space, nor how these realms operated simultaneously. What is needed, Lefebvre asserts, is a reversal of the thinking about space, "a movement from *products* (whether studied in general or in particular, described or enumerated) to *production*" (POS, 26, italics his). Thus the important aspect is how space is produced, which, once understood, will begin to reveal its dimensions as a product or outcome of that production. Merrifield remarks that

The emphasis on production is, of course, very Marxist. To be radical, for Marx, meant "grasping things by the root"...And his obsession with production was designed to do just that: to get to the root of capitalist society, to get beyond the fetishisms of observable appearance, to trace out its inner dynamics and internal contradictions....Lefebvre likewise demystifies capitalist social space by tracing out its inner dynamics and generative moments—in all their various physical and mental guises, in all their materials and political obfuscations...getting at this generative aspect of space necessitates exploring how space gets *actively produced* (Merrifield 2006, 104–105, italics his).

Cutting to the heart of the matter, Elden (2004, 185) notes that "space is produced in two ways, as a social formation (mode of production) and as a mental construction (conception)." In the *Production of Space,* therefore, how these elements of the production of space are characterized, operate, and relate to one another is the large task that Lefebvre has set for himself.

SOCIAL SPACE AS SOCIAL PRODUCT

Lefebvre then moves into the premise or hypothesis that forms the foundation for the rest of his analysis, and that is his well-known premise that "*(Social) space is a (social) product*" (POS, 26, parentheses and italics his). He admits that this is a seemingly obvious statement, even bordering on the tautologous, but insists that it needs to be examined carefully to understand the full implications and consequences. Lefebvre notes that, within the current mode of production, space has taken on "a sort of reality of its own" (POS, 26), not only being a means of production, but also serving as a

tool of thought and of action; that in addition to being a means of production, it is also a means of control, and hence of domination, of power; yet that, as such, it escapes in part from those who would make use of it. The social and political (state) forces which engendered this space now seek, but fail, to master it completely (POS, 26).

Thus, to Lefebvre, social space is not a "collection of things or an aggregate of (sensory) data" or a "void packed like a parcel with various contents" (POS, 27), nor can it be reduced to form or physical materiality. In certain respects, social space is "indistinguishable from mental space (as defined by philosophers and mathematicians) on the one hand, and physical space (as defined by practico-sensory activity and the perception of 'nature') on the other" (POS, 27).

This fact, that (social) space is a (social) product, is largely concealed from us by what Lefebvre refers to as a "double illusion" (POS, 27), each side of which reinforces the other. These two illusions are

1) the illusion of transparency, whereby space is perceived is presumed to be "intelligible," "giving action free rein," and "innocent, free of traps" (POS, 27–28). Under this illusion, space can be accurately described through language, both written and oral, and yet, speaking and writing are themselves ideologically laden social practices.
2) the realistic illusion, whereby space is seen as natural and substantial. This illusion is closer, says Lefebvre, to naturalistic and mechanistic materialism.

Since neither illusion is completely satisfactory on its own, we (as society) commonly shift between them, thus each illusion "embodies and nourishes the other" (POS, 30).

Lefebvre notes that his premise that (social) space is a social (product) has four main implications or consequences. The first of these is that natural (i.e., physical) space is disappearing before our very eyes. While we try desperately to save it, largely through the lens of memories of some previously-known, presumed to be authentic space, nonetheless, natural spaces continue to be ravaged by the mode of production. Soon, Lefebvre muses, "natural space will be lost to view" (POS, 31), or at the very least, will have become background décor.

The second implication is that "every society—and hence every mode of production with its subvariants...—produces a space, its own space" (POS, 31). Historically, then, every society's space will look and feel differently from those spaces that preceded or followed. This unique spatiality occurs because of the interrelationships between the social relations of production (organized via the family, the sexes and different age groups, etc.) and the relations of production (the division of labor and its concomitant social hierarchies and functions). The particular ways that these interrelationships are played out produce a specific and historically-contingent configuration of space. Shields (1999, 159) comments that the idea of production advanced by Lefebvre expands upon concepts put forward earlier by both Hegel and Marx. However, Lefebvre takes the notion of production

from its narrower, industrial sense (production of products, commodities) to include the production of works in the built environment *(oeuvres)* and of spatialised meanings and other codings of the social environment .... However, unlike other commodities or products, space has both a material reality and a formal property that enables it to constrain other commodities and their social relations. It continually recreates or reproduces the social relations of its production .... Social space is simultaneously a means of production as land and part of the social forces of production as space. As real estate property, spatial relations can be considered part of the social relations of production (the economic base). In addition, space is an object of consumption, a political instrument and an element of social struggle (Shields, 1999, 159–60).

In neocapitalist societies, the production of space has been made more complex with three, rather than two, levels of interrelated processes, these being biological reproduction (i.e., the family), reproduction of labor (i.e., the working class) and the reproduction of the social relations of production (e.g., the institutionalization of the particular social relations underpinning capitalism). As well, the interactions among the social relations just noted become even more complicated because they are continually represented through a system of symbols or codes, which serve as the means to promote solidification and cohesiveness. Lefebvre gives the example of the representations of the relations of biological reproduction, which are

Sexual symbols, symbols of male and female, sometimes accompanied ... by symbols of age—of youth and old age. This is a symbolism which conceals more than it reveals, the more so since the relations of reproduction are divided into frontal, public, overt—and hence coded—relations on the once hand, and on the other, covert, clandestine and repressed relations, which precisely because they are repressed, characterize transgressions related not so much to sex per se as to sexual pleasure, its preconditions and consequences (POS, 32–33).

The third implication of Lefebvre's premise is that if (social) space is a (social) product, then "our knowledge of it must be expected to reproduce and expound the process of production" (POS, 36). In other words, our knowledge must shift from "*things in space* to the actual *production of space*" (POS, 37, italics his). This is a tall order, since both things in space and discourses about space can only give us a glimpse of the totality of what is now a global productive process. As well, the traces of past spaces are incorporated into present space, so that space always seems immediate and whole, with all its attendant associations and connections. Thus the "production process and product present themselves as two inseparable aspects, not as two separable ideas" (POS, 37).

It is at this point in the chapter that Lefebvre introduces and elaborates on his now famous conceptual triad. Social space consists of three elements, including:

1. **Spatial practice, or** *perceived* **space:** encompasses production and reproduction, with their particular locations and social arrangements or assemblages. The spatial practice "of a society secretes that society's space" (POS, 38) in a dialectical relationship: social space is produced "slowly and surely" (POS, 38) as it is mastered and appropriated by the mode of production. Spatial practice is manifest in daily life/routines and the ways in which those routines are embedded within the tangible physicality of space— commercial buildings, housing, recreational areas, transportation routes, networks, and so forth. Under neocapitalism, spatial practice takes on a particular logic, which has a certain cohesiveness to it. However, Lefebvre points out that cohesiveness does not necessarily mean coherent. Under a given mode of production, spatial practices produce social space almost organically (for instance, think of the sprawl of endlessly proliferating North American suburbs with the long workday commutes this gives rise to, or the relentless growth and clustering of industrial parks, both of which tend to swallow immense amounts of land with little overall coherence at the macro level).

2. **Representations of space, or** *conceived* **space:** tied to the relations of production, to knowledge and to the system of symbols. This is space as conceived by planners, architects, urban theorists, bureaucrats, engineers, and the like, "all of whom identify what is lived and what is perceived with what is conceived" (POS, 38). Lefebvre asserts that this is the dominant space under any mode of production. Dale and Burrell (2008) characterize conceived space as "organized space," noting that it is a deliberate construction of space to "embody certain conceptualizations (e.g., functionality, control) in materialized form" (2008, 9). They further remark that

   in recent years…there has been a much more deliberate movement in the conscious design of workplaces to achieve certain values and business goals through the manipulation of space. This is not simply in terms of work ergonomics or to gain great efficiency, but as an integral element to the impetus of capturing hearts and minds through the use of spatial politics in attempts to manufacture both organisational culture and appropriate employee identities (2008, 9).

3. **Representational spaces, or** *lived* **space:** spaces as they are experienced particularly through symbolism, which may or may not be coded. These are the spaces of everyday experience, habitation, and imagination, where resistance to prevailing spatial practices may be evident. Representational spaces overlay "physical space, making symbolic use of its objects" (POS, 39). Here we have spaces as represented by a whole host of social groups who want to resist and/or change the ways in which capitalist space is imagined, controlled and used, such as artists, graffiti taggers, back-to-the-land and off-the-grid inhabitants, the homeless, bicyclists, guerilla gardeners, squatters, and, as well, progressive planners and architects who have a different vision from that expressed through prevailing representations of space. Shields refers to this resistance as "new modes of spatial praxis" (1999, 164) and gives the

example of slum dwellers in the cities of some Third World countries who "fashion a spatial presence and practice outside the norms of the prevailing social spatialisation" (1999, 164).

Lefebvrian scholars agree that this triad was never fully or adequately articulated (Merrifield 2006, 109), which can be viewed either as a blessing or a curse. As a result, there are varying interpretations of what the three elements of the triad actually mean, and exactly how they differ. Importantly, Shields (1999, 154) notes that some of this confusion may stem from the translation of Lefebvre's work, with the French word *l'espace* having numerous meanings that are not immediately transferrable to English. He comments that

Because Lefebvre is referring to not only the empirical disposition of things in the landscape as "space" (the physical aspect) but also attitudes and habitual practices, his metaphoric *l'espace* might be better understood as the *spatialisation* of social order. In this movement to space, abstract structures such as "culture" become concrete practices and arrangements in space. Social action involves not just a rhythm but also geometry and spacing....That is, it is not just an achieved order in the built environment, or an ideology, but also an order that is in itself always undergoing change from within through the actions and innovations of social agents (Shields 1999, 154–55, italics his).

Nonetheless, problems of translation aside, what is clear is that, through the triad, Lefebvre is attempting to move away from what he saw as glaring deficiencies in the thinking about space and the social. Earlier in this chapter, we noted that Lefebvre made the point that intellectual inquiry had separated space artificially into the realms of the physical, mental, and social. Clearly, the spatial triad attempts to resist such categorizations through explicating the complex interplay of processes by which space is produced. Accordingly, Lefebvre's triadic processes or conditions (spatial practice, representations of space, and representational space) each have simultaneously operating within them all three realms of the physical, the mental, and the social. Thus *spatial practice* includes not only the ongoing development of the built environment (the physical), but also how we perceive it (the mental) and the ways in which it shapes our lives (the social), all of which forms a type of spatialized practice. Similarly, *representations of space* include not only how we conceptualize, articulate, and plan spaces (the mental), but also what gets built, where and how it is controlled by means of this planning and representation (the physical), and how such representations affect our ideas of what is appropriate behavior or action in any given space or landscape (the social). Finally, *representational space* allows us to portray, through our art, imaginations, actions and daily living (the mental) what it is like to "live" in certain spaces, to challenge various constraining elements of the built environment (the physical) and to disrupt, often in very small ways, the taken-for-granted order of things (the social). Thus physicality, conception, and experience (i.e., the physical, mental, and social) cannot be separated and are integral parts of the production process and the ongoing cycle of recreation and reproduction.

Similarly, the three core concepts (perceived-conceived-lived) of the spatial triad sit in dialectical relationship to one another. As Merrifield (2006, 111) notes, this is no "simple binary between lived and conceived but a triple determination: each instance internalizes and takes on meaning through other instances." The relationships between the perceived, conceived, and lived are not linear and not stable but rather are fluid and dynamic, each feeding on the other in a process of continual production and reproduction. Shields (1999, 160) describes this interplay as a "three-part" or triple dialectic, further commenting that

All three operate at all times. However, the varying balance and degrees of repression of one aspect or the domination of another marks out *historically specific,* as well as socially produced, spatialisations....All three aspects can be latent, ideological or expressed in practice in a historical spatialisation, and may either reinforce or contradict each other in any given site or moment (Shields 1999, 167, italics his).

Schmid (2008, 28) asserts that this triadic dialectic is one of Lefebvre's most original and most overlooked contributions. Although Lefebvre initially drew upon Hegelian dialectics, he was critical of it for its inapplicability to the material world. Schmid points out that Lefebvre has, in fact, developed a "three-dimensional" dialectic (Schmid 2008, 33), one which takes into account the complexities of social reality and which even some Lefebvrian scholars have truly failed to grasp. Accordingly, Lefebvre's dialectic is unique and "has no parallel in philosophy and the history of knowledge." (Schmid 2008, 33). For Schmid, understanding Lefebvre's dialectic is key to the understanding of the *Production of Space.*

    Finally, returning to the four implications of Lefebvre's premise that (social) space is a (social) product, the fourth and last is that the production of space (including its reality and representations) necessarily involves history. However, Lefebvre warns that the history of space does not always correlate with dated historical events, or with the evolution of specific socio-economic structures, laws, customs, or ideologies. Rather, since space is produced, it changes as the mode of production changes. This type of change is often longer than the human life span and so may not be completely revealed until after the fact, even as the next type of space is being produced. To complicate things further, current space incorporates certain elements of past space within it, albeit changed through our discourses and cultural representations. Lefebvre comments that

The production of space, having attained the conceptual and linguistic level, acts retroactively upon the past, disclosing aspects and moments of it hitherto uncomprehended. The past appears in a different light, and hence the process whereby that past becomes the present also takes on another aspect (POS, 65).

To illustrate the fourth implication, Lefebvre introduces two new concepts, which he also develops more fully in later chapters of the book. The first of these is historical or absolute space, which is "religious and political in nature...a product of the bonds of consanguinity, soil and language, but out of it evolved a space which was relativized and *historical*" (POS, 48, italics his). Absolute space is the foundation of early religious, magical, and political symbolism. Within this space, the town with its surrounding countryside was the important locus of social reproduction and social relations.

    However, as the processes of accumulation developed (including the accumulation of wealth, resources, knowledge, technology, money, precious objects, etc. POS, 49), and labor became separated from biological reproduction, absolute/historical space, though still existing, was overtaken by abstract space. Abstract space is the space of capitalism—the illusory and seemingly transparent space where what is perceived or experienced is not what is actually going on. It is the space of "the world of commodities, its logic and its worldwide strategies, as well as the power of money and that of the po-litical state" (POS, 53). Lefebvre maintains that abstract space conceals within it (by means of the double illusion noted earlier) its true "subject," that being state political power. It is also a space that is governed by instrumentality—the manipulations of space by the various kinds of "authorities" and bureaucracies of the capitalist system (POS, 51). Abstract space is founded on the

vast network of banks, business centers...motorways, airports and information lattices. Within this space, the town—once the forcing-house of accumulation, fountainhead of wealth and centre of historical space—has disintegrated (POS, 53).

Abstract space is a totalizing space—it seeks to reinforce homogeneity and to eradicate difference. The only thing preventing abstract space from "taking over the whole planet and papering over all differences" (POS, 55) is class struggle, including parts of classes and groups, such as minorities. Class struggle is, to Lefebvre, one of the most signifi-cant factors in the production of space because it is only through various sorts of class struggle that true difference (i.e., not intrinsic to economic production) can arise and be sustained. Furthermore, the expression of this difference is crucial to the production of space—it is difference, after all, that gives rise to the next mode of production and its attendant spatial formations.

THE RISE OF CONTRADICTORY AND DIFFERENTIAL SPACE

In the second to fifth chapters of POS, Lefebvre expounds more fully upon the nature of social space, absolute space, and abstract space and discusses the transitions from one to another. He also revisits the notion of "production," tracing earlier under-standings of the word, its use in Marxian analysis, and contemporary misuses of the term (such as the production of knowledge) which only serve to hide who is doing the producing, and why. At the end of these discussions, Lefebvre provides an important summary of the simultaneous nature of social space. He writes

We may say of social space that it simultaneously
1. has a part to play among the *forces of production,* a role originally played by nature, which it has displaced and supplanted;
2. appears as a product of singular character, in that it is sometimes simply *consumed* (in such forms as travel, tourism or leisure activities) as a vast commodity, and sometimes, in metropolitan areas, *productively consumed* (just as machines are, for example), as a productive apparatus of grand scale;
3. shows itself to be *politically instrumental* in that it facilitates the control of soci-ety, while at the same time being a means of production by the way it is developed (...metropolitan areas are no longer just works and products but also means of production, supplying housing, maintaining the labor force etc.);
4. underpins the reproduction of production relations and property relations (i.e., ownership of land, of space; hierarchical ordering of locations; organization of net-works...class structures;...
5. is equivalent...to a set of institutional and ideological superstructures that are not presented for what they are (and in this capacity, social space comes complete with symbolisms and systems of meaning...);

6. contains potentialities—of works and reappropriations—existing, to begin with, in the artistic sphere but responding above all to the demands of a body "transported" outside itself in space (POS, 349).

In chapter five, Lefebvre discusses the idea that while abstract space (i.e., the space of capitalism) has a homogenizing tendency, critical analyses very quickly reveal the contradictions lurking below the surface, contradictions that are not somehow separate from social space but are inherent within it. Then, in the penultimate chapter six, Lefebvre attempts to identify and clarify some of the contradictions apparent in abstract space, or what he refers to as *contradictory space*. In particular, he discusses six major elements of contradictory space, four of which are noted as follows. Lefebvre is quick to point out, however, that these contradictions are not merely binary oppositions, but are "three-point" interactions (POS, 354), whereby movement is from one to the other and back again in an ongoing and evolving spatial ballet:

a) **quantity vs. quality** – Abstract space can be quantified, measured, and manipulated (units of production, output measures, etc.) but at the same time, people seek to escape the relentless empiricism of abstract space by demanding certain qualitative characteristics of space (rest, relaxation, adventure, etc.). The search for this qualitative space through leisure leads to the consumption of space (i.e., leisure sites such as parks, beaches, restaurants, theaters, historic sites, etc.). Thus, abstract space contains "two kinds of regions: regions exploited for the purpose of and by means of *production* (of consumer goods) and regions exploited for the purpose of and by means of the *consumption of space*. Tourism and leisure becomes major areas of investment and profitability" (POS, 353). Lefebvre gives the example of the Spanish coast, whereby the very qualities that attracted tourists to it have drawn unprecedented industrial and residential development, thus somewhat negating the original qualities of the region. Lefebvre comments that even while "the contradictions become more acute…the urbanites continue to clamour for a certain "'quality of space'" (POS, 353).

b) **production vs. consumption** – Although there are many elements to the binary concepts of production and consumption, Lefebvre points out in particular the contradictions between "consumption in the ordinary sense…necessitating the reproduction of things" (POS, 354) and the spaces of production, which involve the flows of networks and bureaucratic practices, in turn using and consuming the very spaces of production of which they are a part.

c) **global processes of homogenization vs. fragmentation** – While globalizing capitalism tends to homogenize as it globalizes (e.g., labor faces the same problems/issues no matter where the factory is situated), fragmentation is also inherent: fragmentation by "administrative subdivision…by scientific and technical specialization.…and indeed most of all, by the retail selling of space (in lots)" (POS, 355). So while there is the tendency for neocapitalist processes to homogenize by seeking the replication of certain conditions of production, nonetheless, within this homogenization are elements of fragmentation that cannot be eliminated. Lefebvre states that homogenized space is "fragmented and fractured, in accordance with the demands of the division of labor and of the division of needs and functions" (POS, 355). He later refers to this fragmentation as "the subdivision of space for the purposes of buying and selling" (POS, 365).

d) power vs. knowledge – Lefebvre equates power with violence and knowledge with understanding but, as he points out, these two concepts do not sit purely in opposition to one another. The contradiction ensues that knowledge is constructed in relation to power and so often represents and hides the very ideologies of power. This leads to dominated spaces, overtly evident through the violence of "military and political (strategic) models" but less overtly because such space is the "bearer of norms and constraints" (POS, 358). Lefebvre also suggests that today, the homogenization of space may have less to do with economic imperatives than with political power since "abstract space is overwhelmingly a tool of power" (POS, 391). In the grander scheme of things there is a spatial strategy or logic that works to support dominant economic interests while seeming to be for the common good. As an example of this, Lefebvre notes that gasoline taxes are collected to be used to further the infrastructure of highways, which "benefits both the oil companies and the automobile manufacturers: every additional mile of highway translated into increased car sales, which in turn increase petrol consumption, hence also tax revenues and so on.... [This] production of space is carried out with the state's intervention... yet this production *seems* to answer solely to the rational requirements of communication between the various parts of society, as to those of a growth consistent with the interests of all "users" (POS, 375).

Contradictions such as these give rise to *differential* spaces, which are those spaces on the edges or margins of "the homogenized realm" (POS, 373). Differential spaces in turn give rise to various sorts of resistances, which may or may not persist given the homogenizing tendencies of the dominant space. Lefebvre cites the rise and persistence of shantytowns as one example of differential space.

For Merrifield (2006), the idea of the right to difference and differential space is one of Lefebvre's major contributions in the *Production of Space*. He brings his reading of Lefebvre to a very personal conclusion when he writes:

When writers and scholars enter the Lefebvrian fray, when they write about daily life and global space, they should think very carefully about whose daily life they're talking about, whose (and what) space they mean. When they write about radical intellectuals like Lefebvre, they should think about their own role as radical intellectuals, turning Lefebvrian criticism onto themselves, analyzing their own daily life and space at the same time as they analyze global capitalism.... Guts, as well as Lefebvre, are needed to resist the growing professionalization of ideas and university life, where, before all else, abstractions and cybernanthropes, evaluations and economic budgets sanction knowledge claims.... When scholars write about emancipation, about reclaiming space for others, we might start by emancipating ourselves and reclaiming our own work space (Merrifield 2006, 119–20).

In summary, it must be noted here that this commentary on Lefebvre's *Production of Space* is, at best, partial given the breadth and scope of his writings. As Shields (1999, 2–3) points out, Lefebvre's oeuvre spans many decades, representing very different periods of his thought. The *Production of Space* was written very late in his life and during what might be termed his Anglophone period. Nonetheless, in a comment that resonates strongly with the public service goals of librarianship and the role of the library in society, Shields remarks that

What unites all of [Lefebvre's] work—from his first to most mature works—is his deeply humanistic interest in alienation.... Humanism... he argues, is the key motivation for Marx and for social change anywhere. It is not technological progress, the absence of war, or ease of life, or even length of life, but the chance for a *fully lived life* that is the measure of a civilisation. The quality of any society lies in the opportunity for the unalienated and authentic life experience that it gives all its members. Grounded in anything else, democracy falls short of what it could be (1999, 2, italics his).

LEFEBVRE IN THE LIS LITERATURE

Henri Lefebvre's work has not been explored, to any great degree, in the library and information science literature to date. In most cases, Lefebvre's ideas receive only passing mention. Hope A. Olson (1998) references *The Production of Space* (1991) by drawing links between Lefebvre's notion of transparent space and Lorraine Code's idea of rhetorical space. Jacqueline Cook's (2006) exploration of art ephemera and libraries references this same work in a footnote discussing Cook's recognition of "the building of an art library collection as a representation of spaces" (34); Adele Seeff's (2004) work also references Lefebvre only in a brief footnote. Jutta Haider and David Bawden (2007) also quote from *The Production of Space,* but do not examine Lefebvre's work in any detail. Similarly, David Berry's (2004) article on Internet research refers only briefly to Lefebvre's concept of alienation, from his *Critique of Everyday Life* (1947).

Unfortunately, these discussions provide little direction for readers interested in applying Lefebvre's work to other contexts or to advanced study within LIS. Rekha Murthy's (2006) article, "Story Space: A Theoretical Grounding for the New Urban Annotation," examines the work of Lefebvre in more depth, alongside the works of Jean Baudrillard, and Paul Virilio. Here, Murthy examines the implications of Lefebvre's writings for in-depth explorations of spatial annotation, or "the practice of linking a communication instance—a thought, a story, a piece of information, a call to action, an exchange among users—to a specific geographical location" (para. 2). This is a very promising piece, as it connects Lefebvre's work on physical space to virtual representations of location (e.g., Global Positioning Systems).

However, few scholars within LIS have explored Lefebvre's work in the context of empirical research studies. Lisa M. Given, for example, used Lefebvre's work to examine undergraduates' use of space on a university campus. She, and co-author Virginia Wilson (2004), presented a paper on Lefebvre's spatial triad (perceived-conceived-lived space) that used this theory as a guiding model for the design of qualitative research to incorporate the physical in explorations of personal experience. The paper presented results of qualitative interviews with mature undergraduates to illustrate connections between Lefebvre's triad and students' conceptions of university life. Similarly, Matthew Griffis (2010), a doctoral candidate at the University of Western Ontario, used Lefebvre's spatial triad to examine the Owen Sound Carnegie Library (in Ontario, Canada). Griffis' qualitative case study approach (involving site visits, interviews with library staff, observations of patrons, and photographic methods) was also well grounded in an historical research methodology. He used Lefebvre's triad as a theoretical lens for understanding the place of the library in the community.

LEFEBVRE AND LIS: SUGGESTIONS FOR FUTURE WORK

There are a number of scholars working in information-related fields (such as education, sociology, and other disciplines) who have drawn on Lefebvre's ideas to explore
virtual spaces—an area of study that holds a great deal of promise for future investigations within library and information science proper. Diana Saco's (1998) doctoral
dissertation is one of a number of research projects in the last decade that link Lefebvre's
work to cyberspace; she argues that cyberspace meets all of Lefebvre's criteria for the
ways that social spaces are socially produced. Dale Bradley's (1998) dissertation pursued
a similar line of inquiry, using Henri Lefebvre's work to complete a discursive analysis
of power relations in cyberspace. John Wise (1995) also used Lefebvre's work to explore
technology as a social space. Given the ubiquitous nature of the Internet/cyberspace,
including chat forums and other virtual "spaces" within the field of LIS, the application
of Lefebvre's work to these online contexts holds great promise for future study.

At the same time, the LIS literature is rife with studies of information literacy in
various library settings—which raises the possibility of applying Lefebvre's work to
studies of learning spaces. Indeed, in education, scholars have applied Lefebvre's work
to classrooms and other (less formal) learning environments; these studies give rise to
possibilities for LIS scholars and librarians to examine library-based learning spaces
through Lefebvre's theoretical lens. Paul Temple (2007) presents a review of the literature is his text *Learning Spaces for the 21st Century,* including lengthy discussions of
Lefebvre's work. Similarly, Benjamin Fraser's (2009) work connects critical pedagogy
to the social space of cities, drawing on Lefebvre's work alongside other urban scholars
(such as Jane Jacobs).

Finally, it is important to consider Lefebvre's work in the context of the social production of space within library and information milieus. The inclusion of corporate
sponsors (such as the Gates Foundation) in academic library computing labs, or the
introduction of coffee shops in public libraries, have profound implications on the design and use of social spaces by library patrons. Indeed, the influences of neo-capitalist
modes of production on the design of the library's physical space is not well understood
and is rarely examined in the LIS literature. Using Lefebvre's work as a theoretical lens
for analysis can enhance our understanding of the sociocultural forces that converge
and are evident in the design, presentation, perception, use, and ongoing management
of these types of social spaces.

CONCLUSION

Lefebvre's *Production of Space* has been, and still is, a groundbreaking work. It
shaped the thinking of a whole generation of spatial scholars, and brought to the fore
what are now seen as key ideas about the nature of space in advanced capitalism, doing
so without forgetting about the everyday and embodied experiences of ordinary people and how those experiences reflect and reveal the very tensions inherent in abstract
space. Dale and Burrell (2008) express the impact of Lefebvre's scholarship very well
when they state:

Lefebvre's work provides an opening for understanding the interconnections between different
levels of how social space is produced and reproduced; indeed, that all spaces are social, however
global or abstract they might appear to be (2008, 16).

A Lefebvrian theoretical lens allows us to examine the "place" of libraries and other information-related settings in new ways. His approach is one of the few theoretical frameworks that pays attention to the spaces of the larger neocapitalist environment in which institutions like libraries are embedded, while at the same time, giving us a conceptual perspective and a language (i.e., spatial practices, spaces of representation, and representational spaces) to explore the ways in which specific spaces are created, imagined, and lived in by the people who use them every day. This unique blend of the macro- and micro-levels makes a Lefebvrian analysis very powerful and potentially revealing of the sometimes opaque, sometimes transparent ways that libraries function as social spaces, the perceptions that we have of them, and their larger role within our rapidly changing and increasingly globalized social milieu.

REFERENCES

Berry, David M. 2004. "Internet Research: Privacy, Ethics and Alienation: An Open Source Approach." *Internet Research* 14 (4): 323–32.

Bradley, Dale Alan. 1998. "Unfolding a Strategic Space: A Discursive Analysis of Cyberspace's Power Relations." PdD diss., York University, Canada.

Cooke, Jacqueline. 2006. "Heterotopia: Art Ephemera, Libraries, and Alternative Space." *Art Documentation: Bulletin of the Art Libraries Society of North America* 25 (2): 34–39.

Dale, Karen, and Gibson Burrell. 2008. *The Spaces of Organisation and the Organisation of Space: Power, Identity and Materiality at Work.* London: Palgrave.

Elden, Stuart. 2004. *Understanding Henri Lefebvre: Theory and the Possible.* London: Continuum.

Fraser, Benjamin. 2009. "The 'Kind of Problem Cities Pose': Jane Jacobs at the Intersection of Philosophy, Pedagogy, and Urban Theory." *Teaching in Higher Education* 14 (3): 265–76.

Given, Lisa M., and Virginia Wilson. 2004. "Place, Spaces and Henri Lefebvre: Incorporating the Physical in Qualitative Research." Paper presented at *Advances in Qualitative Methods: The 5th International Interdisciplinary Conference.* Edmonton, AB, January.

Griffis, Matthew. 2010. "Living History: The Carnegie Library as Place in Ontario." *Canadian Journal of Information and Library Science* 34 (2): 185–211.

Haider, Jutta, and David Bawden. 2007. "Conceptions of 'Information Poverty' in LIS: A Discourse Analysis." *Journal of Documentation* 63 (4): 534–57.

Harvey, David. 1973. *Social Justice and the City.* Baltimore: John Hopkins.

Lefebvre, Henri. 1968. *Dialectical Materialism.* Trans. John Sturrock. London: Cape.

Lefebvre, Henri. 1991. *Critique of Everyday Life.* Trans. John Moore. London: Verso.

Lefebvre, Henri.1991. *The Production of Space.* Trans. Donald Nicholson-Smith. Oxford: Blackwell.

Lefebvre, Henri. 1996. *Writings on Cities.* Selected, translated, and introduced by Eleonore Kaufman and Elizabeth Lebas. Oxford: Blackwell. John Sturrock. London: Cape.____. 1968.

Merrifield, Andy. 2006. *Henri Lefebvre: A Critical Introduction.* New York: Routledge.

Murthy, Rekha. 2006. "Story Space: A Theoretical Grounding for the New Urban Annotation." *First Monday (Online)* no. 4, Special Issue.

Olson, Hope A. 1998. "Mapping beyond Dewey's Boundaries: Constructing Classificatory Space for Marginalized Domains." *Library Trends* 47 (2): 233–254.

Saco, Diana. 1998. "Cyberspace and Democracy: Spaces and Bodies in the Age of the Internet."
     PhD diss., University of Minnesota.

Schmid, Christian. 2008. "Henri Lefvebre's Theory of the Production of Space: Toward a Three-
     Dimensional Dialectic." In *Space, Difference, Everyday Life: Reading Henri Lefebvre,*
     ed. 27–45. Eds. Kanishka Goonewardena, Stefan Kipfer, Richard Milgrom and Chris-
     tian Schmid, 27–45. New York: Routledge.

Seeff, Adele. 2004. "Recovering the History of the African Theatre." *Quarterly Bulletin of the Na-
     tional Library of South Africa* 58 (4): 159–67.

Shields, Rob. 1999. *Lefebvre, Love and Struggle: Spatial Dialectics.* London: Routledge.

Shields, Rob. 2004. Henri Lefebvre. In *Key Thinkers on Space and Place,* ed. Phil Hubbard, Rob
     Kitchin, and Gill Valentine, 208–13. London: Sage.

Temple, Paul. 2007. *Learning Spaces for the 21st Century: A Review of the Literature.* London:
     The Higher Education Academy.

Wise, John MacGregor. 1995. "Technology and Social Space Beyond the Modern Episteme."
     PhD diss., University of Illinois at Urbana-Champaign.

18

Herbert Marcuse: Liberation, Utopia, and Revolution

Ajit Pyati
University of Western Ontario, Canada

BIOGRAPHICAL BACKGROUND

Herbert Marcuse (1898–1979) was an important and influential philosopher, public intellectual, and social activist of the 20th century. At times called the Father of the New Left (Kellner 2005, 35), Marcuse often served as an inspiration to the various student and revolutionary social movements of the 1960s. Among Marcuse's many works, *One-Dimensional Man* (1964) and *Eros and Civilization* (1955) remain his most famous. The themes of domination and liberation animated much of Marcuse's writings, as he was concerned with the technological rationality and repressive tendencies of advanced industrial societies (in both their capitalist and state socialist forms). Marcuse was a utopian thinker who envisaged the potential of radical revolutionary moments to create an aesthetically rich and nonrepressive society.

Marcuse was born in 1898 in Berlin to a Jewish family and served in the German Army during World War I before completing his PhD in literature at the University of Freiburg in 1922. He then worked in publishing before returning to Freiburg in 1928 to study philosophy with Martin Heidegger. The influence of Heidegger on Marcuse cannot be underestimated; however, Heidegger's political views and association with the Nazi Party disturbed Marcuse (Kellner n.d.-a). He eventually left Freiburg in 1933 to join the Institut fur Sozialforschung (Institute for Social Research) in Frankfurt, which came to be known later on as the Frankfurt School. This association had a lasting influence on Marcuse, as he began to develop models for critical social theory.

Marcuse left Germany in 1934 and spent the rest of his life in the United States. He was affiliated with Columbia University for a number of years and also worked for the U.S. government in antifascist efforts during the 1940s and early 1950s. He served as a professor at Brandeis University from 1958 to 1965, after which he took up his final academic post as a professor at the University of California, San Diego. The influence of Marcuse as a social theorist has diminished in recent years (Kellner 1998), but recently published writings from the Marcuse archives (edited by Douglas Kellner) have the potential to revive interest in Marcuse's work. He has not had a major influence in LIS, but some recent scholarship by this author (Pyati 2006; 2009) has introduced Marcusean concepts into the LIS discourse. Marcuse's critiques of technological rationality and the technological society have particular relevance for LIS.

MARCUSE AND THE FRANKFURT SCHOOL

Marcuse's work needs to be situated within the wider context of Frankfurt School critical theory, which came out of the Institute for Social Research. This institute was founded in 1923 and was the first Marxist-oriented research institute in Germany, and was composed largely of German-Jewish intellectuals. During the time of its most influential director, Max Horkheimer, the institute attempted to revise both the Marxian critique of capitalism and the theory of revolution in order to address the new social and political conditions that had evolved since Karl Marx's death (Bronner and Kellner 1989). The term *critical theory* did not emerge until 1937; however, after the majority of the institute's members had immigrated to the United States after Hitler's victory, the term stuck and was used to define the general theory of contemporary society associated with Max Horkeimer, Herbert Marcuse, T. W. Adorno, Leo Lowenthal, and Frederick Pollock (Bronner and Kellner 1989). The term represented a code of sorts, which belied its roots in Marxist social theory, particularly in a time of increased hostility to socialist-inspired academic and political projects (Kellner 1989). The main contributions of the Frankfurt School were its sharp critiques of industrial capitalism, mass consumer society, technological society, and the relationship between technology and culture. Of particular concern to many Frankfurt School theorists was the ability of the new communication technologies (such as radio, films, and newspapers) to indoctrinate audiences into the dominant capitalist culture of mass consumption.

The experience of fascism certainly influenced many of their analyses and theoretical positions, as they saw firsthand the role of mass communication tools in perpetuating dominant political and economic interests. Some notable works associated with the Frankfurt School include Lowenthal's studies of popular literature and magazines (Lowenthal 1961), Horkheimer and Adorno's and famous (and perhaps infamous) study of the culture industries in *Dialectic of Enlightenment* (2002), Walter Benjamin's (1969) work on media and cultural politics, and Habermas' work on the democratic public sphere (1989). *Dialectic of Enlightenment* (2002) argued that the system of cultural production (i.e., film, radio, newspapers, and magazines) was under the control of consumer capitalism and produced conformity to the dominant system (Kellner n.d.-b). This particular work has become symbolic of the Frankfurt School in general and has been criticized as reductive, elitist, and totalizing in its approach (Kellner n.d.-b). In particular, some critics argue that it is too pessimistic in its analysis of popular culture and does not leave room for the possibility of positive tendencies in mass communication technologies and their role in resistance to dominant political and economic systems. This critique is certainly valid, but it should be noted that the Frankfurt School is not a monolithic entity, as it accommodated a diversity of theoretical viewpoints. Thus, the work of Walter Benjamin (1969), with its focus on the role of new technologies in creating new and potentially transformative subjectivities, is a counterpoint to some of Adorno and Horkheimer's (2002) major themes.

Like Walter Benjamin, Marcuse does not easily fit into a set of neat descriptions about the Frankfurt School. For instance, while Marcuse always relates economic influences to the spheres of culture and technology, he sees both emancipatory and dominating potentials in these spheres (Kellner n.d.-a). Marcuse therefore does not focus only on domination but rather places emphasis on the themes of liberation and utopia. In addition, he emphasizes the role of individual liberation and transformation in his work, something that was a departure from major strands of Marxist thought (Kellner n.d.-a). He has provided a wealth of important insights and theoretical reflections and some of his more influential contributions include his critique of technological rationality, his concept of one-dimensional man, the role of art and aesthetics in creating a nonrepressive society, and the notion of the Great Refusal. I will discuss some of these themes and a few others that are relevant to LIS in general. This exploration will include arguably his most famous work, *One-Dimensional Man* (1964), *An Essay on Liberation* (1969), *Eros and Civilization* (1955), and a number of the *Collected Papers of Herbert Marcuse* (1998; 2001; 2005; 2007).

ON TECHNOLOGY AND TECHNOLOGICAL RATIONALITY

One of Marcuse's major concerns was the influence of technological rationality in advanced industrial societies. This form of technological dominance served to "institute new, more effective, and more pleasant forms of social control and social cohesion" (Marcuse 1964, xv). While Marcuse argued that technology had liberating tendencies, he also argued that it often served to dominate nature and further totalitarian goals of control both in its capitalist and communist guises. In our present day context, the focus on technological rationality as a tool of domination is a useful construct for understanding how discourses of information technology are being used to perpetuate capitalist logics of consumption. Marcuse was writing during the height of advanced industrial society, but many of the same ideologies and hegemonic concepts of progress, efficiency, and capitalist consumption are still highly relevant (and perhaps even intensified) today. Advertising culture and the manipulation of public opinion by corporate powers also troubled Marcuse—leading to his condemnation of what he termed the "one-dimensional man." According to him, the one-dimensional man takes part in one-dimensional thought and behavior, "in which ideas, aspirations, and objectives that, by their content, transcend the established universe of discourse and action are either repelled or reduced to terms of this universe" (Marcuse 1964, 12).

Technological rationality, argued Marcuse, is a creation related to "that of an advanced society which makes scientific and technical progress into an instrument of domination" (Marcuse 1964, 16). This concept of technological rationality is related to a notion of purposive-rational action, in which the rationalization of the conditions of life is synonymous with the institutionalization of a form of domination whose political character becomes unrecognizable (Habermas 1989). In other words, the logic of instrumental rationality and technological rationality is politically, economically, and socially institutionalized. These forces of domination lead to conformity and indoctrination, in which one-dimensional men are created. Thus, the logic of instrumental rationality creates conditions where critical thought and emancipatory action are stifled.

The one-dimensional man, in a sense, suffers under a form of "false consciousness," as Lukacs (1971) discusses. Technological and instrumental rationality are the logics of an "ideological state apparatus" (Althusser 2001) that maintains the status quo and perpetuates technological and techno-capitalist ideologies. At the root of Marcuse's argument is the critique of "positive thinking and its neo-positivist philosophy" (Marcuse 1964, 225) and its associated, distorted logics of efficiency, rationality, and progress. Marcuse's fear was that the manipulation of public opinion through the cultural industries (radio, television, newspapers, etc.) led to a situation in which critical thought, emancipatory action, and genuine resistance are stifled. In this context, all forms of opposition are integrated into the established system.

One-dimensional man, however, does not necessarily imply that there is no form of resistance or that society is a completely administered totality. Rather, one could understand "one-dimensional" as "conforming to existing thought and behavior and lacking a critical dimension and understanding of the potentialities that transcend the existing society" (Kellner 1991, xxvii). In other words, one-dimensional thinking is conformist by nature and does not see the possibilities for new forms of existence that are free from domination and allow the full development of individual potentials. To counteract one-dimensional society, Marcuse proposed critical and dialectical thinking that perceived a freer and happier form of culture and society, and advocated a "great refusal" of all modes of repression and domination (Kellner 2005, p. 5). This freedom from one-dimensionality relates to the concept of utopia, which will be discussed in the next section.

While Marcuse's one-dimensional man thesis has been accused of excessive pessimism, this assessment is not entirely accurate. For example, his critique of technology focuses not just on domination but on liberation as well. As Marcuse states:

For freedom indeed depends on technological progress, on the advancement of science. But this fact easily obscures the essential precondition: in order to become vehicles of freedom, science and technology would have to change their present direction and goals; they would have to be reconstructed in accord with a new sensibility—the demands of life instincts. Then one could speak of a technology of liberation, product of a scientific imagination free to project and design the forms of a human universe without exploitation and toil (1969, 19).

Thus Marcuse does not criticize technology per se as a source of repression, but focuses rather on its ideological underpinnings and applications within dominant economic and political systems.

On a related note, a theme that reoccurs in Marcuse's writings is the possibility that technology provides for alleviating misery and poverty. As he discusses:

Utopian possibilities are inherent in the technical and technological forces of advanced capitalism and socialism: the rational utilization of these forces on a global scale would terminate poverty and scarcity with a very foreseeable future (1969, 4).

However, as Marcuse points out in many of his writings, while technology has the potential to create a nonrepressive society, it continues to be used in ways that further domination of nature and a consumerist lifestyle. A technological apparatus that creates societal dependence on "the uninterrupted production and consumption of waste, gadgets, planned obsolescence, and means of destruction" (Marcuse 1966, xii) is a system that perpetuates repression. Envisioning the possibilities for a nonrepressive society is a utopian exercise. This utopian exercise requires both a reconstruction of reason and a radical imagination (Marcuse 1969). The next section takes up these ideas in more detail.

LIBERATION AND UTOPIA

The themes of liberation and utopia are prominent in Marcuse's work and illustrate the redemptive possibilities of his theoretical project. In contrast to postmodern and poststructuralist theories, Marcuse did not shy away from comprehensive approaches to social change and grand visions of liberation (Kellner 1998). This focus on a totalizing utopian vision that sought to reconstruct reason had its basis in Marxist dialectics (Kellner 1998). Dialectical thinking for Marcuse involved the ability to abstract one's perception and thought from existing forms in order to form more general concepts (Kellner 1991). These general concepts can then be linked and compared to ideals and potentialities of human existence, creating utopian frameworks for guiding human and social development.

Marcuse's major work that introduced his concept of liberation and the possibility of a nonrepressive society is *Eros and Civilization* (1955). This book was a significant philosophical foray into Freud and took on the ambitious task of integrating Freud's ideas with Marx. While Freud argued that civilization inevitably involved repression and suffering, Marcuse argued that other elements in Freud's theory pointed towards an instinctual drive in the direction of happiness and freedom (Kellner n.d.-a). Through this reinterpretation of Freud, Marcuse developed the outlines of a nonrepressive civilization that would involve libidinal and nonalienated labor, play, free and open sexuality, and the development of a society that promotes freedom and happiness (Kellner n.d.-a). As Marcuse discusses:

Freud's own theory provides reasons for rejecting his identification of civilization with repression. On the ground of his own theoretical achievements, the discussion of the problem must be reopened. Does the interrelation between freedom and repression, productivity and destruction, domination and progress, really constitute the principle of civilization? Or does this interrelation result only from a specific historical organization of human existence? (1955, 4–5)

This vision of liberation that Marcuse presented in *Eros and Civilization* anticipated many of the values of the 1960s counterculture (Kellner n.d.-a).

In addition to the concept of liberation, the role of the imagination in social change is central to much of Marcuse's philosophy. As he argues, the imagination has become stifled and colonized by the mass media and capitalist logics (Marcuse 1969). But rather than seeing the imagination as a form of fantasy and escape, Marcuse sees it as a productive and potentially radical force for change in society. According to him:

The imagination, unifying sensibility and reason, becomes "productive" as it becomes practical: a guiding force in the reconstruction of reality—reconstruction with the help of a *gaya scienza*, a science and technology released from their service to destruction and exploitation, and thus free for the liberating exigencies of the imagination. The rational transformation of the world could then lead to a reality formed by the aesthetic sensibility of man (Marcuse 1969, 30–31).

The imagination therefore provides a link between aesthetic sensibilities and reason, and is itself a rational form of understanding.

On a related note, art and aesthetics play a role in Marcuse's theory of liberation. Aesthetics and art were central elements of Marcuse's thought, as he argued that art had an important role to play in providing alternatives to the dominant society and facilitating social change (Kellner 2007). The concept of art for Marcuse usually referred to literature, music, and the visual arts, and often was oriented towards "high art." For Marcuse art has a radical potential, as it criticizes and negates the existing social order and hints at the possibility of a new social order (Davis 2005). In this framework, art does not have to be overtly political in character, since the power of the artistic form is often enough to provide glimpses of new possibilities and forms of human existence. Art is an expression or language of the imagination, but Marcuse argues that in the dominant, affluent society art has also been co-opted by existing power structures. In other words:

we would have to say that the crisis of art today is only part of the general crisis of the political and moral opposition to our society, of its inability to define, name and communicate the goals of the opposition to a society, which, after all, delivers the goods. It delivers the goods bigger and perhaps even better than ever before and it exacts, for the delivery of these goods, the constant sacrifice of human lives; death, mutilation, enslavement (Marcuse 2007, 114).

However, Marcuse locates some artistic movements that he feels embody the qualities of radical critique that he valued, in particular the Surrealists. For instance, he states that the

surrealist thesis...elevates the poetic language to the rank of being the only language that does not succumb to the all-embracing language spoken by the Establishment, a "meta-language" of total negation—a total negation transcending even the revolutionary action itself. In other words, art can fulfil its inner revolutionary function only if it does not itself become part of any Establishment, including the revolutionary Establishment (Marcuse 2007, 114–15).

Art thus has significant oppositional tendencies in Marcusean thought, and is an essential component of his theories of liberation. However, one can criticize Marcuse for making rigid distinctions between "high art" and "low art" and not engaging seriously with popular culture (Davis 2005, xiv).

RESISTANCE FROM THE MARGINS

While art and aesthetics were important parts of Marcuse's utopian project, another major source of inspiration for him were the various antiwar, antiracist, and new social movements of the 1960s and early 1970s. Marcuse was a major source of inspiration to the radical student movements of these decades and became known as the Father of the New Left. The Old Left was rigid and doctrinaire and often aligned with Soviet Marxism, while the New Left embraced a wide range of social movements around the issues of class, gender, race, sexuality, the environment, peace, and a variety of other issues (Kellner 2005). One of the clearest articulations of Marcuse's alignment with the New Left is his influential work entitled *An Essay on Liberation* (1969). This short and accessible work was written during the height of the student and anti–Vietnam War movements in the late 1960s, and is imbued with countercultural sentiments. Many of his revolutionary utopian ideas are expressed in this particular work and during the time he wrote this book it appeared that the student and countercultural movements were growing in prominence and strength. He subsequently modified some of his positive evaluation of the counterculture; one can argue that he was carried away by the enthusiasm generated by the struggles of the 1960s and exaggerated the importance of the student movement and countercultural revolts as agents of social change (Kellner 2005). However, Marcuse was one of the first major Marxist theorists who expanded the scope of revolution beyond the traditional Marxist conception of the working classes.

This expansion of the Marxist revolutionary optic included student activists, marginalized minority populations in the inner cities of the United States, and the victims of Western aggression in the Third World. A central idea behind Marcuse's focus on these groups was that they stood outside the dominant economic and political systems. Thus, resistance from the margins of society could potentially show cracks in the dominant system and provide liberatory alternatives to the capitalist warfare state (Kellner 2005). The co-optation of the working classes into capitalist consumerism was one of the key insights in *One-Dimensional Man* (1964). The creation of false needs integrated both the working classes into the dominant systems of production and consumption, with the mass media serving to eliminate any forms of opposition and critique to the system (Kellner n.d.-a). Marcuse discusses the decline of revolutionary consciousness in the middle classes as follows:

The power of corporate capitalism has stifled the emergence of such a consciousness and imagination; its mass media have adjusted the rational and emotional faculties to its market and its policies and steered them to defense of its dominion. The narrowing of the consumption gap has rendered possible the mental and instinctual coordination of the laboring classes: the majority of organized labor shares the stabilizing, counterrevolutionary needs of the middle classes, as evidenced by their behavior as consumers of the material and cultural merchandise, by their emotional revulsion against the nonconformist intelligentsia (1964, 15–16).

With this situation in mind, Marcuse saw an opening for resistance coming out of the predominantly African American populations of American inner cities and the marginalized populations of the Third World. Thus, according to Marcuse:

where the consumer gap is still wide, where the capitalist culture has not yet reached into every house or hut, the system of stabilizing needs has its limits; the glaring contrast between the privileged class and the exploited leads to a radicalization of the underprivileged. This is the case of the ghetto population and the unemployed in the United States; this is also the case of the laboring classes in the more backward capitalist countries (1964, 16).

In addition, Marcuse understood the global reach of the capitalist system and identified potential places of resistance within this system. He discusses how National Liberation Movements in the Third World, such as the Viet Cong and the Cuban revolution, have the potential to cut off global capitalist markets, sources of raw materials, and cheap labor supplies, thereby spurring on other revolutionary movements (Kellner 2005). In other words:

The National Liberation Fronts threaten the life line of imperialism; they are not only a material but also an ideological catalyst of change. The Cuban revolution and the Viet Cong have demonstrated: it can be done; there is a morality, a humanity, a will, and a faith which can resist and deter the gigantic technical and economic force of capitalist expansion (Marcuse 1969, 81).

Marcuse's identification of resistance from the margins of the capitalist system was an important insight; however, one should not assume that Marcuse posited that the counterculture expressions, student movements, or Third World movements were the new agents of revolution. Rather, Marcuse sees radical potential, possibilities, and limitations in these groups (Kellner 2005). Throughout Marcuse's writings he indicates that there can be no revolution without the working class, and does not see strong evidence that the working class is responsive to the New Left (Kellner 2005). The fact that the New Left may not be the new revolutionary agents should not be seen as a refutation of their impact, since they provide insights into revolutionary possibilities. To further this point, Marcuse discusses how:

The search for specific historical agents of revolutionary change in the advanced capitalist countries is indeed meaningless. Revolutionary forces emerge in the process of change itself; the translation of the potential into the actual is the work of political practice (1969, 79).

Thus while he held up the importance of the working classes in socialist revolution, the creation of revolutionary agency is an ongoing process.

On a final note regarding Marcuse's work, it would be remiss not to mention some of his ideas with regard to man's relationship with nature. Marcuse also rooted his vision of human liberation in terms of a reconciliation with nature. He believed that until aggression and violence within human beings was diminished, there would continue to be destruction of nature as well as violence against other human beings (Kellner, n.d. -c). For Marcuse, the destruction of nature was a natural outgrowth of capitalist expansion and a less exploitative relationship with nature would require a change in the sensibilities of human beings. This new sensibility

emerges in the struggle against violence and exploitation where this struggle is waged for essentially new ways and forms of life: negation of the entire Establishment, its morality, culture; affirmation of the right to build a society in which the abolition of poverty and toil terminates in a universe where the sensuous, playful, the calm, and the beautiful becomes forms of existence and thereby the Form of the society itself (Marcuse 1969, 25).

In other words, this new sensibility would require a change in individual consciousness, in which the drive towards destructive and dominating attitudes towards the natural world would be diminished. In a world today that faces the perils of global climate change, these theoretical explorations of Marcuse remain highly pertinent.

MARCUSE'S RELEVANCE TO LIS

With a wider sense now of Marcuse's many theoretical concerns, we turn to the issue of how some of these ideas might apply to LIS. While there is no explicit model to follow in applying some of Marcuse's key ideas to LIS, we can explore how his ideas might bring social justice concerns more front and center within the discipline. In particular, his theoretical approach emphasizes constructive critique with a keen eye towards counteracting repression, domination, and injustice. Marcuse has been criticized for an overly pessimistic approach at times; however, he had hope for the liberating possibilities of technological society as well. While Marcuse's work predated the Internet, the Internet (despite an increasing commercial presence) and new media technologies in general still offer the possibility for enhancing democratic and progressive politics. The field of LIS, for instance, can take a more critical look at the corporate domination of information technology development and the pervasiveness of technological determinism in wider society. LIS can thus take many of Marcuse's ideas to heart, specifically in the articulation of less repressive and more just visions of an information society.

While there is debate on this topic, the information society has arguably served to perpetuate the interests of technocratic elites in governments and corporations (Webster 2006). In particular, the private sector has developed much of the infrastructure for the Internet in many parts of the world without much governmental regulation, and the privatization and commercialization of information continues to intensify (Schiller 2007). In fact, this dimension of the information society, an overreliance on market and capitalist logics, is a defining characteristic that has far-reaching consequences. Thus, despite the claims of many postindustrial and postmodern thinkers about the radical "newness" and discontinuities with the past, the information society can be seen as a continuation (or perhaps an intensification) of capitalist practices (Webster 2006). The information age has been highly beneficial to capitalism's increasing global reach and spread, ushering in an era of informational and techno-capitalism. While the dynamic nature of capitalism and the innovative uses of ICTs have spread benefits across the globe, only certain segments of the world's population have been at the receiving end—one would be remiss to ignore that income inequalities throughout the world have increased during the information age (Harvey 2005). To note this fact is not a condemnation of the information age or ICTs; however, it cannot be ignored that the political agendas associated with the information society have exacerbated global inequities.

Many of Marcuse's worst fears resonate in the information society. For instance, with the discourse of the information society being largely driven by the private sector, one cannot escape the advertising bombardment of technology giants such as Microsoft and Apple, as well as ignore the advertising revenue–intensive model of search engine giant Google. Many of the hopes, dreams, and aspirations of the information age are shaped and limited (e.g., Do you want to be a Mac or a PC?) by the hegemony of powerful corporate players. Genuine public sector alternatives, which might consider open source software solutions for instance, are often not part of the wider public consciousness. The extension of Marcuse's ideas to the information society can also be applied to issues such as information overload, information anxiety, the globally unjust distribution of information work, and the growing environmental problem of electronic waste (in which countries of the Global South suffer inordinately). These issues get short shrift within LIS, as they are often obscured by an overemphasized focus on the benefits of ICTs and information access. A Marcusean approach to LIS could highlight some of these inequities and also point to more liberatory possiblities in the information society. Thus, having more access to information and technology are not ends in themselves and do not justify progress; rather, we need a form of critical theory that allows us to differentiate between aspects of the information society that either further domination or promote greater human freedom.

Marcuse's particular form of critical theory also forces LIS to critically assess its foundations and its construction of a modern notion of information. This modern construction of information is intimately tied with the growth and rise of science and the ideologies of technological and instrumental rationality that Marcuse criticizes. Information, which was often associated with the process of informing, became an increasingly reified and commodified entity in a modern, post–World War II environment (Day 2001). Other Frankfurt School theorists, including Adorno and Horkheimer, were also interested in this idea of how knowledge became divorced from information and norms from facts (Bronner 2004). Information, in its modern sense, became dissociated from affective, contextual, and cultural processes, thus making it much easier to be commodified, reified, and abstracted.

In addition to reclaiming and rethinking modern constructions of information, Marcuse's work gives the field of LIS an opportunity to influence discourses of technology. While LIS as a discipline is engaged with the role of technology in society, it arguably does not theorize technology to a sufficient degree. In response to this shortcoming, Marcuse provides substantive insight into the role of technology in contemporary societies and provides critical perspectives on society and technology that challenge us to distinguish between emancipatory and oppressive forces and tendencies (Kellner 1998). These insights help avoid simply seeing all technology and society as a vast apparatus of domination, or seeing all science, technology and industry as progressive (Kellner 1998). Marcuse's approach can thus help mediate between the often unproductive extremes of technophobia and technophilia that are present in the field of LIS and in society at large. A critical engagement with discourses of technology can have broad implications in the field, beyond the usual implementation of technology for enhancing information access.

Lastly, Marcuse reminds us that intellectuals have an important role to play in public life. While we may not all be radicals like Marcuse, he offers a path for both academics and working professionals in the field to be active public intellectuals. As a field that bridges both the academic and professional worlds, LIS is in a unique position to train public intellectuals who can speak for issues in the public interest and advocate for socially just outcomes in the information society.

CONCLUDING REMARKS

This chapter has reviewed some key points from Marcuse's large body of work, with a focus on how some of these ideas might be applicable to LIS in general. An exploration such as this one by its very nature cannot be exhaustive; however, the ideas presented here are meant to stimulate further inquiry and interest in Marcuse's theoretical legacy. Marxist-oriented critique in LIS has focused on a number of issues throughout the years, including the commodification of information and the decline of the democratic public sphere. A reengagement with Frankfurt School critical theory, as another Marxist form of analysis, would also bring critiques of technology, culture, and ideology to the fore. A Frankfurt School type of critique is increasingly important for LIS, as the discipline attempts to navigate the complex ideological terrain of the information society.

Marcuse, as a trenchant social critic, focused on issues of domination and liberation within a utopian framework. Despite his focus on the negative aspects of technological society, he theorized moments of hope and resistance. His uncompromising utopian idealism may even seem outdated today. An "incurable and sentimental romanticist" (Moyers 2005, 164) may not provide the most practical orientation for such a professionally focused field. However, if we utilized our radical imagination for just a moment, might we be able to create a more socially conscious LIS?

REFERENCES

Althusser, L. 2001. *Lenin and Philosophy, and Other Essays.* New York: Monthly Review Press.

Benjamin, Walter. 1968. *Illuminations.* Trans. Harry Zohn, ed. Hannah Arendt. New York: Schocken Books.

Bronner, S. 2004. *Reclaiming the Enlightenment: Toward a Politics of Radical Engagement.* New York: Columbia University Press.

Bronner, Stephen. E., and Douglas M. Kellner. 1989. Introduction. In *Critical Theory and Society: A Reader,* ed. S. E. Bronner and D. M. Kellner, 1–21. New York: Routledge.

Davis, Angela. "Preface: Marcuse's Legacies." In *The New Left and the 1960s: Collected Papers of Herbert Marcuse, Volume Three,* ed. Douglas Kellner, vii–xiv. London: Routledge.

Day, R. E. 2001. *The Modern Invention of Information: Discourse, History, and Power.* Carbondale: Southern Illinois University Press.

Habermas, Jurgen. 1989. *Jurgen Habermas on Society and Politics: A Reader.* Ed. S. Seidman. Boston: Beacon Press.

Harvey, David. 2005. *A Brief History of Neoliberalism.* New York: Oxford University Press.

Horkheimer, Max, and Theodor W. Adorno. 2002. *Dialectic of Enlightenment: Philosophical Fragments.* Trans. Edmund Jephcott. Stanford, CA: Stanford University Press.

Kellner, Douglas. (n.d.-a). "The Frankfurt School," http://www.gseis.ucla.edu/faculty/kellner/essays/frankfurtschool.pdf

Kellner, Douglas. (n.d.-b). "Herbert Marcuse," http://www.gseis.ucla.edu/faculty/kellner/essays/herbertmarcuse.pdf

Kellner, Douglas. (n.d.-c). "Marcuse, Liberation, and Radical Ecology," http://www.gseis.ucla.edu/faculty/kellner/essays/marcuseliberationradicalecology.pdf

Kellner, Douglas. 1989. *Critical Theory, Marxism and Modernity.* Baltimore: Johns Hopkins University Press.

Kellner, Douglas. 1991. "Introduction to the Second Edition." In *One-Dimensional Man: Studies in the Ideology of Advanced Industrial Society,* xi–xxxviii. London: Routledge.

Kellner, Douglas. 1998. "Technology, War and Fascism: Marcuse in the 1940s." In *Technology, War and Fascism: Collected Papers of Herbert Marcuse, Volume One,* ed. Douglas Kellner, 1–38. London: Routledge.

Kellner, Douglas. 2005. "Introduction: Radical Politics, Marcuse, and the New Left." In *The New Left and the 1960s: Collected Papers of Herbert Marcuse, Volume Three,* ed. Douglas Kellner, 1–37. London: Routledge.

Lowenthal, Leo. 1961. *Literature, Popular Culture and Society.* Englewood Cliffs, NJ: Prentice-Hall.

Lukacs, Georg. 1971. *History and Class Consciousness: Studies in Marxist Dialectics.* Cambridge, MA: MIT Press.

Marcuse, Herbert. 1955. *Eros and Civilization: A Philosophical Inquiry into Freud.* Boston: Beacon Press.

Marcuse, Herbert. 1964. *One-Dimensional Man: Studies in the Ideology of Advanced Industrial Society.* Boston: Beacon Press.

Marcuse, Herbert. 1969. *An Essay on Liberation.* Boston: Beacon Press.

Marcuse, Herbert. 1998. *Technology, War and Fascism: Collected Papers of Herbert Marcuse, Volume One,* ed. Douglas Kellner. London: Routledge.

Marcuse, Herbert. 2001. *Towards a Critical Theory of Society: Collected Papers of Herbert Marcuse, Volume Two,* ed. Douglas Kellner. London: Routledge.

Marcuse, Herbert. 2005. *The New Left and the 1960s: Collected Papers of Herbert Marcuse, Volume Three,* ed. Douglas Kellner. London: Routledge.

Marcuse, Herbert. 2007. *Art and Liberation: Collected Papers of Herbert Marcuse, Volume Four,* ed. Douglas Kellner. London: Routledge.

Marcuse, Herbert. 2007. "Art in the One-Dimensional Society." In *Art and Liberation: Collected Papers of Herbert Marcuse, Volume Four,* ed. Douglas Kellner, 113–22. London: Routledge.

Moyers, Bill. 2005. "Bill Moyers: A Conversation with Herbert Marcuse." In *The New Left and the 1960s: Collected Papers of Herbert Marcuse, Volume Three,* ed. Douglas Kellner, 154–64. London: Routledge.

Pyati, Ajit K. 2006. "Critical Theory and Information Studies: A Marcusean Infusion." *Policy Futures in Education* 4 (1), 83–89.

Pyati, Ajit K. 2009. "Critical Theory and Information Studies: A Marcusean Infusion [expanded]." In *Marcuse's Challenge to Education,* ed. Douglas Kellner, Tyson Lewis, Clayton Pierce, and K. Daniel Cho, 181–92. Lanham, MD: Rowman and Littlefield.

Schiller, Dan. 2007. *How to Think about Information.* Urbana: University of Illinois Press.

Webster, Frank. 2006. *Theories of the Information Society,* 3rd ed. London: Routledge.

19

Chantal Mouffe's Theory of Agonistic Pluralism and Its Relevance for Library and Information Science Research

Joacim Hansson
Linnaeus University, Växjö, Sweden

INTRODUCTION

Democratic societies are today confronted with a challenge that they are ill-prepared to answer because they are unable to grasp its nature. One of the main reasons for this incapacity lies… in the kind of political theory which is dominant today and of the type of rationalistic framework which characterizes most of liberal-democratic theory. It is high time, if we want to be in condition to consolidate and deepen democratic institutions, to relinquish that framework and begin thinking about politics in a different way (Mouffe 2000a, paragraph 1).

Thinking about politics and the political in society in a different way is something that has characterized the writings of Chantal Mouffe. Born in Belgium in 1943, but for many years working in London as professor of Political Science at University of Westminister, she has been a visiting professor at several leading universities, including Cornell, Princeton, Harvard, in the United States, and the Sorbonne, in Paris, France. In this chapter, I will start by outlining her groundbreaking work on discourse theory, and then move on to her theory on the political and "agonistic pluralism." I will end by pointing to some issues within library and information science (LIS) where this theory can be fruitful as a framework for critical analyses of library and information institutions and practices.

POST-MARXIST DISCOURSE THEORY

In the mid-1980s Mouffe was one of the renewers of critical discourse theory. Together with Argentinean political scientist Ernesto Laclau, in 1985 she published the groundbreaking *Hegemony and Socialist Strategy: Towards a Radical Democratic Politics*. As discourse analysis had been struggling in the area between theory and methodology, at the same time acknowledging the heritage from traditional critical theory as well as accepting postmodern viewpoints (thus denying Marxism as a relevant ground scientific inquiry), Laclau and Mouffe introduced a discourse analysis that not only resolved this dilemma, but showed how Marxist fundamentals could be used in contemporary analysis of discursive power relations. They did so by combining theoretical concepts and elements from poststructuralism and Lacanian subject theory. With the full acceptance of postmodernism's relativistic stance it was still possible for them to provide an analytical framework for the analysis of democratic development and specifically socialist ideology in terms of a post-Marxist point of view. This combination turned out well and the work of Laclau and Mouffe is today regarded as perhaps the most powerful critical discourse analysis framework available when studying social and democratic development. Torfing views the Laclau and Mouffe critical theory as post-Gramscian in that they develop and partly reformulate the concept of hegemony: "Hegemony is no longer to be conceived of in terms of unification of political forces around a set of paradigmatic interests that are constituted elsewhere. Rather, hegemony involves the articulation of social identities in the context of social antagonism" (Torfing 1999, 14).

Reinterpreting the concept of hegemony in terms of antagonistic subject positions as the driving forces of democratic creativity, and the emphasis on the political as articulation of social identities, paved the way for a more extensive political theory that Chantal Mouffe developed herself in relation to current movement in the political landscape, not least within the European Union. The point of the argument however is equally applicable in the United States, because the focus of her analysis is the traditionally liberal conception of democracy and political development in society. During the rest of this chapter I will expand upon this political theory and place it within library and information science.

A THEORY OF THE POLITICAL

Chantal Mouffe's theory of the political has been developed in several books and articles over the last decade. The ones I primarily draw from here are *The Democratic Paradox* (2000b) and *On the Political* (2005). Building upon her earlier works on hegemony and post-Marxist (post-Gramscian) social analysis, she now focuses on the problems of liberalism as the dominant political discourse in most Western societies, and on the fact that liberal consensus models make way for global capitalism to grow and strengthen its position at the expense of marginalized and excluded groups via the needs of economic growth and greed. She formulates a sharp critique of contemporary politics by restating the concept of "the political" as something now neglected, but absolutely crucial in developing vital and inclusive democracies. The idea of the political is based on legitimate conflicts of different political views and reference systems—a kind of conflict she calls "agonism" or "agonistic pluralism." Now, let us have a look at what she is actually turning against. What is the problem of liberalism as we see it today?

The Problem of Liberal Universalism

When defining the problem of the political in contemporary society, Mouffe turns to a development that is sketched very clearly in different points in her writing. Contemporary politics is built on a model of consensus based on a social liberal ground of reason. This reason states that if we only get the institutions and the political procedures right, then we will be able to create a society in which growth is in the interest of each and every one. Such a way of thinking of course requires that everyone accept the institutions and procedures when and as they develop. Of course, claims Mouffe, this is not the case. In formulating her critique of the liberal consensus model she argues explicitly against philosopher John Rawls, who in his book *Political Liberalism* (1993) provides an important theoretical discussion that explains the ideas behind liberalism as a reasonable consensus model. When arguing for such a model one of the classical paradoxes of liberal politics discloses itself—the search for maximum individual freedom and the simultaneous view that there exists a set of universal human rights which are equal for all. In the case of Rawls, this paradox becomes a problem when having to deal with conflicts of interest and political disagreements. In order to resolve the problem of political conflict, liberal theory (and practice) adopts two sets of basic arguments, both of which become the target of Mouffe's theoretical claims. Firstly, the political is reduced to procedure, making it a purely intellectual endeavour—democracy can be structured and represented not only by elected representatives, but through the establishment of a representative structure of public institutions that administer the chosen form of democratic structure. Secondly, all "good" people are actually liberals since, for instance, the set of basic human rights is universal. If you do not agree to universals like these you are wrong and can only be accepted as legitimate in your standpoints if you abide to the basic view of liberal thought—if not you must be taught to do so.[1] To be able to achieve a consensus of what is good and right liberalism today tends to look away from those outside of its ideological realm, simply by not accepting them as legitimate. In political practice this is seen in the reluctance to still accept the traditional left/right scale of political diversity. By doing this, a formation in the political middle (social liberalism) is attracting most major political parties—as well as theorists. The decrease of legitimate political struggle and the procedural intellectualisation of the political are defined as "progress."

Agonistic Pluralism as an Alternative to Consensual Liberalism

In creating a viable and stable theory of the political, Mouffe turns away from thought concerning "harmonious" conflicts as described in liberalism—differences may occur, but they are all safe as they are intellectual constructions and they accept the basic universalism of reason as the basis of politics. Instead she claims that conflict is the very driving force of vital democracy, and the only way of maintaining its strength is to accept antagonism as socially constructive. In doing so, she takes her departure from several controversial theorists and combines their thinking in a very original way. In an article entitled "Wittgenstein, Political Theory, and Democracy", she uses the combined thinking of Ludwig Wittgenstein, Jacques Derrida, and Richard Rorty as a theoretical basis for criticism of a Habermasian liberal conception:

Democratic citizenship can take many diverse forms and such a diversity, far from being a danger for democracy, is in fact its very condition of existence. This will, of course, create conflict and it would be a mistake to expect all those different understandings to coexist without clashing. But this struggle will not be one between "enemies" but among "adversaries" since all participants will recognize the positions of the others as legitimate ones. This type of "agonistic pluralism" is unthinkable within a rationalistic problematic because it, by necessity, tend to erase diversity (Mouffe 2000a, paragraph 30).

Antagonism as the struggle between interests is here replaced by a related term—agonistic pluralism—the legitimate positions of adversaries in the political discussion creating a viable foundation for democracy. This formulation of what kind of conflict is necessary for democratic development takes its departure in thought constructions far from general mainstream liberals. One simple, but profound, example is found in a question put in Wittgenstein's *Philosophical Investigations:* "Following a rule is analogous to obeying an order. We are trained to do so; we react to an order in a particular way. But what if one person reacts in one way and another in another to the order and the training? Which one is right?" (Wittgenstein 1958, paragraph 1.206). From a liberal point of view this is a subversive thought. To theorists like Jürgen Habermas and John Rawls, the thought of a contradicting reaction to political universals, which by necessity would underlie the order, is fundamentally inconceivable. The question, Which one is right? is a nonissue—since rules and orders are rational in relation to the universals creating their legitimacy.

Apart from Ludwig Wittgenstein, Mouffe uses the controversial political theorist Carl Schmitt as a point of departure, not only for her critique, but to further the formulation of her own theory of agonistic pluralism. Using Schmitt as a reference for a formulation of an emancipatory, left-oriented political theory, as Mouffe does, might seem not only controversial due to Schmitt's affiliation with German Nazism during the time of Hitler, but also theoretically inconvenient, as Schmitt was a strong advocate of totalitarianism and dictatorship.[2]

There are, however, two arguments in Schmitt's work that have been found to be fruitful in the construction of agonistic pluralism. The first one is formulated in his first major work from 1921, *On Dictatorship* [*Die Diktatur*], where he proposes the idea that crises and states of emergency should not be seen as extreme exceptions from a political normality based on rational consensus, but instead as fundamental for any political construction. The existence of social interests that are in direct opposition to the governing power must always exist and strive to create unrest and ultimately chaos among the orderly majority. The second argument is proposed in his most famous essay, *The Concept of the Political* [*Der Begriff des politischen*], from 1932. He states that there is a difference between "politics" and "the political," the latter being a deeper and more constitutive concept that the former, including the thought of friend/enemy dichotomy that must be the very basis of every regulatory political construction, democratic or not.

What Mouffe does with these proposals, in order to obtain legitimacy for Schmitt's theories, turns them against him, pointing to what will happen to a democratic society that has declared itself beyond ideology and treats political struggle as something obsolete. Accepting general democratic institutions and the fundamentally democratic system as the best political construction, she is able to show that when agonistic pluralism, that is, legitimate political conflict, is present the system accepts "the political"—the fundamental struggle of opposing interests acknowledging the other's right to exist, even though its claims are debated. If, on the contrary agonistic pluralism is not allowed, or is neglected, as is the case in contemporary Europe and in the United States, there is always a ground for nonlegitimate movements and political positions to grow strong—as for instance the extreme right or the extreme left. These political positions are considered illegitimate because they do not accept the universals underlying current liberal democracy. Here is one of the crucial points of Mouffe's argument: since different opinions, reference systems, ideologies, norms, values, and beliefs always will be present in a variety that widely supersedes that which may be grasped by liberal consensus, this variety must be acknowledged and valued as the very foundation of democratic thinking. If not there will be a number of these opinions, and so forth, that will work outside the borders of the legitimate and thus create a real threat to a democracy based on fundamentals. We have been able to see the consequences of such political neglect before, not least in the rise of Nazism in Germany in the 1920s. She thus manages to turn the arguments of Carl Schmitt against his own ambitions and political position, and instead place them in the service of radical emancipatory political theory.

At the same time Mouffe turns the argument against contemporary democratic development. Neglect of agonistic pluralism comes from a belief in politics as the administration of universals—this is true whether we speak of Nazism or social liberalism. Both of these systems provide answers to Wittgenstein's rhetorical question quoted above. They know who is right in responding to orders and training—and who is not. True democracy does not build on static universals—simply because they do not exist, but on a pragmatic basis where negotiation is the means, not to find procedures, but to handle conflicts. Maintaining political conflict is thus a way of securing democratic vitality. This is a role that traditionally has been given to the political left. As social democratic parties, not least in Northern Europe and Scandinavia, are leaning more and more towards global capitalism and universalist liberalism in order to win votes and gain political influence, there is a crisis for left-wing parties. Social antagonism; injustice; economic, social, sexual, and ethnic segregation; and discrimination are neglected, and those who point out the obvious fact that these issues are as real and present in society as ever before are seen as disturbances and illegitimate voices that need not be taken into consideration. This is a major problem. As the political left collapsed ideologically in the 1990s there was suddenly an empty space that has yet to be filled. The critical voice that was previously legitimate has now become illegitimate and uttered by the extreme right.

The growth of the extreme right is of course a major—and growing—problem in contemporary politics, in Sweden and in Europe as a whole. Why? Because when there still was a radical left there was a movement which strived for emancipation, advocating a sort of agonistic pluralism where injustice and discrimination could not only be exposed, but formulated in an ideological terminology that could compete on the arena of legitimate adversaries. The extreme right may formulate what it considers to be injustice of discrimination—but it does not have an element of emancipation. Instead fear and jealousy are main ingredients, and from that comes nothing good, only distrust and violence. Distrust and violence are two forces not to be neglected when defending the democratic institutions.

Several of the democratic institutions were built up in an era where agonistic pluralism existed—signified by a living and ever present left/right scale of politics representing true values, and an environment for thought where politics was not reduced to procedure and intellectual solutions managed by expertise managers, but instead consisted of passion and the necessary blend of heart and mind that is the very essence of any political movement. These facts have made some of these institutions strong and vital and—although many have tried to displace them—relevant in the changes of the political and social landscape. One of these institutions is the library. When we are speaking of "democratic institutions" we perhaps primarily think of public libraries. Academic libraries, for instance, serve their democratic purpose as part of various educational and research institutions. When considering how the theory of agonistic pluralism may be used in library and information science, the library as a social and democratic institution will serve well as a point of departure.

RELEVANCE FOR LIBRARY AND INFORMATION SCIENCE

Library and information science has traditionally been exceptionally empirical and not very theoretically oriented in any of its subfields. Critical and emancipatory perspectives have rarely been seen. During the last decade however, there has been a general development in strengthening theoretical claims, and different perspectives have been tried out on more or less traditional empirical environments. This has also led to not only a call for critical theory in general, as formulated by, for example, Hansson (2004) and Benoit (2007), but also de facto effort to summarize and use existing empirical knowledge in defining emancipatory elements in both LIS as an academic field of research and librarianship as a social practice. In the United States a number of influential monographs have been produced, such as McCabe (2001), Buschman (2003), and Budd (2008). Anthologies have presented different social and critical perspectives and tools, using and trying them out in different practical situations and scholarly investigations. Examples of such anthologies are Rayward (2004), Buschman and Leckie (2007), and Lewis (2008).

There are primarily two areas in library and information science where different versions of critical theory have come in handy: public library research and knowledge organization. In none of these areas have theories of agonistic pluralism been used to any real extent. The traditional understanding of critical theory is well rooted in a tradition of liberal thinking, making, for instance, Jürgen Habermas one of the most quoted and discussed theorists. This is not surprising. Public libraries are to a certain extent the archetypical liberal institution.

Public Library Research

The rise of public libraries is, in whatever country we study, tightly woven into the fabric of the institutions that establish and secure a liberal political construction. There are of course many forms of liberalism, ranging from extreme neoliberalism to contemporary European social democracy, but public libraries correspond to some of the universals underlying the liberal project—the value of culture and education. Here, the paradox mentioned earlier between self-interest and absolute equality is clearly shown. Education, or perhaps even more *Bildung,* a term that interestingly enough does not exist in English, is seen as, on the one hand a concern for each individual, and on the other a means to raise and secure a standard of living for the many. To various degrees, education supported by library services is tied to economic growth or development of social identity. The former meaning has during the last two decades become increasingly important—at the expense of the latter.

The liberal character of the traditional public library might be seen in at least two aspects of the professional practice of librarianship: striving for neutrality and moral judging of good taste and manners. The librarian as a custodian of good taste and cultural sophistication was one of the founding characters in the early days of public librarianship (Garrison 1979). It is today not as predominant since users are seen as the driving force for change in the library sector. This shift from a custodian librarian to a service- and user-oriented role is fully taking place within the realm of a liberal consensus model—currently changing from the universal of cultural taste to user-driven free market thinking where the free choice of the individual is the remaining universal. A liberal consensus model inevitably leads us to the question of library neutrality. This is also perhaps the area where the theories of Mouffe most come in handy.

The idea of the neutral library was from the outset fostered by public librarianship in the mid-19th century, particularly when it comes to the development and occurrences in society surrounding the library. The public library has as its basic mission to mirror society in representing all its forms and different opinions to be exposed through collection development or various non-book-related activities, such as exhibitions or lectures. This is accepted as long as we can keep this exposure within the realm of the liberal conception of the good and what is regarded as legitimate opinion or positions in relation to specific social issues. As is so clearly shown in the volume of essays collected from the journal *Progressive Librarian,* titled *Questioning Library Neutrality* (Lewis 2008), there is no such thing as a "neutral" public library. It is only neutral if we accept the liberal standpoint that only those views that come in harmoniously into the set of universals underlying liberal society and institutions are exposed, and others excluded. Neutrality is a shutting of the eyes at alternative interpretations of the world, the socially good, and the political differences that de facto exist in a multicultural society of today.

Agonistic pluralism as a theoretical point of view analyzing libraries is fruitful in that it provides a basis for looking at neutrality in a way that is not previously tied to liberal universals. Such a position makes way for analyses of many different kinds, primarily of how various alternative conceptions of political issues and society as a whole are exposed or excluded. This brings a strong emancipatory force. It also places a lot of responsibility on the libraries themselves, as their role in a vital democracy based on agonistic pluralism is not one of neutrality and kindness, but one of political activity and proaction. The library can be analysed as a social arena for competing legitimate struggles of ideas and political positions.

This idea is gaining significance by the day: a strong paradigmatic hold of the liberal consensus model in Europe is getting stronger and stronger. Groups with different realities and sets of references are increasingly marginalized, and as LIS researchers we may contribute to the exposure of this movement by focussing on such marginalized groups. In the fall of 2009, a Swedish research project based on agonistic pluralism began and empirical analysis of the treatment of national ethnic minorities in public libraries. Accepting the different worldviews of such groups as the Sami people and Gypsies, a full-scale survey of all public libraries in Sweden will be undertaken and the results of how these groups are visualized and treated in program activities and collection development analysed within the realm of agonistic pluralism. This is to the extent of my knowledge the first major empirical library research project working explicitly with Mouffe's ideas on agonistic pluralism as a theoretical foundation.[3]

Knowledge Organization

The second major area of library and information area where critical theory has been used is knowledge organization. It is within classification research we have seen the most explicit analyses based on theoretical frameworks of, for instance, power theory and feminist theory (Olson 2002). A general discussion of the potential and value of critical theory as a tool for emancipatory research within LIS was made by Hansson (2006). More than in public library research, classification research has questioned the very basis of the liberal consensus model. It has been done implicitly though by showing, for instance, how different subjects have been prioritized in classificatory hierarchies, while others have been marginalized or made invisible. Conducting such analyses based on (for instance) feminist theory, queer theory, or postcolonial theory is all well and good, but they all focus on very specific issues and perspectives and mostly miss the broader picture: they are largely unable to present a viable alternative to the given classifications—at least if we look at the major library classification systems we use today. "Standpoint epistemologies" (Trosow 2002) are valuable analytical tools, but there is a need for a development beyond them, a development that may put the whole practice of classification and knowledge organization into question. Agonistic pluralism is the very opposite of a regulatory practice of subject analysis where no matter what system certain values, issues groups, or occasions are made invisible for the benefit of a harmonious whole. In no other library practice, perhaps, is this clearer than in the subject analysis subfield of knowledge organization. How can libraries use classification schemes and indexing systems to promote agonistic pluralism instead of using those same tools to hide away unwanted or inconvenient views and—as a result—documents? The tools of knowledge organization are powerful. Not many still see them as neutral in any real sense of the term, but not many have discussed how they can—and should—be used. They have a potential to oppress and they have the potential to emancipate. LIS research can contribute to the choices that have to be made—the theory of agonistic pluralism can provide a theoretical framework within which a constructive discussion can be maintained.

CONCLUSION

Chantal Mouffe's theory of agonistic pluralism is slowly gaining significance within critical perspectives in political science. Its fundamental questioning of the basic universals underlying most of today's national and international politics is radical, controversial, and revealing. Libraries are part of the institutional construct necessary to uphold a democratic society. Librarianship as a profession has an active responsibility to keep the library institution alive and relevant in times of drastic political, social, economic, and technological change such as those we are experiencing today. Mouffe offers an alternative reading of current politics. She offers an alternative, pluralist, nonconforming, and emancipatory thinking at a time when these characteristics are the very opposite of those propelling current political hegemony. As researchers in library and information science we are able to draw from theory like this, and provide analyses that tell us new things about the things we thought we knew so much about—libraries, librarians and librarianship.

REFERENCES

Benoit, Gerald. 2007. "Critical Theory and the Legitimation of Library and Information Science." *Information Research* 12 (4) http://informationr.net/ir/12–4/colis/colis30.html

Budd, John M. 2008. *Self-Examination: The Present and Future of Librarianship.* Westport, CT: Libraries Unlimited.

Buschman, John E. 2003. *Dismantling the Public Sphere: Situating and Sustaining Librarianship in the Age of the New Public Philosophy.* Westport, CT: Libraries Unlimited.

Buschman, John E., and Glora J. Leckie, eds. 2007. *The Library as Place: History, Community and Culture.* Westport, CT: Libraries Unlimited.

McCabe, Ronald B. 2001. *Civic Librarianship: Renewing the Social Mission of the Public Library.* Lanham, MD: Scarecrow Press.

Gottfried, Paul E. 1990. *Carl Schmitt: Politics and Theory.* New York: Greenwood Press.

Hansson, Joacim. 2004. "The Social Legitimacy of Library and Information Studies: Reconsidering the Institutional Paradigm," In *Aware and Responsible: Papers of the Nordic-International Colloquium on Social and Cultural Awareness and Responsibility in Library, Information and Documentation Studies (SCARLID),* ed. Boyd Rayward, 49–69. Lanham, MD: Scarecrow Press.

Hansson, Joacim. 2006. "Knowledge Organization from An Institutional Point of View: Implications for Theoretical and Practical Development." *Progressive Librarian* 27 (Summer): 31–43.

Laclau, Ernesto, and Chantal Mouffe. 1985. *Hegemony and Socialist Strategy: Towards a Radical Democratic Politics.* London: Verso.

Lewis, Alison, ed. 2008. *Questioning Library Neutrality: Essays from* Progressive Librarian. Duluth, MN: Library Juice Press.

Mouffe, Chantal. 2000a. "Wittgenstein, Political Theory and Democracy." *Polylog.* http://them. polylog.org/2/amc-en.htm

Mouffe, Chantal. 2000b. *The Democratic Paradox.* London: Verso.

Mouffe, Chantal. 2005. *On the Political.* Abingdon: Routledge.

Mouffe, Chantal. 2007. "Artistic Activism and Agonistic Spaces." *Art and Research* 1 (2 Summer). http://www.artandresearch.org.uk/v1n2/mouffe.html

Olson, Hope. 2002. *The Power to Name: Locating the Limits of Subject Representation in Libraries.* Dordrecht: Kluwer.

Rawls, John. 1993. *Political Liberalism.* New York: Colombia University Press.

Rayward, W. Boyd, ed. 2004. *Aware and Responsible: Papers of the Nordic-International Colloquium on Social and Cultural Awareness and Responsibility in Library, Information and Documentation Studies (SCARLID).* Lanham, MD: Scarecrow Press.

Torfing, Jacob. 1999. *New Theories of Discourse: Laclau, Mouffe and Žižek.* Oxford: Blackwell.

Trosow, Samuel E. 2002. "Standpoint Epistemology as an Alternative Methodology for Library and Information Science." *Library Quarterly* 71 (3): 360–82.

Wittgenstein, Ludwig. 1958. *Philosophical Investigations.* Oxford: Blackwell.

NOTES

1. Here, an important short note on the view on liberalism is needed. Both Rawls and Mouffe are forming their arguments around a traditionally European conception of liberalism. This is slightly different from the US meaning of the term. A liberal in the European sense is much more in the middle of the political left-right scale, where an American liberal is considered more as a person belonging to the left on the traditional political scale—this in relation to the general political scale in the United States, which is considerably far more to the right than in Europe.

2. Schmitt was one of the leading political theorists of Nazi Germany during the 1930s and 1940s. After World War II he was captured by the allies and imprisoned; he was released in 1946. Due to his commitment to the Nazi cause, he was expelled from mainstream academia for the rest of his life. This, however, did not prevent him from working, and several contemporary scholars now refer back to relevant parts of his work. Schmitt died in Germany in 1985, at the age of 95 (Gottfried 1990).

3. The project, called Public Libraries and National Minorities, is a collaboration between the Swedish Library Association and the Department of Library and Information Science at the Linnaeus University, Växjö. Its final report will be published in May 2010. The leader and contact person for the project is the author of this chapter.

20

Antonio Negri on Information, Empire, and Commonwealth

Nick Dyer-Witheford
University of Western Ontario, Canada

INTRODUCTION

What could be the relevance to librarians and information scientists of a thinker whose intellectual starting point was the strikes and sabotage of industrial assembly-line workers, who composed several books while imprisoned for terrorism, and whose recent writings have been called a 21st-century *Communist Manifesto* (Žižek, 2001)? Yet despite the apparent gulf between such dramatic life-circumstances and the normal context of academic LIS studies, the work of Antonio Negri is, I suggest, a source of insight into the conditions of information labor, conflicts over information property, and the concept of an information commons.

BIOGRAPHY AND EARLY WORK

Negri was born in Italy in 1933 and began his intellectual career as meteoric young professor of political science at the University of Padua. Initially a left wing Catholic activist, he rapidly became a key member of the *operaismo* ("workerism") tendency that in the late 1960s and '70s connected Marxist intellectuals to shop floor struggles in industrial factories such as those of Italian automobile giant Fiat (for a selection of early writings, see Negri 2005; for background on *operaismo,* Cleaver 1977; Wright 2002 and 2005). *Operaismo* theorists such as Negri and his comrades, Mario Tronti, Raniero Panzieri, and Sergio Bologna, took as their premise not the power and dominion of capital, but the creativity and autonomy of labor. Capital attempts to control the inventive, cooperative capacity of workers, on which it depends for profit. However, labor resists, driving capital to expand its territorial mobility and technological intensity in successive rounds of reorganization aimed at destroying worker power. Such restructurings only generate new forms of labor, and new strategies and tactics of struggle, so that the composition of the working class is an incessant process of mutation.

Historically, *operaismo* discerned two major turns in this cycle of struggles, the epochs of the *artisan* (sometimes called professional) and *mass* worker. In the late 19th century managerial control was stymied by the power that the craft skills gave workers over key production processes. Capital responded with the deskilling and automating regimes of Taylorism and Fordism (see Stevenson, this volume). In doing so, however, it generated the mass worker of the industrial assembly line with the organizational power to shut down entire factories with strikes and sabotage—a potentially revolutionary force. Negri and his comrades aligned themselves with the most radical sectors of a huge wave of industrial militancy that in the late 1960s and '70s swept the factories of northern Italy, paralyzing business and throwing the country into protracted political crisis that resembled the French student-worker strikes of 1968 but exceeded them in scale and duration.

It was, however, already apparent that the peak of mass worker power might be past. By the end of the 1970s, capital was beginning a new round of restructuring, globalizing production and using digital technology to disassemble and relocate the industrial factory and undermine the base of worker activism. This effort was soon assisted by right wing governments such as those of Reagan and Thatcher, throwing a neoliberal counterpunch that all but knocked out the labor parties and trades unions that had constituted the left for a century. The cycle of struggles appeared to have ended—and badly for those who thought it up.

Negri refused this conclusion. His political involvement was moving from the industrial militancy of *operaismo* to the *autonomia* (autonomy) movement—a percolating synthesis of marginalized sectors, including students, unemployed and precarious workers, and feminist movements demanding "wages for housework" (Dalla Costa and James 1972, 5), whose combined resistance to cutbacks and austerity measures continued the long crisis of the Italian state (see Lotringer and Marazzi, 1980). As he made this shift, Negri came up with a new theoretical proposition: out of capital's restructuring was emerging another cycle of struggles. In the era of the artisanal worker, capital concentrated itself in the factory; in the era of the mass worker, the factory became central to society. Now, in the epoch of the "socialized worker," Negri (1980) said, the factory disseminates out into society; labor is deterritorialized, dispersed and decentralized in the "social factory" or "factory without walls" (Negri 1986, 89). Work (production), education and training (reproduction), and leisure (consumption) all become points on an increasingly integrated circuit of capitalist activity so that "the whole of society is placed at the disposal of profit" (1986, 89).

In a world where capital has insinuated itself everywhere, the industrial shop floor is no longer a central locus of antagonism. Rather than dying away, however, conflict over exploitation fractally replicates, manifesting in myriad new movements that contest the logic of capital not only in new kinds of workplaces, but also in homes, schools, universities, hospitals, and media. From *autonomia* came the term that thenceforward would characterize Negri, who is often called the leading theorist of "autonomist Marxism" (for the complexities behind this designation see Wright 2008).

Meanwhile, the Italian political situation was heading towards an appalling crisis. In a context of increasingly violent confrontations between *autonomia* and other social movements on one side, and Italian security forces and fascist counter-movements on the other, clandestine, armed-struggle cells sprung up on the left. The most notorious, the Red Brigades, started to kidnap and assassinate corporate executives and political leaders; in 1978 they abducted, and then executed, the president of the Christian

Democratic Party, Aldo Moro. The massive state-security clampdown that followed destroyed *autonomia*. Thousands of activists were detained and held for long periods without trial; hundreds fled abroad. Many were imprisoned on the slimmest of evidence (see Balestrini 1989).

Negri, accused of masterminding the Red Brigades, was one of these. He was exonerated from Aldo Moro's kidnapping; no links with the Red Brigades were proven; the majority of charges against Negri were dropped shortly after his arrest. He was, however, eventually found guilty of instigating violence and planning the overthrow of the state, although objections raised by organizations such as Amnesty International to the many irregularities in the trials of *autonomia* activists throw doubt on these findings. During his trial he was incarcerated in Italy's infamous Rebibbia high security prison, where he passed time working on a book on Spinoza (Negri 1991); he was there when bona fide Red Brigade militants seized control of a cell block that was then recaptured in a rooftop helicopter landing by the Italian army. In 1984, still in prison awaiting sentencing, Negri was elected to the Italian legislature from a constituency in Rome. Under an obscure statute, Italian parliamentarians were exempt from imprisonment: the authorities had to release him. Knowing that the law that had rescued him would be immediately rescinded, he fled to France, where he lived in exile for the next 14 years.

He supported himself by teaching at Paris universities, and worked with a group of radicals gathered around *Futur Antérieur,* a journal that bought *autonomia* veterans such as Negri and Paolo Virno together with French and American left intellectuals like Jean Marie Vincent, Michael Hardt, and Maurizio Lazzarato (see Virno and Hardt 1996). He continued to work on the socialized worker thesis. Even some of his former comrades thought he was so entranced by the a priori logic of the cycle of struggle concept as to create a mirage of renewed resistance where none existed. However, as opposition to neoliberalism began to revive in the late 1980s, Negri found fresh vindication. Looking over new French and Italian movements of students, nurses, and environmentalists he discerned a wave of struggles completely different from those of the mass worker, characterized by "radically democratic form of organization... the rediscovery of a social perspective by the old sectors of the class struggle, the emergence of the feminist component, of workers from the tertiary sector and of 'intellectual' labor'" (Negri 1992, 18). It is at this point that Negri's thought begins to intersect with LIS concerns.

COMMUNICATION AGAINST INFORMATION

In discussing what he termed the "socialized worker," Negri (1980) began to give ever-increasing importance to the intellectual qualities of a post-Fordist proletariat enmeshed in the computers and communication networks of high technology capitalism. The "factory without walls" is also the "information factory," a system whose operation depends on "the growing identity between productive processes and forms of communication" (1989, 239):

Capital has penetrated the entire society by means of technological and political instruments... not only to follow and to be kept informed about, but to anticipate, organize and subsume each of the forms of laboring cooperation... to generate a higher level of productivity... [It] must appropriate the communicative capacity of the labor force, making it flow within the stipulated technological and administrative channels. This is *the form which expropriation takes in advanced capitalism*—or rather, in the world economy of the socialized worker (1989, 116).

While the mass worker labored on a factory assembly-line, the socialized worker's productivity emerges at the terminal of fiber optic lines, as a nurse monitoring cardiograms, a bank clerk handling on-line transactions, a teacher in a computer lab, a programmer or a video technician, or, indeed, as a digital librarian. Her productivity depends on an elaborated network of informatic systems.

However, this technological envelopment does not merely result in intensified subjugation. As the system of machines becomes all encompassing and familiar, Negri argues, the socialized worker enjoys an increasingly "organic" relation to technoscience (1989, 93). Although initiated by capital for purposes of control and command, as the system grows it becomes for the socialized worker something else entirely, an "ecology of machines"—an everyday ambience of potentials to be tapped and explored (93). The elaboration and alteration of this techno-habitat becomes so pervasively socialized that it can no longer be exclusively dictated by capital. Other theorists had suggested that a new working class, based in the skilled cadres of advanced industry, was in the process of creation (Mallet 1975). Negri, however, did not posit a select intelligentsia of technical workers but a generalized form of labor power needed by a system now suffused in every pore with technoscience; the new communicative and technological competencies were manifesting even among the contingent and unemployed labor force, not so much the products of a particular training or specific work environment as the prerequisite of everyday life in a system permeated by machines and media.

In a rich, if cryptic, passage Negri claims that "communication is to the socialized worker what the wage relationship was to the mass worker" (1989, 118). This does not mean that YouTube videos replace wages. Rather, Negri is suggesting that communicational resources now constitute part of the bundle of goods and services capital must deliver to workers to ensure its own continuing development. Just as in the era of the mass worker, Keynesian capital institutionalized wage increases as the motor of economic growth and generalized the norms of mass consumption, so today, neoliberal capital institutionalizes the information infrastructure into which it plugs its socialized workforce into, familiarizing labor with the networks through which instructions can be streamed and feedback channeled. The analogy, however, suggests more. In the Keynesian era, attempts to domesticate pay demands as part of capitalist growth plans ultimately failed and became a focus for struggle. Similarly, Negri sees the control of communication resources as an emergent arena of tension. By informationalizing production, capital seems to augment its powers of control, but simultaneously stimulates capacities that threaten to escape its command.

Although characteristically abstract, *The Politics of Subversion* (1989), Negri's most sustained statement of the socialized worker thesis, gives a sense of the concrete events fuelling this optimism. It opens with a lyrical invocation to the French student strikes of 1986, a movement that not only highlighted the centrality of education to high-technology capitalism, but was also one of the first social movements organized via computer networks, using the French predecessor to the Internet, Minitel (see Marchand 1988). In the context of this early experiment in hacktivism, Negri writes of the conflict between *communication* and *information* as central to the struggles of the socialized worker. Communicative activity is "current," distributed, transverse, dialogic; information is centralized, vertical, hierarchic, and inert. Capital tries to capture the intellectual capacity of the labor force the forms of information "like a flat, glass screen on which is projected, fixed in black and white, the mystified cooperative potentialities of social labor—deprived of life, just like in a replay of *Metropolis,*" while the direct current of communication takes transverse "polychromatic forms" (1989, 117–18). In the era of the socialized worker "*science, communication and the communication of knowledge*" is the raw material from which management must extract productivity—and from which subversion can blossom (1989, 116). Vivid as Negri's formulations on this topic are, however, they would probably have remained obscure but for some unexpected developments both in his own life and in political events at the very closing years of the 20th century.

EMPIRE AND MULTITUDE

In 1997, Negri returned to Italy to voluntarily serve the remainder of his sentence (which had been reduced on appeal from 30 to 17 years), in the hope that this would raise awareness of the predicament of other *autonomia* exiles and prisoners and help heal rifts within the remnants of the movement. Released in the spring of 2003, he emerged as a political and intellectual celebrity. For while in prison he had been at work on a book coauthored with Michael Hardt, which had been greeted as a manifesto for a new wave of anticapitalist activism that was unexpectedly erupting around the world. That book was *Empire* (2000).

Empire's topic of is nothing less than "globalization"—the world order created since 1989 by the apparently total victory of capitalism over all other social formations. This, Hardt and Negri claimed, is a new planetary regime in which economic, administrative, military, and communicative components combine to create a system of power "with no outside" (2000, xii). Earlier imperialisms, such as those of ancient Rome, 16th-century Spain or 19th-century Britain were rooted in specific nations that dominated the world map. What distinguishes Hardt and Negri's Empire (upper case) from these empires is that it is not directed by any single state. Rather, it is a system of rule crystallized by what Marx called the "world market." This domination is, Hardt and Negri (2000, 167) say, a "network power." Its decentered, multilayered institutional agencies include nation-states, but extend to include multinational corporations, like Microsoft and Sony, world economic bodies, like the World Trade Organization and the International Monetary Fund, international organizations like the United Nations, and even nongovernmental organizations, like Red Cross. What results from the interaction of these nodes is an imperium more comprehensive than any that preceded it.

Empire is, however, not just, or even primarily, an analysis of international relations. Rather, Hardt and Negri offer an ambitious account of conditions of work, forms of subjectivity, and types of struggle in contemporary capital. Empire is, they say, global not only in terms of its geographic reach but also of its social scope. Capital now siphons off its subjects' energies at multiple points: not just at work (as labor-power), but also as consumers (the mindshare targeted by marketers), in education and training (university degrees as vocational preparation), and even as a source of raw materials (the biovalue extracted for genetic engineering). Empire is thus a regime of "biopower"—a concept borrowed from the philosopher Michel Foucault (1990, 135–45)—exploiting social life in its entirety.

Yet if this picture of a world swallowed by capital was all there was to *Empire,* it would be just another left account of corporate domination of a very familiar sort. What made people take notice was that it spoke about opposition to capitalism—even of alternatives to it. That touched a contemporary nerve. The book came out at the high-water mark of the struggles against corporate globalization that were racing around the planet from the jungles of Chiapas to the streets of Seattle, variegated revolts all declaring "another world is possible" (see News from Nowhere 2003; Mertes 2004). Hardt and Negri (2000, 393–414) declared that this wave of activism signaled a new revolutionary power—"the multitude."

Precisely because capital is increasingly everywhere, and has subsumed everything, rebellion against it upsurges at many points, from work to school to leisure, and from many agencies, including workers and unions, but also indigenous communities struggling over land rights, students opposing the corporate campus, antipoverty groups fighting for a living wage, migrants contesting the oppression of borders, environmentalists demanding ecological conservation, open-source advocates promoting knowledge sharing…The multitude is thus a force made up of many protagonists, many distinct "singularities," but all pushing for a more democratic deployment of global resources (2000, 103). Transnational connections, cultural hybridities, and new technologies are seen by Hardt and Negri as containing immense potential for the multitude. Crucially, they spoke not of antiglobalization, but of a movement for another, different globalization, an alter-globalization, and an "exodus" from capital (2000, 210). Compared with characteristic left gloom, their book was a breath of hope.

Empire attracted wide attention, not only from academics, but also from activists and journalists (see Eakin 2001). This was extraordinary, since it was written both in a highly philosophic style and from an openly radical, anticapitalist position. Its success was due to timeliness: the reek of tear gas from the streets of Genoa, Seoul, or Washington seemed to rise off the page. But *Empire* also had intellectual and political credentials. Behind it lay not only Negri's extraordinary personal political history, but also a novel engagement with the work of philosophers such as Gilles Deleuze, Félix Guattari, and Michel Foucault. *Empire* was an experimental fusion of Marxist militancy and poststructuralist theory. It circulated novel concepts—biopower, multitude, exodus—amongst students of globalization and its discontents, and, in the process, catalyzed considerable excitement.

It also, however, drew fierce criticism, much of it coming from the left (see Balakrishnan 2003; Passavant and Dean 2004; Boron, 2005). There was, for example, intense debate between theorists of Empire as set out by Hardt and Negri and analysts of imperialism; for many Marxists, the concept of a decentered transnational Empire seriously underestimated the continuing importance of the nation-state for capitalist power (Wood 2003). In particular, it fatally downplayed the importance of US hegemony as a force driving globalization, and, along with this, the continued subordination of the global South to Northern capital (Arrighi 2003; Seth 2003). Thus the idea of multitude, which Hardt and Negri (2000, 60) seemed to propose as a replacement for that of the working-class, was charged with being nebulous and romantic, resting on a rosy confidence in a revolt that would spontaneously self-organize itself from wildly disparate sources (see Laclau, 2004).

Criticisms gained force from the dramatic turn of global politics in 2001. Only a year after the publication of *Empire,* the attack on the World Trade Center and Pentagon, and the subsequent war on terror, appeared to end the very project of corporate globalization of which *Empire* was in many ways an interpretation. The supernationalism of the Bush regime, the Iraq war, and the associated rift between the United States and its European allies, all made the idea of a unified international capitalist regime dubious. The times suddenly seemed more conducive to analyses such as David Harvey's (2005) account of a new imperialism—essentially, a continuation of old imperialisms based on resource-grabs by nationally, and particularly US-based, corporations (see also Chomsky 2003; Lens 2003). The chill of post-9/11 wartime politics also subdued the Seattle-era oppositional optimism to which Hardt and Negri gave voice.

Nonetheless, Hardt and Negri's follow-up to *Empire, Multitude* (2004), more or less reiterated and enlarged on its argument, emphasizing the role of military force in maintaining capitalist order, citing global mobilizations against the Iraq war as an example of the multitude in action, and arguing that the protracted fiasco of the occupation demonstrated "go-it-alone" US unilateralism was, in fact, unsustainable. Five years later, when the third volume of the trilogy, *Commonwealth* appeared, Hardt and Negri's rather defensive tone had changed to a triumphant "I told you so": the ignominious collapse of the Bush administration, Wall Street's financial crisis, the manifest decline of US economic power all suggested that their analysis of Empire had proven correct, while the election of the Obama regime also made it seem possible that the politics of the multitude, in however a refracted and reformist mode, was on the rise again.

THE IMMATERIAL LABOR DEBATE

Within their account of Empire, Hardt and Negri ascribe an especially important place to "immaterial labor" (2000, 289–94). This concept was originally developed within the *Futur Antérieur* group (see Lazzarato 1996; Virno and Hardt 1996), which used the terminology *immaterial labor* to replace Negri's *socialized worker* formulation but continued many of its themes. Immaterial labor is work involving information and communication, "the labor that produces the informational, cultural, or affective element of the commodity" (Virno and Hardt 1996, 262). As commodities come to be "less material," and "more defined by cultural, informational, or knowledge components or by qualities of service and care," so the labor that produces them undergoes a "corresponding" change (Virno and Hardt 1996, 262). Such work is immaterial because it is not primarily about making an object, like the work that makes a car roll off an assembly line, or extracts coal from a mine. Rather, it involves the less tangible symbolic and social dimensions of commodities. Immaterial labor is less about producing things and more about the production of subjectivity, or, better, about the way the production of subjectivity and things are in contemporary capitalism deeply intertwined. It is the "distinctive quality and mark" of work in "the epoch in which information and communication play an essential role in each stage of the process of production" (Lazzarato and Negri 1994, 86).

In *Empire* (2000), Hardt and Negri divide immaterial labor into three subcategories. The first is industrial production "informationalized" by computer and communication technologies; the second is "symbolic analytic" work, involving social coordination and communication; and the third category is work involving the "production and manipulation of affect," the generation of a sense of ease, well-being, satisfaction, excitement or passion: here they stress the importance of female labor, with its traditional burden of "caring" work, as a component of immaterial labor. Immaterial labor is, Hardt and Negri say, the leading or hegemonic form of work in the global capitalism of Empire (2000, 290–94).

In one sense the idea of immaterial labor isn't very original: it is a Marxian mirror image of the knowledge work celebrated by managerial savants, from Peter Drucker through Daniel Bell to Alvin Toffler and Robert Reich, all of whom share a belief that the critical form of labor power in high-technology capital labor is communicational and intellectual. What distinguishes Hardt and Negri's version is that while business futurists see in such immaterial work the salvation of capitalism from its history of class conflict, find a new agent of subversion.

Immaterial labor is, they claim, very difficult for capital to measure and control: much of it depends on aptitudes and skills acquired and exercised outside the formal workplace. It depends on high levels of cooperation amongst workers, cooperation that is often self-organized without much direct managerial supervision. In many cases, it gives workers a do-it-yourself production capability—for example, to make their own media or digital applications. *Futur Antérieur* had suggested that the growing importance of immaterial labor pointed towards the emergence of "general intellect" the socialized, collective intelligence prophesied by Marx in a famous passage known as the "fragment on machines" (1973, 699–743). Hardt and Negri continued in this vein: "In the expression of its own creative energies, immaterial labor...seems provide the potential for a kind of spontaneous and elementary communism" (2000, 294).

Their thesis was inspired by, and struck a chord with, digital activists. The same anti- or alter-globalization movement that was on the streets in Seattle and Genoa was also on the Net, generating indie media centers—examples of autonomous production whose slogan was "Don't hate the media, become the media." Struggles over intellectual property by open-source programmers, creative commons groups, and daily downloaders of digital music also seemed to exemplify capital's problem in containing immaterial labor. The mobilization of a high-technology workforce had called into a being a resistant shadow-world of piracy, free-software and peer-to-peer networks that corroborated Hardt and Negri's assertions about the subversive power of immaterial labor.

If the idea of immaterial labor roused excitement, it also, however, provoked skepticism: indeed, it was probably the single most fiercely criticized element in *Empire* (see Wright 2005; Camfield 2007; Dowling et al. 2007). There were a number of reasons for this. First, immateriality could easily be read as occluding some very corporeal components of high-tech work—digital palsy, repetitive strain injury and carpal tunnel syndrome, eyestrain and radiation hazards, ruptured circadian rhythms, terminal isolation, and workplace epidemics of hyperstress—all of which should surely be included in critique of information capital.

Second, the priority Negri and his collaborators gave immaterial labor seemed to diminish the continued importance in the post-Fordist economy of a vast mass of all-too-physical and material work—domestically, in the service sector, and internationally, in everything from *maquiladora* manufacturing to coffee plantations to the trade in body organs. These omissions could be pointedly related to the fact that the authors of the idea were men located in Europe or North America. The new circuits of capital, it could be argued, look a lot less "immaterial" to the female and Southern workers who do so much of the grueling physical toil demanded by a capitalist "general intellect" whose metropolitan headquarters remain preponderantly male and Northern. George Caffentzis (1998), another autonomist Marxist, accused Negri and his colleagues of celebrating immaterial labor while ignoring the "renaissance of slavery" in the factories, agribusinesses and brothels of the global South; Negri, Caffentzis said, needed to "expand his revolutionary geography."

Third, immaterial labor overlooked differences between the types of labor it treated together. By including information, communication, and affective labor Hardt and Negri conflated within a single category the very different work of say, a network system administrator, a latte-serving *barista* and a sex-worker—laborers for whom conditions and rewards are manifestly different. Again, many of these divisions run along gender lines, with women doing a lot of the low-end affective work in situations very different from that of well paid symbolic analysts (see Dowling 2007; Weeks 2007); while Hardt and Negri cite the abundant feminist work on such emotional labor, it often seem that they've not entirely absorbed the implications in terms of the workforce stratification. This neglect also throws in question the optimistic estimate of emancipatory possibilities of immaterial labor. Even if one looks at digital, online work—arguably the paradigm case of immaterial labor—we can see huge differences between the creative freedom exercised by say, video game designers and the controlled, routinized, and Taylorized conditions of workers in call centers: looking at the latter group, rather than the former, is likely to produce a bleaker analysis of the prospects for digitally self-organized anticapitalist revolt.

Hardt and Negri replied to these criticisms in *Multitude* (2004, 107–15). *Im*-material labor, they said doesn't mean *non*-material; it is, they emphasize, no less corporeal than intellectual, involving both bodies and brains. To critics such as Caffentzis they replied that the ascendancy of immaterial labor is not quantitative—of course not everyone works with computers or in a creative industry—but qualitative: immaterial labor is the activity advanced capital depends on its most dynamic and strategic sectors. When Marx claimed a lead historical role for the industrial proletariat it, too, was a tiny minority of the global workforce that numbered only a few thousands, mostly in Manchester. They acknowledge the segmentations or stratifications in immaterial workers created by the capitalist division of labor, but continue to suggest that it is a new modality of work that has the potential to overflow these stratifications. *Multitude* and *Commonwealth* go to some lengths to show that their analysis covers the struggles of the global poor, not just high-tech dissidents. It is, however, also notable that these works, while not abandoning the idea of immateriality give it less preeminence than it had in Empire. In contrast, an idea that was present in *Empire* but that comes to the fore in the later works is that of "the common."

FROM COMMONS TO COMMONWEALTH

Talk of commons has become, well, common on the left in recent years. The concept is old, going back to the common lands of feudal Europe enclosed in primitive accumulation from the 15th to the 18th centuries, a process then exported around the planet by colonialism, but its revived usage dates back about a decade. Faced by the onrush of privatizing, deregulating, and expropriating neoliberalism, activists and theoreticians in an array of struggles found in image of the common a point of intellectual and affective inspiration. From land wars in Mexico or India to creative commons initiatives of digital culture to attempts to avert ecological calamity resistance to the "second enclosures" of globalized capitalism spoke of itself as a defense of the commons (see Bollier 2002; Nonini 2007). This rediscovery of the commons was important to activists because it provided a way of speaking about collective ownership without invoking a bad history—that is, without immediately conjuring up, and then explaining (away) communism, conventionally understood as command economy plus a repressive state. The term *commons* instead suggested the possibility of thinking about new forms of democratic and participatory control of social and environmental resources.

In *Empire* (2000, 300–302), Hardt and Negri remark that struggles over ownership of commons have been a long-term feature of the rise of capitalism, starting with the enclosure of common lands by early agribusinesses, going on the recreation of new forms of social collective provisions in the welfare state, which are then in turn privatized by neoliberal capital. The latest turn in this spiral is, they say, the conflict between private and collective ownership of information and energy resources:

we participate in a productive world made up of communication and social networks, interactive services and common languages. Our economic and social reality is defined less by the material objects that are made and consumed than by co-produced services and relationships. Producing increasingly means constructing cooperation and communicative commonalities (2000, 302).

The inescapably common basis of communication comes into increasing conflict with the attempt to impose private ownership over these resources, whose actual conditions of production, circulation, and consumption make such efforts "increasingly nonsensical" (2000, 302).

At first, commons were a minor component in Hardt and Negri's work, but it became increasingly important. In 2008 Negri and another colleague, Cesare Casarino, published a book of essays and conversations entitled *In Praise of the Common*. In *Commonwealth* (2009) the common becomes the centerpiece of Hardt and Negri's argument for "the need to institute and manage a world of commonwealth, focusing on and expanding our capacities for collective production and self-government" (xiii) Philosophically, the common as a category grasps "a certain social generality," as conveyed by terms such as "common sense" or "common knowledge" (2009, 121). This is, however, a sociability that is naturally given but is, rather, always produced in collective practice, so that one is dealing not with a natural state of "being in common" but with an ongoing process of "making the common" (123). Institutionally, the common signals participative, democratic, distributed governance, an alternative to both the capitalist concept of private ownership and the state ownership that has defined "socialism":

The political project of instituting the common…cuts diagonally across these false alternatives—neither private nor public, neither capitalist nor socialist—and opens a new space for politics (ix).

The "collective production of the common" is, Hardt and Negri say, both "an intervention in the current relations of force aimed at subverting the dominant powers," and an "alternative production of subjectivity" (2009, 126–27).

Commons struggles involve both "natural common"—"embedded in the material elements of land, minerals, water and gas"—and "artificial common" that "resides in languages, images, knowledges, affects, codes, habits and practices" (250). A key site of the "artificial commons" is the city, the metropolis, with all the many struggles around private property, gentrification, public space and activities (249–60); such struggles have, it might be added, reached an exceptional intensity with the burst of the US housing bubble and the wave of foreclosures and evictions, and resistance to these events.

A central place in Hardt and Negri's idea of a new society based on commons continues, however, to be allotted to issues of communication. As they put it in one of their most lucid formulations, "People don't need bosses at work. They need an expanding web of others with whom to communicate and collaborate; the boss is increasingly an obstacle to getting work done" (Hardt and Negri 2009, 353). It is in the development of new means of communication—and, crucially, in all the social and subjective aptitudes

that come with this—that they see the possibility for the development of highly participatory and democratic forms of governance. They acknowledge that these hopes may
seem utopian, and that early writings on the topic sometimes generate hopeful myths—
such as "that the transparency of networks is always good, and that the cybernetic swarm
is always intelligent" (357). Nonetheless, they say, "experience with network technologies has…led to the development of novel decision-making processes characterized by
multiplicity and interactivity;

Whereas the old socialist elites used to dream of a "decision-making machine," the experience of
networkers and net users have configured an institutional decision-making composed of a myriad
of micropolitical paths (2009, 358).

Already in *Empire* (Hardi and Negri 2000), they had sketched out some of the elements
they thought would constitute a society beyond capital—including the abolition of
border restrictions on the mobility of labor, a "social wage," and the democratic control,
or "reappropriation" of science and technology (Hardi and Negri 2000, 396–407). Now
they suggest three "platforms" for a "commonwealth" (Hardi and Negri 2009, 380–82).
The first is "[a] global guaranteed income and basic health care." The second is planetary provision of "[b]asic education, and a series of basic social and technical knowledges and skills" to ensure "equality against hierarchy, allowing everyone to become
capable of participating in the constitution of society…something like a global citizenship…which provides both the means and the opportunity to participate equally in the
government of global society" (Hardi and Negri 2009, 380–82). The third component is
"access to commons"—in particular, to various forms of information commons:

Governments must support, in particular, the accumulation of knowledge, scientific knowledges
and codes, of course, which are increasingly central in production, but also social knowledges and
skills, the means of avoiding social conflicts and facilitating felicitous encounters, the means of
promoting productive encounters and exchange (Hardi and Negri 2009, 381–82).

These three platforms are, they suggest, the building blocks for a society that avoids
the catastrophes of both capitalism and socialism, and for "instituting happiness"
(2009, 376).

NEGRI AND LIBRARY AND INFORMATION SCIENCE

Negri's work has attracted attention not only from political and sociological theorists
but from media activists and scholars. A decade ago, I suggested that his discussions of
communication could be seen as a counter to concepts both of an information society
that that transcended class divisions, and also of left pessimism about inevitable corporate media dominance (Dyer-Witheford 1999). Other authors have developed this argument; for example, Jason Soderberg (2008), in his recent examination of the Free and
Open Source Movement, says that the history of hacking and the computer underground
validates Negri's idea that struggle and dissent drive innovation—making capital dependent on the resistances it provokes—and generate new forms of class struggle focused
around control of information.

The use of Negri's ideas within LIS scholarship, in a strict sense, has, however, been
limited. Ronald Day (2002) invokes Negri's work to argue that the rise of the discipline

of Knowledge Management as a "prescriptive management and consulting discourse" aimed at "'mining,' 'tapping,' or 'capturing' of socially produced skills and affects" (2002, 1075) is symptomatic of the subsumption or envelopment of life by capital, and the growing corporate need to capture the dimensions of productivity that arise outside the formal workplace, as properties of "general intellect." More recently, I have attempted to analyze librarians increasing interest in virtual worlds such as *Second Life* by using the *operaismo* concept of cycles of struggle to describe the various phases of subversion and commodification in the short, fast history of the Internet (Dyer-Witheford 2008). These are, however, rare exceptions.

There are reasons for this neglect: Negri's work is politically militant, suffers in translation, and is extravagantly abstract in a way that infuriates empiricists. Nonetheless, there are three interlinked aspects of Negri's thought that should be of interest to LIS scholars.

The first is his rethinking of the conditions of labor in a capitalist order saturated by information technologies and communicative practice. The idea of immaterial labor (along with its predecessors, the socialized worker) is an account of changing conditions of labor that speaks directly to librarians and informational professionals. Despite its sometimes hyperbolic formulation (see Dyer-Witheford 2001; 2005), Hardt and Negri's account of immaterial work as a new mode of cooperative practice with both technological and affective dimensions is significant. One has only to think of the situation of, say, a reference librarian helping a patron with a query while using search engines and data banks, or a Web design consultant trying to help a client publicize her enterprise, to see a convincing example immaterial labor at work.

Second, Negri offers an analysis both of the positive, emancipatory possibilities offered by these developments and the obstacles that often block their realization. Unlike many left academics, he does not see in new information technologies only instruments of domination, but rather opportunities for human self-development that, however, constantly come into conflict with commodification, managerial control, and, particularly, capitalism's infatuation with intellectual property. His work thus speaks to activist scholars engaged in movements such as free and open-source software, creative commons licenses and other forms of "copyleft," open-access publication and democratic and participatory media.

Third, by placing these issues in the context of a larger conflict between Empire and multitude, and linking the idea of an information commons to other experiments in other types of ecological and social commons, Negri provides an audacious and hopeful horizon for thinking about how work in librarianship and information science can contribute to wider, systemic initiatives for a more equalitarian and secure world, perhaps even a world beyond capital.

REFERENCES

Arrighi, Giovanni. 2003. "Lineages of Empire." In *Debating Empire,* ed. Gopal Balakrishnan, 29–43. London: Verso.

Balakrishnan, Gopal, ed. 2003. *Debating Empire.* London: Verso.

Balestrini, Nanni. 1989. *The Unseen.* London: Verso.

Bollier, David. 2002. *Silent Theft: The Private Plunder of Our Common Wealth.* New York: Routledge.

Boron, Atilio. 2005. *Empire and Imperialism: A Critical Reading of Michael Hardt and Antonio Negri.* London: Zed Books.

Boyle, James. 2003. *The Second Enclosure Movement and the Construction of the Public Domain.* Duke Law School Public Law and Legal Theory Research Paper Series. Research Paper (53, December).

Caffentzis, George. 1998. "The End of Work or the Renaissance of Slavery? A Critique of Rifkin and Negri." Paper presented at the *Globalization from Below Conference,* Duke University, Feb 6. Available at http://www.ecn.org/finlandia/autonomia/theend.txt

Camfield, David. 2007. "The Multitude and the Kangaroo: A Critique of Hardt and Negri's Theory of Immaterial Labor." *Historical Materialism* 15:21–52.

Casarino, Cesare, and Antonio Negri. 2008. *In Praise of the Common.* Minneapolis: University of Minnesota Press.

Cleaver, Harry. 1977. *Reading Capital Politically.* Brighton, UK: Harvester.

Dalla Costa, Mariarosa, and Selma James. 1972. *The Power of Women and the Subversion of the Community.* Bristol, UK: Falling Wall Press.

Day, Ronald E. 2002. "Social Capital, Value and Measure: Antonio Negri's Challenge to Capitalism." *Journal of the American Society for Information Science and Technology* 53 (12): 1074–82.

Dowling, Emma. 2007. "Producing the Dining Experience: Measure, Subjectivity and the Affective Worker." *Ephemera* 7 (1), 117–32.

Dowling, Emma, Rodrigo Nunes, and Ben Trott, eds. 2007. Issue on "Immaterial and Affective Labor: Explored." *Ephemera* 7 (1).

Dyer-Witheford, Nick. 1999. *Cyber-Marx: Cycles and Circuits of Struggle in High-Technology Capitalism.* Urbana: University of Illinois Press.

Dyer-Witheford, Nick. 2001. "Empire, Immaterial Labor, the New Combinations, and the Global Worker." *Rethinking Marxism* 13 (3–4): 70–80.

Dyer-Witheford, Nick. 2005. "Cyber-Negri: General Intellect and Immaterial Labor." In *Resistance in Practice: The Philosophy of Antonio Negri,* ed. Timothy S. Murphy and Abdul-Karim Mustapha, 136–62. London: Pluto Press.

Dyer-Witheford, Nick. 2009. "Cycles of Net Struggle, Lines of Net Flight." In *Information Technology in Librarianship: New Critical Approaches,* ed. Gloria J. Leckie and John Buschman, 136–62. Westport, CT: Libraries Unlimited.

Eakin, Emily. 2001. "What Is the Next Big Idea? The Buzz is Growing." *New York Times,* July 7. http://www.nytimes.com/.

Foucault, Michel. 1990. *The History of Sexuality: Volume 1: An Introduction.* New York: Vintage.

Hardt, Michael, and Antonio Negri. 2000. *Empire.* Cambridge, MA: Harvard University Press.

Hardt, Michael, and Antonio Negri. 2004. *Multitude: War and Democracy in the Age of Empire.* New York: Penguin.

Hardt, Michael, and Antonio Negri. 2009. *Commonwealth.* Cambridge, MA: Belknap/Harvard University Press.

Harvey, David. 2005. *The New Imperialism.* Oxford: Polity.

Laclau, Ernesto. 2004. "Can Immanence Explain Social Struggles?" In *Empire's New Clothes: Reading Hardt and Negri,* ed. Paul A. Passavant and Jodi Dean, 21–30. London: Routledge.

Lazzarato, Maurizio. 1996. "Immaterial Labor." In *Radical Thought in Italy Today,* ed. Paolo Virno and Michael Hardt, 133–47. Minneapolis: University of Minnesota Press.

Lazzarato, Maurizio, and Toni Negri. 1994. "Travail immatérial et subjectivité." *Futur Antérieur* 6: 86.

Lotringer, Sylvère, and Christian Marazzi, eds. 1980. *Italy: Autonomia—Post-Political Politics.* New York: Semiotext(e).

Mallet, Serge. 1975. *Essays on the New Working Class.* St. Louis: Telos.

Marchand, Marie. 1988. *The Minitel Saga.* Larousse: Paris.

Marx, Karl. 1973 [1858]. *Grundrisse.* London: Penguin.

Mertes, T., ed. 2004. *A Movement of Movements: Is Another World Really Possible?* London: Verso.

Negri, Antonio. 1980. *Del Obrero-Masa al Obrero Social.* Barcelona: Editorial Anagrama.

Negri, Antonio. 1984. *Marx Beyond Marx: Lessons on the Grundrisse.* South Hadley, MA: Bergin and Garvey.

Negri, Antonio. 1988. *Revolution Retrieved: Selected Writings on Marx, Keynes, Capitalist Crisis and New Social Subjects.* London: Red Notes.

Negri, Antonio. 1989. *The Politics of Subversion: A Manifesto for the Twenty-First Century.* Cambridge, UK: Polity.

Negri, Antonio. 1992. Luttes sociales et control systémique." *Futur Antérieur* 9: 15–20.

Negri, Antonio. 1991. *The Savage Anomaly: The Power of Spinoza's Metaphysics and Politics.* Minneapolis: University of Minnesota Press.

Negri, Antonio. 2005. *Books for Burning: Between Civil War and Democracy in 1970s.* Ed. Timothy S. Murphy. London: Verso.

Nonini, Donald. M., ed. 2002. *The Global Idea of the Commons.* New York: Berghahn.

Notes from Nowhere. 2003. *We Are Everywhere: The Irresistible Rise of Global Anticapitalism.* London: Verso.

Passavant, Paul A., and Jodi Dean, eds. 2004. *Empire's New Clothes: Reading Hardt and Negri.* London: Routledge.

Seth, Sanjay. 2003. "Back to the Future." In *Debating Empire,* ed. Gopal Balakrishnan, 43–51. London: Verso.

Soderberg, Johan. 2008. *Hacking Capitalism: The Free and Open Source Software Movement.* New York: Routledge.

Virno, Paolo, and Michael Hardt, eds. 1996. *Radical Thought in Italy: A Potential Politics.* Minneapolis: University of Minnesota Press.

Weeks, Kathi. 2007. "Life within and against Work: Affective Labor, Feminist Critique, and Post-Fordist Politics." *Ephemera* 7 (1): 233–49.

Wood, Ellen Meiksins. 2003. "A Manifesto for Global Capital?" In *Debating Empire,* ed. Gopal Balakrishnan, 61–82. London: Verso.

Wright, Steve. 2002. *Storming Heaven: Class Composition and Struggle in Italian Autonomist Marxism.* London: Pluto.

Wright, Steve. 2005. "Reality Check: Are We Living in an Immaterial World?" *Mute* 2 (1) URL: http://www.metamute.org/node/417

Wright, Steve. 2008. "Mapping the Pathways within Italian Autonomist Marxism: A Preliminary Survey." *Historical Materialism* 16, 111–40.

Žižek, Slavoj. 2001. "Have Michael Hardt and Antonio Negri Rewritten the Communist Manifesto for the Twenty-First Century?" *Rethinking Marxism* 13 (3): 190–98.

21

Ferdinand de Saussure: Duality

Paul Solomon
University of South Carolina, USA

INTRODUCTION

I was first inspired by Saussure's work in the mid-1980s as I began graduate study in library and information science (LIS). I was challenged to wonder how the various tools of the information field (e.g., indexes, thesauruses, classifications systems) helped or hindered people as they negotiated the tangle of information systems, databases, and the like to extract the "stuff" maintained by these systems and databases. I happened across the fundamental distinction made by Saussure between *langue* and *parole*. While my sense of this distinction, which involved the difference or separation between the abstraction of the formal structure of language and richness of language in use, was somewhat naïve and probably off from that intended by Saussure, this was a crystallizing distinction for me. At the time I was struggling with the "gaps" (Dervin 2003) between the formalizations or structures provided by LIS and the understandings provided by people as they move through life and work.

I offer this background because Saussure's contributions are likely to influence those who encounter and use them in different ways in the course of their intellectual development. In my case the *langue* and *parole* distinction provided a springboard for considering the value and utility of linguistic formalizations and tools for understanding the pragmatic and discourse aspects of conversations in information seeking contexts (Solomon 1997). Yet, my use of Saussure simply involved the contrast suggested by these two terms (i.e., *langue* and *parole*) and was not based on a deep and extensive analysis of the work attributed to Saussure. (In fact, Saussure [1959] paid only minor attention to *parole* in comparison to *langue*.) Thus, in this case my intellectual debt was less about understanding and comprehension than interpretation and application. It seems to me that this approach of contrasting understanding, comprehension, interpretation, and application provides a point of departure for approaching, in general, the role of language in library and information science, and more specifically, Saussure's contributions to such.

Beyond the information field, I have been struck by the wide variance in viewpoint and interpretation of what has been presented as Saussure's ideas related particularly to linguistics and semiotics/*sémiologie*. I find much of the commentary puzzling in that it seems to judge Saussure's ideas without consideration of such facts as Saussure himself has not directly contributed to the development of linguistics and semiotics since at least 1913, when he died at the age of 55, and that these contributions were not put into publishable form by Saussure, himself. Beaugrande, for example, suggests that Saussure's work, along with other structuralists, was "seriously misguided in their projects to make linguistics into a formal science by disconnecting language from its discursive, cognitive, and social functions" (1997, 89). As Beaugrande has made noteworthy contributions to text linguistics and the study of discourse, I take his comments in a positive sense of seeing Saussure's elaborations on general linguistics, written or delivered before 1913, as not necessarily fitting with Beaugrande's contemporary views on linguistics. Ricoeur (1976) sees Saussure as focusing on *langue* to the relative exclusion of *parole*. While *parole* is hardly mentioned in the *Cours de linguistique générale* (CLG) (Gordon 2004), I wonder if this lack of development is less about interest and importance in Saussure's mind than Saussure's early death as he clearly saw *langue* and *parole* in the context of *langage*/language. From another point of view, Thibault (1997) suggests that *parole* may be an instantiation of *langue* and not in opposition to it. My own view is that Saussure's contributions provide a foundation for consideration of the duality (or complementarity) (Gordon 2004) between *langue* and *parole,* similar to Giddens' (1984) duality of structure and action.

Given this backdrop regarding my discovery and continued use of Saussure's duality, the rest of the paper provides further background for interpretation of Saussure's contributions through a biographical note, an outline of those of Saussure's intellectual contributions that are in my view of most significance for LIS, and a summary of the use of Saussure's ideas in information science.

BIOGRAPHICAL NOTE

Saussure was born in Geneva, Switzerland, on November 26, 1857 and died on February 22, 1913. He was something of a prodigy as he became interested in comparative Indo-European linguistics in his early teen years and produced an essay that has been characterized as both naïve and lacking in sound conclusions (Davies 2004). Yet, this work showed a "clarity of argumentation and…professional" writing style (Davies 2004). Saussure continued to learn various languages and began to produce short articles following this initial contribution. During 1878, his 21st year, Saussure produced his only book-length work. This was titled in English, *Memoir on the Original System of Vowels in the Indo-European Languages.* This work received general acclaim and provided a foundation and impetus for the method of comparative linguistics. The *Mémoire* and his doctoral dissertation, which focused on the use of the genitive absolute in Sanskrit—completed in 1880 and published in 1881—established his reputation among his contemporaries as a linguist of the first rank, which carried over during the remainder of his life, though these are not the works for which he is typically remembered today.

The work for which Saussure is most known today is the *Course in General Linguistics* (1959). This work was originally published in 1916 as the *Cours de linguistique générale* and is often referred to by its initials CLG. It is important to note that the CLG in any of its forms—there are several versions complied by various people—does not necessarily contain Saussure's actual words. Rather, the CLG is an amalgam of the lecture notes of students in a series of three courses that he offered at the University of Geneva, with an apparently minimal contribution of lecture notes from Saussure, which were reportedly largely incomprehensible (Davies 2004), as input. It is also reported that Saussure undertook these lectures on general linguistics as part of his contract as professor of linguistics at the University of Geneva—the implication being that his assignment to lecture on general linguistics led him to bring together the ideas of his contemporaries on general linguistics as he developed his own ideas and approach to their expression.

Ultimately, two contemporaries of Saussure, C. Bally and A. Sechehaye, undertook the task of bringing together these lecture notes from students and Saussure to create the first edition of the CLG. Bally and Sechehaye were well regarded linguists in their own right and it is said that, particularly in the case of Sechehaye, who was also a student of Saussure's, that there was likely an interchange of ideas with Saussure prior to his passing. Engler (2004) notes the likelihood that some of the ideas presented by Saussure in the three courses actually came from Sechehaye, possibly as clarifications or elaborations, either as contributions to Saussure's thinking prior to his death, or as a means of bridging the scant expression of ideas in the various lecture notes of students and in Saussure's own pieces of writing. There were at least two other attempts to bring together the evidence of Saussure's ideas on general linguistics, which did not occur until the late 1960s and early 1970s, by R. Engler and T. de Mauro. Davies (2004), Sanders (2004), and Engler (2004) provide additional details and interpretation of Saussure's intellectual development and place in relation to the linguists who were his contemporaries. It is worth noting that additional pieces of Saussure's work were found in 1996 at the Saussure family home in Geneva, including "the substantial outline of a book on general linguistics" (Saussure 2006, xvi). These newly found contributions appear in *Writings in General Linguistics* (Saussure 2006). Scholars are still making sense of these belated contributions and their influence on library and information science remains to be seen.

THEORETICAL CONTRIBUTIONS

Epistemology, Philosophy, and Social Science of Language

Saussure engaged in a critique of the necessary conditions of the study of comparative grammar, particularly historical phonetics (or the development and evolution of sound patterns) across (Indo-European) languages. Saussure's efforts to bring attention to the development or evolution of language, particularly with his attention to comparisons across various languages, is a significant contribution to social science methodology that led to important theoretical developments in diachronic linguistics, while continuing to mine structures in synchronic linguistics. Thus, his contributions to understanding human meaning systems involved both a philosophical vein in the tradition of the times, but also introduced a social science approach to the study of language. It is perhaps from this line that Saussure earned the name of Father of Linguistics.

Sémiologie (Semiotics)

Both epistemology and the combined philosophical/social science approach to the study of language seem to have provided a foundation for Saussure's contributions towards the development of a social science of signs, which he labeled *sémiologie*.

Saussure, along with Charles Sanders Peirce, is frequently mentioned as laying the foundation for the development of semiotics as a domain of study. Saussure never published any work on *sémiologie* and the kernels of his ideas were presented in his lectures and correspondence (Bouissac 2004). Thus, he provided a foundation upon which others built. Saussure and Peirce seem to have followed somewhat parallel paths, which converged in the years following their deaths—Peirce in 1914. While Saussure offered the term *semiology* (*sémiologie*), Peirce preferred the term *semiotics* and his choice of terminology seems to have passed the test of time (Pankow 1995).

Sign: Signifier and Signified

In focusing on semiotics, Peirce, taking a philosophical approach, began with consideration of the cooperation between three subjects: a *sign,* its *objects,* and its *interpretant* as a means of studying the action or influence of signs or symbols of various sorts. While Peirce's ideas regarding the nature of signs and symbols evolved over many years beyond his ideas surrounding this initial triadic relation, Saussure's notions underlying his call for a science of semes—sémiologie—are largely confined to those reported in CLG and other materials, which were not found and published until long after his death (Saussure 2006).

Saussure contributed a dualistic notion of signs by relating the *signifier,* as the form of the word or phrase uttered, to the *signified* as the mental concept (Joseph 2004). It is important to note that, according to Saussure, the sign is completely arbitrary: that is, there was no necessary connection between the sign and its meaning, except through the arbitrary mapping of a particular language at a particular time. Words stand as expressions of content. The borrowing of words across languages seems to support Saussure's observation of the signifier/signified relationship.

The arbitrariness of the sign seems fundamental to Saussure's distinction between *langue* and *parole.* Beyond Saussure's structural view, he also recognized and studied language change. Thus, his interest in the sign recognized historical and social change as dimensions of the study of language as a whole (Joseph 2004). Further, his structuralist description of language through components of various sorts was done with the overriding view of language as a system, which formally recognized its arbitrariness, values, and differences (Alasuutari 1995; Normand 2004).

Syntagmatic and Paradigmatic (Associative) Meaning Relationships

Another of Saussure's contributions of interest in LIS involves his distinction between syntagmatic, which involves positioning that is internal to a text (intratextuality), and paradigmatic (Saussure called these associative relationships), which involves substitution that is external to the text (intertextuality). Together they provide a structural context for signs creating meaning through interactions and associations. Green (1995) explicates the importance of the syntagmatic/paradigmatic distinction with particular attention to the syntagmatic for library and information science.

USES RELATED TO INFORMATION SCIENCE

It is intriguing that Saussure's influence has continued on long after his death as the influence of many of the greats—Jesse Shera, Patrick Wilson, Lester Asheim, and

Lawrence Heilprin, among others—of the information field seems to have waned. This section highlights the ways in which Saussure continues to influence or at least cause pause in the thinking of scholars of the information field.

With regard to causing pause, Saussure's ideas as expressed in the CLG have provided a foil for considering related ideas. Most recently, Campbell (2009) considers language versus discourse as vehicles for supporting advances in knowledge organization. He builds his argument on a consideration of Ricoeur's (1976) critique of Saussure's emphasis on *langue* and the impact of that emphasis in blinding linguistic theorists to the important role of *parole*. Campbell highlights Ricoeur's emphasis on semantics over semiotics in focusing on acts of organization over standards and tools (among other contributions).

Mai (1997; 2001) considers Saussure's ideas related to semiology in relation to those of Pierce's semiotics as a means of understanding subject indexing or, more generally, the subject matter of digital documents as an interpretative process. While Mai emphasizes Pierce's triadic view of signs (sign, referent, meaning derived from the sign) over Saussure's two-sided view (expression and content), he suggests that Pierce's theory may be supplemented by Saussure's.

Hjørland (2000; 2002) too mentions Saussure's ideas as both influential in considering meaning and as blocking, along with other structuralist approaches, consideration of domain-based approaches such as Language for Special Purposes (LSP).

Chalmers (1999) charts a course in the development of linguistics from positivism to the structuralist influences of and promotion of semiotics by Saussure and on to poststructuralist influences of the development of such views as hermeneutics. He uses this foundation as a means of conceptually comparing different approaches to information access.

In some sense, Campbell, Mai, and Hjørland's use of Saussure is to point out apparent deficiencies in his ideas or approach as expressed in the CLG or in their interpretation and use of others with respect to the problems of knowledge organization that they are interested in. Chalmers' exposition seems to take a more matter of fact approach by recognizing Saussure's contributions as a link in a chain of intellectual development. Bourdieu (1973) indicates that his ideas with regard to *habitus* are based in the contributions of a number of scholars including Saussure, especially commenting on the importance of Saussure's *langue/parole* distinction in language as structure and language as practice.

Whatever the point of view, Saussure's work continues to have the power of influencing contemporary thinking about the role of discourse, subject analysis, indexing, access, and other such concerns with respect to addressing problems of identifying meaning, which are fundamental in the information field. This statement seems to capture the spirit of Derrida's ideas regarding deconstruction or *différance,* which allow picking and choosing the resulting pieces of the puzzle to create new approaches (Bennington 2004).

Beniger's (1988) citation analysis, from several points of view, suggests that, at least through the mid-1980s, Saussure, along with other structuralists, have had a major impact on the development of the communication and information fields. Pettigrew and McKechnie (2001) also mention Saussure (semiotics) as one of the humanities theorists who have been used in library and information science research.

STRUCTURALISM

Radford and Radford (2005) focus on Saussure's contributions from a structuralist point of view (by way of the CLG), and Michel Foucault's contributions, from a poststructuralist point of view. Through their consideration of the contributions of these two theorists, the authors focus on ways of conceptualizing the role of the library. The authors view Saussure's contribution as involving the identification of a variety of elements that together comprise the whole of language. These elements create a system, where the value of any one element depends on the others. They note that meaning through language is created by patterns and not by a correspondence between a thing and its label. Radford and Radford see Foucault's poststructuralist view of language as continuing the consideration of the organizing principles of language with a shift from an objective scientific view of language to one that takes note of the place of context in the creation of meaning. Meanings become contingent on the arbitrary configurations of signs in contrast to some independent reference point.

Radford and Radford meld Saussure's structuralist view with Foucault's poststructualist views to create something new that highlights the evolution of thinking on language as a vehicle for helping people make sense of their worlds. While Saussure focused on *signs,* Foucault emphasized discursive formations, which highlight configurations or regularities in concrete items present as humans communicate. This view embraces the cumulative nature of science as it recognizes that seemingly disparate contributions may offer a deeper understanding of the social phenomena related to language in theory and in use. Thus, Saussure propelled us forward in our understanding of language by highlighting structural elements (e.g., sign), while others (e.g., Foucault) have been enabled to move beyond abstract structure per se to concrete understandings of language in use as a generator for communication and the creation of meaning in context. Building on this basis, Radford and Radford lead us to an understanding that libraries (and other information institutions) are not mere storehouses, but generators of knowledge through the connections in support of communication and meaning generation that they enable.

DISCOURSE ANALYSIS, SEMIOTICS, AND INFORMATION SCIENCE

Budd and Raber (1996) and Raber and Budd (2003) are works rich in the integration of Saussure's ideas into the fabric of LIS. Saussure is something of a tipping point in these articles as his distinctions—*langue/parole,* synchrony/diachrony, syntagm/paradigm, and semiotics/the sign—all shape the views of communication, information, and their interactions into the beginnings of a system for viewing the challenges and solutions of library and information science.

Saussure, for the most part, has been criticized for neglecting the pragmatic/discourse aspects of language. In contrast, Budd and Raber develop Saussure's ideas regarding *parole* to show the applicability of his work to the pragmatic aspects of library and information science. Budd and Raber (1996) suggest that: "Probably the most notable pioneer is de Saussure..., who posited a distinction between language (*langue*) as a collective and abstract entity, and speaking (*parole*) as an individual use of language for communication purposes" (219). Speakers seldom possess the full range of knowledge of the structure of language implied by use of the term *langue.* The authors suggest that the important contribution of Saussure is stimulation of the difference between language and speech. The challenge for LIS is bridging the gap between the formalities of structured information storage and retrieval languages (e.g., index languages, subject headings, metadata elements) and the ways people use discourse to communicate among themselves and with information systems.

Raber and Budd (2001) consider information as sign as a means of considering "information" as a thing versus information as culturally contextualized. In particular, they point out that: "Both semiotics and information science are concerned with the nature of the relations between content and its representation, between signifier and signified, between reference and referent, and between information objects and their meaning" (507). These pairings begin to elucidate the challenges that we face whenever we construct something of an idealized nature (i.e., an information system) for use within the context of the everyday discourse of work and life. The term *information* muddles our understanding as it is a word, which takes on new shapes as it is considered from different points of view: speech/thought, text/content, and so forth. Yet, information also unites speech with thought, text with content, and so on. They suggest that Saussure's idea of a sign with its signified/signifier distinction may lead to a clearer understanding of what information may be.

Ultimately, information is made up of signs. Recognizing that the sign and its element language are carriers of information, Raber and Budd build an argument for applying Saussure's work to information and its use, noting the importance of contextualization in supporting the creation of meaning that is fundamental to informing. In part, context is syntagmatically shaped at the moment of creation of something that has the potential of being informing. Context is also paradigmatically shaped by relations of intertextuality.

Bouquet's (2004) comments on the unfinished aspects of Saussure's work seem to round out Raber and Budd's exposition. In particular, Bouquet provides numerous examples of Saussure's concern for the discursive element in language as he notes how the compilers of the first CLG (Bally and Sechehaye) chose to substitute their words for Saussure's in response, for example, to a student's question on the *langue/parole* distinction. Overall, Bouquet makes a compelling argument for Saussure's interest in the interplay of *langue* and *parole* with regard to the intentionality of a speaker in discourse.

CONCLUSION

There is a subtle thread underlying the presentation above related to Ferdinand de Saussure that needs to be highlighted as part of his contribution, in particular, to LIS. This has to do with the challenges that his work, taken as a case of interest to library and information science, presents through the information life cycle—from creation through representation, storage, and retrieval. While all of Saussure's work is related to linguistics, his contributions are varied: from comparative linguistics and phonology to general linguistics and *sémiologie*. His work, though connected by his attention to the sign, varies from the detail of vowels to other aspects of language that connect an utterance to meaning. There is the variety of types of publications containing his ideas, from those written by his own hand in his own words to those that were in some sense given life by his (several) interpreters. There is the existence of incomplete papers and manuscripts as well as student class notes and fragmentary class notes. There is the hermeneutic problem of interpreting what are presented as Saussure's writings without the benefit of an understanding of the context in which they were written. This also suggests issues related to changes in the social, technical, and physical world that surrounds us as time marches on. It is difficult to make sense the mass of his work as it is available today without imposing some relatively arbitrary context or point of view. The case of Ferdinand de Saussure seems a challenge that information science has not faced, though in a digital world with many more pieces of people's lives seemingly being preserved in digital repositories of various sorts, this challenge of contextualization will only intensify.

At this point in time, Saussure seems more of a symbol—a sign?—than a man, whose distinctions, methods, and the substance that holds them together, are clearly represented and understood. In the way of the world, there are those who praise him and those who do not. Yet, through either of these extremes of praise or criticism (or in between), the fundamental distinctions that *he* has left us as his legacy (e.g., *langue/parole,* synchrony/diachrony, synatagmatic/paradigmatic, the sign and the signifier/signified) are bedrocks among the sands of time, providing a foundation for dualities related to semiotics, language, and information science that are yet to come (Koerner 1971).

REFERENCES

Alasuutari, Pertti. 1995. *Researching Culture: Qualitative Method and Cultural Studies.* London: Sage.

Beaugrande, Robert-Alain de. 1997. "On History and Historicity in Modern Linguistics: Formalism vs. Functionalism Revisited." *Functions of Language* 4: 169–213. Available at http://www.beaugrande.com/History.htm

Beniger, James R. 1988. "Information and Communication: The New Convergence." *Communication Research* 15: 198–218.

Bennington, Geoffrey. 1995. "Saussure and Derrida." In *The Cambridge Companion to Saussure,* ed. Carol Sanders, 186–202. Cambridge: Cambridge University Press.

Bouissac, Paul. 2004. "Saussure's Legacy in Semiotics." In *The Cambridge Companion to Saussure,* ed. Carol Sanders, 240–60. Cambridge: Cambridge University Press.

Bourdieu, Pierre. 1973. "The Three Forms of Theoretical Knowledge." *Social Science Information* 12:53–80.

Bouquet, Simon. 2004. "Saussure's Unfinished Semantics." In *The Cambridge Companion to Saussure,* ed. Carol Sanders, 205–18. Cambridge: Cambridge University Press.

Budd, John, and Douglas Raber. 1996. "Discourse Analysis: Method and Application in the Study of Information." *Information Processing and Management* 32:217–26.

Campbell, D. Grant. 2009. "Tensions between Language and Discourse in North American Knowledge Organization." In *Proceedings 2009 North American Symposium on Knowledge Organization* Vol. 2, ed. Elin K. Jacob and Barbara Kwasnik, 10–16. Syracuse, NY: North American Symposium on Knowledge Organization. Available at http://dlist.sir.arizona.edu/2627

Chalmers, Matthew. 1999. "Comparing Information Access Approaches." *Journal of the American Society for Information Science* 50:1108–18.

Davies, Anna M. 2004. "Saussure and Indo-European Linguistics." In *The Cambridge Companion to Saussure,* ed. Carol Sanders, 9–29. Cambridge: Cambridge University Press.

Dervin, Brenda. 2003. "Sense-Making's Journey from Metatheory to Methodology to Method: An Example Using Information Seeking and Use as Research Focus." In *Sense-Making Methodology Reader: Selected Writings of Brenda Dervin,* ed. B. Dervin and L. Foreman-Wernet, 133–64. Cresskill, NJ: Hampton Press.

Engler, Rudolf. 2004. "The Making of the *Cours de linguistique générale.*" In *The Cambridge Companion to Saussure,* ed. Carol Sanders, 47–58. Cambridge: Cambridge University Press.

Giddens, Anthony. 1984. *The Constitution of Society: Outline of the Theory of Structuration.* Berkeley: University of California Press.

Gordon, W. Terrence. 2004. "Langue and Parole." In *The Cambridge Companion to Saussure,* ed. Carol Sanders, 76–87. Cambridge: Cambridge University Press.

Green, Rebecca. 1995. "Syntagmatic Relationships in Index Languages: A Reassessment." *Library Quarterly* 65:365–85.

Hjørland, Birger. 2000. "Documents, Memory Institutions and Information Science." *Journal of Documentation* 56:27–41.

Hjørland, Birger. 2002. "Domain Analysis in Information Science: Eleven Approaches— Traditional as Well as Innovative." *Journal of Documentation* 58:422–62.

Joseph, John E. 2004. "The Linguistic Sign." In *The Cambridge Companion to Saussure,* ed. Carol Sanders, 59–75. Cambridge: Cambridge University Press.

Koerner, Ernst Frideryk Konrad. 1971. "Ferdinand de Saussure: Origin and Development of his Linguistic Thought in Western Studies of Language: A Critical Evaluation of the Evolution of Saussurean Principles and their Relevance to Contemporary Linguistic Theories." PhD diss., Simon Fraser University. Available at http://ir.lib.sfu.ca/ bitstream/1892/4637/1/b11119603.pdf.

Mai, Jens-Erik. 1997. "The Concept of Subject in a Semiotic Light." In *Digital Collections: Implications for Users, Funders, Developers and Maintainers. Proceedings of the ASIS Annual Meeting* 34:54–64.

Mai, Jens-Erik. 2001. "Semiotics and Indexing: An Analysis of the Subject Indexing Process." *Journal of Documentation* 57 (5): 591–622.

Normond, Claudine. 2004. "System, Arbitrariness, Value." In *The Cambridge Companion to Saussure,* ed. Carol Sanders, 88–104. Cambridge: Cambridge University Press.

Pankow, Christiane. 1995. "Semiotics." In *Handbook of Pragmatics,* compiled by Jef Verschueren, Jan-Ola Östman, Jan Blommaert, and Chris Bulcaen, 469–76. Amsterdam: John Benjamins.

Peirce, Charles S. 1931. *Collected Papers of Charles Sanders Peirce.* Cambridge, MA: Harvard University Press.

Pettigrew, Karen E., and Lynne (E. F.) McKechnie. 2001. "The Use of Theory in Information Science Research." *Journal of the American Society for Information Science and Technology* 52:62–73.

Raber, Douglas, and John Budd. 2002. "Information as Sign: Semiotics and Information Science." *Journal of Documentation* 58: 507–22.

Radford, Gary P., and Marie L. Radford. 2002. "Structuralism, Post-Structuralism, and the Library: De Saussure and Foucault," *Journal of Documentation* 61: 60–78.

Ricoeur, Paul. 1976. *Interpretation Theory: Discourse and the Surplus of Meaning.* Fort Worth: Texas Christian University Press.

Sanders, Carol. 2004. "The Paris Years." In *The Cambridge Companion to Saussure,* ed. Carol Sanders, 30–44. Cambridge: Cambridge University Press.

Saussure, Ferdinand de. 1959. *Course in General Linguistics.* Ed. Charles Bally and Albert Sechehaye, trans. Wade Baskin. New York: Philosophical Library.

Saussure, Ferdinand de. 2006. *Writings in General Linguistics.* Ed. Simon Bouquet and Rudolf Engler, trans. Carole Sanders and Matthew Pires. Oxford: Oxford University Press.

Solomon, Paul. 1997. "Conversation in Information Seeking Contexts." *Library and Information Science Research* 19:217–48.

Thibault, Paul J. 1997. *Re-reading Saussure.* London: Routledge.

22

Investigating the Textually Mediated Work of Institutions: Dorothy E. Smith's Sociology for People

Rosamund K. Stooke
University of Western Ontario, Canada

INTRODUCTION

The Canadian sociologist, Dorothy E. Smith is best known as the creator of institutional ethnography, an alternate sociology (DeVault and McCoy, 2002, 751) that she first conceptualized as a mode of inquiry from the standpoint of women and later developed as a "sociology for people" (Smith, 2005). An activist and leading theorist in the feminist movement since the 1960s, Smith was awarded the American Sociological Association's Career of Distinguished Scholarship Award in 1999. The chair of the award committee, Sarah Fenstermaker, wrote:

As few before her, Dorothy Smith engages us in a debate with ourselves over the ideas to which we are most devoted: the relationship of the researcher to the researched; the nature of text and language as social form; the role of historical and political context in fundamentally linking individual agency and social structure and the power of staring from margin rather then [*sic*] center. Smith's...argument for a focus on the everyday, concrete social relations that constitute lived experience, and the conceptual nature of power have directed sociology and shaped scholarship across the discipline (Fenstermaker 1999).

In an autobiographical essay (Smith n.d.), Smith tells of her early career. Born in the north of England in 1926, she began her working life as a secretary in a publishing firm and only applied to the London School of Economics to study social anthropology at the age of 25 because she thought an undergraduate degree might increase her chances of finding a better secretarial job. At the London School of Economics she discovered a passion for sociology and went on to graduate studies at the University of California at Berkeley, working with Erving Goffman and earning a PhD in 1963. The academic world of the 1960s was inhospitable to the idea that women could be scholars and researchers and Smith, who was by that time a single mother of two young children, struggled at first to find a full-time academic appointment. She taught courses at

Berkeley and at the University of Essex before joining the Department of Sociology at the University of British Columbia in 1967 where, together with three other feminist scholars she developed and taught one of the first women's studies courses in Canada. In 1977 she accepted an appointment at the Ontario Institute for Studies in Education (OISE), now part of the University of Toronto. Currently she holds the titles of professor emerita in the Department of Sociology and Equity Studies at the University of Toronto and adjunct professor in the Department of Sociology at the University of Victoria, British Columbia.

Smith has published numerous scholarly articles and books in sociology, women's studies, and education, most notably *The Everyday World as Problematic: A Feminist Sociology* (1987), which was translated into Spanish and for which she was awarded the Canadian Sociology and Anthropology Association's John Porter Award, *The Conceptual Practices of Power: A Feminist Sociology of Knowledge* (1990a), *Texts, Facts, and Femininity: Exploring the Relations of Ruling* (1990b), *Writing the Social: Critique, Theory and Investigations* (1999a), *Institutional Ethnography: A Sociology for People* (2005), *Mothering for Schooling* (Griffith and Smith 2005) and an edited collection of papers focused on *Institutional Ethnography as Practice* (2006).

Smith's work presents a peculiar challenge for a collection of chapters devoted to critical theory. On the one hand, she shares with critical theorists a longstanding commitment to social justice and democratic process. On the other, she is deeply suspicious of practices that fit the actualities of people's lives into theoretical frameworks. "Sociology's stylistic conventions constitute subject positions that locate the reader-inquirer outside the social world in which the text is read and written and where the positioned subject does her work, lives her life, and cares or does not care about the people she investigates" (Smith, 1999b, 67). The practice of nominalization is one such convention. Smith writes that "[a]ll you had to do was find a verb, dress it up a bit, leave the subjects out...convert it into a noun and you had a new social phenomenon: aggression, violence, interaction, motivation, alienation" (Smith 1986, 2–3). The postmodern-poststructural notion of a subject constituted in discourse is another convention. Smith argues that the idea of a subject constituted in discourse parallels the earlier sociological notion of role because it too "establishes the knower's discursive position as transcending the everyday worlds of people's experience" (Smith, 2005, 50). It would be a mistake, however, to conclude that Smith eschews theory. Her ideas are "fully original yet deeply resonant with sociology's foundations" (Fenstermaker 1999). Marx and Engels, Alfred Schutz, George Herbert Mead, Harold Garfinkel, and Russian language theorists A. R. Luria, Valentin Volosinov, and Mikhail Bakhtin have all informed her work (Smith 2005).

I could not imagine beginning all over again, and I learned, quite unscrupulously, from anyone whose work was of use to me in discovering an alternative to the methods of thinking I had been stuck with. But I am not a symbolic interactionist, nor a phenomenal sociologist, nor a Marxist sociologist, nor an ethnomethodologist. The sociological strategy I have developed does not belong to or subject itself to the interpretive procedures of any particular school of sociology (Smith 1987, 9).

Smith goes on to explain that the strategy she developed "is constrained by the project of creating a way of seeing, from where we actually live, into the powers, processes, and relations that organize and determine the everyday context of that seeing" (Smith 1987, 9). For more than thirty years, now, she has been teaching that strategy to others, not as theory, but as political practice. This chapter will first introduce readers to Smith's early theoretical writing in the sociology of knowledge; it then describes institutional ethnography and discusses the potential of institutional ethnography to support a critical project for LIS research and practice.

EARLY WORK: THE SOCIAL ORGANIZATION OF KNOWLEDGE

At the heart of Smith's early theoretical writing is a critique of a phenomenon she calls "the gender subtext of the rational and impersonal" (Smith 1987, 4). Smith attributed the feelings of alienation she experienced as a woman academic during the 1960s and 1970s in part to the obligation to "work in a discourse that describes and provides the working concepts and vocabulary for a landscape in which women are strangers" (Smith 1987, 51). She says, "When I looked for where I was in my discipline, I discovered that I was not there" (Smith 2007, 410). Her frustration with sociological language was only exacerbated by misgivings about sociological practices that tended to objectify the people it studied, even when its goals included emancipation. She writes, "It seemed not possible to take up a topic sociologically without transforming people and people's doings into objects" (Smith 2005, 28). Smith theorized her experience of alienation as a disjuncture between the conceptually organized world of the academic sociologist and the embodied world in which she as a wife and mother lived outside of her professional world. She was drawn into the second-wave feminist movement, but her activism extended beyond securing for women better access to the professions and other positions of power in public life. She theorized a standpoint for women and developed the widely acclaimed critique of the "the conceptual practices of power" (Smith 1990a) that later provided the theoretical grounding for institutional ethnography.

The consciousness raising groups formed by feminists during the 1960s and 1970s motivated several feminist scholars to theorize a women's standpoint. "Consciousness-raising was a foundational organizing device, assembling women as *women* to explore, discover and recognize a community of experience" (Smith, 2002, 49). Through consciousness raising, it became clear to many feminists that the overt sexism of men was not the only challenge facing women. Rather "the struggle was as much within ourselves, with what we knew how to do and think and feel, as with that [masculinist] regime as an enemy outside us" (Smith, 2005, 7). Standpoint theories have nevertheless been roundly criticized. Campbell (2006, 91–92) notes three common critiques: arguments "against the notion of a 'unitary subject' and against white, heterosexual, middle-class feminists' appropriation of women's experience, arguments that refute a perceived essentialist belief in the authority of women's voices," and questions about the "status of experiential accounts produced by people whose knowledge is discursively organized." In response to such critiques, Campbell notes that Smith uses experiential accounts not as windows on reality, but only as entry points into inquiries. Smith herself concedes that early standpoint theorizing "became at once a basis on which women came together for what we discovered we had in common and on which women found difference and questioned nascent hegemonies within the movement itself" (Smith 2002, 49), but later points out that "standpoint" can be used politically as well as referentially. When used politically, women's standpoint coordinates "struggle against the masculinist forms of oppressing women that those forms themselves explicitly or implicitly universalize" (Smith 2005, 9). Standpoint, then, can open for women, "a subject position in the public sphere and more generally, one in the political, intellectual and cultural life of the society" (Smith 2005, 9).

A salient characteristic of Smith's notion of standpoint is that it is always located in the actualities of people's lives, their everyday worlds. Smith proposes that a divide between the public and domestic spheres was produced in the same historical trajectory as the rise of capitalism and the market process in Europe during the modern period. By the beginning of the 18th century the domestic sphere had emerged in Europe as separate from commerce, governance, and the professions; by the end of the 19th century an analogous division was discernable in the institutional structures themselves.

The bureaucratization of the state and the advancing organization of corporate management created a demand for workers who...would be in charge of the material side of texts and documents, transforming words into texts, texts into documents and records, filing, finding files, doing the work of producing and organizing the memory of the firm, and so on (Smith 2002, 50).

People who participate in the public sphere, but not as agents within the discourses of ruling are required to suppress embodied forms of knowledge when accounting for their work although they are also required to draw upon such knowledge in order to competently fulfill their work roles. The work of practitioners in the human services, for example, must be made accountable in terms of the concepts and categories that frequently render the most salient aspects of the work invisible. A standpoint in the everyday world affords opportunities for people to speak about what they know as embodied subjects and to critically interrogate the discourses of ruling that are organizing their experiences as workers or as recipients of services.

The discourses of ruling are not easily discerned from within. People may experience vague feelings of alienation. They might come to suspect that their well-intentioned actions are being harnessed to promote the interests of privileged groups or to maintain the status quo. More often than not, however, the processes by which their actions are supporting projects not of their own choosing remain hidden from view. As noted in the previous section, Smith's project has been to create a way of seeing "into the powers, processes, and relations that organize and determine the everyday context of that seeing" (Smith 1987, 9). Maintaining a standpoint "at the level of the embodied subject" allows individuals to ask: "Just how do we encounter the 'expanding' social relations, whether of capital or of ruling, in which we are active" (Smith 1999b, 73). "Knowing how things work...is invaluable for those who often have to struggle in the dark" (Smith 2005, 32).

INSTITUTIONAL ETHNOGRAPHY

Having established a place from which to look at the workings of power, Smith theorized an ontology that conceptualizes the workings of power as a "complex field of coordination and control (DeVault and McCoy 2002, 751). Institutional ethnography is the strategy she developed for bringing into view the processes of coordination. Its ontology is that of a social world constituted by the concerting and coordinating of individuals' activities and its unit of analysis is "work," a term that gathers whatever people do that requires effort and a degree of acquired competence (McCoy, 2006). This generous view of work "directs us to its anchorage in material conditions" and to the fact that work gets done "in real time" (Smith 1987, 165).

Liza McCoy explains that work is a helpful analytic concept for keeping the workings of power in view because it "directs the researcher's attention toward precisely that interface between embodied individuals and institutional relations" (McCoy 2006, 110). A generous definition of work makes available for analysis activities usually not present in workplace documents, some of them not recognized as work, even by the people who do the work. McCoy (2006, 110) explains that work is an "empirically empty term" whose value lies not in distinguishing work from other activities. Rather it directs "analytic attention to the practical activities of everyday life in a way that begins to make visible how those activities gear into, are called out by, shape and are shaped by, extended translocal relations of large-scale coordination" (110–11). Finally, a generous definition of work allows for language and thought to be incorporated into "the scope of institutional ethnography's ontology" (Smith, 2005, 69). Campbell (2006, 93), for example, documented "a creeping colonization of minds and hearts of the caregivers with the goals and values of the market" in the wake of a "Total Quality Management" exercise in a Canadian long-term care home. Campbell's research illustrates well the idea that consciousness itself is a social accomplishment, a product of the coordination of ideas and of doing things in and with language.

The concerting and coordinating of people's activities is carried out within sequences of actions called social relations. Smith proposes that the social order of any setting is produced by people interacting with one another in the local setting and by people in the local setting interacting with others elsewhere and at other times—which is to say that social relations connect the actions of individuals working in diverse sites who may not be known to one another. Individual actions are thus organized by "translocal social relations that pass through local settings" and in so doing "carry and accomplish organization and control as 'relations of ruling'" (DeVault and McCoy 2002, 752). Mapping social relations is the goal of institutional ethnography inquiry. It is a political practice aimed at "expanding people's own knowledge" of how their everyday/everynight activities are being hooked into "the ruling relations" and also a collective political project. No single study can map a large area of institutional terrain, but individual maps overlap or interlock with one another to open up larger areas of institutional landscape ethnographically.

It is helpful when reading accounts of institutional ethnography inquiries to keep in mind that the terms "relations of ruling" and "institutional relations" may be used interchangeably. The term "institution" refers not to an organization or agency such as an academic library or information service, but to a "cluster of text-mediated relations organized around specific ruling functions, such as education or health care" (DeVault and McCoy 2002, 753). The Market is an institution, but the New York Stock Exchange is a local site of market activities. Health care is an institution, but a hospital is a local site of health care activity. Smith's definition of a text is less inclusive than her definition of work. Visual and media texts as well as print texts in paper and electronic formats are of interest to the institutional ethnographer as long as they can be replicated. Replicable texts are important because each person who interacts with the text is interacting with the same material artifact. Researchers therefore pay close attention to ways in which people produce and interact with replicable texts because they can be "read, seen, heard, watched, and so on in particular local and observable settings" (Smith 2006, 66), and yet, at the same time draw people's actions into the "relations of ruling." Smith's definition of a discourse originates with Foucault's (1972, 49) characterization of discourse as "practices that systematically form the objects of which they speak." For example, the frequently cited "mothering discourse" (Griffith and Smith 1987, 2005) systematically forms the relations that coordinate the work of mothers and teachers in relation to children's schooling. The power of a discourse to coordinate and concert people's actions in local settings derives in part from its ability to communicate at a tacit level. Discourse eschews critique because members of a discourse community draw on mutually comprehensible practices that obviate the need for explanations. It is worth noting that texts are always discursively organized. Discourse is a powerful organizer of text production. Discourse can also mediate activities in the absence of replicable texts. Recently institutional ethnographers have paid particular attention to textually-mediated work processes in which people's actions are entered into translocal relations associated with the New Economy (DeVault 2008). Globalization and the blurring of boundaries between the public and domestic spheres of activity in the wake of unprecedented technological change ensure that the concerting and coordinating of people's everyday/everynight activities are increasingly organized by New Economy discourse (DeVault 2008, 11).

CONDUCTING AN INSTITUTIONAL ETHNOGRAPHY INQUIRY

The first three sections of the chapter aimed to contextualize institutional ethnography, to sketch its ontological grounding, and to define key terms such as work, social relation, ruling relations, institution, text, and discourse. Stated simply, institutional ethnography is a strategy for empirically investigating the ruling relations from the standpoint of an individual or group of individuals whose actions are caught up in the ruling relations, but who are, themselves, positioned outside them. Institutional ethnography is both a routine way of looking at social life and a highly systematic mode of inquiry.

Discovering how activities are being coordinated to produce or maintain institutional processes is "an analytic project that can be realized in diverse ways,…rather like grabbing a ball of string, finding a thread, and then pulling it out" (DeVault and McCoy 2002, 755). Moreover, there is often no recognizable planning phase for the inquiry. Rather, the process of discovery proceeds in a recursive manner, a characteristic of institutional ethnography that sometimes creates difficulties for researchers who are expected to document plans for data collection and analysis when they apply to funding agencies and complete ethical review protocols. The following sequence provided by DeVault and McCoy (2002, 755) is a guide rather than a prescription:

- The researcher and informants identify the experience that constitutes the point of entry for the inquiry;
- The researcher identifies some of the institutional processes that are shaping the experience;
- The researcher investigates the processes in order to describe analytically how they operate as grounds of the experience.

Accounts of experience(s) that constitute(s) the entry point for an inquiry direct the researcher to a problematic, that is "a possible set of questions that are 'latent' in the actualities of the experienced world" although they "may not have been posed" yet and may not yet exist as puzzles (Smith 1987, 91). In many settings, but especially in human services settings, it is not uncommon for a study to be developed in response to a vague but nagging and persistent concern about a situation whose determinants seem to elude those people most affected by the situation. Institutional ethnographers have investigated a broad range of problematics (DeVault and McCoy 2002, 751). The experiences of people living with HIV in relation to treatment options (McCoy 2006), of community activists in relation to planning policies (Turner 1995), police responses to domestic violence against women (Pence 1997), the regulation of sexuality (G. Smith 1998), the discursive organization of ecotourism (Grahame and Grahame 2000), job training for immigrant women (Grahame 1999), and the organization of mothers' work in relation to schooling (Griffith and Smith 1987), which Smith (1987) employs as an exemplar of early institutional ethnography, have all been topics of investigation. Campbell and Manicom's (1995) *Knowledge, Experience and Ruling Relations,* DeVault and McCoy's (2002) essay on interviewing in institutional ethnography, Smith's (2006) *Institutional Ethnography as Practice,* and DeVault's (2008) *People at Work* contain numerous and diverse examples of institutional ethnography problematics.

In order to identify the institutional processes shaping the experiences at the inquiry's point of entry, researchers often begin by documenting what people are doing, or what people can tell the researcher about what they and others are doing in relation to the situation (DeVault and McCoy 2002, 751). Together the researcher and informants explore how the activities are being coordinated to produce "institutional processes as they actually work" (Smith 2005, 60). Fieldwork techniques are the most common approaches to data collection for institutional ethnography inquiries. These include individual and focus group interviews, participant observation and reflections on one's own experiences, but can be as informal as "just talking to people" (DeVault and McCoy 2002, 757). Copious amounts of data may be gathered as the researcher learns about the work carried out in a setting, but relatively small amounts of data may prove relevant to the identified problematic. For example, an examination of data may lead to the exploration of sequences of action in which specific texts are implicated. Sometimes the inquiry moves directly to examining an administrative or professional work process.

Data collected in institutional ethnography inquiries are analyzed in two ways: first to learn concretely about the issue or situation being investigated and second to identify institutional processes active in the coordinating and concerting of work. The second approach requires that the researcher's knowledge of the context for the inquiry go beyond what informants within the setting can tell them. Policy texts can help orient the inquiry to ways in which informants' work is being coordinated. So can background literature, since it too can be approached in two distinct ways: first for "conventional reasons, to discover the scope of research knowledge in the area" (Campbell and Gregor 2002, 51), and second to explore the discursive organization of the literature. Stooke's (2003) analysis of the *Early Years Study* (McCain and Mustard 1999) demonstrates these two approaches to reading background literature. Stooke examined the text in order to learn about the research base for Ontario's new social policies for families with young children, but she also critiqued the report to show how it functioned as a rhetorical device to justify policies already being implemented and how it was shaped by neoliberal principles of efficiency and competition.

Another way to learn about the context is to interview people who work outside the local setting. Campbell and Gregor explain: "To understand the workings of any setting involves learning how people, seemingly positioned outside the setting, are nevertheless active inside it" (2002, 60). DeVault and McCoy note in this regard that the accounts of agency staff are important sources of data for institutional ethnography inquiry because agency staff are often the people who are charged with making the "messiness of everyday circumstance" fit into "the categories and protocols of a professional regime" (2002, 760). In seeking external accounts, however, it is important to avoid describing people's activities in relation to existing theories and categories as, for example, the ALA's *Every Child Ready to Read @ Your Library (ECRR)* does when it represents social class as a determinant of parents' behaviour and children's future literacy achievements.

Institutional ethnography does not subscribe to the epistemological warrants embedded in outputs or outcomes-based measurement practices. Hence, exploring a problematic does not involve strategies typically employed in evaluation research, even qualitative evaluations (e.g., Patton 2001). Neither are institutional ethnography studies of one kind. An analysis might examine regimes of accountability in the public sector (e.g., Griffith and André-Bechely 2008), how work in local sites can be coordinated in the absence of overt regulation (Stooke, 2004; Stooke and McKenzie, 2009), or how one work process could be reorganized through a rewriting of texts (e.g., Pence, 1997). What the above analyses share is summed up by Smith herself. In an article written for *The Handbook of Feminist Research,* Smith (2007, 413) lists five key components for institutional ethnography. First, institutional ethnography starts from the experience(s) of people in their everyday lives; second, it takes a standpoint "in their experience" and aims to learn from them; third it stays with people's experiences as it explores the institutional relations that coordinate the experiences; fourth, it pays attention to texts and discourses as they are activated by people; and fifth, it aims to produce maps that people can use to expand their knowledge of how their daily activities are being coordinated.

WHAT CAN SMITH'S IDEAS CONTRIBUTE TO LIS?

Smith brings to her writing and her teaching a respect for work that is often not recognized as work, even by those who do the work, and a nuanced understanding of organizational life. It is not surprising that human service professions such as nursing, teaching, and social work have provided particularly fertile settings for institutional ethnography inquiries (Campbell and Gregor 2002). As intermediaries between systems and people, human services practitioners negotiate the disjuncture between the rational, impersonal, and embodied "ways with words" many times during a work shift. It is surprising that Smith's ideas have not been widely employed in LIS. However, LIS studies often display at least one institutional ethnography characteristic. For example, as did Pence, Harris, and Dewdney (1991) identified ways in which texts mediated access to safety and support for victims of domestic violence. Moreover, Harris's (1992) critique of professionalization movements in librarianship echoed Smith's critique of the rational and impersonal when she called for a revaluing of caring work in librarianship. Another feminist researcher, Suzanne Hildenbrand (1996), proposed that understanding librarians' absence from policy discussions could be found by examining their work rather than their personality traits, while classification theorists, Bowker and Star (2000), discussed the challenges of bringing visibility to relational work in the creation of a work classification scheme for nursing. More recently McKenzie (2006) mapped textually mediated information practices in midwifery care; McKenzie and Stooke (2007) identified the work carried out by adult and child participants and librarians to produce a library storyhour and Stooke and McKenzie (2009) identified textually and discursively mediated educational work processes carried out in library-based recreational programs for very young children.

Three doctoral dissertations at the University of Western Ontario drew directly on Smith's theoretical writing. Lundberg (1991) investigated the social organization of birth control information in public libraries and classification theorists. More recently Carey (2003) examined the discursive organization of information practices in a lupus support group from the standpoint of the group members, while Stooke (2004) analyzed children's librarians' work as gendered work and uncovered mechanisms by which their work was being coordinated with the American educational reforms and OECD policies for early child development.

One purpose for this chapter has been to show that Smith's ideas have much to offer a critical project in LIS. Librarianship shares with human services such as nursing, social work, and teaching an ethical imperative to promote social justice and care for people (Harris, 1992), and LIS professionals routinely act as mediators of systems for users. They understand the value of navigational tools and well appreciate that while the work of making navigational tools sometimes demands highly technical skills, the tools themselves must be intelligible to users.

LIS researchers and practitioners are also used to thinking about the organization of texts and the ways in which knowledge and power come together in practice to organize what happens to people (Campbell and Gregor 2002, 12). And yet librarians are vulnerable to the "creeping colonization of minds and hearts... with the goals and values of the market" that Campbell (2006, 93) recognized among health care practitioners. Library workplaces are sites of numerous and diverse forms of institutional work processes that too easily draw actions into "the ruling relations." Libraries are organized as hierarchies and bureaucracies whose smooth running depends on routines that can easily subordinate the interests of users to those of the organization. As agencies that depend on public funding they are regulated by regimes of accountability that are firmly hooked into the relations of the New Economy.

In closing I would draw readers' attention to a comment made by Marjorie DeVault. DeVault (2008, 295) writes, "It is the distinctive capacity of institutional ethnography to underscore the sometimes startling power of text-based management, which organizes activity in ways that may not be obvious." I contend that institutional ethnography offers LIS practitioners and researchers strategies with which to interrupt their involvement in processes that privilege the interests of powerful groups and reinforce hegemonic discourses of competition and the principles of the market. Pence's groundbreaking work serves as one exemplar. By working with agency staff, Pence reorganized the reporting process to promote safety for victims rather than bureaucratic efficiency. LIS researchers and practitioners might also revise routine work processes to promote equity and social justice goals. They might, for example, employ Smith's generous view of work to open up topics such as "barriers to access" as socially organized accomplishments that people can "do" differently. Most important, institutional ethnography's commitment to maintain a standpoint with the people who actually experience the situations being investigated and to produce accessible maps that people can use for their own purposes are important ingredients for a critical project in LIS.

REFERENCES

American Library Association. *Every Child Ready to Read @ Your Library*. http://www.ala.org/ala/mgrps/divs/alsc/ecrr/projecthistory/researchearlyliteracy/researchearlylit.cfm. Accessed August 15, 2009.

Bowker, Geoffrey C., and Susan Leigh Star. 2000. *Sorting Things Out: Classification and Its Consequences*. Cambridge, MA: MIT Press.

Campbell, Marie. 2006. "Institutional Ethnography and Experience as Data." In *Institutional Ethnography as Practice*, ed. Dorothy E. Smith, 91–108. Lanham, NJ: Rowman and Littlefield.

Campbell, Marie, and Ann Manicom, eds. 1995. *Knowledge, Experience and Ruling Relations: Studies in the Social Organization of Knowledge*. Toronto, ON: University of Toronto Press.

Campbell, Marie, and Frances Gregor. 2002. *Mapping Social Relations: A Primer in Doing Institutional Ethnography*. Aurora, ON: Garamond Press.

Carey, Robert F. 2003. "Narrative and Information: An Ethnography of a Lupus Support Group." PhD diss., University of Western Ontario.

DeVault, Marjorie. L. 1991. *Feeding the Family: The Social Organization of Caring as Gendered Work*. Chicago: University of Chicago Press.

DeVault, Marjorie L. 1999. *Liberating Method: Feminism & Social Research*. Philadelphia: Temple University Press.

DeVault, Marjorie L. 2008. *People at Work: Life, Power and Social Inclusion in the New Economy*. New York: New York University Press.

DeVault, Marjorie, and Liza McCoy. 2002. "Institutional Ethnography: Using Interviews to Investigate Ruling Relations." In *Handbook of Interviewing*, ed. Jaber F. Gubrium and James A. Holstein, 751–75. Thousand Oaks, CA: Sage.

Fenstermaker, Sarah. 1999. Citation, Career of Distinguished Scholarship Award. In *Footnotes* 27, 7. http://www.asanet.org/footnotes/sepoct99/task5.html. Accessed August 15, 2009.

Garfinkel, Harold. 2003. "Socially Negotiated Knowledge." In *Social Construction: A Reader*, ed. Mary Gergen and Kenneth J. Gergen, 11–14. London: Sage.

Grahame, Kamini M. 1999. "State, Community and Asian Immigrant Women's Work: A Study in Labor Market Organization." PhD diss., University of Toronto.

Grahame, Peter, and Kamini M. Grahame. 2000. "Official Knowledge and the Relations of Ruling: Explorations in Institutional Ethnography." *Journal for Pedagogy, Pluralism & Practice*, 5. http://www.lesley.edu/journals/jppp/5/grahame.html. Accessed August 15, 2009.

Griffith, Alison, and Dorothy E. Smith. 1987. "Constructing Cultural Knowledge: Mothering as Discourse." In *Women and Education: A Canadian Perspective*, ed. Jane Gaskell and Arlene Tigar McLaren, 87–103. Calgary, AB: Detselig Enterprises Ltd.

Griffith, Alison, and Dorothy E. Smith. 2005. *Mothering for Schooling*. New York: Routledge Falmer.

Harris, Roma M. 1992. *Librarianship: The Erosion of a Woman's Profession*. Norwood, NJ: Ablex.

Harris, Roma M., and Patricia Dewdney. 1994. *Barriers to Information: How Formal Help Systems Fail Battered Women*. Westport, CT: Greenwood Press.

Hildenbrand, Suzanne. 1996. *Reclaiming the American Library Past: Writing the Women In*. Norwood, NJ: Ablex.

Lundberg, Norma J. 1991. "The Social Organization of Birth Control Information in Public Libraries." PhD diss., University of Western Ontario.

McCain, Margaret, and J. Fraser Mustard. 1999. *Reversing the Real Brain Drain: Early Years Study, Final Report.* Toronto, ON: Canadian Institute for Advanced Research.

McCoy, Liza. 2006. "Keeping the Institution in View: Working with Interview Accounts of Everyday Experience." In *Institutional Ethnography as Practice,* ed. Dorothy E. Smith, 109–26. Lanham NJ: Rowman and Littlefield.

McKenzie, Pamela. J. 2006. "Mapping Textually-Mediated Information Practice in Clinical Midwifery Care." In *New Directions in Human Information Behavior,* ed. Amanda Spink, and Charles Cole. Dordrecht: Springer.

McKenzie, Pamela J., and Rosamund K. Stooke. 2007. "Producing Storytime: A Collectivist Analysis of Work in a Complex Communicative Space." *Library Quarterly* 57 (1): 3–19.

Patton, Michael Q. 2001. *Qualitative Research and Evaluation Methods,* 3rd ed. Thousand Oaks, CA: Sage.

Pence, Ellen. 1997. "Safety for Battered Women in a Textually Mediated Legal System." PhD diss., University of Toronto.

Smith, Dorothy E. 1986. *Feminism and the Malepractice of Sociology* No. 3. Toronto, ON: Centre for Women's Studies in Education.

Smith, Dorothy E. 1987. *The Everyday World as Problematic: A Feminist Sociology.* Boston: Northeastern University Press.

Smith, Dorothy E. 1990a. *The Conceptual Practices of Power: A Feminist Sociology of Knowledge.* Toronto, ON: University of Toronto Press.

Smith, Dorothy E. 1990b. *Texts Facts and Femininity: Exploring the Relations of Ruling.* London: Routledge.

Smith, Dorothy E. 1999a. *Writing the Social: Critique, Theory and Investigations.* Toronto, ON: University of Toronto Press.

Smith, Dorothy E. 1999b. "From Women's Standpoint to a Sociology for People." In *Sociology for the Twenty-First Century: Continuities and Cutting Edges,* ed. Janet L. Abu-Lughod, 65-83. Chicago: University of Chicago Press.

Smith, Dorothy E. 2002. "Feminist Consciousness and the Ruling Relations." In *Knowledge and Discourse: Towards an Ecology of Language,* ed. Colin Barron, Nigel Bruce, and David Nunan, 49–62. Harlow, UK: Longman.

Smith, Dorothy E. 2005. *Institutional Ethnography: A Sociology for People.* Lanham, NJ: AltaMira.

Smith, Dorothy E. 2006. *Institutional Ethnography as Practice.* Lanham, NJ: Rowman and Littlefield.

Smith, Dorothy E. 2007. "Institutional Ethnography: From a Sociology for Women to a Sociology for People." In *Handbook of Feminist Research: Theory and Practice,* ed. Sharlene Nagy Hesse-Biber, 409–16. Thousand Oaks, CA: Sage.

Smith, Dorothy E. n.d. "Dorothy E. Smith." Available at http://faculty.maxwell.syr.edu/mdevault/dorothy_smith.htm. Accessed August 15, 2009.

Smith, George W. 1998. "The Ideology of 'Fag': The School Experience of Gay Students." *Sociological Quarterly* 39: 309–55.

Stooke, Rosamund. 2003. "[Re]visioning the Ontario Early Years Study: Almost a Fairy Tale—But Not Quite." *Journal of Curriculum Theorizing* 19 (2): 91–101.

Stooke, Rosamund. 2004. "Healthy, Wealthy and Ready for School: Supporting Young Children's Education and Development in the Era of the National Children's Agenda." PhD diss., University of Western Ontario.

Stooke, Rosamund, and Pamela J. McKenzie. 2009. "Leisure and Work in Library and Community Programs for Very Young Children." *Library Trends* 57 (4): 657–75.

Turner, Susan M. 1995. "Rendering the Site Developable: Texts and Local Government Decision-Making and Land Use Planning." In *Knowledge, Experience and Ruling Relations: Studies in the Social Organization of Knowledge,* ed. Marie Campbell and Ann Manicom, 234–48. Toronto, ON: University of Toronto Press.

NOTE

The author wishes to thank Dr. Smith for her encouragement and comments on an early draft of the chapter.

23

Gayatri Chakravorty Spivak: Deconstructionist, Marxist, Feminist, Postcolonialist

Hope A. Olson
Melodie J. Fox
University of Wisconsin–Milwaukee, USA

INTRODUCTION

Gayatri Chakravorty Spivak purposely eludes categorization. Nevertheless, she most commonly is categorized as a feminist, Marxist, deconstructionist, and/or postcolonialist. Her complex viewpoints, nominally in literary criticism but in practice across the board, fit into sociology, history, women's studies, and now, into library and information science (LIS). Initially, her works seem tangled and impenetrable, but familiarity reveals recurring themes. Her international perspective challenges conventional Western thinking and accessibility of intellectual work. Themes spill across essays; she revises her views within the same essay in postscripts that refocus what was just written. The relationships between her "-isms" are purposefully complicated and sometimes conflicting. This inability to be pigeonholed is intentional; any definition of her stance is constantly deferred. Spivak views her own work as a method of reading that is "sensitive to gender, race, and class" (1985a, 81), but resists the essentialism that could lead to a generalization about gender, race, or class. In LIS, her work pushes us to recognize our complicity as "custodians of culture" and provides methods of analyzing our praxis.

Previous LIS research using Spivak's work appears to be limited to Olson (2001, 2002, 2003, 2007). However, wider use of her theoretical perspectives in LIS can be readily imagined by exploring the concepts she develops, such as: the subaltern, ideology, strategic essentialism, translation and representation, and the "telematic society of information command" (Spivak 1999, 393). In this chapter we introduce Spivak and her context, offer an overview of her theoretical foundations, and examine her interpretations of the sample of five conceptual constructs listed above. We include examples of potential LIS applications throughout.

Biography

Gayatri Chakravorty Spivak's biographical and scholarly background is an integral part of her work. She was born in 1942 in Calcutta, India, and earned a degree there in English (meaning British) literature from Presidency College at the University of Calcutta in 1959. She earned her MA from Cornell in 1962 and continued to work with Paul de Man on her dissertation while teaching at the University of Iowa, completing her doctorate in 1967. She completed a fellowship at Cambridge and has earned honorary doctorates from the Universities of Toronto and London. Spivak currently holds the Avalon Foundation Professorship of the Humanities and directs the Institute for Comparative Literature and Society at Columbia University. She is known as a literary critic, yet her work and reputation cross disciplinary and international boundaries. She sees the role of the humanities "as the arena of cultural explanations that question the explanations of culture" (1979, 117). She often parallels the marginalization of the humanities within the academy to the marginalization of women or the oppressed. Well aware of her status as an elite Indian-born female, she avoids playing "native informant" to the academy, instead questioning all explanations of culture regardless of origin.

A prolific writer and translator, her authored books include *Myself Must I Remake: The Life and Poetry of W. B. Yeats* (1974), *In Other Worlds: Essays in Cultural Politics* (1987), *The Post-Colonial Critic: Interviews, Strategies, Dialogues* (1990), *Thinking Academic Freedom in Gendered Post-Coloniality* (1993), *Outside in the Teaching Machine* (1993), *The Spivak Reader* (1995), *Imperatives to Re-Imagine the Planet* (1999), *A Critique of Postcolonial Reason: Towards a History of the Vanishing Present* (1999), *Death of a Discipline* (2003), *Other Asias* (2005), *Who Sings the Nation-State? Language, Politics, Belonging* (2007, with Judith Butler), and *Red Thread* (forthcoming). Additionally, she has translated, most famously, Derrida's *Of Grammatology* and the works of the Indian writer Mahasweta Devi. She has published multiple collections of interviews and is the subject of many books and countless articles.

THEORETICAL OVERVIEW

To understand Spivak's work and then apply it, one must understand her relationships with the four critical perspectives from which she draws and to which she contributes: (1) poststructuralism in the form of deconstruction, (2) Marxism, (3) feminism, and (4) postcoloniality. Spivak interprets and employs these perspectives in distinctive ways that result in a unique theoretical basis for her surprisingly pragmatic approach.

Deconstruction

Those slightly familiar with Spivak are likely to know that she translated Jacques Derrida's opus *Of Grammatology*, which introduces the process of deconstruction. She has continued to apply deconstruction in her work, but not always in a classically Derridean form. Before looking at Spivak's interpretation, we will summarize deconstruction basics (something that Spivak notes Derrida never does). Deconstruction is a critical practice that is applied to texts, interpreting the concept of text broadly. In LIS, texts can include foundational works, but also policies, pathfinders, circulation statistics, informetric data, classification schemes, Web portals, signage, Machine-Readable Cataloging (MARC) coding, metadata schemata, survey data, databases, reference interviews, and social tagging.

Deconstruction can be described as having three steps: identify a binary opposition, reverse the binary by reading the text(s) focusing on the subordinate, and the binary dissolves. Identifying the binary opposition requires first singling out a key concept (say, the public sphere) and its implied opposite (the private sphere). The two elements in a binary opposition are in a hierarchical relationship with each other. One is dominant (public) and is sometimes referred to as the *one;* the other is subordinate (private) and is referred to as the o*ther.* The *one* requires the presence of the *other* for its own existence. The difference between the two defines the *one.* In the second step, reversing the binary, the texts selected for analysis are read closely with a focus on the subordinate member of the binary and its expression in the texts. This reading can take many forms, but the purpose is to highlight the traces of what is obscured: the *other.* For example, the private sphere is traditionally associated with women and "women's work," so mentions of women's work in a text may be placeholders for the private sphere even if they occur in the public sphere (teaching and librarianship come to mind). The third step just happens. As the reading progresses, it becomes apparent that the difference between the *one* and the *other* is not innate, it is constructed (some women's professions only became defined as such in the last century and a half, as when Melvil Dewey recruited "college-bred women" into librarianship; into the 19th century teachers and librarians were men). Further, the difference is not conclusively defined; rather, its definition is constantly deferred. That is, the boundary between the two concepts in the binary opposition is constructed which means that it is mutable. So there is never any final, permanent definition. This becomes apparent during the second stage of deconstruction and constitutes the third stage. In the example, it becomes apparent as one reads relevant texts that the issue is not who does the cleaning or the laundry. The issue is a constructed boundary between the public and private spheres that has stifled women's opportunities and enhanced men's opportunities, but a close look suggests that the abilities of women to be active in the public sphere are not negligible or even inferior to men's abilities. So the definition of the difference between the two can never be solidified. The gendered nature of the public/private binary will continue to shift. We can never pin it down. From this deferral of difference comes Derrida's notion of *differánce,* a concatenation of the French words for difference and defer. It is with the concept of *differánce* that the unstable nature of the limit between the *one* and the *other* becomes apparent and finally falls apart.

Derrida did not see deconstruction as a methodology, but rather as a critical approach to text. Spivak is not satisfied with leaving it at that.

I am still moved by the reversal-displacement morphology of deconstruction, crediting the asymmetry of the "interest" of the historical moment. Investigating the hidden ethico-political agenda of differentiation constitutive of knowledge and judgment interests me even more (1985a, 84).

She combines deconstruction with political programs, notably feminism and postcoloniality, which include an ethical demand for action. In that sense Spivak values deconstruction because rather than denying truth, "[i]t is constantly and persistently looking into how truths are produced" (1994, 27). Deconstruction, because it reveals definition as an always-deferred process, maintains a constant questioning. In the case of the public/private binary opposition, Spivak recognizes that feminists apply deconstruction by working to reverse the hierarchy of the binary to value the private over the public:

The shifting limit that prevents this feminist reversal of the public-private hierarchy from freezing into a dogma or, indeed, from succeeding fully is the displacement of the opposition itself. For if the fabric of the public sector is woven of the so-called private, the definition of the private is marked by a public potential, since it *is* the weave, or texture, of public activity. The opposition is thus not merely reversed; it is displaced. It is according to this practical structure of deconstruction as reversal-displacement, then, that I write: the deconstruction of the opposition between private and public is implicit in all, and explicit in some, feminist activity. The peculiarity of deconstructive practice must be reiterated here. Displacing the opposition that it initially apparently questions, it is always different from itself, always defers itself (1979, 103).

Spivak goes beyond Derrida in this addition of agency to deconstruction, instead of abandoning deconstruction due to its shortcomings. She sees deconstruction as

a method of analysis that would fix its glance upon the itinerary of the ethico-political in authoritarian fictions; call into question the complacent apathy of self-centralization; undermine the bigoted elitism (theoretical or practical) conversely possible in collective practice; while disclosing in such gestures the condition of possibility of the positive (Spivak 1980b, 101).

That is, deconstruction can identify the constructed nature of conceptual difference relative to ethico-political movements, can call our attention to the *other,* and can help us make our practices open to the voice of the *other.* It can do this not by relying on negative critique, but by an honest effort to understand how questionable some of our underlying presumptions are.

As part of exploring the ethico-political, Spivak values deconstruction for its potential for reflecting back to a political movement what it is actually doing. In the context of feminism, she writes, "[i]t is not just that deconstruction cannot found a politics, while other ways of thinking can. It is that deconstruction can make founded political programs more useful by making their in-built problems more visible" (1993a, 121). Her *A Critique of Postcolonial Reason* includes "[o]ne task of deconstruction [that] might be a persistent attempt to displace the reversal, to show the complicity between native hegemony and the axiomatic of imperialism" (1999, 37). That is, Spivak invokes deconstruction to keep the political movement, in this case postcoloniality, conceptually honest.

Traces of deconstruction can be seen throughout Spivak's work as she reverses and then displaces concepts that we presumed had stable boundaries. She goes further to apply it to herself, questioning her own previous writings, as will be seen in the discussion of essentialism later in this chapter. LIS is rich with binary oppositions that would benefit from deconstruction with agency. Some are obvious, such as: free text/controlled vocabularies; print/digital; librarianship/information science ("L-word"/"I-word"). Other binaries are more subtle in that the *one* is obvious, but the *other* needs some thought to deduce: service/*neglect?economy?;* sharing/*inefficiency?contextualization?;* neutrality/*bias?sensitivity?;* intellectual freedom/*censorship?sensitivity?* Any topic will have an implied opposite apropos of different situations.

Marxism

Classical Marxism forms the foundation of Spivak's work but is refracted through the prism of feminism, deconstruction, and postcoloniality. She spends much time working through Marx's historical and economic works, applying and adapting his theories to postcolonial or feminist contexts. Unlike Marx's nationalist, desexualized Western European labor force, her context is the diverse, gender- and class-bound Third World, which provides much opportunity to emend his works. A rudimentary understanding of Marxism greatly enriches the reading of Spivak's work, so a few basic concepts will be introduced here in simplified form. In Marxism, a powerful, central capitalist nation-state exploits a peripheral margin of workers—the proletariat or peasants. The proletariat contributes labor to the capitalist system, yet the workers are alienated from their product, since they only exist as a cog of a large industrial complex and do not see the end product. In Spivak's postcolonial interpretation, the First World represents a colonizing nation-state that exploits the subaltern class, or "those removed from the lines of social mobility" with no political voice (2004, 531). Marxism analyzes the unjust relationships between power and the exploited in order to effect social change by empowering the proletariat or subaltern. Spivak also critiques imbalanced power structures begotten by capitalism, but identifies them as imperial or gendered.

Marxism's economic theories correspond to power relationships evident in several areas of LIS. Classification and thesauruses are hierarchical structures that award position based on conceptualization by a central power (bibliographic utility, classification system, or cataloger) whose worldview purports to reflect the values of the population. In Spivak's interpretation the population exists without a self-definition; they are defined by the discourse of the imperial power. Moreover, as purveyors of culture, libraries are instrumental in forming the ideology of the community. The community's ideology, in part formed by the library, is the source from which the alleged values are drawn. The circular "consistency loop" omits feedback from the user and "fence[s] out" difference (Spivak 1979, 114).

Spivak also draws from Marx's concepts of self-sameness and difference, by which she means how individuals identify themselves as opposed to how they are identified by others, particularly by imperialist forces. In other words, a system of self-representation "establish[es] self-identity through access to a self-determination that will annul the difference established by history" (Spivak 1999, 78). History may impose an identity, but self-determination can minimize it. Such user-centered technologies as social tagging may exist as a means for singular users to identify with multiple realms, creating a dynamic and user-organized social classification system.

Feminism

Much of Spivak's work on feminism originally appeared as critiques or commentary on French feminists such as Luce Irigaray, Hélène Cixous, and Simone de Beauvoir. Her work can frustrate feminists because she resists any hint of essentialism that underpins some feminist thought, calling it "a trap" (Spivak 1985a, 89). Like most of her work, Spivak's feminism is informed by Marxism, but she recognizes that "[h]ardcore Marxism at best dismisses and at worst patronizes the importance of women's struggle" (82). Marx imagined a nonsexed labor force, but as a feminist, Spivak recognizes the capitalist system to be the domain of men. Spivak often points out the shortcomings of Marx's views by discussing the structural importance of women in society, the tendency for women to be treated as property, and their unacknowledged contributions to labor. She expands and "corrects" Marx's definition of labor to include women's unpaid work, and considers the womb as a place of production.

Spivak avoids defining "woman" in order to avoid setting up the binary of man/woman, since the opposition assumes a dominant and an *other,* believing "the ideological construction of gender keeps the male dominant. If, in the context of colonial production, the subaltern has no history and cannot speak, the subaltern as female is even more deeply in shadow" (Spivak 1998, 287). She challenges any practice or institution so that it can be recognized as a masculine structure, including the discourses that make up society. She advocates for women to "infiltrate the male academy and redo the terms of our understanding of the context and substance of literature as part of the human enterprise" (Spivak 1985a, 81). Women's materials already infiltrate the library collection by living "in the master-text as well as in the pores" (92). That women's materials have no classificatory home mirrors the unappreciated structural importance women hold in society.

Canonical, male-centric texts do not "deconstruct themselves" (Spivak 1980a, 18), and Spivak proposes rewriting rather than revising the male-dominated history:

Part of the feminist enterprise might well be to provide "evidence" so that these great male texts do not become great adversaries, or models from whom we take our ideas and then revise or reassess them (1985a, 81).

The great male texts of American librarianship are, of course, the Dewey Decimal Classification (DDC), the Library of Congress Classification (LCC), and the Library of Congress Subject Headings (LCSH). What Spivak suggests could mean a radical reworking of classificatory systems, constituting a violent event that displaces one system with another. The upheaval of a powerful "sign-system is a violent event. Even when it is perceived as 'gradual,' or 'failed,' or yet 'reversing itself,' the change itself can only be operated by the force of a crisis" (Spivak 1985b, 197). The "violence" resulting from Sandy Berman's *Prejudices and Antipathies* or Joan Marshall's *On Equal Terms* spurred needed change to LCSH, although Spivak would rather build a user-designed new system that allows all stakeholders to have a voice.

Spivak sees feminist compatibility in Marx's concept of value. Because women continually produce more than they get back through unpaid labor, reproduction, or low wages, they are highly profitable for the "man who owns her" or the "capitalist who owns *his* labor power" (Spivak 1985a, 79; emphasis Spivak's). Women produce more surplus value, or profit, making them valuable but exploitable employees. Although a woman produces a child (or commodity), property rights belong to the man or company, so he maintains possession of the woman's product. A parallel could be drawn to bibliographic utilities that assume ownership of surrogate records or professional organizations that benefit from unpaid work contributed for the betterment of the profession (or collective). Catalogers who upload original records or committee volunteers add surplus value in excess, beyond the exchange-value of the product or service produced.

As a female-intensive profession with a disproportionate number of men in charge, one suspects that an economic strategy is in place, given the surplus value that women add. The male-dominated "putative center" of management in large public and academic libraries "welcomes selective inhabitants of the margin in order to better exclude the margin" (Spivak 1979, 107). So by celebrating and tokenizing a few women, who "can only be tolerated if [they behave] 'like men'" (109), the center is excused from displacing the margin. Furthermore, the male/female ratio in LIS education risks a masculine authority attempting to speak for a female-dominated profession, or as Spivak notes, "Feminism in its academic inceptions is accessible and subject to correction by authoritative men" (Spivak 1982, 133).

Postcoloniality

Linking her feminism to postcoloniality Spivak writes: "the name 'woman'... has shifted for me into the subaltern of contemporary colonization" (1993a, 140). Spivak's subaltern (discussed later in this chapter) is a result of her postcolonial critique. To put it in context, Spivak locates three periods:

colonialism—in the European formation stretching from the mid-18th to the mid-20th centuries—*neocolonialism*—dominant, economic, political, and culturalist maneuvers emerging in our [20th] century after the dissolution of the territorial empires—and *postcoloniality*—the contemporary global condition (1999, 172).

Postcoloniality examines the inheritances from colonialism and the effects of neocolonialism that have resulted in and continue to shape the contemporary condition. Spivak uses the term "postcoloniality" rather than "postcolonialism," associating the latter with elitist academic activity that benefits the scholars, not the subaltern from whom it maintains a distance (1999, 358).

In exploring postcoloniality, Spivak employs several themes, including diaspora and the legacies of imperialism/colonialism. The concept of postcolonial *diaspora* is the scattering of people around the globe as the result of colonialism and its aftermath. Colonists moved to colonies, but, more significant to Spivak, the colonized migrated away from their colonized and decolonized homes. Diaspora places people like Spivak in the role of "assimilated-colonial-ethnic-minority" who are without a home—living in a metaphorical hotel (1991b, 175–77). Most notably, women migrate, as observed and lived by Spivak, to avoid conflict and oppression, to leave poverty for opportunity, and to find justice—all for themselves and their children (Spivak 1999, 398).

The concepts valued in decolonization are "coded with the legacy of imperialism: nationhood, constitutionality, citizenship, democracy, socialism, even culturalism" (1990, 60). Spivak notes that these concepts based largely in Eurocentric liberal individualism are the goals of teleological change, a Eurocentric approach. They have no historical antecedents in decolonized states. A different sort of legacy is that of language. She notes that academics and readers from different former colonies can interact with each other because they share the language of their colonizers (Spivak 1990, 60). Conversely, Spivak compares the use of English in India to a child of rape:

It's an act of violence. On the other hand, if there is a child, that child cannot be ostracized because it's a child of rape. To an extent, the postcolonial is that. We see there a certain kind of innate historic enablement which one mustn't celebrate, but toward which one has a deconstructive position, as it were. In order for there to be an all-India voice, we have had to dehegemonize English as one of the Indian languages (1994, 19).

Spivak takes a postcolonial critical stance in interpreting the contemporary condition. For example, she uses her critical approaches to identify skewing of culture, as in ersatz ethnicity in clothing and architecture (1999, 319n), and homogenization of people, as in the naming of "third world women" or "women of color" (165). Further, she employs literary texts, especially but not exclusively Indian classics and texts by contemporary Indian authors, to demonstrate her points, as in her interpretation of Hegel's interpretation of the *Srimadbhagavadgitā* with the *Gitā* itself to uncover the use of Time to manipulate history (37 ff).

In her characterization of the new female immigrant from the decolonized South, Spivak takes her postcolonial interpretation to the diaspora. In the United States in particular the immigrant, escaping from the political and economic oppression of her home, encounters white supremacist culture and liberal multiculturalism (as well as racist white supremacists). White supremacist culture wants to spread the superior (Western) values of individual freedom, democracy, and human rights through capitalism. While claiming a sort of resistance, "liberal multiculturalism is determined by the demands of contemporary transnational capitalism" (Spivak 1999, 397). However, "[l]iberal multiculturalism without global socialist awareness simply expands the U.S. base, corporate or communitarian" (402). "The obstinate among us might want a broader perspective that does not merely *refer* to the international division of labor, but also takes the trouble to acquire transnational literacy in the New World Order that has come and is coming into being in the last decade of the second millennium: command, if you like, of a diversified historical and geographic information system" (398). That is, some, "the obstinate," will work to learn the historical and economic context of decolonized nation-states and, ideally, also subaltern languages to be able to comprehend the post-Soviet New World Order that is being spread via an electronic global communication system. Transnational literacy means learning to examine the universalization that this system spreads (Spivak 2001, 15). These facets of postcoloniality as well as deconstruction, Marxism, and feminism play out in a range of concepts that Spivak develops in her work, some of which we elaborate in the following.

POTENTIAL APPLICATIONS OF SPIVAK'S THEORETICAL WORK

Spivak's theoretical background sets the stage for understanding her work, its subtleties, and its potential application in LIS research. We have chosen five conceptual constructs—the subaltern, ideology, strategic essentialism, translation and representation, and the "telematic society of information command"—to demonstrate how themes from Spivak can reveal LIS issues and enhance their interpretation, but other researchers will undoubtedly find other concepts in Spivak equally fruitful.

Subalternity

Spivak builds on Marx's proletariat and the subaltern classes of Antonio Gramsci's *Prison Notebooks* in her work on the subaltern. As discussed above, by subaltern, she means "the margins (one can just as well say the silent, silenced center) of the circuit marked out by this epistemic violence, men and women among the illiterate peasantry, the tribals, the lowest strata of the urban subproletariat" (Spivak 1998, 283), who library users might recognize as the homeless, economically disadvantaged, or those in ethnic, racial, or religious minorities. Her most well-known and controversial essay, "Can the Subaltern Speak?" originates from a critique of the Subaltern Group Studies collective, a group of historians ostensibly writing to give a voice to the marginalized in South Asia. Along with "Subaltern Studies: Deconstructing Historiography," it contends that providing a voice from the privileged perch of academia objectifies the very group that academics are attempting to liberate. If the subaltern classes are being "given" a voice, they still lack any real sort of agency, and thus maintain their subalternate status. Those in power also have responsibility to what Spivak calls "unlearning one's privilege" or to become "able to listen to that other constituency" and "speak in such a way that one will be taken seriously by that other constituency… [and] recognize that the position of the speaking subject within theory can be an historically powerful position when it wants the other actually to be able to answer back" (Spivak 1986, 42). By asserting her own voice to a willing audience, the subaltern transforms into a subject with agency, and consequently the subaltern will no longer exist. Spivak believes that the act of studying the subaltern as a group requires the essentialist assumption that a collective consciousness exists, that the group thinks and acts as one. She objects that "'[c]lass' is not, after all, an inalienable description of human reality" (Spivak 1985b, 205), but rather an artificial construct created by colonial or intellectual authority.

Imposing a collective consciousness on a group, marginalized or not, is what is done daily in LIS when creating standards and services based on a collective user. As far back as Charles Ammi Cutter, the "convenience of the public" has driven classification decisions, yet the singular public was meant to embody a multitude of ethnic, racial, and gender differences, not to mention characteristics influenced by socioeconomic status, education level, occupation, or a host of other variables. Standards such as classification and subject headings have the capability to colonize by impressing upon a diversity of users the essentialized definitions, explanations, and preferred vocabulary that reflect the values of the bibliographic utility. Furthermore, standards and the institutions that maintain them can be monolithic and powerful. When the marginalized themselves challenge the authority, "the reason for failure most often given is the much greater scope, organization, and strength of the colonial authorities" (Spivak 1985b, 199). Catalogers can attempt to correct misrepresentations by formally suggesting changes to DDC, LCC, or LCSH; however, Spivak would object that as intermediaries, catalogers are attempting to speak for a marginalized group, thus continuing the subalterns' status. The librarian, similarly to the Western intellectual, "is either caught in a deliberate choice of subalternity, granting to the oppressed either that very expressive subjectivity which s/he criticizes or, instead, a total unrepresentability" (209). Without input from groups as users or formal advisors, the subaltern in the library will be unable to speak.

How can librarians allow subalterns to speak without speaking for them? Collection development, programming, outreach, and the reference interview all hold potential to predict and impose what the user supposedly wants or needs, and information retrieval systems and subject access estimate the presumptive lexicon of the user. Creative methods of collecting feedback from individual users and user groups are worth exploring to empower voices that are rarely heard. On the technological side, Web 2.0 techniques may provide a means to achieve a voice for users by allowing design, tagging, and networking all centered on the user rather than a central authority.

Ideology

To Spivak, ideology is comprised partly of the product of intellectuals: explanations. Intellectuals must be aware of their own responsibility and complicity in the creation of ideology because under the capitalist system, too often their labor is subverted into producing official explanations that make up state ideology. As she uses it, the concept of ideology relates closely to the work of the library:

Our assigned role is, seemingly, the custodianship of culture....Our role is to produce and be produced by the official explanations in terms of the powers that police the entire society, emphasizing a continuity or a discontinuity with past explanations....As we produce the official explanations, we reproduce the official ideology (Spivak 1979, 108).

Just as intellectuals do, librarians serve as "custodians of culture" and have the power through collection development, cataloging, and programming not just to mirror, but to unintentionally or intentionally shape culture in the communities in which the library exists. Also, those ideologies that reflect a masculine-focused, mainstream-reinforcing voice should be identified for what they are, rather than as a representation of the norm. She cautions that "[t]he first mistake of ideology is that a 'popular prejudice' mistakes itself for 'human nature'" (Spivak 1985b, 211), and warns of the fallacy of believing that "structural explanations can indeed be ideology-free" (Spivak 1979, 111). The messages put forth by the library or other cultural institutions must be conscious of "hidden agendas [that] might pass themselves off as the goes-without-saying-ness of truth" (Spivak 1993a, 131). Ideology is not inherently bad; it merely reflects how society sees itself. However, the society's self-image should not intentionally marginalize its members on the basis of gender, ethnic origin, religion, or socioeconomic status, the danger being that they become fenced out of society's center without a voice.

The tools of librarianship reinforce the cultural agenda or ideology. Consulting selection lists, purchasing works that have already been filtered through the publishing process, organizing, displaying and eventually weeding them constitute value judgments that reveal the agenda of the library. The subject representation work of catalogers, standards developers, and bibliographic utilities shape ideology by naming topics and placing them in a hierarchy, thus asserting value and adding connotative baggage. The collection, cataloging standards, LCSH, scope notes, reading recommendation lists, bibliographies, programming, pathfinders, Web portals, and any other texts that carry the discourses of the library are the literature that results in the formation of cultural ideology. Engels's view of the illusory quality of ideology suggests how the ideologies formed by the discourses in the library can influence society's ideas of itself. Intentional censorship or inadvertent omission also can shape values. Spivak recommends awareness of this self-fulfilling influence in order to avoid harm from ideology and work toward change. "One cannot of course, 'choose' to step out of ideology. The most responsible 'choice' seems to be to know it as best one can, recognize it as best one can, and, through one's necessarily inadequate interpretation, to work to change it" (Spivak 1982, 120).

Strategic Essentialism

Essentialism is "the assumption that groups, categories or classes of objects have one or several defining features exclusive to all members of that category" (Ashcroft, Griffiths, and Tiffin 1999, 77). In critical theory, essentialism is viewed as a reductionist oversimplification leading to stereotyping. However, there has been some suggestion that strategic essentialism, the employment of essentialized categories to gain certain desirable ends, may be an acceptable practice. If you search "strategic essentialism" on the Web you will retrieve several sites beginning with Wikipedia that attribute the term, accurately, to Spivak. However, most of these resources do not include the information that Spivak changed her mind on this topic.

Interviewed in 1989, Spivak says, "I have, then, reconsidered my cry for a strategic use of essentialism" (1993d, 5). She describes the use of a "mobilizing slogan or masterword like *woman* or *worker*" as an "impossible risk of a lasting strategy" (3). That is, once essentialism is used in a strategic way to gain a particular point, it may already have become entrenched. Essentialism glosses over differences and must, in Spivak's view, be constantly questioned, critiqued, and contextualized—for Spivak, by using deconstruction. She points out that strategies are tricks for specific instances, not theories that can be applied regardless of context. This questioning of essentialism is necessary as "an acknowledgement of the dangerousness of something one cannot not use" (5). According to Spivak, an essence is what remains, *ce qui reste,* after differences are stripped away—it is minimalizable. However, within essential categories, are various diversities. Spivak notes that as an essence is diversified it "oozes away" (18), so there is no stable minimalizable essence.

Spivak also raises the question of the audience of a text. When we write, who do we think is reading our writing? Or, in LIS, who are our users? "The audience is not an essence, the audience is a blank. An audience can be constituted by people I cannot even imagine,...Yet, in the narrow sense, when an audience is responsible, responding, invited, in other words, to coinvestigate, then positionality is shared with it" (Spivak 1993d, 22). Inviting the audience to be a partner is what Derrida called "responsibility to the trace of the other" (Spivak 1993d, 22). It deconstructs the investigator/audience binary opposition by acknowledging the differences within the audience and the commonalities between the audience and the investigator.

As an alternative to essentialism Spivak suggests identity. "We 'write' a running biography with life-language rather than only word-language in order to 'be'" (1993d, 4). Yet in the identity that we write for ourselves as individuals we are also "instantiations of historical and psychosexual narratives" (6). That is, we have been inserted into a particular history. Our running biography has a context. Identity is both individual and culturally linked.

The idea of the essence of the audience being deconstructed is the most obviously applicable to LIS. Our audience consists of our users, and therefore we need to deconstruct the professional/user binary opposition. Our users are most at risk of being essentialized by us as we develop policies, services, and standards for them. Even if we think we are helping, we may be forming an ideology harmful to a marginalized group or culture. Instead Spivak proposes that groups and cultures be allowed to speak for themselves and those of us with privilege unlearn it and learn to listen. Other research that could apply Spivak's thinking about essentialism relates to the image and role of librarians and to the "L-word" versus "I-word" debate. The stereotypical librarian can readily see her perceived essence ooze away under close examination and librarianship and information science can be revealed not to be opposites except as they have been constructed as such. If the stereotype of the librarian is an essentialized category then the same might be said of both librarianship and information science. Another area to consider is whether or not controlled vocabularies, perhaps especially classifications, are essentializing in their quest for mutually exclusive categories. Finally, Spivak's suggestion of identity puts us in a position to understand ourselves as professionals who come from specific contexts and have been influenced by specific narratives or discourses. Issues such as how to recruit a more diverse student body into LIS education require that we understand our identity and our privilege as individual professionals and academics and that we recognize that each student has her or his own identity as well.

Translation and Representation

Spivak's observation "that the politics of translation takes on a massive life of its own if you see language as the process of meaning-construction" (1993c, 179) is of interest to us as a field that often translates, in a loose sense of the word. We translate from texts to descriptive cataloging, subject headings, classifications, index entries, metadata, abstracts, bibliographies, and so forth. We translate information needs into searches. We translate our collections into pathfinders. We translate Web sites into links in Web portals. In that process of translation, something is always changed. Typically, in LIS, the text with which we begin is larger than the text that results from our translation. We are creating representations of these texts to function as surrogates for them. We seek neutrality, which Spivak endorses as a goal but recognizes to be futile: "The desire for neutrality and dialogue, even as it should not be repressed, must always mark its own failure.... The idea of a neutral dialogue is an idea which denies history, denies structure, denies the positioning of subjects" (1987, 72). Spivak offers a Marxist distinction that is potentially useful in this regard.

Drawing on Marx, Spivak identifies two senses of representation: first, *vertreten,* the notion of a representative representing, as legislators represent their constituencies; and, second, *darstellen,* a *re*-presentation depicting something (1999, 257–59). To be represented politically means not only that the group cannot speak for itself, but also that one essentialist voice is substituted for the voices of many. Representation in the "portrait" sense implies a more accurate reflection of the will of the people and empowers them by eliminating intermediaries. A surrogate created for the purpose of organizing information seems clearly the portrait type of representation, but something like a reference interview in which a librarian represents a user's needs in the form of a search is fuzzier, since the search terms serve as a proxy for the information need. In that instance, it is helpful to look at Spivak's views on translation, in particular the role of rhetoric: "[l]ogic allows us to jump from word to word by means of clearly indicated connections. Rhetoric must work in the silence between and around words in order to see what works and how much" (1993c, 181). To reflect the rhetorical as well as the logical aspects of texts, Spivak says that "the translator must surrender to the text" (183). Thus, "the translator must be able to discriminate on the terrain of the original" (189). Surrendering to the text is a giving over of oneself to the feel of the text. It is an emotional response to the text—an empathy. Being able to inhabit the terrain of the original requires empathy, but also logic in analyzing and understanding its context and relating it to something comprehensible to the translator. An in-depth application of Spivak's ideas regarding representation and translation could address topics such as objectivity and neutrality in various aspects of LIS practice; whether or not objectivity and neutrality should ultimately be our ideals; and how it all affects our relationship to texts whether written or oral. Perhaps those catalog records are not only *re*-presentations— perhaps they are also texts created by professionals acting as representatives of the originals just as reference librarians may be the representatives of users. Most of these representations are disseminated via information systems that are part of what Spivak calls the "telematic society of information command."

The Telematic Society of Information Command

Spivak identifies a dimension of the contemporary postcolonial condition in writing that:

The actual postcolonial [decolonized] areas have a class-specific and internationally controlled limited access to a telematic society of information command, which is often also the indigenous contact-point or source of the discourse of cultural specificity and difference." (1999, 361)

This telematic control is, in Spivak's view, a part of the apparatus for "worlding" the "Third World"/"South." (1999, 114)

Worlding is a term that Spivak borrows from Heidegger and uses to describe the process of the First World defining the Third. She includes in the "telematic society of information command" the "computerized and videographic" popular culture that fails to consider cultural identity and the voices of migrants in a postcolonial world (Spivak 1991a, 239). She also includes the electronic capitalism that allows business to be done without face-to-face contact and the exploitation of biodiversity via database. Spivak observes that "[f]rom the infinite care and passion of learning [e.g., about ecology] we have by-passed knowledge (which is obsolete now) into the telematic postmodern culture of information command" (1999, 391–92).

To counter, Spivak offers transnational literacy as a means of discerning "the uneven relationship of different nation-states with the agencies of universalization" (2001, 15). Transnational literacy asks the questions: "Who needs and leads the movement for universalization? Who celebrates it? In what interest? Why? There's never a satisfactory answer to these questions, but learning to ask them is required" (15). It is in that way that we can understand and unlearn our (unwitting) complicity and our level of privilege.

How does this relate to LIS research? Clearly libraries and other information entities are a part of the telematic society of information command. We play a role either intentionally or unintentionally in the worlding of the Third World/the South. Topics that might benefit from scrutiny in this light include issues such as: the role of the International Federation of Library Associations and Institutions (IFLA) as a United Nations-like body fostering library services and developing library standards; library cooperation with digital dissemination of resources such as Google Books; the de facto international dissemination and impact of standards designed for the dominant culture, such as our cataloging standards and tools; the global marketing of our practice as through WorldCat and its potentially universalizing effect; LIS education of students from the South and the practices they take home or the brain drain of professionals if they do not return; and the impact of electronic capitalism on the publishing industry.

CONCLUSION

Spivak is ultimately pragmatic in the application of her theoretical frameworks. For example, her article "Righting Wrongs" (2004) is almost entirely about the need for and pedagogy required to educate subaltern children—the children of the rural poor—beyond basic literacy and numeracy if global human rights are to be approached, much less achieved. She is familiar with the rote learning of subaltern children compared to the critical thinking taught to their wealthier counterparts and the disadvantage that creates. This ability to bridge theory and practice makes her work particularly applicable in a professional field like LIS that requires both. Spivak can also help us to look at ourselves—to constantly question our presumptions and institutions and to unlearn our privilege. LIS is benefited by our willingness to adopt theoretical perspectives from a range of disciplines. In recent decades such theory has come mainly from the social sciences and sciences. It is time for us to look to the humanities. LIS research has largely avoided humanistic approaches, perhaps largely because we are an applied field. However, Spivak makes cogent arguments for applying text-based humanities analysis to concrete everyday issues. Given that so many of us in LIS are grounded in the humanities, looking to Spivak as a humanities scholar who applies her theoretical understanding to real life issues seems, nay, not seems, 'tis, an obvious approach.

REFERENCES

Parenthetical page references in the text are to the more readily available collections of Spivak's work, but dates are for the original when essays in the collections are reprints.

Ashcroft, Bill, Gareth Griffiths, and Helen Tiffin. *Key Concepts in Post-Colonial Studies.* London: Routledge, 1999.

Olson, Hope A. 2001. "The Power to Name: Representation in Library Catalogues." *Signs: Journal of Women in Culture and Society* 26 (3, Spring): 639–68.

Olson, Hope A. 2002. *The Power to Name: Locating the Limits of Subject Representation in Libraries.* Dordrecht, Netherlands: Kluwer Academic.

Olson, Hope A. 2003. "Transgressive Deconstructions: Feminist/Postcolonial Methodology for Research in Knowledge Organization." In *Tendencias e Investigación en Organización del Conomcimiento/Trends in Knowledge Organization Research,* ed. José Antonio Frías and Críspulo Travieso, 731–40. Salamanca, Spain: Ediciones Universidad de Salamanca.

Olson, Hope A. 2007. "How We Construct Subjects: A Feminist Analysis." In *Special Issue: Gender Issues in Information Needs and Services,* ed. Cindy Ingold and Susan E. Searing. *Library Trends* 56 (2): 509–41.

Spivak, Gayatri Chakravorty. 1979. "Explanations and Culture: Marginalia." In *In Other Worlds,* 103–17. New York: Routledge, 1988.

Spivak, Gayatri Chakravorty. 1980a. "Finding Feminist Readings: Dante–Yeats." In *In Other Worlds.* 15–29. New York: Routledge, 1988.

Spivak, Gayatri Chakravorty. 1980b. "Revolutions That as Yet Have No Model: Derrida's 'Limited Inc.'" In *The Spivak Reader,* ed. Donna Landry and Gerald MacLean, 75–106. New York: Routledge, 1996.

Spivak, Gayatri Chakravorty. 1982. "The Politics of Interpretations." In *In Other Worlds,* 118–33. New York: Routledge, 1988.

Spivak, Gayatri Chakravorty. 1985a. "Feminism and Critical Theory." In *In Other Worlds,* 77–92. New York: Routledge, 1988.

Spivak, Gayatri Chakravorty. 1985b. "Subaltern Studies: Deconstructing Historiography." In *In Other Worlds,* 197–221. New York: Routledge, 1988.

Spivak, Gayatri Chakravorty. 1986. "Strategy, Identity, Writing." In *The Post-Colonial Critic: Interviews, Strategies, Dialogue,* ed. Sarah Harasym, 35–49. New York: Routledge, 1990.

Spivak, Gayatri Chakravorty. 1987. "The Post-Colonial Critic." In *The Post-Colonial Critic,* ed. Sarah Harasym, 67–74. New York: Routledge, 1990.

Spivak, Gayatri Chakravorty. 1988. *In Other Worlds: Essays in Cultural Politics.* New York: Routledge.

Spivak, Gayatri Chakravorty. 1990. "Marginality in the Teaching Machine." In *Outside in the Teaching Machine,* 53–76. New York: Routledge, 1993. Originally published as "Poststructuralism, Marginality, Postcoloniality, and Value" in 1990.

Spivak, Gayatri Chakravorty. 1991a. "How to Teach a 'Culturally Different' Book." In *The Spivak Reader: Selected Works of Gayatri Chakravorty Spivak,* ed. Donna Landry and Gerald MacLean, 237–66. New York: Routledge, 1996.

Spivak, Gayatri Chakravorty. 1991b. "Not Virgin Enough to Say That [S]he Occupies the Place of the Other." In *Outside in the Teaching Machine,* 173–78. New York: Routledge, 1993.

Spivak, Gayatri Chakravorty. 1993a. "Feminism and Deconstruction, Again: Negotiations." In *Outside in the Teaching Machine.* 121–40. New York: Routledge.

Spivak, Gayatri Chakravorty. 1993b. *Outside in the Teaching Machine.* New York: Routledge.

Spivak, Gayatri Chakravorty. 1993c. "The Politics of Translation." In *Outside in the Teaching Machine,* 179–200. New York: Routledge.

Spivak, Gayatri Chakravorty, 1993d. "In a Word: Interview." Interview by Ellen Rooney, 1989. In *Outside in the Teaching Machine,* 1–23. New York: Routledge.

Spivak, Gayatri Chakravorty. 1994. "Bonding in Difference: Interview with Alfred Arteaga." In *The Spivak Reader: Selected Works of Gayatri Chakravorty Spivak,* ed. Donna Landry and Gerald MacLean, 15–51. New York: Routledge, 1996.

Spivak, Gayatri Chakravorty. 1996. *The Spivak Reader: Selected Works of Gayatri Chakravorty Spivak,* ed. Donna Landry and Gerald MacLean. New York: Routledge.

Spivak, Gayatri Chakravorty. 1998. "Can the Subaltern Speak?" In *Marxism and the Interpretation of Culture,* ed. Cary Nelson and Larry Grossberg, 271–313. Urbana: University of Illinois Press.

Spivak, Gayatri Chakravorty. 1999. *A Critique of Postcolonial Reason: Toward a History of the Vanishing Present.* Cambridge, MA: Harvard University Press.

Spivak, Gayatri Chakravorty. 2001. "Questioned on Translation." *Public Culture* 13 (1): 13–22.

Spivak, Gayatri Chakravorty. 2004. "Righting Wrongs." *South Atlantic Quarterly* 103 (2/3): 524–81.

Index

About the Editors and Contributors

JOHN M. BUDD is a professor in the School of Information Science and Learning Technologies at the University of Missouri, Columbia. His 2001 book, *Knowledge and Knowing in Library and Information Science: A Philosophical Framework,* was awarded the 2002 Highsmith Library Literature Award, and he is the recent author of *Self-Examination: The Present and Future of Librarianship* (Libraries Unlimited, 2007). John has published recently on undergraduate students and library resources in *College & Research Libraries* and in *Library Resources & Technical Services.* He holds a BA from Louisiana State University, an MA from the University of Texas, an MLS from Louisiana State University, and a PhD from the University of North Carolina.

JOHN E. BUSCHMAN is associate university librarian for scholarly resources and services at Georgetown University Library since 2007. Immediately prior to this, he was department chair and head of collection development at the rank of professor-librarian at Rider University Library in Lawrenceville, New Jersey, for 19 years. He has published four previous books before this volume: *Critical Approaches to Information Technology in Librarianship: Foundations and Applications* (Libraries Unlimited, 1993), *Dismantling the Public Sphere: Situating and Sustaining Libraries in the Age of the New Public Philosophy* (Libraries Unlimited, 2003), *Library as Place: History, Community and Culture* (Libraries Unlimited, 2006, coeditor with Gloria J. Leckie) and *Information Technology in Librarianship: New Critical Approaches* (Libraries Unlimited, 2009, coeditor with Gloria J. Leckie). In 2004, his work *Dismantling the Public Sphere* received the American Library Association's Futas Award and the New Jersey Library Association's Research Award. John is a coeditor of the journal *Progressive Librarian,* is on the Progressive Librarians Guild Coordinating Committee, and served for three years on the National Council of the American Association of University Professors (AAUP). Recent publications include articles on democratic theory and LIS in the *Journal of the American Society for Information Science and Technology,* and an article on the intellectual and academic freedom for librarians in *Academe.* He holds a BS in history and sociology and an MLS, both from Ball State University, an MA in American Studies from St. Joseph's University, and is a candidate for the doctor of liberal studies degree at Georgetown University.

HANS DAM CHRISTENSEN is the dean of research, School of Library and Information Science, Copenhagen, Denmark. His main research areas are visual media, art history, visual culture, and museology. He has written numerous articles on these subjects and has coedited several books as well. He is a member of the international program committee, Assigning Cultural Values (2008–12; Research Council of Norway), founding editor of the academic journal *Periskop. Forum for kunsthistorisk debat* (financially supported by the Danish Research Agency), member of the organizing committee of the Novo Nordisk Foundation Art History Project (in cooperation with the University of Copenhagen's Doctoral School in Cultural Studies, Literature, and the Arts), and member of the steering group, Nordic Network on Visual Studies, as well as Vision of the Past: Images as Historical Sources and the History of Art History (both financial supported by NordForsk, the Nordic Research Board). He holds a PhD from the University of Copenhagen.

RONALD E. DAY is an associate professor at the School of Library and Information Science at Indiana University, Bloomington. He is the author of *The Modern Invention of Information: Discourse, History, and Power* (2001), the coeditor (with Claire McInerney) of *Rethinking Knowledge Management: From Knowledge Objects to Knowledge Processes* (2007) and coeditor and cotranslator (with Laurent Martinet and Hermina G. B. Anghelescu) of Suzanne Briet's *What Is Documentation?* (2006). Dr. Day is the author of numerous articles engaged with critical information theory. He has his MA in philosophy and his PhD in comparative literature (interdisciplinary with philosophy, specializing in theory) from the State University of New York, Binghamton, and he has an additional MLIS from the University of California, Berkeley.

JOSEPH DEODATO is a assistant professor and web services librarian at the College of Staten Island, City University of New York (CUNY). His primary research interest lies in critical theories of libraries, archives, and museums with a focus on issues of power, mediation, and social responsibility. His essays on the application of postmodernist perspectives to archival theory have received awards from the University of Maryland's College of Information Studies as well as the Progressive Librarian's Guild. Deodato holds a BA in History from Rutgers University, an MLS from the University of Maryland and an MA in Liberal Studies from the College of Staten Island.

NICK DYER-WITHEFORD is associate professor and associate dean of the faculty of information and media studies at University of Western Ontario in London, Ontario, Canada. He is author of *Cyber-Marx: Cycles and Circuits of Struggle in High-Technology Capitalism* (University of Illinois, 1999); co-author, with Stephen Kline, and Greig de Peuter, of *Digital Play: The Interaction of Technology, Culture, and Marketing* (McGill-Queen's, 2003); and co-author, with Greig de Peuter, of *Games of Empire: Global Capitalism and Video Games* (University of Minnesota, 2009). He has also written several articles on the work of Antonio Negri and on autonomist Marxism.

MUSTAFA YUNUS ERYAMAN is the vice president of the Turkish Educational Research Association and assistant professor in the Department of Elementary Education,

Canakkale Onsekiz Mart University (Turkey). He has served as a council member in the European Educational Research Association and World Education Research Association. He received his MEd from University of Missouri, Columbia and his PhD from the University of Illinois, Urbana-Champaign. He is the author of *Teaching as Practical Philosophy* (2008), and editor of *Peter McLaren, Education, and the Struggle for Liberation* (2009).

MELODIE J. FOX is a doctoral student in information studies at the University of Wisconsin, Milwaukee. She holds an MA in English from the University of Illinois, Chicago and an MLIS from the University of Wisconsin, Milwaukee. Melodie currently is the dean of instruction at Bryant and Stratton College in Milwaukee. Her research interests include subject representation and the social consequences of the organization of information from a feminist critical theory perspective. Most recently, she has worked on a database of the contents of the Woman's Building Library from the 1893 World's Columbian Exposition and has presented the results nationally and internationally.

LISA M. GIVEN is a professor in the School of Library and Information Studies and adjunct professor in humanities computing at the University of Alberta. A former director of the International Institute for Qualitative Methodology, Lisa has received numerous research grants and has published widely on topics related to individuals' information behaviours, Web usability, and qualitative inquiry. Her research interests include the social construction of knowledge, spatial analysis, information literacy, research methods, and information issues in higher education. One of her current projects is funded by the Social Sciences and Humanities Research Council of Canada ("Participatory Design for a Visually-Based Drug Information Interface: Web Usability in the Context of Consumers' Health Information Behaviours.") Lisa serves on a number of editorial boards for international journals and is currently associate editor of the *International Journal of Qualitative Methods*. She is editor of *The Sage Encyclopedia of Qualitative Research Methods* (2008).

JOACIM HANSSON is a professor in Library and Information Science at the School of Cultural Studies, Linnaeus University, Växjö, Sweden. His research has mainly centred around three themes: ideological aspects of knowledge organisation systems; the identity of librarianship and of libraries as social organisations, and history and theory development in library and information science. He has written five books, most recently *Libraries and Identity—The Role of Institutional Self Image and Identity in the Emergence of New Types of Libraries* (2010). He holds a BA from Lund University, an MLIS from the Swedish School of Library and Information Science, and a PhD from Göteborg University.

LISA HUSSEY is an assistant professor at the Graduate School of Library and Information Science at Simmons College in Boston. Her main teaching focus is on management in LIS and reference services, while her research interests include diversity and management, leadership, and the role of theory versus practice in teaching library science. She has recently published an article based on her dissertation, "Why Librarianship? An Exploration of the Motivations of Ethnic Minorities to Choose Librarian and Information Science as a Career," in *Advances in Library Administration and Organization*.

Dr. Hussey holds a BA in history from the University of Miami, an MLS from the University of Arizona, and a PhD in LIS from the University of Missouri.

ANDREW J. LAU is a doctoral student in the Department of Information Studies at the University of California, Los Angeles, and adjunct faculty at Glendale Community College. He teaches a course on new media, information, and society, with a focus on community organizing and activism. He is currently working on his dissertation, focusing on artists' documentation practices and their relationships with collecting institutions. This is part of a larger research agenda to bridge distributed theoretical discussions about the archive in arts, humanities, and professional archival discourses. Andrew is a current editor and former book review editor for *InterActions: UCLA Journal of Education and Information Studies*. He holds a BA in psychology with a specialization in research methodology and an MLIS, both from the University of California, Los Angeles.

GLORIA J. LECKIE worked for a decade as an academic and government librarian before returning to academia pursue her MA and PhD in geography in the mid 1980s. She is currently an associate professor and LIS program coordinator in the Faculty of Information and Media Studies at the University of Western Ontario. Her research interests include academic librarianship, library as place, information literacy, information behaviour, and critical theoretical approaches. Dr. Leckie is the editor of two previous collections: *Library as Place: History, Community and Culture* (Libraries Unlimited, 2006, coedited with John Buschman) and *Information Technology in Librarianship: New Critical Approaches* (Libraries Unlimited, 2009, also coedited with John Buschman). She is currently working on a project to update her previous research on the issues surrounding faculty status for Canadian academic librarians.

HOPE A. OLSON is professor and associate dean in the School of Information Studies at the University of Wisconsin, Milwaukee. Her research addresses classification theory and problems of bias in subject access to information using feminist, poststructural, and postcolonial perspectives. Among her current interests are the cultural specificity of classificatory structure, gender and the structure of knowledge, subject access to indigenous knowledge, knowledge structures and vocabularies suited to how searchers search, and the nature of conceptual relationships in social tagging. Dr. Olson has published in a wide range of journals in library and information studies, women's studies, and semiotics; authored *The Power to Name: Locating the Limits of Subject Representation in Libraries* (2002); edited *Information Resources in Women's Studies and Feminism* (2002); coauthored with John Boll *Subject Analysis in Online Catalogs,* 2nd ed (Libraries Unlimited 2001); and was editor-in-chief of the journal *Knowledge Organization* from 2000 to 2004.

MICHAEL R. OLSSON is graduate coordinator of information and knowledge management at the University of Technology, Sydney, where he teaches in both the undergraduate and postgraduate programs. Michael is an active researcher in the field of information behaviour/practices research and his work has appeared in the leading international research journals and conferences in the field, including journals *Information Research, Library Quarterly*, and *Libri*; and the Conceptions of Library & Information Science, International Communication Association, Canadian Association for Information Science, and Information Seeking in Context conferences. His research focuses on information practices and knowledge sharing in academic, professional, and artistic communities, and his most recent research includes an international study of how theatre professionals (actors, designers, directors) make sense of Shakespeare and (in collaboration with researchers at the universities of Western Ontario and Tampere) a study of the information practices of journalists. This work seeks to develop a discourse analytic approach to information research with a particular focus on the social construction of knowledge and the interrelationship of meaning and authority (*pouvoir/savoir*). Michael holds a BA from the University of Sydney and an MA (Information) and PhD from the University of Technology, Sydney.

AJIT PYATI is an assistant professor in the Faculty of Information and Media Studies at the University of Western Ontario. His MLIS and PhD degrees are from the Department of Information Studies at the University of California, Los Angeles. He actively publishes and conducts research in the areas of information policy, international library development, globalization and immigration studies, and information and communication technologies (ICTs) for development. Dr. Pyati is currently pursuing research on issues of equitable information access and democratic participation in India's "knowledge society."

DOUGLAS RABER has been a subject specialist at the State University of York, Buffalo, director of the public library in Harvard, Illinois, and as head of reference at Monroe County Public Library in Bloomington, Indiana. He returned to the University of Missouri after teaching at the University of Tennessee where he served as interim director from 2003 until 2005, and is now director of Ferndale (MI) Public Library. His book, *The Problem of Information: An Introduction to Information Science,* was published in 2003 by Scarecrow Press, and he has published articles and reviews in *American Libraries, Library Quarterly, Information Processing & Management, Journal of Education for Library and Information Sciences,* and *Public Libraries.* His research is in the areas of information policy and politics, information society and culture, First Amendment and copyright, Internet filtering, and public libraries. He holds a BA, an MA, and a PhD—all from Indiana University, and an MALS from Northern Illinois University.

MARTINA RIEDLER is an assistant professor of art education at Canakkale Onsekiz Mart University (Turkey). Her current research focuses on the role of national museums and identity formation, questions of critical pedagogy in art museums, and issues of contemporary museum studies. Before being awarded a Fulbright Fellowship to pursue her doctorate in art education and museum studies at the University of Illinois at Urbana-Champaign, Martina worked with the adult interpretive education programs at the Solomon Guggenheim Museum New York and in the education programs at ZKM/ Center for Art and New Media Karlsruhe (Germany). In addition to her lecturer positions with the University of Art and Industrial Design in Linz (Austria) and the Carl von Ossietzky University in Oldenburg (Germany), she has worked as a secondary school art educator in the public school systems of New York City and Vienna. An editorial board member of the *International Journal of Progressive Education* and an advisory board member of the *International Journal of Education and the Arts,* she earned her MA in art education at the Academy of Fine Arts Vienna (Austria).

HOWARD ROSENBAUM is the associate dean and an associate professor of information science in the School of Library and Information Science at Indiana University and has been on the faculty since 1993. He is the director of the Master of Information Science program and a codirector of the Graduate Certificate in Information Architecture program in SLIS. He studies social informatics, e-business, information architecture, and community networking. Rosenbaum has presented his work at the Association for Information Systems, the American Society for Information Science, the Association of Internet Researchers, HCI International, and other organizations. He is a fellow in the Rob Kling Center for Social Informatics at Indiana University and in the Center for Digital Commerce at Syracuse University. He has been recognized often for excellence in teaching and for the innovative use of technology in education. He received the Frederic Bachman Lieber Memorial Award for Teaching Excellence, Indiana University in 2005, a statewide MIRA Award for Technological Innovation in Education from Techpoint in 2003, the Indiana Partnership for Statewide Education Award for Innovation in Teaching with Technology in 2002, and was named one of the first SBC Fellows at Indiana University in 2000.

PAULETTE ROTHBAUER is an assistant professor in the Faculty of Information and Media Studies at the University of Western Ontario. Her recent research has focused on the reading cultures of contemporary young women who claim alternative sexual identities and of rural youth who are geographically isolated from access to reading materials and active reading cultures (see, for example, "Exploring the Placelessness of Reading Among Older Rural Teens in a Canadian Municipality," *The Library Quarterly* 79 (3): 465–83, 2009). Currently, she is studying the emergence of the modern Canadian young adult novel and how it dovetails with our changing conceptualization of the teenage reader in Canada. She holds a BA (in English) from the University of Toronto, and an MLIS and PhD (in library and information science) from the University of Western Ontario.

PAUL SOLOMON is associate professor in the School of Library and Information Science, University of South Carolina, holding a BS (Penn State), MBA (University of Washington), and MLS and PhD (University of Maryland). His research focuses on social studies of information, which try to identify what information is to people as they engage in life and work tasks, in such contexts as schools, government agencies, and universities, and with such diverse populations as children, managers, academic chemists/chemical engineers, and the elderly. Paul's teaching has been focused in the areas of research methods, management and administration, and user perspectives. He is the author of numerous information and library science publications, many of which have been widely cited and several have been recognized as "best papers" by the American Society for Information Science and Technology. Paul is a member of the American Society for Information Science and Technology, the Association for Library and Information Science Education, the American Library Association, and the Academy of Management.

SIOBHAN STEVENSON is an assistant professor in the Faculty of Information at the University of Toronto. She holds an MLIS and a PhD from the University of Western Ontario. Dr. Stevenson worked for ten years with an agency of the Ontario government responsible for the coordination of autonomous public library boards through the development of policies, programs, and funding opportunities designed to that end. The problems she addresses in her research revolve around issues she encountered in the field, specifically the role of class struggle in the public policy process and the meaning of social struggle with respect to competing visions of citizenship, work, and consumption. The object of her analysis is often the local public library because, among other reasons, its ubiquity and banality combine to make it a compelling site for the study of the complex ways in which state institutions serve to legitimate and reproduce the status quo. Current projects include a historical study of labour relations in public libraries across Canada from the early 1950s through to today's information economy, and the political economy of corporate philanthropy in less developed countries, specifically at the unlikely intersection of public libraries, intellectual property rights, the World Trade Organization, and the World Bank. Her work has been published in *Information Society, Canadian Journal of Library and Information Science, First Monday,* and *Library and Information History.*

ROSAMUND K. STOOKE is an assistant professor in the Faculty of Education at the University of Western Ontario, where she teaches courses in curriculum studies and the development of literacy. She holds an MLIS, MEd, and PhD from the University of Western Ontario. Her research investigates young children's literacy from a sociocultural perspective and explores the social organization of educational work in community settings such as public libraries.

SANNA TALJA is a senior lecturer in the Department of Information Studies and Interactive Media (INFIM), University of Tampere, Finland. She teaches in the areas of knowledge organization and knowledge management. Her current research focuses on organizational learning, knowledge sharing, and knowledge management. She also studies the mutual shaping of ICTs, digital resources, and scholarly communities from a domain analytic and practice based perspective. Since 1996, she has published several articles about metatheories and theories within information science, and about theories and conceptions of information technology. Dr. Talja has written and coedited six books, among them *Practicing Information Literacy: Bringing Theories of Learning, Practice and Information Literacy Together* (2009, coedited with with Annemaree Lloyd). She has contributed articles to a number of journals, including *Journal of the American Society for Information Science and Technology; Journal of Documentation, Information Processing and Management; Journal of Information Science, Library and Information Science Research,* and *Information Research.* She holds a PhD from the University of Tampere.

WILL WHEELER currently serves as head of research and instruction at Georgetown University's Lauinger Library, as adjunct faculty in the School of Continuing Studies, and additional music faculty in the Department of Performing Arts. From 1998–2008, Wheeler served in library positions at Yale University, North Carolina State, and Stanford. From 1999–2009, Dr. Wheeler was adjunct assistant professor at the University of Illinois Graduate School of Library and Information Science and also taught LIS at the University of North Carolina, Chapel Hill, and University of Maryland, College Park. Wheeler holds a PhD from Indiana University in ethnomusicology, folklore and anthropology and two MAs (one in LIS) from the University of Illinois. Wheeler has various publications in the field of LIS, including *Saving the Time of the Library User*

Through Subject Access Innovation (2000); "The Impact of the Internet on Cataloging," (chapter 4 in *The Impact of the Internet on Libraries,* ed. Lewis Liu, Greenwood Press, 2001); and "Decision Support Databases: Three Cases and A Brief Review of Disparate Literatures," *Journal of Electronic Resource Librarianship* (2008). Wheeler's major interests in LIS are science studies and the ethnography of work at the digital divide, including data analysis, information mapping, and digital transformations of research in the social sciences.